More

More

The Politics of Economic Growth
in Postwar America

ROBERT M. COLLINS

OXFORD
UNIVERSITY PRESS
2000

OXFORD
UNIVERSITY PRESS

Oxford   New York
Athens   Auckland   Bangkok   Bogotá   Buenos Aires   Calcutta
Cape Town   Chennai   Dar es Salaam   Delhi   Florence   Hong Kong   Istanbul
Karachi   Kuala Lumpur   Madrid   Melbourne   Mexico City   Mumbai
Nairobi   Paris   São Paulo   Singapore   Taipei   Tokyo   Toronto   Warsaw

and associated companies
in
Berlin   Ibadan

Library of Congress Cataloging–in–Publication Data
Collins, Robert M.
More : the politics of economic growth in postwar America / Robert M. Collins.
p.   cm.
Includes bibliographical references and index.
ISBN 0-19-504646-3
1. Wealth—United States—History—20th century.   2. United States—Economic policy.
3. United States—Economic conditions—1945-.   4. Liberalism—United States—
History—20th Century.   5. National characteristics, American.   I. Title.
HC110.W4C65   2000
338.973—dc21   99–022524

Design by
Adam B. Bohannon

9 8 7 6 5 4 3 2 1
Printed in the United States of America
on acid-free paper

For My Parents

Contents

Preface

A bit of personal serendipity nearly three decades ago inspired this book. In 1971 I visited Washington, D.C., and happened upon an artifact of the American Century that has stayed in my mind ever since. It was the so-called GNP clock, and the story behind it fascinated me.

The GNP clock was an appropriately outsized toteboard full of lights and numbers that the Department of Commerce had constructed to keep track of the nation's economic growth. The aim was to record and publicize the point at which the U.S. economy achieved a rate of growth that would, if continued for one year, yield a $1 trillion gross national product.[1] At the appropriate moment, all the bells and whistles of the Nixon administration's public relations machinery would announce to the world yet another milestone in the progress of the world's richest economy.

By prearrangement, the numbers on the board were to flash the $1 trillion figure at noon on a winter's day late in 1970, at which time President Richard Nixon would usher in the economic millennium with a few celebratory remarks. Alas, the president's arrival was delayed. Mild panic set in as technicians scrambled madly to turn the machine back. But the board seemed to take on a life of its own, and despite their best efforts it flashed the $1 trillion figure at 12:02. By the time Nixon finally arrived at 12:07, $2.3 million more had been added as the machine began calculating the GNP at a wildly accelerating rate.[2] Some Americans, less enamored of economic growth than the Republican president, saw this victory of machine over man and of matter over mind as ominously symbolic.

In outline, the story of the GNP clock seemed to feed all of my prejudices. At the time, I felt a left liberal's powerful antipathy toward Nixon, whom I and my friends called the Trickster even before Watergate; and reflecting my graduate student penury and the influence of counterculture values on even an aspiring middle-class professional, I embraced a weak but exceptionally smug antimaterialism that held in contempt not my own quite strong desire for acquisition but rather my culture's somewhat more abstract (but still indisputably real) and surely less refined materialism. All in all, the GNP clock story struck me at the time as an apt metaphor for economic growth, materialism, and technology all run amok.

It was only years later, when I read the full text of Richard Nixon's remarks on that occasion, that I came to suspect that perhaps the GNP clock episode expressed something more complicated—and more interesting—than the rather arch morality play I had first envisioned. In the land where, John Kenneth Galbraith had sworn just a decade earlier, the cult of production held absolute sway, Nixon's remarks sounded a strangely defensive note: "I think that rather than apologizing for our great, strong, private enterprise economy, we should recognize that we are very fortunate to have it." "Don't look at it," he urged, "simply in terms of a great group of selfish people, money grubbing." The real significance of the trillion-dollar achievement, he stressed, was not production for its own sake but rather what an economy of that size and strength made possible. Plans for improving the income, health, education, and housing of America's poor and middle classes were fanciful unless backed by such productive capacity: "Unless we produce the wealth, all of those great dreams, those idealistic plans for doing things for people, aren't going to mean anything at all." Nixon stood for growth, defiantly but not mindlessly. Here, at what had appeared at first blush to be little more than a civic celebration of Mammon, Nixon gave thanks that "as a result of our moving forward on the economic side . . . we can now turn more to the quality of life and not just to its quantity."[3] Reading Nixon's speech after the fact, it occurred to me that perhaps America's embrace of economic growth had been more complex, more nuanced, more ambiguous, and perhaps even more ambivalent, than either contemporaries or historians have generally recognized. The chapters that follow explore that possibility.

This book, then, is about how the pursuit of economic growth came to become a central and defining feature of U.S. public policy in the half-century after the end of World War II. Commentators in the 1950s coined the term "growthmanship" to describe the seemingly single-minded pursuit of exuberant economic growth that was then appearing to dominate the political agenda and the public dialogue throughout the Western industrialized world, nowhere more dramatically than in that bastion of materialistic excess, the United States. I examine the origins of the postwar embrace of growth and trace how that initial growthmanship evolved over time.

Over the last half of the twentieth century, American political leaders, policymakers, and intellectuals created a succession of growth regimes, all of which emphasized growth both as an end in itself and, more important, as a vehicle for achieving a striking variety of other, ideological goals as well. In one regard, I follow the lead of many observers in seeing the pursuit of growth as a time-honored way of avoiding hard questions and evading tough decisions about the distribution of wealth and power in America. At the same time, however, I depart from the view that Americans in the postwar era "substituted economic performance for political ideology."[4] Rather, I contend that growth did not suspend or supersede ideological conflict so much as embody and express it. The political economy of growth became an important arena for ideological expression and conflict in the postwar era; throughout, ideology shaped conceptions of growth, while, at the same time, growth itself influenced ideology. As a result of this interpenetration, economic growth over time emerged as a much more complex and heavily freighted phenomenon than the rhetoric of many of its champions and most of its detractors allowed. It is my intention to make that complexity both more discernible and more comprehensible.

Of course, I do not mean to suggest that it was only in the postwar era that growth came to be recognized or valued. Economists since Adam Smith have long recognized the importance of growth for a rising standard of living; Smith himself wrote in 1776 that "it is not the actual greatness of national wealth, but its continued increase, which occasions a rise in the wages of labor."[5] From the time of Alexander Hamilton's Report on Manufactures in 1791 and its gradual implementation in the early nineteenth century, the federal government used land and trade policies to encourage national development. Similarly, fears about the end of growth or about limits to growth, usually expressed as anxiety regarding the disappearance of the frontier, became a staple of American discourse as early as the 1880s.[6]

What made the postwar pursuit of growth distinctively modern was the availability of new state powers and means of macroeconomic management dedicated to achieving growth that was more exuberant, more continuous and constant, more aggregately quantifiable, and also more precisely measured than ever before. Perhaps we can best appreciate what made postwar growthmanship distinctive by looking at the context from which it emerged, for it was the ambivalence of New Deal economic policy that made the subsequent emergence of growthmanship seem like a striking departure.

Acknowledgments

Writing is a solitary exercise, but completing a book is a collective achievement. This book has been a long time in coming, and my indebtedness to others has grown accordingly over the years. Many friends and colleagues read portions of the work in progress, and Colin Gordon and Michael Hogan read the penultimate draft in its entirety. I have benefited from their helpful criticism, even if I did not always follow their suggestions. The Hagley Center for the History of Business, Technology, and Society, the National Endowment for the Humanities, the Lyndon B. Johnson Foundation, and the University of Missouri Research Council all provided welcome financial support. The staffs of the superb presidential libraries and archival repositories mentioned in the notes, as well as that of the University of Missouri libraries, helped with an unobtrusive professionalism we researchers sometimes take for granted. Oxford University Press was patient in dealing with me and expeditious in dealing with my work, a combination I have come to appreciate greatly. Finally, Betsy Rives Collins contributed to the project in countless ways large and small. My heartfelt thanks to all.

More

Prologue

The Ambiguity
of New Deal Economics

O ver the years, economists have developed several
definitions of economic growth. Usually they use
the term to mean either an absolute or per capita increase
in an aggregate measure of national income, such as the
well-known gross national product (or its more recent
variation, the gross domestic product). Refining the matter even further, economists often take care to distinguish
between economic expansion, which entails increasing the use of existing
capacity, and economic growth, which involves increasing the economy's productive capacity itself. Few Americans, however, have used the
term with such precision. Rather, they have generally con-
strued growth to mean a significant increase in
something: more economic activity, more production, more consumption. In this century,
growth has also assumed unmistakable conno-
tations of technology, industrialism, materialism, and consumerism—forces often as disorienting as they are
rewarding. It was precisely this broader, richer, popular understanding of economic growth that drove some Americans to question its
desirability even as the events that heralded the Great Depression were making growth, however defined, increasingly problematic.

I. Ambivalence

Attitudes regarding economic growth varied widely during the Great
Depression. The twelve Southerners who in 1930 contributed to the sympo-

sium entitled "I'll Take My Stand: The South and the Agrarian Tradition" conjured up a malignant combination of growth, progress, industrialism, and materialism—and then rejected the image with all the power of young poets possessed. They were a small band of agrarian guerrillas, occasionally addressing each other as "General," engaged in a campaign against the belief in bigger and better machines, against the faith that holds the acquisition of things to be a means of personal or social salvation. All had been born in the South and most were, or had been, connected with Vanderbilt University. The best-known among them—John Crow Ransom, Donald Davidson, Allen Tate, and Robert Penn Warren—were already among the South's preeminent men of letters and their embrace of yet another Lost Cause merely added poignancy to their appeal. Their campaign extended through the Depression decade, and its echoes reverberated even as the modernized South they so dreaded finally took shape in the aftermath of World War II.[1]

It would be a mistake, however, to see the Agrarians' protest as simply a doomed lament against industrialization. It was that, of course, but they denounced as well the endless, unbridled growth that was "the fundamental thesis underlying the industrial system." They found the mindlessness of what they called "moreness" particularly offensive. Such progress, they observed, "never defines its ultimate objective, but turns its victims at once into an infinite series. Our vast industrial machine . . . is like a Prussianized state which is organized strictly for war and can never consent to peace." Their alternative was a South that "never conceded that the whole duty of man was to increase material production, or that the index to the degree of his culture was the volume of his material production."[2] They realized, all too well, that their South was already slipping away.

For other Southerners, the future promised by economic growth and development could not arrive quickly enough. Henry Grady and other boosters of a "New South" had been courting industrial development for over half a century, but the region stubbornly remained the nation's poorest and most backward. In 1935, Hugh Lawson White, a wealthy retired lumberman, won the governorship of Mississippi pledging to provide the "greatest industrialization in this state that has ever been known." White shepherded the Mississippi Industrial Act through the state legislature and quickly put into place a "Balance Agriculture with Industry" program, which authorized the use of municipal bonds to construct factories for firms willing to commit to local employment and payroll guarantees. The Mississippi program yielded results only slowly and even then generated chiefly low-wage, nonunion jobs in labor-intensive textile and apparel plants, but the idea spread to neighboring states and later, after the war, gained favor across the South as states resorted to an increasing variety of public subsidies in their effort to buy industrial development.[3]

An even more ardent celebration of economic growth appeared in the faraway Northeast. As the nation waited expectantly for the newly elected Franklin D. Roosevelt to take the oath of office, a movement known as Technocracy became, for a brief season, the object of cultlike attention. Technocracy stole the national limelight from businessmen, politicians, and gangsters alike. It was "all the rage," exclaimed the *Literary Digest* in December 1932; everywhere it was "being talked about, explained, wondered at, praised, damned." The *Nation*, in a bit of wishful thinking, called it "the first step toward a genuine revolutionary philosophy for America." Less certain, Will Rogers joked, "This technocracy thing, we don't know if it is a disease or a theory." In reality, it was a little of both.[4]

Technocracy grew out of the ideas of Howard Scott, an eccentric, self-taught engineer from Greenwich Village. Scott had known the iconoclastic Thorstein Veblen, and served for a time as a consultant to the radical International Workers of the World union. He believed that capitalism's artificial price system had created an imbalance between production and consumption; consequently, technological progress and increasing production brought only growing unemployment and debt. Technocracy's answer was to replace the old price system with a new one based on energy, on ergs and joules rather than gold. The results would be revolutionary, "banishing waste, unemployment, hunger, and insecurity of income forever . . . replacing an economy of scarcity with an era of abundance." But the price system proved to be more durable than the movement that attacked it.[5]

Technocracy collapsed almost as quickly as it had appeared. After several months, Americans had to admit to themselves, if not to others, that the movement's jargon was impenetrable. Scott's credibility as a master engineer collapsed with the revelation that his contribution to the Muscle Shoals power project had been made as the foreman of a cement-pouring gang. Soon Columbia University severed its ties with the movement's proposed Energy Survey of North America, and adversity and personal disputes caused the movement to split in two. The parts lingered on, for the vision of perpetual growth and permanent abundance was not without appeal, but the contending factions operated increasingly on the fringe of American utopianism.

Although it is difficult to chart public opinion with precision in an era when scientific polling was only in its infancy, it seems reasonable to specu-

late that most Americans' attitudes toward growth in the 1930s fell somewhere between the extremes of the Agrarians' outright denunciation on the
one hand and the desperate courtship of the Mississippi Industrial Commission and the uncritical embrace of the Technocrats on the other. In that
hazy middle ground, attitudes were likely more complicated and equivocal,
and we can discern a hint of that ambivalence in the appeal of the era's two
great demagogues, Huey P. Long and Father Charles E. Coughlin. As Alan
Brinkley has written, both the Louisiana politician and the radio priest created dissident political movements by contesting, albeit indirectly, "modernization itself—and the idea that human progress rested on continuing
economic growth and organization." Yet because it was rhetorically and
politically difficult to attack something so powerful yet ineffable, at once
sacrosanct and problematic, Long and Coughlin took care to specify their
approval of material progress. The Kingfish promised a new order in which
"as much would be produced as possible so as to satisfy all demands of the
people." "It is only an untrained and cowardly mind," asserted Coughlin,
"which will disparage our high-powered tools, our better arrangement of
materials, our more efficient management." Both men appealed strongly to
those who feared that the spread of industrial society had grievously weakened community life and allowed the concentration of wealth and power in
distant places and sinister hands.[6] Clearly, even in hard times attitudes were
colored by both the promise of what growth would do *for* a community and
the realization of what it could do *to* a community.

As the Great Depression's hold on society and the economy tightened,
doubts about the desirability of growth were superseded by a new uncertainty: whether economic growth—desirable or not—was likely or, indeed,
even possible in a highly developed capitalist economy. While we have
quantitative measures by which to gauge the swiftness and depth of the
nation's economic collapse after 1929, it is more difficult to recapture the
collapse of New Era optimism and the rise of the new pessimism in economic thought that accompanied the Great Depression. Herbert Hoover
had in his 1929 inaugural address proclaimed, "I have no fears for the future
of our country. It is bright with hope," but his opponent in the 1932 presidential campaign spoke of a rather different new era, an epoch defined by
economic maturity. "It seems to me probable," Franklin D. Roosevelt
observed, "that our physical economic plant will not expand in the future at
the same rate at which it has expanded in the past. We may build more factories, but the fact remains that we have enough now to supply all of our
domestic needs, and more, if they are used." The nation could already

make more shoes and more steel than it could use. In the future, he added prophetically, Americans would of necessity think less about the producer and more about the consumer.[7]

Roosevelt's uncertainty about the future of the economy surfaced most clearly in his campaign address at the Commonwealth Club in San Francisco in September 1932. He noted at the outset that the world in depression seemed "old and tired and very much out of joint." In contrast, he observed, "America is new. It is in the process of change and development. It has the great potentialities of youth." But the proclamation of vigor immediately gave way to a portrait of a mature, indeed sclerotic economy:

Our industrial plant is built; the problem just now is whether under existing conditions it is not overbuilt. Our last frontier has long since been reached, and there is practically no more free land. . . . We are not able to invite the immigration from Europe to share our endless plenty. We are now providing a drab living for our own people. . . . Clearly, all this calls for a re-appraisal of values. A mere builder of more industrial plants, a creator of more railroad systems, an organizer of more corporations, is as likely to be a danger as a help. . . . Our task now is not discovery or exploitation of natural resources, or necessarily producing more goods. It is the soberer, less dramatic business of administering resources and plants already in hand . . . of adapting existing economic organizations to the service of the people.[8]

Hoover challenged FDR's pessimism in a subsequent campaign appearance at New York's Madison Square Garden, attacking "the whole idea that we have ended the advance of America, that this country has reached the zenith of its power, the height of its development." What his opponent had "overlooked," the beleaguered president explained, was "the fact that we are yet but on the frontiers of development of science . . . and . . . invention," the fact that there were "a thousand inventions . . . in the lockers of science . . . which have not yet come to light." To argue otherwise was "the counsel of despair," which would itself help lock America into a "decline and fall." Hoover repeated this argument throughout the 1930s, and other Republicans, including the GOP's 1936 standard-bearer, Governor Alf Landon of Kansas, echoed the point. The theme of economic maturity would, Theodore Rosenof has argued, serve as "the primary divide" separating New Dealers, progressives, radicals, and conservatives in their approaches to the problems of the Great Depression. The tension between the vision of the United States as a youthful, expansive economy on the one hand and an overbuilt, mature economy on the other, reverberated throughout the Depression decade.[9]

The specter of maturity bred a brand of scarcity economics that dominated the New Deal's initial policies for both industry and agriculture. Production controls to limit output were central to both the National Recovery
Administration and the Agricultural Adjustment Administration. The price-
fixing provisions of the NRA's individual industrial codes generally had the
effect of limiting production. "Balance" was a key word in discussions of
early New Deal economic policy, and it implied a recovery that aimed to
restore a previous level of prosperity but little more. The emphasis of so
many New Deal programs on "security"—indeed, perhaps the single most
important thread unifying what critics characterized as the New Deal
hodgepodge—bespoke a similarly pessimistic reading of the nation's present condition and future chances. Many liberals came to view massive
unemployment as a permanent problem. Harry Hopkins, the New Deal's
chief relief administrator, predicted in 1937 that "a probable minimum of
4,000,000 to 5,000,000" would remain without work "even in future 'prosperity' periods."[10] A full decade after the stock market crash, Corrington
Gill, assistant commissioner of the Works Progress Administration, spoke
of "the new economic order of things" characterized by "chronic underemployment" and "threatened economic stagnation." "The big expansion of
our economy is over," he wrote, "at least for some time."[11] Taken together
and in retrospect, the New Deal's pursuit of recovery, balance, and security
provides a rather sober counterpoint to FDR's personal jaunty optimism.
Perhaps there *was* much more to fear than just fear itself.

The emergence late in the 1930s of a full-blown school of economic
thought built on the idea of secular stagnation reinforced the New Deal's
practical emphasis on balance and security. The classic formulation of the
stagnationist analysis appeared in Alvin Hansen's presidential address to the
American Economic Association in December 1938. The United States, the
Harvard economist told his colleagues, had reached economic maturity:
population increase had slowed dramatically, and territorial expansion was
now a thing of the past. Technological innovation had produced no great
industrial boom since the automobile, and it was doubtful that technological change could be counted upon to stimulate the economy with any regu-
larity. The result was secular stagnation—"sick recoveries which die in their
infancy and depressions which feed on themselves and leave a hard and
seemingly immovable core of unemployment."[12] Hansen's fiscal policy
seminar at Harvard attracted a large and influential group of students and
had an impact on both academe and government. In 1938, a group of young
Harvard and Tufts economists influenced by Hansen published a stagna-

tionist manifesto entitled *An Economic Program for American Democracy*. The book made an appearance on Washington's best-seller list and when, in February 1939, James Roosevelt discussed with his father the possibility of an educational film on the program and objectives of the New Deal, the president suggested the work of the Harvard-Tufts group as a good summation of the administration's economic philosophy.[13]

It should be remembered, however, that the New Deal's embrace of scarcity economics and stagnationism was often ambivalent, a source of tension and contention. Some New Dealers spoke longingly of the day when they would be able to ease off on the economic brakes and step on the gas. "Rationalize it any way we have to," said Rexford Tugwell, "we can't make a religion out of growing or making fewer goods with this whole country and the whole world in bitter need." As early as 1934, Tugwell and other Department of Agriculture economists, notably Mordecai Ezekiel, sought to devise programs for industrial and agricultural expansion rather than restriction, a kind of "AAA in reverse." "The only way each of us can enjoy bigger income slices," wrote Ezekiel, "is by making the whole pie of production and income bigger."[14]

As secretary of agriculture, Henry A. Wallace became perhaps the nation's most visible restrictionist and a prime example of the New Deal's ambivalence. In two short months in 1933, Wallace oversaw the plowing under of ten million acres of cotton already in the fields and the slaughter of six million piglets whose existence threatened a future glut in the hog market. The uproar was immediate. "To hear them talk," Wallace complained, "you would have thought that pigs were raised for pets." But he felt keenly the obscenity of attacking poverty in the midst of plenty by eliminating the plenty. "We of this administration," he wrote the next year, "are not committed indefinitely to crop control or to NRA codes." It was a matter of playing the hand you were dealt; the failures of the past made scarcity economics necessary. Agriculture had to be brought into some sort of balance with industry. Significantly, however, Wallace remained uncertain whether the goal was "balance and continuous stability" or "a continually moving but balanced state."[15]

The ambivalence exemplified by Wallace was expressed in, and compounded by, the inconsistency of New Deal policy. Although it is probably unrealistic, especially in a boisterous democratic republic, to expect national policies to march in lockstep toward a well-ordered set of goals, the confusion of what the historian Alan Brinkley has described as the New Deal's "combination of vacillation and eclecticism" was nevertheless striking.[16] Much of that confusion derived from the fact that throughout the 1930s there existed beneath the main current of the New Deal's scarcity economics and state cartelism a subsidiary policy stream best characterized as state capitalism or, more simply, public investment.[17]

Even as the major New Deal policies for industry and agriculture—the NRA and AAA—sought to control production and curtail competition, a variety of other New Deal measures aimed at economic development. Spearheading this effort at the outset was the Reconstruction Finance Corporation, which FDR inherited from the Hoover administration. The RFC served at first as a safety net—a source of public capital—for the banks and railroads that constituted a crucial part of the nation's economic infrastructure. Later in the decade, the RFC sought to become, Jordan Schwarz has written, "a catapult of growth for entrepreneurs." Throughout its lifetime, the agency financed a host of capital improvement projects that created the infrastructure on which later economic growth would be based. Other New Deal public investment focused on power development. The Tennessee Valley Authority (TVA), created in 1933, quickly became the largest power producer, private or public, in the United States, and especially after David E. Lilienthal became TVA chairman in 1938, the agency took the lead in bringing large manufacturing plants to the South. The New Deal's Rural Electrification Administration (REA) prepared the way for the economic development of rural America. The REA's Electric Home and Farm Administration financed the purchase of electric appliances in the hope of hastening the spread of electricity across the American countryside.[18]

A host of other building projects contributed the hydroelectric power, roads, and bridges that would later help bring the underdeveloped West into the national economy. Beginning with the construction of Boulder Dam outside Las Vegas, the federal Bureau of Reclamation shifted its emphasis from irrigation to multipurpose projects that helped create the power infrastructure for western industrial development. The western construction firms making up the fabled Six Companies consortium that built Boulder, Grand Coulee, and Shasta Dams effectively launched their careers with those New Deal construction contracts, and went on to become prominent participants in the subsequent modernization of the West. In both the South and the West, the spectacular economic growth and industrial development of the World War II years were built on a foundation laid by the New Deal.[19]

Skepticism and outright opposition to scarcity economics intensified over the course of the Depression decade. In 1938, Phil La Follette, the governor of Wisconsin, founded a new political party based on a philosophy of increased production. La Follette's National Progressives of America adopted as their emblem a blue X circumscribed by a red circle, all on a white background. "The X," La Follette explained, stood "for multiplication of wealth instead of less."[20] The party sought to replace the old era of "horizontal development," now exhausted, with a new one characterized by what La Follette called "vertical development." He declared, "We have tried to give the farmer high prices by restricting agricultural production. We have tried to give industry high prices by restricting . . . production. . . . We have tried to give labor high wages by restricting the output of the worker. . . . A little simple arithmetic gives the . . . [result]: *less* from agriculture, *less* from industry . . . and *less* from labor." At the same time, a group of congressional liberals led by Maury Maverick, Jerry Voorhis, and Tom Amlie fought for an Industrial Expansion Bill that would use NRA-type mechanisms to plan for abundance rather than scarcity. But the bill went nowhere.[21]

As the 1930s came to a close, the tension between state cartelism and state capitalism remained unresolved. In the early years of the New Deal, scarcity and stability predominated as the administration sought to provide a modicum of security for all of the various segments of society. Later in the decade, the balance shifted, slightly but perceptibly, toward growth and development. In 1937, FDR struck an uncertain expansionist note with his commitment to address the needs of the one-third of the nation that remained "ill-housed, ill-clad, ill-nourished."[22] The administration followed up this lead a year later by haltingly adopting a Keynesian spending policy, although its efforts in this direction were largely rebuffed by congressional conservatives until the coming of war.[23] But at the same time, Roosevelt toyed with the idea of reinstituting an NRA-like arrangement, and government-sanctioned cartels continued to function successfully in agriculture and in individual industries such as oil, coal, and air and truck transportation, as well as in the distributive and service trades.[24]

While the twists and turns of public policy highlighted the interplay between stability and growth, the tension between them assumed a cultural dimension as well. The clearest illustration of this came in the New York World's Fair of 1939, which the cultural historian Jeffrey Meikle has described as "a microcosm of the machine-age world." Meikle argues persuasively that the fair's distinctive symbols, a slender, 620-foot-tall triangular needle and a sphere 180 feet in diameter and 18 stories high, both painted the purest white, stood as metaphors for the chief cultural tension of the age: the Trylon represented "limitless flight into the future," the Perisphere "controlled stasis." As the Great Depression finally came to an end, the World's Fair's monumental art expressed surprisingly well a defining political, as well as cultural, ambivalence of the Depression era.[25]

II. A Gross National Product War

The coming of World War II resolved the ambivalence of the Depression era, tipping the balance decisively away from the economics of scarcity and toward economic expansion. The goals of balance and recovery gave way to the pursuit of all-out production and full employment. The reorientation was more difficult and uneven than our social memory of the war suggests, but the forces behind expansion were ultimately overpowering. Defense orders from Europe, followed by the necessity of arming the nation's own military forces, created demand and energized the economy in a way that the New Deal's necessarily more limited spending for civilian purposes never could.

As the mobilization for war got under way, the expansionist tendencies of the administration's growing cadre of Keynesian economists became clear and the New Dealers worked to keep the fire that had been lit under the economy at a white heat. They were determined to use the opportunity presented by the defense buildup to attack the persistent stagnation that had afflicted the economy for over a decade. Consequently, they worried far less about the danger of overheating the economy and the risk of inflation than did John Maynard Keynes himself. "I have tried to persuade [Richard] Gilbert and [Don] Humphrey and [Walter] Salant that they should be more cautious," Keynes wrote of his U.S. colleagues in 1941, but "I am afraid I have only partially succeeded." The American Keynesians firmly believed, as Salant later recalled, that the "repression of demand by [premature] tax increases would inhibit an otherwise attainable expansion of output."[26] In 1940-41 they sought simultaneously to maintain New Deal programs, sustain civilian consumption, and arm the nation, thereby pushing the economy to full employment at a new, higher level of output.

In their battle to push the pace of economic expansion, the Keynesian "all-outers" gained an important advantage by virtue of their expertise in national income analysis.[27] The expansionists were also aided by the belief of many New Dealers that the real obstacle to long-term recovery was the system of administered markets that allowed firms in highly concentrated industries to maintain or raise prices while limiting output. Expansion would eliminate these bottlenecks by creating new capacity, increasing output, and inducing price reductions. Thus, New Dealers came to view expansion as both an economic goal in its own right and a way to strike at monopoly power; it appealed to both the fiscalists and the structural reformers among Roosevelt's followers. The "sitdown strike by capital" would finally be broken. Anything less than maximum expansion, warned Marinner Eccles, head of the Federal Reserve Board, would result in "a static economy frozen at a level of underemployment."[28]

Some businessmen, however, viewed stasis as preferable to expansion. The automobile, electric power, petroleum, and railroad industries all shared a reluctance to expand capacity. The struggle over steel, however, constituted the main event between the forces John Kenneth Galbraith would later aptly label the "maximalists" and the "minimalists."[29] The issue appeared deceptively simple: America's steelmakers did not want to expand. Indeed, the industry had a long tradition of preferring stability over expansion; over the years, the large steelmakers had used the tariff, the basing-point system of pricing, and the international steel cartel to build an industry impervious to change. The journalist I. F. Stone complained midway through the 1940-41 steel struggle about the wisdom of leaving "decisions of expansion to men who had spent a lifetime fighting to maintain scarcity."[30] Other critics viewed the situation in immediate, moralistic terms: the steel manufacturers wanted to exploit the shortages caused by the defense buildup in order to extort excessive profits.

In reality, the steelmakers opposed expansion more out of fear than avarice. Both publicly and, more important, privately, they worried that expansion for the defense effort would leave them with excess capacity and glutted markets—"the nightmare of a generation of redundancy overhanging the market," in the words of one observer—when the emergency had passed.[31] Their motivation was complex, and undoubtedly colored by commercial self-interest and oligopolistic tradition; but it was also the consequence of a long and psychologically grueling depression. As Bruce Catton, the liberal director of information for the War Production Board, later recalled, "A grim specter haunted these men's minds in those days; the specter of going back, some day, to ordinary peacetime pursuits and finding the nation equipped with more productive capacity than could profitably be employed." No less than other Americans, business leaders had been scarred by the Great Depression, which seemed to teach that the ability to produce more could perversely turn into the necessity of getting by with less. A "too ardent" defense effort now could bring unhappy consequences later. "Genuine abundance," Catton wrote, "can be the most horrifying of all concepts."[32]

The all-outers, from FDR on down, alternately badgered, bribed, and reassured the hesitant business leaders. Privately, they wondered whether the nation's businessmen would, as Galbraith put it, ever get off their asses.[33] The administration attempted to encourage expansion by relaxing its antitrust and labor law enforcement, offering accelerated tax write-offs for investment, and creating the Defense Plant Corporation to build new facilities for private firms with government funds. In the case of steel, it also threatened to underwrite the entry of new competitors such as Henry J. Kaiser, the highly visible drum major of all-out production. Finally, in 1941 the steel industry surrendered and accepted the inevitable: a $1.2 billion expansion of basic capacity by 13 million tons, practically all of which would be federally financed.[34]

The New Deal also found it difficult to shift gears from scarcity to abundance in agriculture. The mechanism put into place in the 1930s to restrict production and raise prices did not work effectively to meet the new task of all-out agricultural production for war. Department of Agriculture personnel were divided into four different field operations (the Extension Service, the Agricultural Adjustment Agency [AAA], the Farm Security Administration, and the Soil Conservation Service), and these agencies varied considerably in their receptivity to the new wartime exhortations for increased production. Secretary of Agriculture Claude Wickard noted in 1941 that agriculture officials "have not found it easy to shift their thinking over from peacetime to wartime requirements. . . . The sudden need for more production . . . has found them unprepared." It was not until 1944, two full production years after Pearl Harbor, that the AAA formally ended all acreage allotments—the basic form of production control—except those for burley and flue-cured tobacco. Old programs, conceived in another era, lived on uneasily in the new maximalist environment.[35]

Despite the difficulties, the all-outers ultimately prevailed. Their efforts contributed to the expansion of capacity in steel and other basic industries, to the development of the government's all-out "Victory Program" for mobilization in 1941, and to FDR's proclamation of even more ambitious production goals in January 1942. And in the end, the productivity of the American economy counted heavily in what one military historian has characterized as a "gross national product war"—a contest that turned largely on the matter of which coalition could outproduce the other.[36]

America's industrial might allowed her both to serve as the so-called arsenal of democracy and to adopt for her own military the strategic tradition identified with the Civil War general Ulysses S. Grant: the "relentless application of vast military power until the enemy surrendered unconditionally." In practice, both roles, arms-maker and combatant, were defined so as to maximize the nation's material contribution and minimize the expenditure of American lives. And behind both roles lay what Winston Churchill once impatiently called the "American clear-cut, logical, large-scale, mass production style of thought."[37]

American factories made the arsenal of democracy concept a reality. In the European theater, the United States supplied an estimated 35 percent of all the munitions expended against Germany and her satellites by the Allied powers. In the Pacific, an estimated 85 percent of all the munitions expended against Japan came from American manufacturers. Overall, the United States accounted for approximately one-half of the combat munitions produced by the anti-Axis coalition.[38]

The same industrial strength facilitated the mobilization of the nation's own armed forces. At the beginning of the European hostilities in 1939, the United States Army had fewer than 200,000 troops, 1,800 obsolescent aircraft, and only 329 tanks. Many of its basic weapons dated back to World War I, and even those were in short supply. By the end of the war, the United States had mobilized about 12 percent of its continental population (compared with Russia's 13 percent, Britain's 12 percent, Germany's 14 percent, and Japan's 13 percent). In August 1945, the size of the army stood at 8.1 million, the navy at 4 million.[39]

The equipping of a huge, modern army, navy, and air force was one of the fundamental economic accomplishments of the war effort. Over the 1940-45 period, American factories turned out 88,410 tanks, 46,706 self-propelled weapons, 2,382,311 military trucks, and 2,679,819 machine guns. In the same years, the navy added to its already formidable fleet 10 battleships, 18 large and 9 small carriers, 110 escort carriers, 45 cruisers, 358 destroyers, 211 submarines, and over 82,000 landing craft of various types. American shipyards launched 5,777 tankers and cargo vessels to ply the all-important ocean supply routes.[40] The efficiency of the shipyards increased dramatically over the course of the war, taking on the aspect of assembly line production: the construction time for a Liberty-type cargo ship that had taken nearly 10 months to build during World War I was down to 105 days in 1942, a little over 50 days a year later, and 40 days in 1944.[41] Shipbuilder Henry J. Kaiser enjoyed telling his fellow businessmen of the young daughter of a state governor who stood on a platform in his company's yard, champagne in hand, ready to christen and launch a new ship. "But where is the ship?" she inquired. "Well, sister, don't be uneasy about it," shouted a nearby worker. "You just start your swing; the ship will be there."[42]

III. Visions of Abundance

The movement away from scarcity economics toward a new economics of abundance gathered impetus steadily throughout the war years, but for a brief moment the two constellations of attitudes and aims appeared to stand in equipoise. The two reports issued by the National Resources Planning Board and sent in tandem by FDR to Congress on March 10, 1943, expressed the equilibrium. The first, entitled *Security, Work, and Relief Policies*, was commissioned in 1939 and transmitted to Roosevelt in late 1941. It hearkened back to the 1930s, emphasizing that "serious maladjustments" in the economy necessitated a large, permanent public aid program to provide "access to minimum security for all our people."[43] Its vision and tone were darkened by a pessimistic reading of stagnationist economic theory and by the experiences of the 1930s. The second NRPB report, on the other hand, entitled *National Resources Development*, reflected the experience of wartime mobilization. Its view of the future was expansive and confident. The United States, it asserted, stood "on the threshold of an economy of abundance"; with proper planning, "this generation has it within its power not only to produce in plenty but to distribute that plenty."[44]

Although it is heuristically useful to freeze these reports at the moment of their public debut in 1943, it would be a mistake to overlook that the one represented the past and the other the future. In effect, the divergent politico-economic worldviews embodied in the two NRPB studies passed each other, one in ascendancy, the other in decline. The Board pointed the way to the future in its final correspondence with Roosevelt before its dissolution: "Our expanding economy," it wrote in August 1943, "is likely to surpass the wildest estimates of a few years back and is capable of bringing to all of our people freedom, security and adventure in richer measure than ever before in history."[45]

In the last years of the war, the emergence of the new constellation of abundance, high or full employment, and economic stability gathered momentum. Alvin Hansen, the intellectual godfather of the secular stagnation school of economic analysis, gravitated to an optimistic assessment of economic maturity. In suggesting that an abbreviated "White Paper on Employment Policy" be prepared for inclusion in the 1944 Democratic platform, he directed, "The draft should make a clear declaration that the government accepts as a primary responsibility the maintenance of full employment; and the prevention of depression and deflation on the one side and of inflation on the other."[46] If such steps were taken, Hansen was, he wrote to a colleague in 1945, "really very optimistic about our prospects." America was not "through": "We can make adjustments to the changed situation [described in his theory of economic maturity] and go on to higher living standards and as great, if not greater, opportunities for private enterprise as we have had in the past." Such confidence, he reported, set him apart from Keynes himself, who in 1944 and 1945 took a much dimmer view of America's prospects for full employment.[47]

The new goal of abundance and the optimism that underlay it appeared in a number of different political guises. Liberals planned for a further extension of the New Deal, based on economic growth instead of balance and security. At the same press conference in 1943 at which Roosevelt related the parable of Dr. New Deal and Dr. Win the War, the president spoke of a "new program" built around "an expanded economy," and in the 1944 election campaign he sketched out the vision of a full-employment economy offering sixty million jobs.[48] Henry A. Wallace's call for a postwar Century of the Common Man amplified the themes of abundance and full employment.[49] Walter Reuther, a leading expansionist throughout the war, proclaimed, "The road leads not backward but forward, to full production, full employment and full distribution in a society which has achieved economic democracy within the framework of political democracy."[50]

Few businessmen favored a resurgent, hyperactive New Deal, but the optimism that inspired liberal visions of a new political economy encouraged many executives as well. Paul Hoffman, head of the Studebaker Corporation and chairman of the Committee for Economic Development, recalled that the Depression had given birth to "some strange thinking on the part of business, labor, agriculture, and government—thinking which in turn found expression in weird policies." These policies, he declared, had been "designed to fasten upon us an economy of scarcity." But the war had changed all that, and had opened the way to a "peacetime economy of abundance."[51] General Robert E. Wood of Sears, Roebuck, who in the late 1930s had quoted Hansen's views on economic stagnation approvingly—"It means," he observed rhapsodically, "that the sun has passed its zenith and the shadows of afternoon have begun to fall"—would backtrack soon after the war and declare the idea of economic maturity to be "the greatest of the many fallacies enunciated in the 1930s by the New Deal."[52]

For business executives, the battle between visions of abundance and forebodings of scarcity could have concrete consequences. Wood acted on his newfound optimism in 1945 by taking the biggest gamble of his long merchandising career and investing $300 million in a gigantic postwar expansion program at Sears. Within two years, Sears's profits more than tripled and the company left in the dust its formerly fierce competitor, Montgomery Ward, whose chief executive, Sewall Avery, made the irretrievable business mistake of liquidating Ward's holdings in preparation for a horrific postwar depression that never came.[53]

The emergent consensus on the economics of abundance was tested during the debate over full employment in 1945 and ratified by the enactment of the Employment Act of 1946. Despite the significant dilution of the bill by congressional conservatives, the Employment Act's final declaration of the government's "continuing policy and responsibility . . . to promote maximum employment, production, and purchasing power" signaled the formal recognition of "high" employment and economic stability as the chief aims of macroeconomic policy. Signing the act into law in February 1946, Truman commented that the law expressed "a deep-seated desire for a conscious and positive attack upon the ever-recurring problems of mass unemployment and ruinous depression."[54] The Employment Act represented both an extension of the developments of the Great Depression and a departure from them. With its passage, the focus of national economic policy formally shifted from the problem of curing a gravely, perhaps permanently, sick economy to maintaining a healthy one.

In addition to its declaration of policy, the Employment Act also established the Council of Economic Advisers (CEA) as a mechanism to ensure that the president would in the future benefit from expert economic advice on a regular basis. Created at the point when the economics of abundance, with its goals of high employment and economic stability, superseded the Depression's stress on recovery, balance, and security, the Council of Economic Advisers would in its first years of existence add to the dominant constellation of goals a fresh, self-conscious emphasis on economic growth, an emphasis that would in time become the centerpiece of the postwar political economy.

1

The Emergence of Economic Growthmanship

Although focused and articulated most clearly by the new Council of Economic Advisers, the postwar interest in economic growth per se was not the Council's unique discovery or intellectual property. Talk of abundance, hopes of abundance, plans for abundance were all in the air as the war drew to a close. Even before the war's end, an informal committee that included Alvin Hansen and Gerhard Colm of the Bureau of the Budget's Fiscal Division had noted that "after the war, the volume of demand and production . . . will have to increase steadily from year to year in order to sustain full employment as the productive power of our country expands."[1] But in such thinking, growth remained more the by-product of sustained full employment than a primary end in itself. In a similar fashion, the Committee for Economic Development, a prominent business organization, recognized when developing its suggestive and influential "stabilizing budget policy" in 1947 that "reasonable stability of total demand at an adequate level . . . means a steadily rising level of demand as our productive capacity grows."[2] Here too, however, growth remained subordinate to economic stability as the focus of policy.

Chester Bowles, the wartime head of the Office of Price Administration, viewed economic growth as a more central matter. The New Deal, he recalled, had been "only half a success," and "many frustrated economists told us that there was little more that we could do about it. . . . We must learn to live with a certain amount of scarcity in the midst of plenty." But that was "a recipe for class warfare," Bowles believed, "and for a dog-eat-dog society in which no group could prosper except at the expense of some other group."[3] Bowles foresaw a different future. In 1946 he published *Tomorrow Without Fear*, a liberal tract that had at its heart the question "Where is our productive capacity going to be ten years hence, twenty years from now?" His answer was optimistic: "Our population isn't going to stop growing, technology isn't going to stand still, and all these new plants and machines, bought by an average of 30 billion dollars a year in business investment spending, will steadily increase our ability to produce."

Bowles predicted that "by the late 1960s our national production . . . will have grown to the breathtaking total of 400 billions of dollars a year!"[4] Significantly, he shifted the discussion from economic expansion (that is, the putting to work of idle resources, the elimination of economic slack, and the achievement of full employment) to what economists regard as pure economic growth—the long-term growth of economic potential, of potential output. Still, it remained for Truman's new Council of Economic Advisers to develop fully the concept of growth and give it a place of primacy among the other goals—notably full employment and economic stability—that guided postwar economic policy.

I. The Council of Economic Advisers and the Doctrine of Growth

The CEA began operation in August 1946, with a membership diverse in background, temperament, and politics. Edwin G. Nourse was a moderate conservative with excellent professional credentials; he had headed both the American Economic Association and the Social Science Research Council, and was a vice president at the Brookings Institution when selected to lead the Council. Leon H. Keyserling had been in the vanguard of the New Deal. A graduate of the Harvard Law School, he did not hold a doctorate in economics but had proven himself a brilliant student of political economy during his long government service, most notably as a trusted adviser to New York's senator Robert F. Wagner. John D. Clark had made a fortune in the oil business, then retired while in his early forties to study economics and undertake an academic career; he was serving as dean of the business school at the University of Nebraska when Truman tapped him to serve on the Council.

The CEA members were an unusual mix in terms of economic philosophy as well. Although not strict Keynesians, all were familiar with Keynesian analysis and ready to accept many of the most basic Keynesian pre-scriptions. Indeed, an early CEA memorandum to the president spoke of the "wise policy of deficits under adverse business conditions."[5] But the three also had strong institutionalist leanings and a keen interest in micro-economic phenomena.[6] As Keyserling subsequently observed:

The whole basis of economic analysis is to analyze where your resource maladjust-ments are, where allocations are going wrong, where your income flows are going wrong. And you correct it by applying the stimulus or the restraint at the right points, which really gets back to what I said in 1948. . . . We don't have the kind of economy where you can just throw a blunderbuss at the whole thing. Here again, economists are beginning to say that we need micro economic as well as macro eco-nomic policies.[7]

Thus, it was out of what can only be described as a unique brand of eco-nomic eclecticism that the Council forged the new emphasis on growth as the nation's foremost economic task.

A gradual but clearly perceptible quickening of interest in growth can be traced in the unusually philosophical year-end reports submitted by the CEA between 1946 and 1950. The first such report in December 1946 recog-nized the legitimacy of stabilization as a fundamental policy aim: "The passing of the Employment Act . . . would have been no more than a sense-less gesture," the president's advisers commented, "if it did not express a considered belief that . . . we could moderate in the future the devastating periods of business depression." But they also cautioned that mere stability was not by itself a wholly satisfactory criterion of success. Indeed, the "greatest danger of recent years" had been "a more or less permanent equi-librium at a low or 'stagnation' level."[8] High employment per se did not constitute a completely trustworthy measure of economic success either. "Maximum *employment*," the Council warned in 1947, "may be achieved in a rich economy or in a poor economy, in a static economy or in a dynamic and growing economy." Indeed, experience had already demonstrated the "inadequacy" of aiming merely at a high number of jobs. "We were aston-ished," the CEA declared, "to find, after the country had reached the ideal-ized figure of 60 million [postwar] jobs, that the volume of production still was disappointing."[9]

At the end of 1947, the CEA suggested that the attention already given to economic stability and full employment be complemented by an increased emphasis on "maximum production," the "belatedly added phrase" in the

Employment Act's declaration of policy that "should be kept foremost in our analysis of conditions and trends and in our efforts toward better-ment."[10] The CEA's view of production was rich and complex. It favored a proactive rather than reactive approach: "Government economic activities should be carefully designed to add to the resourcefulness, the productivity, and the growth of our business system as a whole instead of being regarded mainly as a device for applying poultices to that system when it becomes infected."[11] But, the CEA warned in picturesque language, maximum pro-duction should not be interpreted to mean a life of grinding toil and depri-vation so that "Pa can raise more corn to feed more hogs to buy more land to raise more corn to feed more hogs *ad infinitum.*" Instead, the CEA pre-sented the vision of a redistributive mass consumption society in which "the enlarging production" would "go increasingly to filling in the con-sumption deficiencies of the erstwhile poor."[12]

The direction of the Council's thinking during its first two years under Nourse's leadership was clear. The full-fledged growthmanship that would emerge when Leon Keyserling took over the effective leadership of the Council in 1949—an increasingly focused, self-conscious, single-minded emphasis on growth as the overriding (but not sole) national economic goal—was not a sudden departure in its thinking but rather the culmina-tion of a trend already well under way.

Written under Keyserling's direction, the CEA's 1949 report constituted growthmanship's declaration of principles. In it, the Council sought to offer "new ideas" to a "new generation," thereby distinguishing the liberalism of Truman's Fair Deal from its New Deal predecessor and from conservative alternatives. Accordingly, the report stressed that "the doctrine of secular stagnation no longer finds place in any important public circle with which we are familiar." In its stead, the Council offered "the firm conviction that our business system and with it our whole economy can and should continue to grow." Moreover, the CEA maintained that economic growth deserved prior-ity over efforts to redistribute the nation's current product. In the Council's view, such an emphasis on growth promised to reduce "to manageable pro-portions the ancient conflict between social equity and economic incentives which hung over the progress of enterprise in a dynamic economy." Indeed, the report found in growth the standard or criterion that could be applied to the troublesome problem of "balance" in the economy, balance between pro-duction and consumption, and balance among wages, profits, and prices.

Here was a macroeconomic goal that contained a key to the solution of society's most vexing relational problems. Growth provided an economic yardstick that would allow factual economic analysis to be applied to the contending claims of consumers, labor, management, capital, agriculture, and government. For the Council, it promised the opportunity to move issues of social strife out of the political arena and into the court of "scientific analysis": "It then becomes possible, albeit not easy, for business-men, workers, and farmers to seek that share of the total product which is most conducive to the progress of the whole economy and thus to their own best interests in the long run." Daring in its conception and articulate in its presentation, the 1949 CEA report came close to raising growth from an overriding economic goal (first among equals) to a new organizing prin-ciple for a neo-corporatist political economy.[13]

Keyserling believed strongly that the Council's emphasis on growth was a significant departure, and he stressed the point repeatedly. The emphasis on "growth economics" was, he later observed, "the one really new thing" in Democratic programs since the New Deal, the "one really innovating fac-tor." It was a departure as well from Keynesianism, "really a static econom-ics" that "doesn't deal with economic growth at all."[14] Keyserling also contrasted the CEA's emphasis on growth with the updated restrictionism advocated by others on the right, who held that a truly healthy economic readjustment after the war and the immediate postwar boomlet necessi-tated, in Keyserling's words, "not only a shrinkage of the price level but also a shrinkage of markets, also a shrinkage of employment . . . also a some-what lower level of production and distribution than we had in 1948."[15]

The CEA distinguished between the new goal of growth, now primary, and the longer-standing but now decidedly secondary aim of economic sta-bility. In May 1950, Gerhard Colm, now a senior economist with the CEA, assessed the United Nations Report on National and International Measures for Full Employment, which had been produced by a staff of experts appointed by the UN secretary general. The UN economists, he reported, placed their greatest stress on compensatory measures to offset fluctua-tions, while the Truman administration gave "primary attention" to "mea-sures that promote steady expansion and [thereby] increase the shock resistance of the economy." Compensatory stabilization programs, while closely related, "should be kept in readiness as a second line of defense."

The difference in priority had important analytical origins and policy consequences. The Council believed that "economic disturbances *originate* in maladjustments, not of the aggregate, but of economic relationships." A countercyclical policy aimed at cushioning booms and declines, Colm wrote, necessarily "accepts defect" [sic] in the primary effort to establish and maintain healthy relationships between consumption and investment and among wages, prices, and profits. Thus, countercyclical policy aimed at correcting aggregate symptoms rather than addressing root causes. The "more affirmative policy" of "promoting sustained expansion" led to "the necessity of focusing on crucial economic relationships as much [as] if not more than on the development of aggregates." In the CEA's view, growth-manship was not a retreat from microeconomic complexities but rather a way of merging and engaging a variety of macro- and microeconomic problems and objectives.[16]

By 1949 the emergent growth orientation was exerting a strong influence in discussions of economic policy both within the Council and outside it. The historian Charles S. Maier has written that the "American organizing idea for the postwar economic world" was what he has labeled "the politics of productivity," a set of actions and ideas that aimed to supersede class conflict with economic growth.[17] The chief international instrument for the politics of productivity was the Marshall Plan, which sought to spread both the message and the reality of growth to war-ravaged Western Europe.[18] By 1949, the effort was having great success. As one well-placed observer, Jean Monnet, the patron saint of European integration, noted at the time: "We Europeans are still haunted by past notions of security and stability. Today the principal idea is that of expansion. That is what is hap-pening in the United States. They are always ready to evolve and search out progress."[19]

At home, the president's economic messages sounded the battle cry of economic expansion and growth throughout the year, with a constancy that was particularly striking in light of the fact that the concern with inflation that had dominated the start of the year was soon replaced by worry about deflation as the policymakers belatedly recognized the recession of 1949. In January's State of the Union message, Truman observed that it was not enough "to float along ceaselessly on a postwar boom until it collapses" or "merely to prepare to weather a recession if it comes": "Instead," he pro-claimed, "government and business must work together constantly to achieve more and more jobs and more and more production . . . which will mean more and more prosperity for all the people."[20] In the fall, Truman echoed Keyserling's rhetoric when he told a Kansas City audience that the United States could achieve a $300 billion economy and double the income of a typical family. "This is not a pipe dream," he insisted. "It can be done. But can't happen by itself. And it can't happen if we have a lot of 'pull-backs' at the helm of government."[21]

Similarly, in Congress economic expansion and growth appeared the keynote in a variety of legislative initiatives that claimed to address the problems of both inflation and recession. At the beginning of the year, the Spence Economic Stability Bill of 1949 (H.R. 2756) offered expansion as a weapon against inflation, following very closely the lines of draft legislation prepared under the direction of the CEA.[22] The Economic Expansion Bill of 1949 (S. 281), introduced in July by Senator James Murray (after much redrafting) as an amendment to the expansionary Full Employment Bill of 1950 originally proposed by the National Farmers Union, used a similarly ambitious growth approach, which its supporters claimed would address the problem of deflation. This measure, too, was actively supported by Keyserling, although Truman withheld administration support from it for reasons that are not entirely clear. Both the Spence and Murray bills died aborning, but growth, it seemed, was in the air—a cure for all ills.[23]

Both big business and organized labor saw in growth an opportunity to reconfigure postwar labor-management relations to their particular advantage. For unions, arguably the most dynamic element in Roosevelt's New Deal coalition, the emergence of growthmanship in the mid- and late 1940s coincided with a fundamental reorientation away from labor's previous commitment to economic planning, structural reform, and social solidarity, toward a new effort to create a private-sector welfare state through collective bargaining over wages, benefits, and pensions.[24] The relationship between General Motors and the United Automobile Workers exemplified the new turn in class relations. General Motors had embarked on a massive $3.5 billion postwar expansion program designed to boost production by more than 50 percent over prewar levels, building new plants in California, Texas, Ohio, and New York and increasing its blue-collar workforce by 25 percent. To safeguard this expansion, GM needed stability and predictability. On the other side, the UAW wanted higher pay, better benefits, and relief from the press of postwar inflation. In 1948, GM and the UAW agreed on a contract incorporating both a quarterly cost-of-living adjustment (COLA) tied to changes in the consumer price index and an "annual improvement factor" (AIF) wage increase based on the increase in GM productivity. Two years later, the auto giant and the trendsetting union expanded the agreement in an unprecedented five-year contract—the so-called Treaty of Detroit— that sweetened the COLA and AIF provisions of the earlier deal, guaranteed workers a 20 percent increase in their standard of living over the life of the contract, and committed GM to provide a corporate pension and to underwrite half the cost of a new health care insurance plan.[25] The linking of wages, benefits, inflation, and productivity paved the way for the banner production years of the 1950s. It also constituted a self-conscious elevation of growth at the micro level that meshed perfectly with the growthmanship taking shape at the macro level. It is little wonder that Truman promptly gloated that the Treaty of Detroit was an answer to those "who have been making fun of the idea that our economy has to grow continually."[26]

The CEA's direct impact on events increased further in 1950. The January 1950 *Economic Report to the President* declared, "Maximum production and maximum employment are not static goals; they mean more jobs and more business opportunities in each succeeding year. If we are to attain these objectives, we must make full use of all the resources of the American economy."[27] Within months, the nation's national security policymakers, working under Keyserling's tutelage, incorporated the doctrine of growthmanship into Cold War strategy. In the wake of the "loss" of China and the Soviet development of an atomic bomb, they undertook a sweeping reassessment of America's Cold War stance. Truman first read the resulting document, the famous NSC-68, in April; after the worldview expressed in NSC-68 appeared to have been validated by the outbreak of fighting in Korea in June, Truman finally approved the document in September 1950.

NSC-68 suggested that economic growth could be used to generate the funds required for a massive rearmament and a redefinition of the nation's global responsibilities. As the authors of the plan wrote, "The necessary build-up could be accomplished without a decrease in the national standard of living because the required resources could be obtained by siphoning off a part of the annual increment in the gross national product." Growth would provide the vast resources necessary for what the diplomatic historian John Lewis Gaddis has characterized as a "symmetrical version of containment," which would seek to give the United States a kind of perimeter defense against communism. All points on the perimeter would be equally important; in the words of NSC-68, "a defeat of free institutions anywhere is a defeat everywhere."[28] Thus was made a connection between unlimited means and unlimited ends that, as we shall see later, would bring another generation of liberals to grief in the late 1960s.

The combination of NSC-68 and the outbreak of the Korean War touched off a vigorous debate over economic mobilization policy later in 1950, and here, too, growthmanship played an important role. Keyserling later recalled the events in a fashion rather typically unencumbered by humility:

The really great issue that arose at the beginning of the Korean War was the balance between trying to finance the war out of diversion of resources, as against financing the war out of economic expansion. I think the greatest single decision made . . . was the decision to go for a program of very large economic expansion. This involved a very hot battle within the administration, and one which was won completely by the growth people for the first part of the Korean war. I think that my initiation and partic-ipation in that was about as large as that of any one individual could be in influencing policy.[29]

Although self-serving, Keyserling's account was essentially correct.[30] The Defense Production Act signed into law on September 8, 1950, was, in the words of the CEA's executive secretary, Bertram Gross, "a third step in a series started by the Spence Bill and the Murray Economic Expansion Bill, particularly the third title, 'Expansion of Productive Capacity and Sup-ply.'"[31] By the end of 1950, the growth orientation that had been developed gradually since 1946 and articulated clearly in 1949 was firmly embedded in national policy.

II. Growthmanship and Economic Theory

The emergence of growthmanship raises an important question about the connection between public policy and modern social science. To what degree did the postwar turn to growth result from the advancing course of economic knowledge? In this instance, the answer is complex. In both its theoretical and empirical dimensions, the interface between policy and science was richly tex-tured but uneven, and, given early aspirations, somewhat disappointing.

From the beginning, chairman Edwin Nourse conceived of the CEA as "a scientific agency of the Federal Government" that sought "to enlist eco-nomics in the public service."[32] The CEA, he recognized, was "not set up as a great research agency but as a very small synthesizing body." As a result, the agency turned to the economics profession for help in bringing scientific research to bear on its efforts. In 1947, Nourse suggested optimisti-cally that the American Economic Association's research committee "be organized and equipped to see that the scientific resources of economics are enlarged . . . and . . . brought to serve."[33] In May 1948, he was still hopeful about "articulating our program with research activities and interests of the profession through A.E.A."[34]

The relations between the CEA and the economics profession on matters of theory never fulfilled the early hopes and expectations of Nourse and others. John D. Clark noted the difficulties in bringing theory to bear on policy, using the example of business cycle theory. He observed that "there is no professional consensus upon business cycle theory, only professional agreement that each particular theory is inadequate." Moreover, he contended, "cycle theory has seemed to be almost irrelevant in the work the Council must perform. . . . Upon no occasion have the members of the Council raised any point of cycle theory and no agreement upon any point under consideration . . . has ever been delayed while the Council members exchanged their views about the business cycle." The CEA's analysis, Clark added, "does not require resort to cycle theory but can be founded upon simple economic principles which are far more limited." And the situation concerning cycle theory was true more generally as well: "The Council has not found that its ability to reach a conclusion about the probable effect of various economic conditions or about the correct government policy to meet observed problems has often been seriously limited by the lack of a satisfactory economic theory."[35]

Keyserling found attempts to bring economic theory to bear on problems similarly unrewarding. In commenting on just such an effort by Donald H. Wallace of Princeton, a study of "Price-Wage-Profits Relations" undertaken at the CEA's behest, Keyserling wrote: "It seems to me that relatively little attention should be paid to [general theory], not because it is unimportant, but because it is to be assumed that members of the Council and staff are reasonably familiar with general economic theory and keep abreast of it." Keyserling's preference for the empirical over the theoretical was unmistakable: "In the final analysis, we are fairly well in agreement here on general theory and need to get down to the brass tacks of some factual appraisals." Whereas academic economists discussed prices and wages and profits "in the refined atmosphere of theoretical techniques," the CEA and government policymakers of necessity operated "in a world where prices and wages and profits are being *made*."[36] In the real world of policy, Keyserling made it clear, theory played but a small role at best.

With just this perception in mind, Roy Blough, who joined the Council in 1950 as its third member after Nourse's resignation, wrote shortly thereafter that "economics in Washington is, in general, not at the high level of intellectual intensity that is characteristic of the better universities."[37] For the Truman CEA, theory did not inform policy in general or the emergence of growthmanship in particular in any notable way, if theory is taken to mean conceptualization of a specialized, sophisticated sort beyond the general laws of textbook economics.

Why was the relationship between policy and technical economic theory so underdeveloped despite Nourse's early hopes? The answer to this question lies in the interaction of three factors that determined the nature and quality of the relationship between policy and economic knowledge. The first was the state of the scientific knowledge available for policymakers to use and appropriate. The second was the desire and commitment of the policymakers themselves to tap this specialized knowledge. The third was the existence of instruments and agencies that would aid policymakers in exploiting the available theory. Weaknesses in each of these areas contributed to the CEA's theoretical impoverishment during the yeasty Truman years.

Leon Keyserling noted the poverty of growth theory in the late 1940s. "There had been almost no interest in American economics in economic growth," he recalled.[38] It is true that growth had been of continuing interest to economists from the very beginning of economics as a science. As Paul Samuelson has pointed out, Adam Smith's *The Wealth of Nations* (1776) "can be read as a bible of economic development."[39] While Ricardo and Malthus took a gloomy view of the prognosis for growth, and Karl Marx continued their preoccupation with distribution instead of growth, the neoclassical writers retained rather more of Smith's optimism. Despite this continuing interest, however, the question of growth had over the years slipped out to the periphery of economic thought. To be sure, the landscape of growth theory was not quite as barren during the Truman years as Keyserling subsequently remembered. The work of R. F. Harrod in the late 1930s and Evsey D. Domar in the immediate postwar years would later serve as benchmarks for the beginning of "modern" growth theory.[40] But, as sweeping and parochial as his judgment was, Keyserling exaggerated only a little.

When the American Economic Association undertook a review of the various fields of economics in the early 1950s, Moses Abramovitz wrote of the "fragmentary" and "rudimentary" state of the art in the economics of growth. "The theory of growth," he observed archly, "is an underdeveloped area in economics." Harold F. Williamson agreed, commenting that "economists generally have been too much concerned with static models and too culturally bound by a Western European framework of institutions to make the contributions to the subject of the economics of growth that might reasonably be expected from the profession." Simon Kuznets noted "a recent surge of interest in problems of economic growth," but added that it came "after decades during which the problem has been neglected in the traditional corpus of economic theory, and ruled out by some economists as not the proper concern of economics." Symptomatic of such neglect, Paul Samuelson offered virtually no discussion of productivity or economic growth or development in the 1951 edition of his classic introductory economics text, except in connection with Malthus and secular stagnation.[41]

A second reason for the underdevelopment of the relationship between policy and theory was the striking lack of interest in theory per se on the part of key CEA figures and, less surprising, on the part of the leader to whom they reported, President Truman. Nourse noted caustically in September 1949:

Keyserling and Clark were quite impatient with my idea that, since we have to do a great deal of re-thinking of economic theory and business practices, the staff work is heavily weighted with refinement of issues and statements of pros and cons rather than setting forth dogmatic answers. Keyserling said that he knew it was quite possible to get prompt and definitive answers to the problems. When he was in the Housing Administration he had in two and a half months prepared a report that was a perfect example of the succinct laying out of a major economic problem with its proper solution.

He himself, Nourse concluded sardonically, was obviously handicapped in his CEA post "by my long experience as an independent research worker at Brookings and in the SSRC [Social Science Research Council]."[42] In fact, Nourse harbored his own reservations about economic theory. He recognized the "blighting isolation of a great deal of the theorizing that economists have done" and was "mistrustful of the whole idea of a 'general theory' of employment, of money, of economic enterprise, or of any one of the significant segments of the economic process and still more of the idea that there could be a general theory of the economic process as a totality."[43]

Keyserling's war with academe was legendary even during his service on the CEA, and his antipathy for theory had both intellectual and psychological roots. Not possessing a doctorate in economics, Keyserling felt put upon by academics and returned their supposed snubs and disdain with a highly developed and oft-expressed animus of his own. He loved to distinguish between "those who have been challenged by the responsibilities of practical action and particularly by the responsibilities of public office," on the one hand, and "the economist who has to maintain only a theoretical position, or to write his name imperishably (in his belief) into the literature of his profession," on the other.[44] Academic economists had fractured the discipline into esoteric subspecialties and "in that process came to regard those who wanted to take a general view of the economic problems of the nation as a whole and their relationship to one another as being almost apostates from the field of economics."[45] Such views made a disdain of theory into a defense of self.

As the CEA's "boss" and chief consumer of economic advice, Truman manifested no interest in the theory or even the reasoning behind the CEA's recommendations. Nourse could be absolutely devastating in his private assessment of the president's approach to economic problems. After one meeting with Truman, he wrote, "I left with the feeling that his decisions were already pretty well taken, and this on the basis of information that comes to him casually from a variety of sources, with the final determinant his own political judgment. He seems to me quite quick and brittle in his reactions, not at all attracted by a contemplative analysis of basic issues."[46] Even Keyserling, who held Truman in considerable esteem, admitted, "He was not a technical economist, a formal economist. He had the level of understanding that one might expect, shaped by certain profound views that were fundamental to economics and public policy."[47]

Indeed, Truman's attitude regarding theory was less a lack of interest than actual resistance and antagonism. As presidential assistant Joseph Feeny expressed it (with the president's warm approval) in early 1950, "History has shown that the long-range theories of the past have sounded fine in theory but have rarely ever proved beneficial when applied. . . . Our country has reached the soundest and most stable era of prosperity by a realistic approach to each particular problem as it arose."[48] Thus the scientific weakness in growth theory was joined by a disinclination on the part of both adviser and policymaker to use whatever theory might nonetheless be available.

The final factor responsible for the weak influence of theory on policy was the condition and usefulness of the primary instrument available to effect the interaction between policy and knowledge, the Council of Economic Advisers itself. The CEA proved unequal to the task for a number of reasons. First, the press of current events and workaday routine exerted a stultifying influence on the intellectual work of the Council. Donald Wallace complained to Nourse in mid-1947 of the CEA staff's inability to find the time to do or even to oversee basic research, and the problem proved intractable.[49] In 1949 Nourse wrote to Senator Paul Douglas that "the resources of the Council and its small staff are fully taxed by the continuing task of furnishing economic judgments upon concrete problems as they arise. . . . Therefore we have rigorously restricted our discussion of general problems in an abstract setting to a very few that we have dealt with in the Council's annual reports to the President."[50] The next year, when Roy Blough joined the Council, he told a friend: "I suppose there are ways to make this job of mine a nice quiet study of economics, but I do not seem to have learned them. There are a lot of very difficult problems that we get drawn into; many conferences with the leading lights . . . newspapermen who want to get 'background' or at least to satisfy their curiosity about what I look like; speeches to write and deliver." "I am enjoying the work," he wrote to another colleague, "but find there is a good deal of pressure."[51] Moreover, all such pressures of routine, daily crises, and recurrent bureaucratic deadlines were exacerbated by the "start-up" problems that inevitably troubled a wholly new agency like the CEA.

Compounding the deadening influence of daily routine and the press of short-run problem solving were the budget and staffing difficulties that plagued the Council during the Truman years, some the result of political pressure by conservatives and Republicans. The cuts were more than a mere annoyance. According to Nourse, they "precluded our holding topical conferences of academic, business, and labor economists that we had in mind as a means of mobilizing professional thinking on national economic problems."[52]

Finally, the CEA's ability to exploit economic theory was limited by the disunity that characterized the Council during Nourse's tenure. The conflicts that separated Nourse from Keyserling and, to a slightly lesser extent, from Clark were real, encompassing professional (i.e., economic), political, and philosophical disagreements and personality clashes. The most fundamental intellectual disagreement between Nourse and Keyserling involved growth: Nourse believed in economic limits and the necessity of trade-offs and hard choices; he was fond of observing that "the hard facts of economic life" dictated that "you can't eat your cake and have it too"; in his eyes, Keyserling was dangerously oblivious to the threat of an inflationary overheating of the economy.[53]

The disagreement between Nourse and Keyserling over growth and limits proved especially divisive because it spilled over into other important debates. The running controversy over defense spending that occupied the attention of policymakers throughout the immediate postwar decade brought matters to a head. Nourse became a chief spokesman for those "economizers"—including the conservatives Herbert Hoover and Senator Robert Taft, the commentator Walter Lippmann, as well as Truman's own secretary of defense, Louis Johnson, and officials in the Bureau of the Budget—who argued that overspending for defense would weaken the U.S. economy and run the risk of creating a garrison state that would destroy American democracy in the effort to protect it. Keyserling, as we have seen, spoke for the other side, joining Secretary Dean Acheson and other State Department officials, the National Security Council, and the military in advancing a national security ideology that held the U.S. economy capable of doing whatever was deemed necessary for defense of the American way of life and national interests.[54]

Keyserling believed in retrospect that the long-run cost of this discord on the CEA affected both the emergence and then the staying power of the growth orientation. He recalled:

I think that President Truman was completely sold on the general idea of economic growth . . . but I cannot say that I was ever fortunate enough to have at any time, the kind of understanding and support and breadth of support which I think existed, let us say for the policies of the Kennedy economic advisers. . . . It was always a hard battle; it was a hard battle initially because the Council was divided on how it should behave.[55]

In the end, work pressures, budget constraints, and disunity all compromised the CEA's ability to exploit economic theory to any noteworthy degree in the reorientation of policy around the overriding goal of growth.

In summary, growth theory itself was impoverished, the will to use it was feeble, and the instrument designed to foster the application of theory to policy—the CEA—was handicapped in significant ways. In its last year of operation, the Truman CEA continued to seek ways "to bring the thinking of the economics profession to bear upon the work of the Council."[56] The task had originally been undertaken with some optimism in 1946. That the effort seemed to be virtually starting anew six years later testified to the fact that the early hope for a marriage of economic science and national policy remained unfulfilled.

If technical economic theory contributed little to the reorientation of policy around the goal of growth, what about influence running the other way, from policy to theory? Here judgment is more difficult and necessarily more speculative. The decade after 1952 witnessed, in the words of W. W. Rostow, "a most remarkable surge of thought centered on the process of economic growth." As Simon Kuznets observed, this surge of interest was "clearly *not* an organic outgrowth of continuously and increasingly effective work on the problem leading to a scientific discovery, the latter stirring interest and stimulating research on a new foundation," but rather was the result of current events.[57] Among these events, the emergence of a "Third World" of modernizing nation-states and the continuation of a Soviet-U.S. competition for military, economic, and propaganda dominance in the Cold War were undoubtedly central. It is possible, indeed probable, that the prominence the Truman CEA accorded economic growth also contributed to the renewal of interest in the field of growth theory, but that contribution cannot be measured precisely.

III. The Importance of Measuring Things

Although the development of growthmanship relied little on specialized economic theory, the CEA operated rather more effectively in the realm of scientific data management, borrowing and contributing in significant ways. Here, too, on the empirical side of economic science, the relationship between policy and knowledge was governed by the state of the science, the will to use scientific knowledge, and the instruments at hand. All these factors were, on balance, stronger for the exploitation of empirical research and statistical science than for the appropriation of specialized theory.

Stuart Rice, the longtime chief statistician in the Bureau of the Budget, has observed that "statistics, like education, are pervasive in their influence."[58] He might have added that they are omnipresent as well. But for the CEA's formulators of growthmanship, one field of statistical knowledge stood above all others in significance—the concept of national income. National income and its statistical cousin the gross national product (GNP) have long served as the fundamental measures of economic change and, in the minds of many, of national welfare and progress as well.[59] The concept of national income took shape slowly in the 1920s and 1930s, and was institutionalized in its modern form just as the Truman Council began its work.

The modern era of national income accounting began with the efforts of the National Bureau of Economic Research in the 1920s. The Federal Trade Commission ventured into the field in 1926, but its work was terminated when government funding for such basic research was cut off. Ultimately, the impact of three developments—the Great Depression, the advent of Keynesian economic theory, and World War II—combined to propel national income accounting to the forefront of statistical science and economic policymaking. All three placed a premium on measuring aggregate income, outlays, and production. The Department of Commerce began to prepare national income estimates in the mid-1930s, and introduced quarterly estimates of GNP and national income in 1942. Finally in 1947 there appeared an expanded, double-entry set of income and product accounts by sector, which gave these measures their wholly modern form. Thus, at the beginning of its operations the CEA found available a set of highly sophisticated statistical data and an array of analytical tools. The CEA quickly incorporated these into its economic analysis and, by its public pronouncements and published reports, placed them in the national spotlight.

The CEA, divided and deeply ambivalent about the utility of sophisticated economic theory, appeared much more willing to grant the central importance of statistical fact-finding—"the foundation of the work of this Council."[60] The CEA, John Clark reported in 1948, sought "to improve and expedite statistical service, and it has worked to this end with the several fact-gathering agencies."[61] Nor was the CEA's interest merely that of a voracious but passive consumer of data. Staff economist Walter Salant wrote to his colleagues regarding statistical matters:

Speaking for myself alone, I feel that if I do not know the parts that go into the analysis and also how they are put together, I am merely indulging in a kind of informal chatter when I discuss the outlook. . . . Each of us owes it to the Council to use scientific procedures in formulating our independent individual judgments as well as our collective judgment, and that requires that we see everything that goes into the pot.[62]

Whereas the CEA stood alone as the first federal agency expected (by some, if not by all) routinely to bring economic theory to bear on the formulation of policy, in the realm of economic measurement it joined a long-standing, multifaceted federal effort. The Departments of Agriculture, Commerce, Labor, and the Interior, as well as the Federal Reserve Board and the National Recovery Administration, were already engaged in data collection when Roosevelt in 1933 established the Central Statistical Board to coordinate the federal government's statistical services.[63] The Reorganization Act of 1939 subsequently transferred this coordinating function to the Bureau of the Budget.

World War II necessitated a dramatic expansion of the federal government's statistical capability: just to mention such alphabet agencies as WPB (War Production Board) and OPA (Office of Price Administration) is to conjure up the vision of a statistical juggernaut.[64] Soon postwar planning provided a further spur. In August 1944, Roosevelt set off a flurry of activity when he asked the Bureau of the Budget to prepare a comprehensive program of statistics for the reconversion effort.[65] But Stuart Rice warned his superiors that it was "easier to ask for such a program than to develop it" and in the end much of Roosevelt's proposed "Basic Statistics Program" failed to gain congressional funding.[66]

It would be a mistake, then, to paint too rosy a picture of the statistical tools and instruments available to the CEA as it set to work. The failure to fund Roosevelt's Basic Statistics Program was soon compounded by a further round of budget-cutting in 1947; seeing creeping socialism and intrusive bureaucracy everywhere, conservatives attacked federal statistics programs of all kinds.[67] By 1949, the Budget Bureau had simply stopped developing and submitting program proposals "in view of the congressional attitude toward statistics."[68] Despite such problems, however, the CEA inherited a legacy (however troubled) and a statistical arsenal (whatever the gaps) that served as a foundation for some noteworthy achievements on the policy-knowledge front.

The CEA's statistical activities did not usually include the actual gathering of data—other government and private agencies performed that service—but rather focused on the use of data collected by others. The CEA's contributions came in all three of the kinds of information found in the federal statistical system: indicators, frameworks, and basic research.[69] Some were absolutely fundamental to the task of policymaking, and so were unrelated to the emergence of growthmanship per se; others, however, were clearly linked to the CEA's growth orientation. One example of the former was the CEA's compilation of basic economic statistics published under the title *Economic Indicators*. The statistics had originally been published, in an abbreviated form, by the Bureau of the Budget, but at Keyserling's strong urging the CEA took over the effort, expanded its scope and distribution, and arranged for regular monthly publication under the auspices of the Joint Committee on the Economic Report.[70]

The CEA's development of statistical frameworks—systems for illuminating fundamental interrelationships between parts of the economic system—necessarily reflected the conceptual nature of its thinking over the years and thus was clearly linked to the emergent growthmanship. The foremost statistical system adopted by the CEA, first for analytical and then increasingly for heuristic purposes, was the so-called Nation's Economic Budget. First used in the 1946 budget published in January 1945 and summarized in FDR's accompanying budget message, the Nation's Economic Budget was then incorporated into the full-employment proposals that led ultimately to the creation of the CEA. The CEA made it the statistical centerpiece of the yearly *Economic Report of the President*. In the words of Gerhard Colm, the Nation's Economic Budget

simply presents gross national income and gross national expenditures in the two columns of a national ledger. The totals of both sides must, of course, be equal. National income and national expenditures are allocated to consumers, business, international transactions, and government. . . . This presentation not only affords a check on the estimates but also shows the interrelation between transactions of consumers, business, and government.[71]

The Nation's Economic Budget concept combined an analysis of broad economic flows with a view of the interrelationships among profits, wages, and prices. It illuminated present conditions and offered a basis for projections into the future and hence for a degree of what might be called "economic planning." One reviewer of the CEA's initial reports was ecstatic: "This is not somebody's crackbrained theory; it is simple arithmetic."[72]

The Council quickly attempted to extend the temporal range of its statistics. In October 1947, it began work on long-term projections of GNP, national income by demand category, and disposable income for 1950 and 1955 and on the development of "target" figures against which to measure its estimates. The CEA staff then planned to collaborate with the Bureau of Labor Statistics, using the latter's comprehensive input-output table in order to project investment needs for specific industries and public facilities.[73] The results of this project stirred controversy within the CEA when the staff tried to incorporate its ten-year projections into the 1949 *Economic Report* under the title "Basic Objectives for Balanced Economic Growth."

The daring use of such statistical projections to support just the sort of affirmative growth-oriented policy toward which the Council had been moving proved too much for Nourse and Clark. Critical of the projections as "too highly speculative . . . whatever [their] . . . exploratory value for scholars," the two Council members at first sought to excise the offending section, then settled for its inclusion "in a more tentative and sketchy form."[74]

The next year, however, Keyserling, then serving as acting chairman and freed from Nourse's countervailing conservatism, included in the 1950 *Economic Report of the President* a full-employment model of the economy for 1954. Scholars considered the effort a pioneering study. Under Keyserling's leadership, the CEA continued its work on "the preparation of economic objectives for 5- and 10-year periods," and it cooperated with the National Bureau of Economic Research to organize the Annual Conference on Research in Income and Wealth in 1951 on the subject of long-term projections.[75]

The growth orientation helped dictate another basic change in the framing of government statistics. When Keyserling assumed the chairmanship of the Council, the Department of Commerce was reporting the GNP and its component figures only in current dollars. Keyserling recalled:

This was meaningless; you can't tell what the rate of growth has been; or what really happened in current dollars. You have to have constant dollars with different deflators. The Secretary of Commerce said this would cost too much and he didn't see why we should do it. I had to go to the President. The result was that the Secretary . . . was ordered to do it in constant dollars as well as current dollars.

In this way, Keyserling has correctly observed, "the picture in constant dollars and in current dollars with the proper deflators" became available to "economists and everybody else."[76]

In the third area of statistics, basic research, the CEA's growthmanship fostered a major effort to study underdeveloped regions of the country. The regional development research program included studies of the Southeast (1949), New England (1950–51), and the Southwest (1951). Keyserling directed the local economists charged with the New England analysis to study carefully "the possibility that further self-development in this region may be encouraged and facilitated by some national action favorable both to that area and to national economic growth."[77] Thus, in the fields of statistical frameworks and statistical basic research in particular, the CEA in its pursuit of economic growth both borrowed from science and contributed significantly as well.

In the final analysis, the contribution of economics as a social science to the initial reorientation of policy around growth was distinctly uneven. Economic theory provided surprisingly little inspiration or guidance. On the empirical side, however, advances in statistics contributed significantly to the development of growthmanship. Ultimately, the recasting of policy around growth was a political imposition. Rather than science pushing policy, or policy pulling science, the emergence of growthmanship suggests another image: policy and science often marched in tandem, moving farther and faster together than either could have alone, and moving closer together as time passed. But it was policy—an elemental assertion of political will and imagination—that caused the first step to be taken, fundamentally altering the national agenda.

IV. Public Entrepreneurship and Historical Moment

Keyserling's triumphs of 1949-50 did not last, however. In 1951, both his expansionist approach and his concomitant preference for indirect controls suffered defeat. In January, the administration instituted a general price freeze, and later in the year it decided to "stretch out" military procurement programs into 1955 and 1956. Full mobilization of American productivity gave way to minimum mobilization. The CEA also found itself excluded from the Fed-Treasury Accord of March 1951 and generally supplanted by the Office of Defense Mobilization as the leading source of advice concerning economic mobilization.[78]

The return of the Republicans to presidential power in 1953 furthered the decline of growthmanship within the federal government. For the newly reconstituted Eisenhower Council of Economic Advisers, under the leadership of both Arthur F. Burns (1953-56) and Raymond J. Saulnier (1956-61), the tension between the goals of economic growth and stability remained central, but with a decidedly different emphasis. A visceral fear of inflation and a keen sensitivity to the political dangers of recession combined to lay stress on the business cycle and on stability. The result, at least in the minds of growth-oriented Democrats such as Walter Heller, "kept policy thinking in too restrictive a mold in the late 1950s."[79]

The temporary and partial eclipse of growthmanship in the 1950s should not obscure the Truman CEA's considerable achievement in introducing, articulating, and incorporating the new orientation into policy. The achievement owed much to Keyserling's efforts. From the outset, he was the leading force in developing the administration's economic philosophy. Keyserling exerted a powerful influence within the CEA, both while Edwin Nourse headed the agency and thereafter when he himself served as chairman; his intelligence, energy, single-mindedness, combativeness, and political skill made him a truly formidable advocate in Council deliberations.

More important, Keyserling had influence beyond the CEA—he had the ear of the president of the United States. The CEA's emphasis on growth "stems very largely," Truman wrote him, "from your personal convictions"; and the growth orientation, the president maintained, "has set the right framework for meeting many economic situations." Truman's own frugal instincts—he loved poring over budgets and was happiest when they balanced—kept him from fully embracing a growth framework as the solution to all problems, but, as his most searching biographer has written, Truman "consciously and enthusiastically accepted" Keyserling's ideas on growth, approving both their general direction and their expansiveness of vision. Keyserling was, Truman later observed, "the greatest advocate I have ever had around me."[80]

Keyserling also operated behind the scenes, as an occasional writer of White House speeches and as a member of the so-called Wardman Park group, a weekly gathering of administration liberals who began meeting in 1947 in the hope of infusing Truman's presidency with a reformist identity and hence political appeal all its own. Named for its meeting place—the apartment of Oscar Ewing, head of the Federal Security Agency—the group fed its ideas to Truman via two of its members, presidential advisers Clark Clifford and Charles Murphy. Keyserling's was the dominant voice on economic matters, and the refrain was economic growth.[81] In addition, he served as a tireless publicist in the mass media, using the *New York Times* and national magazines to good advantage in popularizing the growth agenda.

In leaving a significant mark on national policy, Keyserling operated in the classic fashion of the public entrepreneur, whose role, according to one theorist, is "to change the flow over time of . . . vast resources, for good or ill, within the framework of a popular democracy and its elected representative institutions."[82] Keyserling did just that, by dint of intellectual power and prickly personal ferocity rather than personal charm or charisma of a more classic sort. Throughout his career, Keyserling exhibited a zest for bureaucratic combat and demonstrated a keen appreciation of where the levers of power were and who operated them. A personal anecdote makes the point: When his Columbia University mentor Rexford Tugwell first sent him to Washington during the early New Deal, Keyserling was interviewed by Jerome Frank, who would soon become chief counsel of the Agricultural Adjustment Administration. "What do you know?" Frank asked. "['Cotton'] Ed Smith," Keyserling answered, naming the all-powerful South Carolina Democrat who happened to be the chair of the Senate Agriculture Committee.[83] Here, clearly, was a lad from Beaufort, South Carolina, who knew the ways of the world.

It would be an oversimplification, however, to view the turn to growth as simply the revelation of an individual or a political coup by a small group. The emergence of growthmanship was a response to broad currents in American life as well. Most immediately, it was a response to the amazing wartime recovery of the U.S. economy. But it also had roots that ran deep in American culture and history. The growth regime expressed in the arena of political economy the ascendant values of the modern consumer culture, which had emerged unmistakably in the 1920s and was now, in the immediate postwar period, assuming the mature shape that would so thoroughly color American life for the remainder of the twentieth century that most Americans simply assumed that the consumer culture *was* America and vice versa. As growthmanship came increasingly to be discussed in explicitly Keynesian terms, with an emphasis on boosting aggregate demand (which came to be translated as: consumption, more consumption), the convergence between the postwar political economy and the voracious postwar culture of consumption became ever more complete. Even more broadly, the emphasis on growth at once expressed and reinforced the tremendous outburst of national optimism sparked by the economic recovery and military victory of World War II. Confidence in the future had long been a noteworthy feature of American life, but one dimmed considerably by the trauma of the Great Depression; now, in the aftermath of the war, American expectations became grand once again, and in this revival of optimism growthmanship operated as both cause and effect.[84]

Finally, the emergence of growthmanship owed much to the fact that the new orientation promised to be so useful: for the CEA, it provided the ultimate yardstick for macroeconomic management and the way to wed macro- and microeconomic objectives; for business, it bid fair to generate sustained prosperity in an increasingly productive mass consumption economy; for workers, it promised a constantly rising standard of living alongside a burgeoning private welfare system of pensions and benefits; for liberal activists, it served as a rationale and a vehicle for reform; for Cold Warriors, it made feasible a new, globalized, and militarized containment policy; and for Democratic partisans, it promised political appeal and electoral success. Few significant departures in public policy have seemed at once so innovative *and* inevitable.

2

The Ascendancy of Growth Liberalism

The prosperity of the 1950s and 1960s proved just how wrong the pessimists of the 1930s had been in their estimation of the fundamental strength of the economy. Jump-started by the demands of war and sustained—to just what degree would become the subject of heated debate—by the subsequent mobilization for a Cold War, the economy moved into a period of unparalleled affluence that would last until the early 1970s, an era that appears in retrospect to have been America's economic golden age. Alvin Hansen's dark vision of secular stagnation brightened considerably during the war, and in 1963 even he observed that the postwar period "must be regarded as one of high stability and growth."[1]

I. The Postwar Boom, 1947–1960

Where had the stagnationists gone wrong? The answer is that the engines of economic progress that Hansen had identified in 1938 had not expired but merely stalled. Population growth rebounded dramatically, as the vaunted baby boom in the years 1946–64 gave America the largest absolute population increase in its history.[2] The frontier experience was replicated in the explosive growth of the crabgrass frontier of suburbia and in the emergence of the Sunbelt. Innovation continued to exert a healthy influence as the auto boom continued into the postwar years, with nearly 8 million passenger cars produced in 1955 (the prewar high had been 4.5 million in 1929).[3] The chemical industry—as Benjamin Braddock learned in the 1960s anthem movie *The Graduate:* "Just one word. . . . Are you listening? . . . *Plastics*"—joined electronics and other defense-related industries to move the economy forward. In other words, on each specific count of their analysis the pessimists were undone by events.

The postwar affluence took hold of the American imagination. Writers found new metaphors for the American experience in the visible institutions of abundance: the supermarket was especially favored. *Life* magazine rhapsodized about shoppers whose market carts "became cornucopias filled with an abundance that no other country in the world has ever known."[4] In his poem "Superman," John Updike archly reported, "I drive my car to the supermarket,/ The way I take is superhigh,/ A superlot is where I park it,/ and Super Suds are what I buy."[5] And Norman Mailer heralded the political triumph of John F. Kennedy in 1960 in an essay entitled "Superman Comes to the Supermart."[6]

The economic reality that underlay the imagery of abundance was impressive. The GNP (measured in constant 1954 dollars) rose from $181.8 billion in 1929 to $282.3 billion in 1947. By 1960, the GNP had increased by a further 56 percent, reaching $439.9 billion.[7] The Federal Reserve Board depicted the advance in yet another statistic: its Index of Manufacturing Production stood at 58 in 1929, reached 100 in 1947, and rose to 163 in 1960.[8] Spending on personal consumption (measured in constant 1954 dollars) increased from $128.1 billion in 1929 to $195.6 billion in 1947, and to $298.1 billion in 1960. Even when the increased size of both the labor force and the overall population are taken into account, the progress is striking: GNP per capita (in constant 1954 dollars) increased 24 percent between 1947 and 1960, and personal consumption spending per capita (also in constant 1954 dollars) 22 percent.[9]

Admittedly, hidden beneath such rosy statistics was a more disquieting aspect of the postwar economic order. By any standard, either comparative or absolute, the income distribution in the United States remained skewed. Using a complicated semi-decile ratio, Peter John de la Fosse Wiles has found that for the late 1960s, the measure of income inequality stood at 3.0 for Sweden, 5.9 for the United Kingdom, 6.0 for the Soviet Union, and 13.3 for the United States.[10] Paul Samuelson stated the matter more picturesquely in 1970: "If we made an income pyramid out of a child's blocks, with each layer portraying $1,000 of income, the peak would be far higher than the Eiffel Tower, but almost all of us would be within a yard of the ground."[11] Clearly, not all Americans shared fully in the postwar boom. Some groups—notably blacks, Hispanics, Native Americans, and the elderly—remained less well off than others. Nevertheless, income distribution in the United States, however skewed, became slightly more equal during the postwar boom. The bottom 40 percent of American families received 12.5 percent of aggregate family personal income in 1929, 16 percent in 1947, and 16.1 percent in 1957; the top 20 percent of families received 54.4 percent of all income in 1929, 46 percent in 1947, and 45.3 percent in 1957.[12]

In a similar way, although blacks did not share as fully as whites in the postwar bounty, their relative position did improve. In 1960, black males received only 67 percent of the salary or wage income of whites; the figure for black females was only marginally better, 70 percent. Yet, before the war, the situation had been even worse, with black males and females receiving only 41 and 36 percent, respectively, of the income earned by their white counterparts.[13] Economic growth did not end discrimination or eliminate its ravages, but it did significantly lessen the existing disparities.

In mid-1955, George Meany, president of the AFL-CIO, observed that "American labor has never had it so good."[14] The same could be said for the majority of Americans. On one important point, however, the stagnationists had been prescient: The postwar affluence was accompanied by the emergence of a governmental presence in the economy that dwarfed even that of the New Deal. Federal spending, which during the 1930s had crested at 10.5 percent of GNP in 1936, averaged 17.3 percent over the 1947-60 period.[15] The increased fiscal presence, combined with the liberation of monetary policy in the famous Fed-Treasury Accord of 1951, greatly increased the federal government's power to influence the pace of economic activity. Meanwhile, the acceptance of government responsibility for maximum employment, production, and purchasing power, which had been put forth somewhat tentatively in the Employment Act of 1946, over time hardened into a firm, bipartisan commitment to manage American prosperity, even though debate continued over how best to fulfill that responsibility.

II. The Republican Interlude

In the early 1950s, Keyserling's assertive growthmanship was eclipsed by events and by alternative judgments regarding the economy's potential and problems. As we have seen, Keyserling's influence waned during the Korean War mobilization. By 1952, there was serious talk in congressional circles about closing down the Council of Economic Advisers altogether, partly in reaction to his abrasive partisanship.[16] More important, the return of the Republicans to presidential power in 1953 brought a renewed emphasis on the other elements in the constellation of concerns guiding policymakers, notably stability and inflation; growth was not completely dismissed, but it was subordinated to these other issues.[17]

Arthur F. Burns, Ike's first CEA chairman, observed that the American people had become "more conscious of the business cycle, more sensitive to every wrinkle of economic curves, more alert to the possible need for contracyclical action on the part of government, than ever before in our history."[18] Whereas Keyserling had maintained that "there is not meaningful stability except *a stable rate of constant growth,*" Eisenhower's advisers placed a premium on stabilizing the business cycle by minimizing fluctuations and on stabilizing prices by vigorously fighting inflation. For Keyserling, growth was the necessary precondition for stability; for Raymond J. Saulnier, Ike's second CEA chairman, price stability was "prerequisite to the attainment of vigorous and sustainable economic growth."[19]

Eisenhower considered the battle against inflation "never-ending" and preeminent.[20] When asked at a press conference whether the administration had worried "a little too much about inflation . . . and perhaps not enough about the slow rate of growth of our economy," Ike answered that he had spoken of "the expanding economy" as much as anyone in public life. But in the end, he maintained, inflation was logically the first priority: "I believe that economic growth in the long run cannot be soundly brought about except with stability in your price structure."[21]

The administration's stance helped make economic growth a matter of controversy in Eisenhower's second term. The growth of the early postwar years slowed distinctly. The real GNP increased at a yearly rate of 3.8 percent from 1947 to 1954, but at a lower 3.2 percent rate from 1954 to 1960. More dramatically, potential GNP (a calculation based on the assumption of full employment) grew at an average of 4.4 percent per year in the earlier period (1947-54) and at only 3.5 percent per year for the years 1954–60.[22] As one expert observed, "Looking at the decade [of the 1950s] as a whole, most persons would judge the growth rate of output as rather sluggish. If the latter part of the decade is made the reference point, the rate would be judged unsatisfactory."[23] Of course, from a more recent perspective, such an assessment seems harsh; in retrospect, the economic performance of the Eisenhower years appears highly satisfactory in most respects. But the loss of economic momentum was sufficient for the question of economic growth to become a major public controversy before the 1950s were over.

The tension between the often competing goals of stability and growth dominated policymaking throughout the Eisenhower presidency. The administration consistently resolved the tension in favor of stability, to the detriment of the vigorous growth that had been characteristic of the immediate postwar years. Often it did so self-consciously. In his final presidential *Economic Report*, in January 1961, Eisenhower summed up his economic philosophy one last time. "Some temporary acceleration of growth might have been achieved," he admitted, if inflationary expectations "had been allowed to persist and to become firmly rooted." But such growth would have been "unsustainable," requiring "far-reaching and painful correction." Precisely because of the administration's "action to maintain stability and balance and to consolidate gains," the nation could now look forward to "a period of sound growth from a firm base."[24] Despite the administration's promises of future well-being, however, the issue of growth flared into public controversy during Ike's second term and moved to the center of national debate during the 1960 presidential campaign.

One important reason for the volatility of the growth issue was the fact that it became a staple of partisan politics. Although both parties accepted the need for both stability and growth, the primacy of the one over the other divided the essentially pro-growth Democrats from the basically inflation-conscious Republicans. Leon Keyserling played an especially important role in keeping economic growth high on the political agenda of liberal Democrats. He left government service at the end of the Truman presidency but remained highly active in public life. He created a personal think tank, the Washington-based Conference on Economic Progress, and worked ceaselessly to spread his one *idée fixe*.

Keyserling imbued the liberal Americans for Democratic Action with a passion for economic growth that served as that organization's grand design for economic policy throughout the 1950s. In an ADA handbook entitled *Guide to Politics, 1954*, Keyserling derided the "depression psychosis" still afflicting a segment of the population; even some liberals, he observed, "have so little confidence as to think that the American economy is going to be capsized again by every little puff of wind." He called upon good liberals to see beyond "stability" to the need for constant economic expansion. Sustained growth would yield a $500 billion to $600 billion economy by 1960, with "at least a one-third increase in the average standard of living."[25] Keyserling's views suffused the ADA's 1956 platform, which proclaimed that sustained growth would make possible a reduction in poverty, an expansion in welfare services, and the assumption of free-world security burdens—all with a balanced budget and without excessive taxation.[26]

Keyserling and his ideas also played a key role in the Democratic Advisory Council, a policy group formed by the Democratic National Committee after the 1956 election to generate winning ideas for the opposition party. Keyserling reported to friends that he was "crusading continuously" against Eisenhower's "spurious and illegitimate crusade against inflation," which was being used "to repudiate and defeat national objectives, including economic growth, far more important than absolute price stability." John Kenneth Galbraith, who chaired the DAC's advisory committee on economic policy, was disturbed by Keyserling's disregard of the dangers of inflation; he was also at the time developing the rationale for a more qualitative liberal economics as an alternative to Keyserling's quantitative approach. These two formidable figures, with attending supporters, locked horns throughout the DAC's early years, but Keyserling scored effectively in their skirmishing and in 1958 led the DAC into a commitment to a 5 percent annual growth rate that would later appear in the 1960 Democratic Party platform. Although Keyserling's influence waned as the 1960 election itself approached, his leadership made the DAC, in the words of the journalist Sidney Hyman, "an early leader in stressing the need for, and the implications of, sustained economic growth."[27]

The Republicans chafed under the partisan Democratic assault, but Eisenhower remained steadfast in his concern for fiscal integrity and price stability. Ike was for economic growth, but when he named Vice President Richard Nixon to head a new Cabinet Committee on Price Stability for Economic Growth, the title of the group betrayed his emphasis on the dangers of inflation. The "deficit-producing, inflation-inviting, irresponsible-spending proposals of self-described liberal Democrats" left Eisenhower cold. Despite Nixon's own frustration with the administration's seeming insistence "that you can't do things—that we can't afford things," the vice president lashed back at the Democrats, accusing them of practicing a puerile sort of "growthmanship." Secretary of Commerce Maurice Stans spoke dismissively of a "cult of growth." Henry Hazlitt, an economics columnist for *Newsweek* friendly to the Republican cause, flayed the "rate-of-growth fetishists," "agitators," and "alarmists."[28]

In the mid-1950s, Cold War competition raised the stakes of partisan political sniping to a new, higher level. In May 1957, Nikita Khrushchev predicted that the Soviet Union would "soon catch up to the U.S. level of per capita output of meat, milk, and butter; then, we shall have shot a highly powerful torpedo at the underpinnings of capitalism."[29] With the threat of mutual nuclear destruction still overhanging the world, the Cold War took on the additional dimension of economic competition. The development of a Soviet nuclear capability and the launching of Sputnik constituted hard proofs, in the eyes of Walter Lippmann, that "the prevailing picture of the Soviet economy as primitive and grossly inefficient was false."[30]

The economic contest between the superpowers focused especially on the matter of growth. Again, Khrushchev made the point with frightening directness: "Growth of industrial and agricultural production is the battering ram with which we shall smash the capitalist system, enhance the influence of the ideas of Marxism-Leninism, strengthen the Socialist camp and contribute to the victory of the cause of peace throughout the world." To American listeners, the threat was clear. The Soviet economy was growing faster than the American, enabling the Soviets to support a powerful military machine and making the Soviet system dangerously appealing to Third World countries looking for models to emulate. With the launching of a new Soviet seven-year plan in 1958, Khrushchev predicted that by 1970 at the latest the Soviet Union would "catch up with and outstrip the United States in industrial output . . . [and] advance to first place in the world in absolute volume of production and in per capita production."[31] The rhetoric was clearly ominous, but the statistical reality of the Soviet threat proved harder to establish.

A 1957 study undertaken by the Legislative Reference Service at the behest of the Joint Economic Committee concluded that "firm conclusions about rates comparisons are fraught with many perils."[32] The problems encountered in comparing Soviet and U.S. growth rates included the sketchy quality of Soviet statistics and the possibility of their falsification for propaganda purposes. More fundamental and more vexing for analysts was the difficulty inherent in comparing economies that differed greatly in organization, structure, and maturity.

Notwithstanding such problems of measurement and analysis, the Legislative Reference Service told Congress that the Soviet Union was expanding its industrial output at roughly twice the rate of the United States. Because of the much larger size of the American economy, the absolute gap between the two vastly favored the United States and was continuing to widen. But if the Soviet growth rate continued to be higher than that of the United States, "in time . . . the absolute gap would begin to narrow sharply."[33]

Allen Dulles, head of the Central Intelligence Agency, painted a similar picture when he testified before the Joint Economic Committee in late 1959.

Soviet industrial production, he reported, "has been growing at a rate at least twice as rapidly as that of the United States since 1950." The Soviet GNP, he added, "has also been growing twice as rapidly as that of the United States over the past 8 years."[34] Dulles's generally scholarly and judicious analysis avoided Cold War hysterics, but he warned, "If the Soviet industrial growth rate persists at 8 or 9 percent per annum over the next decade, as is forecast, the gap between our two economies by 1970 will be dangerously narrowed unless our own industrial growth rate is substantially increased from the present pace."[35]

Observers reacted to the emergence of an economic Cold War in a variety of ways. To some, the matter was nothing but a numbers game.[36] Others, including the outstanding growth theorist Evsey D. Domar, an MIT economist, believed the Soviet growth rate worrisome; he warned that "the influence played by a country in world affairs is related to its economic size." Jay Lovestone of the AFL-CIO believed that America's own domestic well-being required more rapid growth, and that the Soviet threat made the need all the more urgent. Howard C. Peterson of the Committee for Economic Development, a corporate-liberal business group, was less troubled: "Surely we wish to progress as rapidly as in the past, and to do better if we can—but not at any cost." Members of the business community such as Peterson generally worried that an increase in the nation's growth rate might be obtained at the price of increased government intervention in the economy and perhaps higher taxes. Clearly, responses to the Soviet Union's economic challenge were colored by fundamental beliefs as well as immediate Cold War fears.[37]

While the controversy over economic growth reflected both partisan politics and Cold War pressures, it was fueled as well by a generalized anxiety that seemed to come over the nation in the late 1950s. "Woe to them that are at ease in Zion," the Bible warns, and during the latter part of the Ike Age, Americans grew increasingly fearful that the nation had lost its way in the blaze of its own prosperity. The result was an outburst of public soul-searching and numerous attempts to articulate an agenda of national goals that would be worthy of history's most powerful democracy. One such undertaking was the Special Studies Project of the Rockefeller Brothers Fund, organized in 1956.

The Rockefeller project set up panels in six broad areas to define major national problems and "clarify the national purposes and objectives that must inspire and direct the meeting of such great challenges." Behind the effort lay the concern that "our achievements and our strengths, because of their very magnitude, appeared in some ways to have outrun our goals." The overall Rockefeller panel of thirty notable Americans then published the individual reports as they were concluded one by one between January 1958 and September 1960. The economic policy panel report appeared in April 1958. Its message was unambiguous: "We must accelerate our rate of growth." The report viewed growth as the essential means to whatever ends U.S. society would aspire to, and it specified that a 5 percent growth rate was required to provide the public and private expenditures needed to achieve the nation's goals of freedom, abundance, and security.[38]

The discussion of national goals continued with the publication in *Life* magazine in 1960 of a series of articles on the theme of "the national purpose." Time-Life publisher Henry R. Luce caught perfectly the paradoxical amalgam of confidence and anxiety that pervaded the search for national goals: "But what now shall Americans *do* with the greatness of their nation?" he asked. "And is it great enough? And is it great in the right way?" James Reston called attention to "all this concern in the nation among serious men about the higher rate of growth in the U.S.S.R." But "it isn't just the Russians now," Archibald MacLeish noted, "it's ourselves. . . . We feel that we've lost our way in the woods, that we don't know where we are going—if anywhere." For Walter Lippmann, at least, the way was clear: "To use increments of our growing wealth wisely and prudently for public and immaterial ends: that is the goal, so I believe, toward which our national purpose will now be directed."[39]

Even President Eisenhower joined in the search for purpose, appointing a President's Commission on National Goals under the auspices of the American Assembly, a neo-corporatist public interest group that he had founded while president of Columbia University in 1950. The commission received advice from a panel of economists whose members ranged from the Keynesian Paul Samuelson to the monetarist Milton Friedman. Its report, publicly transmitted to the president in mid-November 1960, underscored the importance of growth while straddling most of the issues connected with it. The economy needed to grow, the commission maintained, "at the maximum rate consistent with primary dependence upon free enterprise and the avoidance of marked inflation." As to what that maximum rate should be, the commission noted that there was no consensus among economists and that good faith estimates ranged from 3.4 percent per year growth in GNP to up to 5 percent.[40] What the President's Commission was unable to decide—just what a national commitment to economic growth entailed—became in 1960 one of the crucial issues of the presidential campaign.

As Senator Paul Douglas observed, the matter of growth was "at the heart of politics in 1960."[41] Electoral politics at the presidential level brought the concerns of half a decade into clear focus. The sharpening of the public debate was evident in a series of articles on growth that the *New Republic* ran throughout the electoral season. William R. Allen, an economist at UCLA, agreed that "other things the same, having more goods and services is better than having less." But he cautioned against "putting the goose through the wringer in the attempt to squeeze out the golden eggs faster"—faster growth required hard choices and entailed costs and trade-offs.[42]

Significant divisions appeared even between those more disposed to force the pace of economic growth. James Tobin of Yale University saw the matter in stark terms: "We must devote more of our current capacity to uses that increase our future capacity, and correspondingly less to other uses." Tobin called for a shift of national output from private consumption to public and private investment, and he argued that the key to engineering such flows was increased taxation.[43] In so doing, he echoed the call for fewer tailfins and for more and better public facilities that had been popularized earlier by John Kenneth Galbraith in *The Affluent Society*. Keyserling, however, argued vigorously that such a growth policy would be regressive and that expanded production for private consumption was indeed needed in order to liquidate the large pockets of poverty still existing in American society.[44] The difference was significant: Keyserling asked the quantitative questions, "How much growth, how fast?" Tobin and Galbraith added the important qualitative question, "What kind of growth do we want?"

John F. Kennedy embraced the goal of faster growth from the outset of the 1960 campaign. He called the resumption of economic progress "the number one domestic problem which the next President of the United States will have to meet," and fitted the growth issue into his overall campaign theme—the promise to get the country moving again.[45] On the hustings, he observed:

The United States looks tired. My campaign for the presidency is founded on the single assumption that the American people are uneasy at the present drift in our national course, that they are disturbed by the relative decline in our vitality and prestige. . . . If I am wrong in this assumption . . . then I expect to lose this election. But if I am right . . . then those who have held back the growth of the U.S. during the last years will be rejected.[46]

Stiffening such rhetoric was the Democratic platform, much influenced by Keyserling and the Democratic Advisory Council, which committed the party to a 5 percent annual growth rate. For the party as well as for the candidate, growth would provide the means to great ends. As the platform explained, "Economic growth is the means whereby we improve the American standard of living and produce added tax resources for national security and essential public services."[47]

The Democratic onslaught left the Republican candidate in a difficult position. Vice President Richard Nixon had for some time been troubled by Eisenhower's cautious economic policy, complaining privately about "the standpat conservative economics that [Secretary of the Treasury Robert] Anderson and his crowd are constantly parroting."[48] In the spring of 1960, Arthur Burns, a former chairman of the Council of Economic Advisers, prevailed upon Nixon to urge that the administration adopt a more expansive fiscal policy to stimulate the economy, but the president would not budge.[49] During the campaign, Nixon found himself caught between the need to defend Eisenhower's record and the desire to identify with a more vigorous growth position. He reminded viewers during the first televised debate that the administration "has encouraged individual enterprise and it has resulted in the greatest expansion of the private sector of the economy that has ever been witnessed in an eight-year period."[50] Yet, in late July 1960, just before the Republican convention, Nixon and Governor Nelson Rockefeller of New York struck the so-called Compact of Fifth Avenue, an agreement which specified that "the rate of our economic growth must, as promptly as possible, be accelerated by policies and programs stimulating our free enterprise system—to allow us to meet the demands of national defense and the growing social needs and a higher standard of living for our growing population."[51]

Nixon attempted to edge closer to Kennedy's expansive position on growth while distinguishing the Republican version of such progress. "I would say that my goal," he announced, "and I think the only proper goal, for those who do not buy the theory of government manipulated growth, the only proper goal is a maximum growth rate. It might, in some instances be 3 percent, in some instances 4, in some instances 5."[52] Such efforts failed, however, to dislodge the connection in the public mind between the goal of accelerated growth and JFK's most powerful appeal, his call for action and his promise of greatness. Kennedy was the growth candidate; Nixon was not. And Kennedy won, if but narrowly.

The primal energy in the air after Kennedy's victory was palpable. Richard Goodwin, a Kennedy speech writer, would later recall "the almost sensual thrill of victory—not a culminating triumph, but the promise, almost limitless in dimensions, of enormous possibilities yet to come."[53] Economic growth would be the engine to drive such expansive visions and deeds.

III. Great Societies at Home and Grand Designs Abroad, 1961–1968

Of course, winning elections and making promises are easier than governing a vast nation and delivering on commitments. Kennedy knew as much, even in the heat of the campaign. When he first met Walter Heller, an economist at the University of Minnesota, on a campaign swing through Minneapolis in October 1960, his initial question was: "Do you really think we can make good on that 5 percent growth promise in the Democratic platform?"[54] Introducing Heller as his choice for chairman of the Council of Economic Advisers at a late December press conference, the president-elect said carefully, "What Dr. Heller and I are in agreement with, I hope, is that the economy of the United States must grow at a faster rate than it has been growing during the last five years, and we hope to stimulate that growth."[55]

Although the commitment to increased growth was unshakable, the precise path to that goal was not quite settled. Kennedy's handpicked economic advisers, including Heller, James Tobin, and Paul Samuelson, had doubts about Keyserling's muscular brand of growthmanship. Tobin saw it as "'more spending, more spending, more spending' by everybody" and later recalled that "the group around Kennedy felt politically that a kind of unmitigated Keyserling or old-style Democratic liberalism in regard to economics and fiscal policy wasn't going to pay off politically both during the campaign and afterwards."[56] But in reality Keyserling's conception of growth as the overriding goal—if not his particular prescription of the best means to that end—was now firmly embedded in the moderate liberalism of the New Frontier. In just a few short years, Tobin would write that "in recent years economic growth has come to occupy an exalted position in the hierarchy of goals of government policy."[57]

As president, Kennedy immediately addressed the need to pick up the economic pace. "The American economy is in trouble," he warned in his first State of the Union Address, on January 30, 1961. "The most resourceful industrialized country on earth ranks among the last in the rate of economic growth. Since last spring our economic growth rate has actually receded."[58] Growth was important in its own right as an economic goal, and it was crucial in another fundamental regard as well: growth was to provide the additional revenues needed to fulfill the administration's domestic social aspirations and to achieve its national security objectives. Walt W. Rostow, the MIT economic historian who joined the new administration, told Kennedy that "all our hopes and policies, domestic and foreign, hinged on reconciling higher growth with price stability. . . . I then underlined that his domestic program required more public revenues which only growth could provide."[59]

In fact, the pursuit of growth quickly became one of the New Frontier's distinguishing features. Heller was joined on the Council of Economic Advisers by James Tobin and Kermit Gordon—in Heller's words, "adherents of the Cambridge–New Haven growth school."[60] Tobin recalled, "Growth was a good word, indeed *the* good word." Soon after the inauguration, all the offices and desks in the Commerce Department displayed signs asking "What have you done for Growth today?"[61] The president ordered Heller "not to return from an international economic meeting in Paris until [he] had discovered the secret of European growth"; in November 1961, the administration committed the United States to a twenty-nation Organization for Economic Cooperation and Development agreement to raise the combined GNP of the group by 50 percent in the 1960s. The commitment to growth took on further symbolic and bureaucratic dimensions in 1962 when Heller complained to the president that "our noses are rubbed in the unemployment, price, and balance of payments problem and policies every day—we need some device to keep our noses to the growth grindstone as well." He suggested an interagency committee as "the best way to launch the get-up-and-grow effort," and Kennedy responded by creating a Cabinet Committee on Growth, which included the chairman of the CEA, the budget director, and the secretaries of the treasury, commerce, and labor. The straightforwardness of the new group's name contrasted tellingly with Eisenhower's earlier Cabinet Committee on Price Stability for Economic Growth.[62]

Policy soon followed. Less than two weeks after his inauguration, Kennedy sent to Congress a special message on economic recovery and growth. Cautioning that "we cannot expect to make good in a day or even a year the accumulated deficiencies of several years," he proposed that the nation aim in 1961 to bring production up to existing capacity—economists call this expansion—and in 1962 and 1963 to achieve genuine economic growth, the enlargement of productive capacity.[63] As Heller later characterized the policy reorientation, "Gone is the countercyclical syndrome of the 1950s. Policy now centers on gap closing and growth, on realizing and enlarging the economy's non-inflationary potential."[64]

The new policy of what Heller called "Keynes-*cum*-growth" proceeded along three major lines into the mid-1960s.[65] First, to narrow the gap between current production and existing capacity, the government expanded demand by means of a massive tax reduction—the famous Kennedy-Johnson tax cut, which was first discussed in 1962, formally proposed in 1963, and signed into law in February 1964. Second, to provide cost-price stability, the administration developed wage-price guideposts in 1962 and initiated a policy of "jawboning" business and labor into acquiescence. Finally, to increase the output potential of the economy—to achieve true "growth"—the Kennedy and Johnson administrations encouraged business investment by liberalizing depreciation allowances in July 1962; by instituting a 7 percent tax credit for capital outlays on machinery and equipment in October 1962; and by introducing beginning in 1961 a host of manpower development, education, and retraining programs to increase the quality and ultimately the output of the labor force. In addition, the "monetary twist" policy begun in 1961 raised short-term interest rates in order to minimize the outflow of volatile funds to other countries while holding down long-term interest rates to encourage investment at home.

The results through mid-decade were impressive. Between 1961 and 1965, real GNP increased at a rate above 5 percent per year. Employment grew by 2.5 percent per year, and in January 1966 the unemployment rate sank to 3.9 percent. The percentage of Americans mired in poverty, according to official estimates, dropped from 22.4 percent in 1960 to 14.7 percent in 1966. As these advances unfolded, the rate of inflation remained below 2 percent per year through 1965. By all the usual measures, the economic policies of the early 1960s were unambiguous successes.[66]

The spectacular economic expansion and growth of the Kennedy and early Johnson years made possible a strikingly expansive view of national possibilities. The journalist Theodore White caught the mood when he identified the rise of "a new generation of Americans who saw the world differently from their fathers. [They were] brought up to believe, either at home or abroad, that whatever Americans wished to make happen, would happen." The new expansiveness was underpinned by the belief that economic growth was not merely possible but practically inevitable given the proper policies.[67]

In this regard, Eisenhower stood as the last of the old breed, whose sense of limitations contrasted sharply with the expansiveness of his liberal Democratic successors. Walt Rostow makes the point in a telling story. In 1958, Eisenhower encouraged the creation of a citizens' committee to rally support for the administration's foreign aid proposals. In April 1958, the president received the group in his office: "Expecting a statement of encouragement and an injunction to carry on the good fight," Rostow relates, "most of us were shaken to hear a troubled and wistful monologue about the overriding need to balance the budget, closing with the rhetorical question: 'Where are we going to get the money from?'"[68] Kennedy and Johnson sought to avoid such constraints, and economic growth promised the so-called fiscal dividends that would make that possible. As James Tobin has observed, "The [Kennedy and Johnson] Administrations regarded growth in national production and income not only as an end in itself but as the fount of economic and fiscal resources for meeting national needs." President Johnson expressed the point in his own way in 1964, telling an aide: "I'm sick of all the people who talk about the things we can't do. Hell, we're the richest country in the world, the most powerful. We can do it all. . . . We can do it if we believe it."[69]

The economic policy of "Keynes-*cum*-growth" had become the engine driving U.S. public policy on a variety of fronts. As CEA chief Walter Heller—with the exception of the presidents he served, as important a figure as worked in government during his time—observed, economic growth was "both an end in itself and an instrumentality, both the pot of gold and the rainbow." Prosperity and rapid growth, he wrote in 1966, put at the president's "disposal, as nothing else can, the resources needed to achieve great societies at home and grand designs abroad."[70] Growthmanship made possible a host of new undertakings in the vastness of outer space, in the jungles of Southeast Asia, and in the streets of America's inner cities. Freed for the moment from the discipline of stringency, policymakers redefined what was possible and in the bargain purchased both triumph and tragedy for the nation.

One such new frontier was that of space and science. In May 1961 Kennedy dramatically reversed Eisenhower's space policy by committing the nation "to achieving the goal, before this decade is out, of landing a man on the moon and returning him safely to the earth."[71] The contrast could not be clearer. Eisenhower had vetoed the Apollo manned-moon-shot program in 1960. When told that supporters of the venture likened it to the voyages of Columbus, Ike retorted that he was "not about to hock [my] jewels."[72] Maurice Stans, Eisenhower's budget director, tried to keep the National Aeronautics and Space Administration's budget for fiscal year 1962 at what the NASA administrative history later labeled "an absolute rockbottom level."[73]

The promise of a growing economy allowed Kennedy to view the space race more expansively than his predecessor. As the historian Walter A. McDougall has pointed out, the Democratic administration thought of space exploration "in terms of ends (were they desirable?) rather than means (can we afford it?)." The NASA payroll grew tenfold under the Apollo program. By 1965, the agency and its private contractors employed 411,000. NASA appropriations rocketed from less than $1 billion in fiscal year 1961 to $5.1 billion in fiscal year 1964. Bound only loosely by the budgetary constraints that had so fettered Eisenhower, first Kennedy and then Johnson made the space program, in McDougall's words, "a model for a society without limits, an ebullient and liberal technocracy."[74]

A similar pattern unfolded in the area of national security affairs, but one that ended far less satisfactorily for the United States. Again, the story begins with the Eisenhower presidency. As John Lewis Gaddis has argued compellingly, the Eisenhower administration had moved away from Truman's brand of "symmetrical" containment as embodied in NSC-68. The basic reason for the change was Eisenhower's belief that the means available for national security purposes were limited; the national economy might be bankrupted if driven too hard, or its free enterprise character fatally compromised by a regimented Cold War mobilization. Republican defense policy emphasized not the indivisibility of interests à la NSC-68 but rather the pitting of U.S. strengths against adversary weaknesses, at times and in locations of American choosing—what Gaddis labels "asymmetrical containment."[75] The trick, as Ike saw it, was "to figure out a preparedness program that will give us a respectable position without bankrupting the nation."[76]

The resulting policy was labeled the "New Look," a defense posture that relied on the threat of massive nuclear retaliation at the top end of the ladder of confrontation and on the use of covert action through the CIA at the bottom rungs.[77] The idea, observed Secretary of State John Foster Dulles, was to achieve "a maximum deterrent at a bearable cost." During Eisenhower's first year in office, the National Security Council identified the nation's two chief national security problems as the Soviet menace and the need to react to that challenge without "seriously weakening the U.S. economy or undermining our fundamental values and institutions." The New Look was a doctrine, James Tobin observed at the time, "made as much in Treasury as in State."[78]

That the New Look strategy wore a dollar sign attracted critics as well as admirers. Writing at the time in *Foreign Affairs,* Harvard professor Henry A. Kissinger identified three major influences on military strategy—military doctrine, technology, and fiscal concerns—and concluded that fiscal and technological considerations were outweighing military doctrine in the formulation of U.S. policy.[79] Even within the administration dissident voices could be heard. Vice President Nixon pushed behind the scenes for greater defense spending, and in 1957 the administration's in-house Gaither Committee (named for its chairman, businessman H. Rowan Gaither) faulted the reliance on nuclear deterrence and criticized the state of the nation's conventional capacity.[80] Army generals in particular chafed under the New Look arrangements, feeling squeezed out between the competing demands of the navy and, especially, the most-bang-for-the-buck air force. Maxwell Taylor, the articulate former army chief of staff, decried the reliance on massive retaliation and offered instead what he called the "Strategy of Flexible Response." Taylor's alternative would give the United States "a capability to react across the entire spectrum of possible challenge, for coping with anything from general atomic war to infiltrations and aggressions such as threaten Laos and Berlin in 1959."[81] Flexible response emphasized the middle rungs of the ladder of escalation, not just the extremes. But such an alternative obviously came only at a price, and Eisenhower remained a fiscally conservative master strategist until the end.

The Democrats saw in Ike's fiscally driven, asymmetrical defense policy an opportunity for political advantage. Flexible response fitted with the symmetrical version of containment the Truman administration had forged around NSC-68 in the early 1950s. JFK and LBJ slammed home a partisan message that U.S. national security interests were indivisible. As Lyndon Johnson put it in 1964, "Surrender anywhere threatens defeat everywhere."[82] The Democratic platform in 1960 promised that a new Democratic administration would "recast our military capacity in order to provide forces and weapons of a diversity, balance, and mobility sufficient in quantity and quality to deter both limited and general aggressions." The candidate put an even finer point on the matter: "We must regain the ability to intervene effectively and swiftly in any limited war anywhere in the world."[83]

Once in office, Kennedy moved energetically to implement the policy of flexible response. Over the next three years there ensued what Theodore Sorensen called a "buildup of the most powerful military force in human history—the largest and swiftest buildup in this country's peacetime history, at a cost of some $17 billion in additional appropriations."[84] Under the leadership of Robert S. McNamara, the Department of Defense prepared to fight two and a half wars simultaneously—the extreme contingency of major wars in both Europe and Asia, with a concurrent lesser conflict somewhere.[85] The buildup proceeded on three levels. Strategic forces were bolstered with the expansion of the land-based nuclear missile force to a thousand Minutemen and the strengthening of the Polaris program. By mid-1964 the United States had boosted its deliverable megatonnage by 200 percent. In the area of conventional strength, the army increased its number of combat-ready divisions from eleven to sixteen by 1965; the marines added a fourth division and a fourth air wing; and the air force increased its airlift capacity from sixteen to thirty-eight squadrons. Finally, Kennedy increased dramatically the military's capacity for unconventional war, increasing the size of the army special forces (the favored "green berets") by a factor of five and reorienting them for Third World antiguerrilla warfare.[86] Kennedy's Department of Defense reported implementation of all levels of the flexible response posture "in accordance with the President's directive that military requirements should be considered without regard to arbitrary budget ceilings." Yet, because the economy was growing so fast, the percentage of GNP allocated to national defense actually decreased slightly, from 9.1 percent in fiscal year 1961 to 8.5 percent in fiscal year 1964.[87] The revolution at the Pentagon and the growth revolution at the White House were intertwined from the beginning.

These intertwined revolutions set the stage for tragedy in Southeast Asia. As John Lewis Gaddis has argued, it is budgetary constraint that has "most often forced the consideration of unpalatable options" in postwar foreign policy: "When one knows one has only limited resources to work with, then distinctions between what is vital and peripheral, between the feasible and unfeasible, come more easily."[88] Both the perception and the reality of limits had constrained U.S. policy toward Vietnam in the 1950s. The United States had refused to intervene directly to rescue the besieged French garrison during the climactic battle for Dien Bien Phu in 1954. Several critics of Eisenhower's New Look policy believed it to be partly responsible for this inaction. Army general James Gavin contended that if we had spent only a small portion of our total massive retaliation expenditures on limited-war forces, "we could have settled Korea and Dien Bien Phu quickly in our favor." General Maxwell Taylor contended similarly in 1960 that "unfortunately . . . [the necessary conventional] forces did not then exist in sufficient strength or in the proper position to offer any hope of success [at Dien Bien Phu]."[89] In 1961 Kennedy made Taylor his personal military adviser and some months later appointed him chairman of the Joint Chiefs of Staff. The economic limits of which Taylor had complained would operate only weakly as the Kennedy and Johnson administrations moved toward war in Vietnam.

Southeast Asia provided immediate proof to the incoming Kennedy administration of the correctness of their complaints about Eisenhower's parsimonious New Look posture. According to Arthur M. Schlesinger Jr., a presidential assistant, "Kennedy was appalled to discover a few weeks after the inauguration that, if he sent 10,000 men to Southeast Asia, he would deplete the strategic reserve and have virtually nothing left for emergencies elsewhere." The nation's airlift capacity was such that "it would have taken nearly two months to carry an infantry division and its equipment to Southeast Asia."[90] It was these findings that fueled Defense Secretary Robert S. McNamara's pursuit of what he called "usable power," power in being that could be applied to the variety of tasks Kennedy's symmetrical containment policy would find at hand. Of course, one problem with usable power is that its very existence tempts its use. As Walt Rostow observed to Kennedy in March 1961: "We must somehow bring to bear our unexploited counter-guerrilla assets on the Viet-Nam problem: armed helicopters; other Research and Development possibilities; our Special Forces units. It is somehow wrong to be developing these capabilities but not applying them in a crucially active theater. In Knute Rockne's old phrase, we are not saving them for the Junior Prom."[91]

The abundance of usable power generated by growth economics freed America's Vietnam policy from earlier logistical and fiscal constraints. By the time of Kennedy's assassination in November 1963, the United States had nearly sixteen thousand military personnel stationed in Vietnam and had helped overthrow the regime of Ngo Dinh Diem. When the subsequent South Vietnamese governments proved even more vulnerable to communist pressure than Diem's regime, the temptation to apply America's "usable force" directly to save the South proved irresistible. Two days after signing the Gulf of Tonkin Resolution, which authorized the use of force to assist the government of South Vietnam, President Lyndon Johnson warned, "Let no one doubt for a moment that we have the resources and we have the will to follow this course as long as it may take."[92] His administration and the nation would come to grief in learning that he was, in that statement, wrong on every count.

While economic growth supported grand designs in Asia, it undergirded a massive liberal enterprise at home as well. As with other matters, the effort began slowly and somewhat shakily under Kennedy, and emerged full-blown, perhaps overblown, under Johnson. Domestic reform ran along many lines in the superheated optimism of the early and mid-1960s. The political labels of the day seem in retrospect curiously appropriate. All along the New Frontier there appeared rough, exploratory federal efforts on civil rights, manpower training, area development, education, health care, and poverty. Upon Kennedy's death, Johnson tried to accelerate the pace of innovation and embody the results in a welter of legislative achievements that would cumulatively build a Great Society. LBJ embarked on his domestic crusade in January 1964, when he committed the nation to an "unconditional war on poverty"; the full, utopian character of the undertaking became clear later in the year when he began to invoke the phrase "Great Society" to describe his goal: "a society of success without squalor, beauty without barrenness, works of genius without the wretchedness of poverty."[93] The label quickly stuck and came to describe several hundred legislative initiatives that aimed at achieving civil rights for blacks, victory in the War on Poverty, enhanced educational opportunity, improved health care for the elderly, a more acceptable quality of urban life, better environmental protection, and improved protection for consumers. Because of such efforts, between 1964 and 1972 social welfare expenditures rose from 25.4 percent of the federal budget to 41.3 percent, and from 4.3 percent of the GNP to 8.8 percent.[94]

As with the adventure in space and the engagement in Vietnam, economic growth played a significant role in liberalism's domestic program. "Stable, rapid, noncyclical, noninflationary growth" was, in James Tobin's words, "the underpinning of the Great Society." Arthur Okun, who chaired the CEA under Johnson, wrote: "As long as the economy was growing rapidly and making progress, I believe . . . [LBJ] really did see an opportunity for shifting things to the public sector, for shifting the distribution of public services toward the disadvantaged without having anybody feel it very much because it would be sharing the gains rather than asking for belt-tightening."[95]

Growth was crucial to the emergence of the Great Society in three regards. First, it fueled the basic optimism that made such a grandiose conception appear reasonable. "Hell," LBJ told aides in April 1964, "we've barely begun to solve our problems. And we can do it all. We've got the wherewithal."[96] LBJ's biographer Doris Kearns would later write of "his confidence in the almost limitless capacity of the American nation."[97] Second, growth really did provide the wherewithal of which LBJ spoke. James Tobin has estimated that of the total increase in GNP over the 1961–65 period, roughly one-quarter represented the result of cyclical recovery (especially the reduction of unemployment) and the remainder was attributable to growth in the economy's capacity to produce.[98] The creators of the Great Society assumed that a portion of this growth could be redirected to support the most ambitious liberal program in U.S. history. Economic growth both inspired the vision and promised to provide the means for its realization. Joseph Califano, an LBJ aide, recalled that the president "considered a robust, noninflationary economy so critical to his domestic program that he spent more time on economic matters than on any other subject."[99]

Growth influenced the Great Society in a third way through its impact on the content of that Great Society centerpiece, the War on Poverty. The War on Poverty was based on the promise and reality of economic growth, as Walter Lippmann observed in March 1964: "A generation ago it would have been taken for granted that a war on poverty meant taxing money away from the haves and . . . turning it over to the have nots. . . . But in this generation . . . a revolutionary idea has taken hold. The size of the pie can be increased by invention, organization, capital investment, and fiscal policy, and then a whole society, not just one part of it, will grow richer."[100] But the influence of growth ideas went beyond the belief that the annual increment in GNP could be used to combat poverty. Granted that growth provided wherewithal, how should those expanded resources be used?

The Johnson administration's attack on poverty was dictated by both politics and broader conceptions of political economy. As the CEA observed in its 1964 Annual Report, the affluent majority could conceivably simply transfer money to the poor via taxes and income supplements, which would bring all poor families up to an acceptable minimum income level—for less than one-fifth the annual cost of the defense budget.[101] But as Johnson saw it, any such redistributive scheme would fail on three counts. First, it would run counter to his own Puritan work ethic, which had little use for simple government giveaways. Second, any such redistributive plan would invite precisely the political controversy and division that LBJ's positive sum politics sought to avoid. Finally, simple redistributive proposals ran counter to the growth idea. As Carl Brauer has observed, "To growth- and efficiency-oriented economists, increasing the productivity of the poor was intrinsically preferable to paying them not to work."[102] Lester Thurow, an economist who served as a CEA consultant in the early 1960s, has recalled, "The national desire to accelerate the rate of growth and stay ahead of the Russians meant that nearly all of the early Great Society and war on poverty programs were manpower training programs and not income-maintenance programs."[103]

The goal of the War on Poverty was not simply to enrich the poor but rather to change them so that they, too, could then contribute to the national goal of increased growth. Joseph A. Kershaw, the assistant director of the Office of Economic Opportunity, in February 1965 made the point directly: "Most income transfers simply result in different ways of slicing the income pie. . . . What we need in the longer run are ways to increase the productivity of the poor, ways to make them valuable in jobs and ways of getting them from where they are to where the jobs are. Measures that do this increase the size of the pie, not just the way it is sliced."[104] Such investment in human resources would, Kershaw concluded, enable the poor to be "generating themselves the resources which will help eliminate poverty, not only this year but for all those years to come."[105] Only later, as the 1960s tailed into another era, did the political mainstream begin to reconceive the problem of poverty as a problem of inequality. Both Richard Nixon, with his Family Assistance Plan, and George McGovern, with his Demogrants, would discover the political difficulty of shifting welfare policy from the channels carved by the confluence of growth economics and liberal politics in the heady days of the New Frontier and Great Society.

Thus did economic growth help underwrite and define the central public undertakings of the 1960s. The interpenetration of growth economics and liberal politics produced a defining feature of public life in the 1960s—the ascendancy of what might be labeled "growth liberalism." Growth liberalism linked together two of the most disparate presidents in American history, giving their combined leadership a distinctive identity. Joining other forces for social change that emanated from outside the established political system, growth liberalism imparted to the 1960s an optimism and energy that loom large in both our social memory and our historical understanding of the era. But such was not the whole of the 1960s. If growth liberalism was at its most robust in America's grand public enterprises in space, abroad, and at home in the years 1960–68, it was accompanied almost from the outset by a noteworthy ambivalence and uncertainty, by the need somehow to match its quantitative achievements with attention both to the *quality* of life and to the *ravages* that growth itself visited upon society and environment.

IV. The Complexities and Contradictions of Growth, 1960–1968

By the middle of the 1960s, as its policies were put into place at home and abroad, growth liberalism's complexity came more clearly into view. Growth liberals stressed production and quantitative change. As James Tobin put it in 1965, "The whole purpose of the economy is production of goods or services for consumption now or in the future. I think the burden of proof should always be on those who would produce less rather than more, on those who would leave idle men or machines on land that could be used."[106] Yet alongside the quantitative drive of growth liberalism there coexisted two related but hardly coincident impulses. The first was the desire to transcend the attachment to growth by means of a new emphasis on the pursuit of quality in American life. The second, developing steadily as the decade wore on, sought to cushion and repair some of the apparent consequences of growth, especially the despoliation of the environment.

The notion that material growth represented neither the apotheosis of American civilization nor an adequate basis for public policy was not at all new. There has been a long and notable strain of antimaterialist thought in the United States, running from the Puritans through the transcendentalists to the beats of the 1950s and the counterculture hippies of the 1960s.[107] Moreover, doubt about the wisdom of growth as an end in itself has never been the monopoly of those on the fringes of the political culture. Eisenhower refused to view growth as an overriding goal. His former CEA chairman Arthur Burns observed in 1967 that "the economic growth of a nation is a blind concept unless we consider what is produced as well as the rate of growth of what happened to be produced."[108]

More striking, however, was the emergence among growth liberalism's own advocates and within its own constituency of a profound ambivalence about the relationship between quantity and quality in American life. The tension surfaced first in the 1950s, when Arthur M. Schlesinger Jr. and John Kenneth Galbraith sought to chart a new path for American liberals. They approached the task from slightly different angles, but their arguments overlapped in important regards. Writing in 1957, Schlesinger urged liberals to reorient their creed, to move from a New Dealish concern "with establishing the economic conditions which make individual dignity conceivable—a job, a square meal, a living wage, a shirt on one's back and a roof over one's head" to a new concentration on "enlarging the individual's opportunity for moral growth and self-fulfillment." The shift would move the focus of liberalism "from economics and politics to the general style and quality of our civilization."[109] The enemy was no longer mass deprivation but rather mass culture.

With the approach of a new presidential election season in 1959, Schlesinger elaborated his views in a privately published essay, "The Shape of National Politics to Come," which he circulated among the Democratic faithful. Building on the theory of an inherent cyclical rhythm in national affairs famously advanced by his Harvard historian father, Schlesinger *fils* maintained that America's "growing discontent with purely material ends," along with other symptoms of a "spreading anxiety and frustration in our society," presaged a dramatic shift to a "new political epoch." "The crust is breaking up," he announced. "New forces and values are straining for release in our society." The Democratic Party would be the "chosen instrumentality . . . of national renaissance" only if it shed the qualitative emphasis that smacked of the "scarcity" of the 1930s and adopted in its place a new "qualitative liberalism" better suited to the fact that "today we dwell in an economy of abundance." It was, he wrote, now time to "move on . . . to the more elusive and complicated task of fighting for individual dignity, identity and fulfillment in a mass society."[110]

John Kenneth Galbraith set forth a similar idea. Early in 1956 he testified before the Royal Commission on Canada's Economic Prospects, opining that "sooner rather than later our concern with the quantity of goods produced—the rate of increase in Gross National Product—would have to give way to the larger question of the quality of the life that it provided." Two years later he developed this insight at greater length and applied it to his adopted home, the United States. The result was a best-seller, *The Affluent Society*. In it he wrote, "Liberal economic policy is still deeply preoccupied with production. . . . Platforms, manifestos, and speeches develop the vision of a growing, ever more productive America." But, he warned, the emphasis on aggregate output needed now to be replaced by a new attention to the distribution of the product, to the uses to which production was put. The United States needed to pay less attention to the production of private goods and more to the meeting of public needs.[111]

Predictably, Keyserling found such views heretical, and, characteristically, he attacked them. The controversy unfolded in the pages of various journals of opinion and in private correspondence. Keyserling accused both Schlesinger and Galbraith of underestimating the extent of still-massive private poverty. He agreed on the need for a substantial, sustained increase in public spending, but maintained that "to attempt to do this primarily by redistribution of expenditures—from private consumption to public needs—rather than primarily through high economic growth, defies history and reason."[112] For Keyserling, the issues of growth and social balance as between the private and public use of resources were thoroughly intertwined. Both sides to the dispute were on to something: Keyserling was correct in maintaining that quantity and quality could not be neatly compartmentalized; Schlesinger and Galbraith in pointing to the tension that existed between the quantitative and qualitative orientations.

The tension between quantity and quality remained a hallmark of growth liberalism during its ascendancy in the early and mid-1960s. Intellectuals and ideologues were more troubled by the tension than politicians, yet politicians were not immune. Schlesinger has written of Kennedy that "despite his support of economic growth and his concern over persisting privation, the thrust of his preoccupation was less with the economic machine and its quantitative results than with the quality of life in a society which, in the main, had achieved abundance."[113]

The vision of a Great Society illuminated the tension vividly. Richard Goodwin, the speech writer who coined the phrase, contended in 1965 that "the Great Society looks beyond the prospects of abundance to the problems of abundance. . . . Thus the Great Society is concerned not with how much, but how good—not with the quantity of our goods but the quality of our lives."[114] Not surprisingly, LBJ's speeches articulated the same objectives. In first announcing the Great Society at the University of Michigan in May 1964, Johnson proclaimed, "For half a century we called upon unbounded invention and untiring industry to create an order of plenty for all of our people. The challenge of the next half century is whether we have the wisdom to use that wealth to enrich and elevate our national life, and to advance the quality of our American civilization." Americans had the opportunity to choose between "a society where progress is the servant of our needs, or a society where old values and new visions are buried under unbridled growth."[115]

The tension between quantity and quality affected more than political rhetoric. By the early 1960s, administrators in the Department of Health, Education, and Welfare (HEW) searched for a system of social bookkeeping that would measure quality the way that the federal government already tracked quantitative economic change. At the beginning of the Kennedy administration, the Department of Health, Education, and Welfare had begun publishing two series—the annual *Trends* and the monthly *Indicators*—that compiled social statistics. In March 1966, LBJ pushed farther and requested HEW "to develop the necessary social statistics and indicators to supplement those prepared by the Bureau of Labor Statistics and the Council of Economic Advisers."[116] As a result of this charge, the secretary of HEW forwarded a report on social indicators entitled *Toward a Social Report* to Johnson just before he left the White House.[117] Social reporting would remain in its infancy long after the 1960s had passed, but its forward movement was noteworthy, both in its own right and as testimony to a current of ambivalence that constituted the underside of growth liberalism.

Additional evidence of the complexity of attitudes regarding growth appeared in the mid-1960s, with an increasing number of people both inside and outside government adopting a new environmental sensibility and with the federal government gradually implementing measures to protect the environment from several of the worst ravages of economic growth. Although some commentators date the onset of the ecological age from the 1962 publication of Rachel Carson's *Silent Spring*, Samuel P. Hays argues persuasively that the development of environmental action was too evolutionary to be pinned to one event. According to Hays's stage analysis, between 1957 and 1965 environmentally minded people were most concerned about outdoor recreation, wildlands, and open space; from 1965 to 1972 environmental activists and policymakers focused on the adverse effects of industrial growth.[118] The shift from a conservationist to an ecological orientation marks the 1960s as a crucial turning point in the man-nature relationship.

As in so many areas, Kennedy moved in the new environmental direction only tentatively. His secretary of the interior, Stewart Udall, was a transitional figure, sensitive to quality-of-life issues and possessed of what the historian Martin Melosi has described as "a relatively broad ecological perspective," but still concerned primarily with traditional conservation issues.[119] JFK himself could urge Americans to "expand the concept of conservation to meet the imperious problems of a new age," but his effort was more rhetorical than substantive and his posture more reactive than trailblazing. As Udall reported to Arthur M. Schlesinger Jr., "Intellectually he is fine. He knows the issues and recognizes their importance. When the problems are brought to him, his response is excellent. But he doesn't raise them himself."[120]

Johnson responded to the nascent ecological sensibility more forcefully and effectively. His rhetoric moved beyond Kennedy's both in its urgency and in the perception that economic growth—the central, guiding, and driving force behind his programs—exacted costs even as it bestowed benefits. "Ours is a nation of affluence," he stated in November 1965, "but the technology that has permitted our affluence spews out vast quantities of wastes and spent products that pollute our air, poison our waters, and even impair our ability to feed ourselves. . . . Pollution now is one of the most pervasive problems of our society."[121]

Johnson worked energetically to incorporate the emergent environmental sensibility into his overall Great Society framework. He created nine presidential task forces—a favorite device for focusing attention and forcing action—to address environmental problems and signed into law almost three hundred conservation and beautification measures entailing outlays of over $12 billion. His landmark legislation included the Clean Air Act in 1963, the Water Quality Act in 1965, the Endangered Species Act in 1966, and the Air Quality Act and National Emissions Standards Act in 1967. Meanwhile, Lady Bird Johnson operated as a formidable political force in her own right on behalf of beautification. Udall captured the impact of these developments when he wrote to Johnson in 1968: "No longer is peripheral action—the 'saving' of a forest, a park, a refuge for wildlife—isolated from the mainstream. The total environment is now the concern. . . . The quality of life is now the perspective and purpose of the new conservation."[122]

The concern with quality represented growth liberalism at its richest and most complex. The desire to use economic growth to transcend economic growth was as noble as it was chimerical, and the attention to growth's environmental consequences was as responsible as it was ironic. Still the driving optimism remained: Growth would make the chimerical and the ironic possible. On the horizon, however, lay a confrontation with national mortality, with limits, with Vietnam. Not even the supreme politician Lyndon Johnson could avoid this confrontation and not even growth liberalism could finesse it.

The great undertakings abroad and at home accelerated at mid-decade. In 1965, as LBJ subsequently observed, "two great streams in our national life converged—the dream of a Great Society at home and the inescapable demands of our obligations halfway around the world."[123] On the home front, more than one thousand projects had been initiated since the start of the War on Poverty and in February 1965 Johnson called upon Congress to double the national effort and to appropriate $1.5 billion for antipoverty programs in the next fiscal year.[124] Over the course of 1965, Johnson signed into law Medicare, a federal aid to education act, and the Housing and Urban Development Act of 1965. Total federal social welfare expenditures (measured in real dollars to correct for inflation) increased a stunning 18 percent in fiscal year 1965.[125]

Halfway around the world, America's grand design in Asia in 1965 became the Vietnam War. The United States began a sustained air offensive against North Vietnam in March, and a week later the first regular U.S. combat troops arrived in South Vietnam. Initially limited to defensive operations, the U.S. forces were soon allowed to go on the offensive, and in late June they executed their first "search and destroy" mission in War Zone D northwest of Saigon. In late July the die was cast when Johnson—aware that the United States was, in his words, "going off the diving board" into "a new war"—ordered the commitment of up to 175,000 troops in 1965 with an additional 100,000 in 1966.[126]

The remainder of Johnson's administration would be marked by the confluence of these "two great streams": a major, if not total, commitment in Vietnam and an unparalleled attack on social problems at home. The two endeavors rested on a common economic foundation. In both cases, the administration depended on a constantly expanding economy to provide the wherewithal for the effort, in a fashion that would avoid extensive debate, harsh conflict, and the necessity of painful choices—in short, the discipline of stringency. It followed that the Great Society and the Vietnam War would be connected as well by the threat that an overacceleration of either one would inevitably endanger the progress of the other. Awash in a powerful mixture of vision, ambition, delusion, fear, and duplicity, the Johnson presidency by the beginning of 1968 had stretched the U.S. political economy close to the breaking point.

3

Growth Liberalism Comes
a Cropper, 1968

The ideology driving the Kennedy and Johnson presidencies was an amalgam of growth economics and government activism at home and abroad. Growth liberalism sought to update the nation's still potent reform tradition for the era of affluence, influence, and optimism well captured in Henry Luce's prescient conceit, the "American Century." But, by the late 1960s, growth liberalism's combination of growth-inducing tax cuts, an escalating war in Vietnam, and increased social spending at home had overstrained economic institutions and capabilities. The economic crisis that resulted in 1968 provided irrefutable proof of that strain and figured prominently in the decisions to cap U.S. escalation in Vietnam and rein in the Great Society initiatives at the top of LBJ's presidential agenda. Those decisions—and the problems that elicited them—left growth liberalism in disarray and the American Century in retreat.

In early 1968, the most serious economic crisis since the Great Depression shook the Western world. The disruption exposed a variety of economic ills plaguing the U.S. and world economies, some of recent vintage but others with roots that reached back a decade or more. The problems, both long-term and short-run, were tightly intertwined, and they culminated in March in a speculative run on gold that *Time* magazine called "the largest gold rush in history, a frenetic speculative stampede that . . . threatened the Western world."[1]

The rush on gold did not lack for drama. The Treasury Department's general counsel alerted Secretary

Henry Fowler of the need to airlift $500 million in gold bars from Fort Knox to New York "on a crash basis," without insuring the shipments or arranging for the customary "second" weighing of the gold as it left the Kentucky depository. A single-day record at the London gold market saw over 200 tons of the precious metal change hands. Fistfights broke out when ten times the usual number of buyers jammed the gold pit in the cellar of the Paris Bourse. Edward Fried, a key National Security Council (NSC) adviser on international monetary affairs, recalled that "pandemonium had virtually broken out. Just had gotten completely mad. You could see pictures of even Canadians, farmers, lining up to get gold." It seemed, he remembered, "as though this part of the world had gone completely off its rocker."[2]

As the crisis peaked in mid-March, the stakes appeared large to both onlookers and participants. "The world is lost," warned a British economist, "we're in the first act of a world depression." Peking's New China News Agency observed with considerable satisfaction that "the capitalist monetary system has in fact collapsed." The Polish trade union council showed only a little more caution in observing, "The dollar is doomed. It is possible that joint efforts by world financial circles will stave off the crisis temporarily, but this will only postpone the execution."[3]

Among policymakers in Washington, the mood was appropriately tense. "Everybody was just petrified," recalled Under Secretary of the Treasury Joseph W. Barr. "It was a hair-raising period in which we literally had to watch the gold markets day by day and hour by hour." At the NSC, Fried feared "that this was not something that was any longer under control." President Lyndon Johnson's national security adviser, Walt W. Rostow, briefed the president on the stakes "at a most important moment in postwar history": a misstep, he wrote, "could set in motion a financial and trade crisis which would undo much that we have achieved in these fields in the past twenty years and endanger the prosperity and security of the Western world."[4]

I. The Sources of the 1968 Crisis

The economic crisis of 1968 was dramatic but not entirely a surprise. What made the crisis so daunting, and so difficult to resolve, was not its suddenness but rather the way it tied together a number of serious problems that fed off one another in a perverse synergy. The most deeply rooted such problem concerned the United States' chronic balance-of-payments deficit.

The immediate context for the balance-of-payments difficulty extended back in time to the gathering of seven hundred delegates at the Mount Washington Hotel in Bretton Woods, New Hampshire, in 1944. The Bretton Woods conference created the International Monetary Fund (IMF) and the World Bank, erecting on that foundation a new monetary system that would order the world economy for over a quarter century. The Bretton Woods regime outlawed discriminatory currency practices and exchange restrictions and established pegged exchange rates. In practice, the U.S. dollar was pegged to gold at $35 an ounce, and all other IMF members then pegged their currencies to the dollar. The United States committed itself to exchange gold for dollars at the rate of $35 per ounce upon the demand of foreign governments; the other IMF members agreed to keep their currencies from deviating from their respective dollar parities by more than 1 percent in either direction. The IMF administered an international fund to provide short-term credit for the financing of balance-of-payments deficits, with the understanding that fundamental (i.e., large and chronic) deficits might legitimately occasion a change in par value. The original conferees realized that the new arrangements would have to be phased in, and the transition for the nations of Western Europe lasted until the implementation of currency convertibility in 1958 and the removal of transitional restrictions in 1961. The overall result of the Bretton Woods innovations was an international monetary system based on two major forms of international money—gold and foreign exchange, mostly U.S. dollars and British sterling.[5]

The United States began to suffer chronic balance-of-payments deficits early on under the new order, as four years of surpluses (1946–49) gave way in 1950 to a string of deficits that ran into the 1960s (with the exception of 1957, when the unusual impact of the Suez Crisis helped generate a surplus).[6] At first, the U.S. deficits seemed benign, since they were relatively small and appeared to have the salutary result of pumping dollars into an international economy troubled since the end of World War II by a shortage of dollars, the currency needed by the rest of the world for the purchase of U.S. goods for postwar reconstruction. But, by the end of the 1950s, the deficits began to appear more ominous to technicians, academics, and policymakers alike as they grew in size.

Basic social, political, and economic trends contributed to the growth of the U.S. balance-of-payments deficit. The maturation of America's own consumer culture made tourism an industry, and the spending by American tourists abroad contributed increasingly to the payments deficit. The Cold War occasioned higher expenditures for foreign aid and heavy overseas military deployments. The economic resurgence of Europe and, to a lesser extent at this point, Japan both increased American imports from these areas and increased the outflow of capital, as overseas investment opportunities became more appealing. President John F. Kennedy expressed the problem succinctly in early 1961: "The surplus of our exports over our imports, while substantial, has not been large enough to cover our expenditures for United States military establishments abroad, for capital invested abroad by private American businesses and for government economic assistance and loan programs."[7] By the early 1960s the feared dollar shortage had become a dollar glut.

Events soon forced political leaders to act. Foreign governments and central banks became increasingly reluctant to hold ever more of the dollars cascading overseas, and by 1959 they began to ask the U.S. Treasury to convert their dollar holdings into gold. A growing fear that the dollar might be devalued drove up the price of gold on the London market to over $40 an ounce in October 1960. Remarking that "we can't sit still and see our monetary system destroyed," President Dwight D. Eisenhower sought to bring the balance-of-payments deficit under control. After the November 1960 election, he ordered reductions in the number of military dependents accompanying U.S. forces abroad and sent Secretary of the Treasury Robert Anderson and Under Secretary Douglas Dillon to Germany to enlist European support in financing the costs of American military forces in Europe, especially the Seventh Army in Germany.[8]

John F. Kennedy launched his own balance-of-payments program immediately upon assuming office. He was ill at ease with the complexities of the payments issue, but was nonetheless convinced that it mattered greatly; several of his advisers believed him to be obsessive about the problem. Kennedy's first cabinet meeting focused on the problem, and within two weeks of his inauguration he sent a special message to Congress outlining the administration's plan to attack the balance-of-payments deficit.[9]

Kennedy's balance-of-payments program included both rhetoric and action. The president worked hard to bolster confidence both in the dollar and in the administration's financial probity. The substantive measures were a mixed bag. The administration induced Europe to shoulder more of the burden of the Cold War by supplying more foreign aid and by purchasing military equipment in the United States. The federal government sought to promote American exports in a number of ways, including tying them to U.S. loans to underdeveloped countries. Short-term interest rates were increased to attract and hold volatile capital, and foreign borrowing from the American capital market was restricted. The administration also placed new, lower limits on the amount of goods American tourists could bring home duty-free. No one of the initiatives was earth-shattering, but in combination they brought about some improvement.[10]

Lyndon Johnson continued JFK's initiatives. He brought to the balance-of-payments issue no more intellectual sophistication than his predecessor. Gardner Ackley, the chair of Johnson's Council of Economic Advisers (CEA), observed, "His understanding of the balance-of-payments problems was pretty rudimentary," adding tartly, "indeed, almost every politician's understanding of that was and is rudimentary."[11] Johnson introduced voluntary programs to limit direct investment overseas and to further reduce bank lending, and he continued to try to cut military expenditures abroad. "These things worked reasonably well" in the judgment of LBJ's undersecretary of the treasury for monetary affairs, Frederick Deming, "but [then] Viet Nam came along."[12] Deming was right on both counts: by 1965 the balance-of-payments deficit measured on a liquidity basis had been reduced to $1.3 billion from its 1960 high of $3.9 billion; but the onset in 1965 of full-bore fighting in Vietnam quickly negated such progress. The cost of maintaining U.S. forces in Southeast Asia added substantially to foreign payments, and the inflation unleashed by the war fueled a dramatic increase in imports. By 1967 the balance-of-payments deficit was again running at the level of 1960, nearly $4 billion.[13]

The Vietnam War, then, constituted the second source of the economic crisis of 1968. It aggravated the balance-of-payments problem and sparked off a round of inflation that twisted the economy out of shape, with consequences that would still be felt decades later. "There's no dimension of the American economy in the last three-and-a-half years," asserted LBJ's last chairman of the CEA in 1969, "which hasn't been touched by Viet Nam, Viet Nam changed the entire budget posture. It took all the elbow room away."[14]

Put simply, federal spending for the Vietnam War and the Great Society domestic agenda overheated the U.S. economy, which was already enjoying an expansion spurred by the impact of the 1964 tax cut. In the fourth quarter of 1965, the GNP rose by the largest amount in U.S. history. The rate of inflation (as measured in consumer prices) that had averaged 1.3 percent per year for the 1961-65 period increased to 2.9 percent in 1966, fell back to 2.3 percent for the first half of 1967, and then shot to 3.8 percent for the second half of 1967 and 4.4 percent for the first four months of 1968.[15]

By the end of 1965 the danger of a serious inflation had become clear, if not entirely unmistakable. In December the Federal Reserve Board reacted by hiking the discount rate—the rate that banks pay on loans from the system—in order to apply some braking pressure to the economy. Later that month, Gardner Ackley, chair of the CEA, wrote to Johnson, "The only conclusion I can reach is that an increase of individual and corporate income tax rates should be planned, whatever the FY 1967 budget may be (within the limits we have heard discussed). . . . From an economic standpoint, it needs to be done as soon as possible."[16] The timing of Ackley's assessment, one of the first intimations that the Keynesian growth liberalism of the 1960s was stretching the U.S. economy dangerously thin, was unintentionally ironic, for on December 31 *Time* magazine put John Maynard Keynes on its cover, only the second person no longer living to be so honored (Sigmund Freud was the first). Achieving that extraordinary mark of popular acclaim, the Keynesian creed had already begun its long retreat into disrepute.

At first, Johnson resisted calling for a major tax increase. He sought instead to pursue a policy of guns and butter funded by the growth that the new economics had already unleashed. In January 1966, the president insisted, "We are a rich nation and can afford to make progress at home while meeting obligations abroad. . . . For this reason, I have not halted progress in the new and vital Great Society programs in order to finance the costs of our efforts in Southeast Asia."[17] Throughout 1966 he stuck to his guns—and butter—and refused to push for a major tax hike. In September, he relented sufficiently to announce a spending cut of $1.5 billion in fiscal year 1967 and the suspension of the existing 7 percent investment tax credit. In his January 1967 budget message, Johnson finally proposed a temporary 6 percent surcharge on corporate and individual income taxes. Not until August 1967—more than a year and a half after Ackley had advised LBJ of the compelling need for a tax increase—did the administration present a concrete plan for a temporary 10 percent surcharge on both corporate and individual income taxes to deal with what Johnson now called "the hard and inescapable facts."[18]

Just why the administration dawdled has been a matter of considerable speculation and debate. The fact that LBJ's advisers were themselves divided clouded the issue. Even Paul Samuelson, whom Ackley called "the dean of our kind of economists," came to believe for a time in 1966 that the Federal Reserve's tight money policy had introduced the possibility of a recession and that consequently the need for a tax hike had passed.[19] Treasury Secretary Henry Fowler opposed the increase in late 1965 and early 1966.[20] And Secretary of Defense Robert S. McNamara was, in Ackley's judgment, "strongly against it, not on economic grounds at all but on political grounds." LBJ's chief economist thought that McNamara "realized—perhaps more than anybody else and perhaps sooner than anybody else—that the Vietnam War was going to be an awfully unpopular thing and that a tax increase would just make it all the more unpopular."[21]

In his published memoirs, Johnson defended his foot-dragging on the tax front by emphasizing the lack of support for a tax increase, either in Congress, the business community, organized labor, or his own cabinet. The CEA's Arthur Okun recalled, "Anybody who wanted to slow things down was a killjoy." In 1966 and 1967, both the New York Times and the Washington Post opposed a major tax increase. As late as January 1968, a Gallup poll found 79 percent of the public opposed to raising taxes.[22] Ackley has since contended that Johnson's political pessimism was both genuine and determinative: "I have no question that he [LBJ] was convinced that a tax increase was needed, badly needed, right at the beginning of 1966; and that if he didn't get it, the economy really was going to go to hell and all kinds of problems. . . . And he was also convinced that he couldn't get a tax increase if he tried. I'm sure also, that he wasn't really very enthusiastic about trying, but I really think he was convinced that he couldn't get it, no matter how hard he tried, and that an attempt to get it would do more harm than good."[23]

The difficulty of the task did not, however, fully explain LBJ's reluctance to go all-out for a tax hike. There is little doubt that Johnson realized the seriousness of the problem. But he was playing for the highest of stakes: the fate of his Great Society. To force the issue on the question of a tax hike would allow critics of the Vietnam War to savage the administration; it would also encourage conservatives to demand that the Great Society programs be cut back lest they interfere with the financing of the war. An increase in taxes would invite a political scrutiny that threatened both the administration's Vietnam policy and its domestic reform. So Johnson hesitated on taxes and fudged on the cost of the war. His judgment was partially validated when his long-delayed tax bill, introduced in August 1967, was immediately bottled up in Congress by those who wished to force the administration to trim its domestic spending.

Having hesitated on the tax issue for a disastrously long time, Johnson now found himself stymied by the determination of Representative Wilbur Mills, the Democratic chairman of the House Ways and Means Committee, to exact cuts in domestic spending as the price for congressional action on the administration's tax proposal. It was a clash of legislative titans. Mills had entered Congress in 1939, and by the mid-1960s was perhaps the most powerful figure on Capitol Hill.[24] Tutored by Sam Rayburn, LBJ's former mentor, Mills was a prodigious worker and the acknowledged congressional master of fiscal arcana. Seemingly unchallengeable in his home district in Arkansas, Mills struck Johnson's last health, education, and welfare secretary, Wilbur Cohen, as "the kind of man in politics who is as independent as a human being can be."[25] Kennedy had once said of Mills: "Wilbur Mills knows that he was chairman of Ways and Means before I got here and that he'll still be chairman after I've gone—and he knows I know it. I don't have any hold on him."[26] Recognizing Mills's critical importance in the tax hike campaign, Johnson told him straightforwardly, "I have got everybody on my side except you, and you are the one I have got to have."[27]

Mills, however, saw Johnson as a wastrel, a spender of the old New Deal stripe: "I thought I knew the President well enough to know that if we gave him ten billion dollars more money to spend, that he would spend it if we didn't tie his hands to where he couldn't spend it."[28] The issue was, Mills believed, a fundamental one. To increase taxes without simultaneously cutting expenditures would "have a serious long-range impact upon the direction of our economy." He feared that the president's path "would mean bigger and bigger government with a smaller and smaller range of freedom of activity for the private sector."[29]

Mills's critique was more than the reflexive howl of a powerful but provincial fiscal conservative. Indeed, behind his insistence on spending cuts as the price for a tax increase lay a sophisticated attempt to decouple the defining elements of growth liberalism, to separate growth economics from liberal activism. Mills believed he had been burned by the Kennedy-Johnson tax cut of 1964, which he had ultimately come to support as an application of Andrew Mellon's free enterprise tax policy of the late 1920s— tax reduction that would produce economic growth by unleashing the productive power of the private sector.[30] To Mills's dismay, the Eighty-ninth Congress in 1965 and 1966 had passed a host of Great Society initiatives, and expenditures had "taken off like the Apollo spaceship . . . to . . . the Moon." Instead of constraining federal activism, the 1964 tax cut had underwritten an unprecedented expansion of governmental programs.[31] The heating up of the Vietnam War had exacerbated the problem, and Mills excoriated LBJ's guns-and-butter policy: "I just do not believe," he observed, "that when we are in a war that is costing us $25 to $30 billion a year we can carry on as usual at home."[32]

For Mills, the heart of the matter was growth liberalism's overreach. "Like you," he wrote to a constituent in October 1967, "I have raised the same questions of whether . . . this country is strong enough to be able to police every corner of the world, fight limited wars, attempt to raise the living standards of the peoples of the underdeveloped areas of the world, satisfy our needs of our people at home and go to the moon all at the same time without the creation of unstable deficits."[33] Consequently, Mills fought Johnson not only to cut current expenditures but also to influence the future by cutting both the old and new obligational authority that constituted the pipeline for future spending.[34]

Mills brought to his side a majority of the Ways and Means Committee, which in October 1967 voted 20 to 5 to temporarily table Johnson's 10 percent surcharge proposal. LBJ's budget director, Charles L. Schultze, had confidently predicted to the president that Mills and his committee were playing "chicken" in an "eyeball-to-eyeball" confrontation with the administration, and that Mills would blink first.[35] But the chairman's gaze proved pitiless as the sun, and the Vietnam inflation worsened dramatically in the last quarter of 1967. By exacerbating the chronic balance-of-payments problem and fueling a dangerous inflation, the Vietnam War worked a double whammy on the U.S. economy. In doing so, the war also weakened the U.S. dollar, and that weakness emerged dramatically in the last months of 1967 to challenge policymakers on yet another front.

The assault on the dollar was the third and most immediate of the sources that in their interaction caused the economic crisis of 1968.[36] Ironically, the assault was ignited by the travails of another currency, the British pound. The pound had been weak and vulnerable to raids by speculators through much of the 1960s. In Frederick Deming's words, "You've got a major confidence crisis in sterling about every fall on the fall, so to speak, and there was in '64, '65, '66, and then it culminated in '67."[37] When the pressure against sterling crested in mid-November 1967, Deming, the treasury under secretary for monetary affairs, was already in Paris for regularly scheduled meetings with senior treasury and central bank officials of the major industrial powers (the so-called Group of Ten), and he led an effort to mobilize multilateral support for the pound.[38] But the attempt failed, and on November 17 the British ambassador informed Johnson that the British would on the following day announce a 14.3 percent devaluation.

The British devaluation touched off a frenzy in the gold market. Treasury Secretary Henry Fowler had earlier warned Johnson that one result of devaluation would be "that the gold market would come under very great pressure—and might explode."[39] Demand for gold was already strong because of the uncertainty generated by the summer's Six-Day War in the

Middle East, because industrial use was rising faster than new production, and because the Soviets had refused in both 1966 and 1967 to sell gold on the world market.[40] The chronic weakness of the pound caused further movement away from paper money into gold, and Britain's devaluation provided the final spark that caused the gold market to explode just as Fowler had feared. The so-called gold pool—formed in 1961 by the United States and eight other countries to sell gold when the demand was too great or to buy gold when the supply was too great in order to keep its price in the London gold market close to the official $35 per ounce—intervened to stabilize the gold market and from November 20 through 27 incurred losses of $641 million (of which the U.S. share was 59 percent).[41]

The devaluation of sterling and the financial unrest that followed sent tremors of fear through the U.S. economic establishment. Alfred Hayes, president of the Federal Reserve Board of New York, worried that the gold pool was at the point of disintegrating.[42] Fed chairman William McChesney Martin Jr. observed, "It is the first time in all my 16 years with the Fed that I have seen all the important bankers and directors agree that we face a crisis ahead." "The real question," Fowler told the cabinet, "is can we keep confidence in the dollar. The answer affects all the world."[43]

The United States responded to the British devaluation and its aftermath with a three-pronged defense of the dollar. First, the president made clear the American commitment to keep the price of gold at $35 an ounce. Second, the administration worked to get other nations to agree to maintain their existing exchange rates in order to prevent a chain reaction of competitive currency realignments. Third, Secretary Fowler called upon the bipartisan leadership to build confidence in the dollar: "No single act could more effectively restore and maintain confidence in the dollar, and shore up our balance of payments position—both short and long term—than the passage of an expenditure reduction and tax increase package at this Session of Congress." "Markets don't wait," he added pointedly.[44]

Fowler's remarks underscore how intertwined the problems of the balance of payments, the Vietnam War, and the strength of the dollar had become by the end of 1967. The war and the administration's apparent inability to get the tax hike needed to dampen domestic demand heightened international concern about the U.S. balance of payments, and that concern in turn weakened the dollar by encouraging heavy sales of that currency and purchases of gold in the international market. It was this terrible interlocking combination of problems that became the stuff of the economic crisis of 1968.

II. The Crisis Unfolds

The international monetary system recovered from the British devaluation episode, but it quickly fell prey to further shocks. The week of December 4–8 saw the return of relative calm to the gold market, as the determination of the gold pool countries to hold the line "down to the last bar [of gold]" temporarily stanched their losses and resulted in a net gain for the week of $9 million.[45] In the next week (December 11-15), gold pool losses rocketed back up to $548 million, and Rostow notified the president that "the gold market has come to a boil again."[46] Once again, the gold pool came close to cracking under the pressure. Later, Hubert Ansiaux of the Belgian central bank told William McChesney Martin that "we [the Belgian, German, Italian, Dutch, and Swiss members of the gold pool] were strongly of the opinion until yesterday night [December 14] . . . to recommend that we should stop our intervention in the London market." But the gold pool partners agreed to soldier on, provided that the United States make public a new program for dealing with the balance-of-payments deficit.[47]

The administration had for some time been developing just such a payments program, with the work coordinated by the so-called Deming Group, which included Frederick Deming as treasury under secretary for monetary affairs, J. Dewey Daane and Robert Solomon of the Federal Reserve, Anthony Solomon representing the State Department, Arthur Okun from the CEA, and Edward Fried of the NSC. Now, with the additional prodding by the Europeans, the effort shifted into high gear; LBJ gave his final approval to the package on December 29 and announced it on New Year's Day 1968.

The New Year's balance-of-payments program had two basic thrusts. What Johnson labeled "the first order of business" called for prompt enactment of the administration's anti-inflationary tax increase, for more effective wage-price restraint, and for the elimination of strikes in key industries that affected the balance of payments by reducing exports or increasing imports. The program's second thrust aimed at specific aspects of the balance-of-payments deficit. To arrest the outflow of capital, the president used his existing authority to institute a mandatory program to restrict direct investment abroad and authorized the Federal Reserve to tighten its program restricting foreign lending by U.S. banks. To reduce the net impact of government overseas expenditures, the program called for a new round of belt-tightening and further efforts to get the NATO allies to pick up more of the tab for the U.S. military presence in Europe. To lessen the outflow of tourist dollars, Johnson suggested that Americans defer for two years nonessential travel outside the western hemisphere and promised new proposals to increase the influx of foreign tourists to the United States. Finally, to strengthen the basic trade balance, the New Year's program promised increased spending to promote U.S. exports and intensive efforts to further reduce nontariff barriers to U.S. goods abroad.[48]

The initial public response to the new balance-of-payments program was strongly positive, and a week after its announcement Ackley reported "widespread optimism that speculation in gold should be substantially halted." "But," he added, "in fact, the gold market could flare up over anything."[49] Indeed, Johnson's plan of action soon confronted new realities that threatened to tie the threads of the balance of payments, Vietnam, and the vulnerable dollar into a knot beyond undoing.

The bad news seemed endless. On the payments front, the latest statistics were grim. The CEA informed the president in late December 1967 that the fourth-quarter outflow had been nearly $2 billion, threatening "to turn the year into a disaster" by creating a deficit that "may challenge 1960's unhappy record of $3.9 billion."[50] The economic fallout from Vietnam was equally troubling. Inflation worsened, with consumer prices rising 0.3 percent in January—the fourth straight monthly increase of that magnitude— and the wholesale price index up 0.4 percent in January and 0.6 percent in February. "Price increases," warned the Bureau of Labor Statistics, "are becoming more pervasive throughout the economy."[51] Moreover, the surprise Tet Offensive at the end of January raised the distinct possibility that even more U.S. troops would be committed to the struggle, with any such commitment likely necessitating calling up of the reserves and a general mobilization for war. Meanwhile, the administration began to despair over passage of its tax surcharge proposal, with one official describing the attitude in the House as "one of almost anarchistic willingness to pull down the temple around their ears on the grounds that our budgetary expenditures are out of control."[52] The tax hike difficulty was all the more vexing because, as Rostow acknowledged, "it has become a symbol in Europe of what the U.S. itself is willing to do."[53]

On the dollar and gold front, still other problems worked to frustrate the administration's New Year's plan. American efforts to calm the gold market continued to be hampered by the failure of new gold production to meet the liquidity requirements of the expanding world economy. The leveling off of new gold production, rising industrial use, and heavy speculative demand combined to draw down the total monetary gold stock; at the same time, the increasing hesitancy of other nations to hold reserves in dollars made it impossible to depend on that reserve currency to meet the world's expanding liquidity needs. The end result of this liquidity crunch was greater pressure on the dollar, as speculators increasingly bet that the United States (and the rest of the world) would be forced to raise the price of gold to provide a one-time addition to liquidity.[54] A second problem vexing U.S. policymakers and intensifying the risk of crisis involved the legal requirement that the United States allocate sufficient gold reserves to "cover" 25 percent of the nation's domestic note issue (essentially, the paper money in circulation); this amounted to approximately $10 billion of the nation's gold supply that could not legally be used to fulfill the commitment to dollar convertibility.[55] Attempts were under way to remedy both problems, liquidity and the gold cover, but in the first months of 1968 they had not yet come to fruition, and that fact added to the economic volatility of the moment.

Losses by the gold pool held below a crisis level at $227 million for the first two months of 1968, but pressure continued to build just beneath the surface.[56] The continued wrangling over the tax bill seemed interminable, both to Europeans and to the White House. The administration introduced legislation to solve one problem by removing the gold cover, but the hearings on the proposal added a new note of uncertainty when amendments were proposed that would have restricted gold sales in the face of heavy losses (thus ending absolute dollar convertibility). Still more controversy followed when the president's New Year's proposals on tourism and trade ran into increasing criticism. In addition, Britain's devaluation was not working out well and sterling continued to be weak, which kept pressure on the dollar and fed gold speculation.[57]

The crisis suddenly came to a head in March. "The gold market broke out again last week," Fowler told the president on March 4. "After a few weeks of quiet, gold pool losses last week came to $123 million, including $88 million on Friday. Today losses were $53 million. We face the prospect of increasingly heavy sales during the rest of the week." On Friday, March 8, Rostow reported that the gold pool had that day suffered its third largest loss ever, $179 million.[58] The speculative spiral was out of control. McGeorge Bundy had once quipped that "only the greedy, the frightened, country folk and the Frenchmen love gold"—if true, then it was those groups who now dictated events.[59] On Tuesday, March 12, Rostow told the president, "My own feeling is that the moment of truth is close upon us."[60]

On Wednesday, March 13, losses for the day totaled approximately $200 million, and Federal Reserve chairman Martin called his European counterparts to alert them that the United States might seek to close the gold markets.[61] The administration postponed action so that Congress would have time to pass the pending gold-cover legislation; Thursday, March 14—which Fowler later called "one of the most hectic days of my life"—became the day of decision.[62] As LBJ met twice with his economic advisers, losses for the day reached nearly $400 million. After much debate, the administration, fearful that another's day's losses might run to $1 billion, asked the British to shut down the London gold market on Friday and invited the central bankers of the gold pool countries to Washington for an emergency meeting over the weekend. When it proved impossible to reach some of the foreign officials by phone, Secretary of State Dean Rusk instructed the duty officers at embassies and consulates across Europe to contact them "at once, waking them if necessary." Rusk closed with a flourish, "You must track down these men at all costs."[63] The melodramatic tone was fitting.

III. The Crisis Resolved

Having prevailed upon the Bank of England to close the London gold market and having invited to Washington the governors of the central banks of the gold pool nations, Johnson quickly sought to drive home the message that the price of gold would be held. In a March 15 telegram to West Germany's chancellor Kiesinger, LBJ observed, with a certain populistic vengeance, "The speculators are banking on an increase in the official price of gold. They are wrong."[64] The United States had blinked, unwilling to play the game "to the last bar," but it also refused to give the speculators what they wanted—devaluation. The alternative was to shore up the Bretton Woods system, and that the administration proceeded to do.

The crisis atmosphere of March 1968 produced several immediate changes that, together, returned the international monetary system to working order. The first of these was the implementation of a "two-tier system" for gold transactions. The so-called Washington Communiqué issued at the end of the weekend meetings made it clear that the gold market would henceforth be separated into an official market, where monetary gold for central banking purposes would be governed by dollar-gold convertibility at $35 an ounce, and a private market, where gold for industrial and speculative purposes would be governed by the basic laws of supply and demand.[65] As one Zurich banker put it, "The central bankers are saying to the speculators: 'Take it to the dentist.'"[66] In effect, the central bankers were also saying that in the future they would meet their reserve and liquid-ity needs through a new kind of "paper" international reserve asset rather than through buying more gold. The concept behind the two-tier system was not newly minted at the March 1968 conference; Guido Carli of the Bank of Italy had advanced the idea back in November 1967. But two things had changed in the interim. The plans for the new "paper gold" reserve asset, on which any two-tiered arrangement would rely, were now much farther advanced. And, as Arthur Okun has contended, the experience of the crisis itself had an important effect: "I don't think we could have gotten the other countries on board if we had opted for . . . [the two-tier system] earlier. They had bled a little, and they knew that some accommodations had to be made. They wanted to stop their losses of gold . . . and they became very enthusiastic about this."[67]

A second immediate change to which the March crisis contributed mightily was the removal of the American gold cover. The Washington Communiqué noted specifically and approvingly that the removal of the gold cover "makes the whole of the gold stock of the nation available for defending the value of the dollar."[68] This, too, was a change long discussed. As early as 1961, John Kennedy had been advised to seek repeal of the gold cover commitment, but he feared that any such proposal by him would be wrapped around his neck politically as "Democratic funny-money finagling."[69] In 1965, Congressman Henry Reuss, a Wisconsin Democrat, introduced a bill to eliminate the gold cover, but the initiative failed to win support. Three such bills were introduced in the House and Senate in 1967, and Fed chairman Martin publicly endorsed the proposed freeing of the gold stock "for use as an international monetary reserve—the principal function performed by gold today."[70] Resistance to the suggested change centered on the fact that the gold cover dated back to the creation of the Federal Reserve system and so enjoyed the imprimatur of both time and financial probity.

Johnson asked Congress to remove the cover in his State of the Union address on January 17, 1968, but winning congressional approval proved difficult, and again the March crisis played a role. Treasury Under Secretary Joseph Barr recalled that on the day the Senate voted on the measure, at the peak of the gold crisis, Senate majority leader Mike Mansfield (D., Mont.) called to report that he was no longer sure he had the votes. "So Fowler and I and Bill Martin . . . sat down with the leadership on both sides . . . explained to them that the crisis was getting worse and worse, and that if we did not pass that bill that day, we might be forced to renege the next day on our promise to deliver gold." Finally, at 7:30 in the evening, the Senate approved the repeal of the gold cover by a 39–37 vote. In the future, all of the nation's gold stock would be placed behind its commitment to maintain the price of gold and value of the dollar.[71]

The third immediate result of the March crisis was a renewed and strengthened commitment to a reform already in the works—the creation of a new form of international reserves, the Special Drawing Rights (SDR), designed to serve as a form of paper gold to meet the liquidity needs of an expanding world economy. Indeed, it was, as the Washington Communiqué explicitly stated, the prospect that the SDR would soon be in place that allowed the creation of the two-tier system. With the SDR on the horizon, the central bankers of the gold pool states could agree that the existing stock of monetary gold was sufficient and that they would no longer need to buy gold from the market.[72] The international reserves needed for future economic growth could come from the new paper gold, which would be used alongside real gold and the dollar for settling international accounts.

It is clear that the concept of the SDR was already well advanced by the time of the March crisis. The congressional Joint Economic Committee had as early as 1962 urged the creation of new methods for routinely increasing international liquidity, and discussions on the matter continued among both the Group of Ten and the International Monetary Fund in the mid-1960s. The IMF approved an outline proposal for the creation of SDRs at its meeting in Rio de Janeiro in September 1967, but working out the final details proved to be a difficult and contentious task.[73] Early in 1968, *Time* reported, "There is one big hang-up: these 'S.D.R.s' will probably not be activated until the U.S. and Britain markedly reduce their balance of payments deficits." *Business Week* agreed that "the plan can't be ratified before next year at the earliest."[74] More devoted to the primacy of gold than other nations, France in particular seemed to be dragging its feet.

Once again, the March crisis had an effect, more accelerative than causal in the case of SDRs but significant nonetheless. A Group of Ten meeting in Stockholm at the end of March finally settled the SDR issue. In the judgment of Treasury Secretary Fowler, the gold crisis of mid-March had pointed up the danger of continuing to depend on increased supplies of gold at $35 an ounce as the monetary system's source of additional liquidity: "The gold crisis was draining away from, and reducing, the quantity of gold held in the reserves of Central Banks. So there was a source of diminishing liquidity. This underscored and, indeed, highlighted the need for the Special Drawing Rights facility."[75]

U.S. policymakers believed that the Washington Gold Accord of mid-March and the innovations that underpinned it—the two-tier system, the full commitment of the U.S. gold stock, the development of the SDR—were necessary expedients that provided much-needed breathing room, but as Arthur Okun, LBJ's new chairman of the CEA, pointed out, the accord was "futile unless we get a tax increase."[76] In the end, Wilbur Mills triumphed. Johnson ended the long struggle by signing the Revenue and Expenditure Control Act of 1968 into law on June 28, 1968—two and a half years after CEA chairman Gardner Ackley had first warned of economic overheating. The administration won a retroactive 10 percent surcharge on individual and corporate income taxes but at the price of agreeing to $6 billion in immediate spending cuts for fiscal year 1969, a reduction of $10 billion in new obligational and loan authority for fiscal year 1969, and a future $8 billion recision in unobligated balances of obligational and loan authority carried over from previous years.

The March gold crisis contributed significantly to the final outcome of the tax hike struggle. The tax compromise was a difficult one for Johnson and the liberals in his administration to accept, for it cut to the heart of the Great Society—the reductions would come from domestic programs as well as non-Vietnam defense expenditures. Wilbur Mills believed that the dramatic impact of the March gold crisis helped drive LBJ to accept the hard bargain that Mills and his allies had forced upon him: "President Johnson . . . was scared almost out of his body when he woke up to the fact that people in Europe were having trouble exchanging dollars for foreign currency."[77] For his part, Johnson agreed that the crisis provided important impetus, but he emphasized its impact on *his* opposition: "The international crisis had done what we could not do: arouse the American public and many congressional leaders to the need for decisive action." Mills did indeed subsequently report that the "severe run on the dollar in the international market during the early months of 1968" and the "drastic outflow of gold" were "important to . . . [the Ways and Means Committee] in reaching a decision to agree to the surtax proposal." In retrospect, the March crisis moved both sides toward a resolution of the fiscal impasse. Treasury Under Secretary Frederick Deming correctly observed that "the prime mover in getting action was the fact that the international monetary system seemed to be going to hell in a handbasket."[78]

In this fashion, the worst economic crisis since the Great Depression was resolved. Changes—significant but not truly radical—were made to buttress the Bretton Woods regime, and hard choices were decided upon in the name of fiscal responsibility. In the short run, the innovations seemed to work. Johnson touted the development of the SDR as a "historic step" that "will prepare us for the era of expanding world trade and economic opportunity that unfolds before us."[79] At the end of July, Okun reported to the president that "there is less of a crisis atmosphere now than at any time in the past year"; in September, he noted that the "economy is advancing strongly" and that "the unhealthy boomy pace of the first half has already moderated."[80] Ironically, the balance of payments improved dramatically over the course of 1968. The administration's New Year's program and the tax hike helped to some extent, as did the unrest in Europe when France suffered its May riots and the Soviets invaded Czechoslovakia. As a result, Joseph Barr (who replaced Fowler as treasury secretary in December 1968) recalled, "all the money ran out of Europe and came to the United States so we ended up really in amazing statistical fashion." By the end of the year, the United States enjoyed a small surplus in its balance of payments, calculated on both the liquidity and the official transactions basis.[81]

Looking back, however, it is clear that the resolution of the 1968 economic crisis bought breathing room but settled little. An analysis of how the basic sources of the crisis played out in its aftermath makes the point. The balance of payments quickly turned downward again, as even the trade account (basically, exports and imports of goods and raw materials), long a source of U.S. strength, sank into deficit in the face of stagnating productivity at home and increased global competition.[82] The Vietnam War continued to generate inflationary pressures that would plague the economy, and policymakers, into the 1970s and beyond. Johnson's tax surcharge proved to be too little too late, and appears to have had only a small effect on consumer and business spending.[83] Moreover, it was offset, much to the chagrin of Wilbur Mills, by the easing of credit by monetary authorities in the latter half of 1968.[84] Finally, despite the revamping of 1968, the Bretton Woods international monetary regime was doomed by the continued economic and political resurgence of Europe and Japan, and, after another global monetary crisis in 1971, President Richard M. Nixon closed the gold window, thus ending the era of dollar-gold convertibility. By 1973, a new regime based on floating exchange rates had taken shape.[85]

IV. Reverberations

Thus, in the economic realm the 1968 crisis proved to be more revelatory than revolutionary. Regarding the economy, the crisis was significant more for what it revealed than for what it changed. The episode illuminated trends that could be accommodated and moderated but not arrested or reversed. It revealed and contributed to both the passing of postwar U.S. economic hegemony and the beginning of an awkward transition from the postwar boom to a period of economic stagnation-*cum*-inflation—stagfla-tion—which emerged unmistakably by the mid-1970s. (Indeed, the sugges-tion of such a transition puts the Nixon presidency in a new light and offers a new context and criterion for evaluating its record, in addition to those provided by Watergate and the Cold War. That story is told in our next chapter.)[86] But such revelations aside, the most dramatic and concrete results of the crisis of 1968 were not narrowly economic.

It was, rather, in the wider world of political economy, where economics connects with the political culture and the social fabric, that the most signi-ficant impact of the economic crisis of 1968 occurred. By early 1968, LBJ's attempt to fight a war in Southeast Asia while building the Great Society at home had stretched the U.S. political economy to the breaking point. The economic crisis that culminated in March coincided with the shock of the Tet Offensive in Vietnam, which began on the last two days of January but continued to dominate the war action through February and March. The combined weight of these economic and military reversals finally wrecked Johnson's guns-and-butter policy. As a result, the administration was forced to cap both the long escalation of the Vietnam War and the expansion of the Great Society.

The events in Vietnam flared up with dramatic suddenness. At 2:35 on the afternoon of January 30, a staffer called national security adviser Walt Rostow out of the president's regular Tuesday luncheon with his foreign policy advisers—the so-called Tuesday cabinet—to relay a flash from the national military command center. Returning to the meeting, Rostow reported, "We have just been informed we are being heavily mortared in Saigon. The Presidential Palace, our BOQs [bachelor officers' quarters], the Embassy and the city itself have been hit." "This could be very bad," the president observed, adding without apparent self-consciousness, "This looks like where we came in. Remember it was at Pleiku [in 1965] that they hit our barracks and that we began to strike them in the north."[87] Johnson's immediate reaction highlighted the political problem posed by the commu-nist attacks: If the Tet Offensive was reminiscent of "where we came in," how then to justify or even merely assess the intervening two and a half years of U.S. warmaking?

The Tet Offensive, in Clark Clifford's phrase, "really . . . threw gasoline on the fire."[88] Communist forces struck at district headquarters, provincial capitals, and cities and towns across the length of South Vietnam. Although General William Westmoreland, the U.S. commander in Vietnam, had warned his superiors a week before the Lunar New Year holiday of a likely enemy "country-wide show of strength just prior to Tet," the ferocity, scope, and scale of the communist onslaught rocked the American and South Vietnamese forces back on their heels.[89] On February 5, Westmoreland cabled Washington: "After nearly five days of widespread fighting, the true dimensions of the situation are beginning to emerge. From a realistic point of view we must accept the fact that the enemy has dealt the GVN [the South Vietnamese government] a severe blow."[90]

The military tide turned quickly when the Americans and South Vietnamese counterattacked and inflicted devastating losses on the Communists, especially on the irregulars of the Viet Cong, but the impact of the enemy's initial success proved impossible to erase. The American media's mistaken insistence on interpreting the episode as a disastrous military defeat for the allies contributed to the Johnson administration's woes,[91] but even more telling were the inevitable and wholly realistic questions raised by the ability of the Communists to launch such an undertaking. As George Christian, LBJ's press secretary and special assistant, later admitted, "To me it appeared that if something like that could happen at that late date in Vietnam . . . just the mere fact that they could mount that type of operation was a very negative thing from our standpoint."[92]

The Tet Offensive crystallized doubts and reservations that had been gathering for months and years among both policymakers and the general public. The war was far from over; any light at the end of the tunnel—in Westmoreland's unfortunate phrase—was much dimmer than optimistic official assessments had suggested; clear-cut military victory now seemed either impossible or unacceptably costly.

As if to punctuate the bad tidings, Westmoreland and General Earle Wheeler, the chairman of the Joint Chiefs of Staff, in February requested the commitment of an additional 205,000 troops to Vietnam.[93] The military's request for more troops touched off a controversy within the administration that became a public debate when word of the proposal was leaked to the press, resulting ultimately in a fundamental reassessment of U.S. policy in Vietnam. Coming at precisely the moment when the economic crisis of 1968 came to a head in the March run on gold, the reexamination of war policy provoked by the post-Tet troop request involved economic consider-ations fully as much as political calculation and military strategy.

The economic implications of the troop request were troubling. To pro-vide the requested reinforcements for Vietnam would require the rebuild-ing of the military's seriously depleted strategic reserve as well, and so the Westmoreland-Wheeler request would necessitate the call-up of over a quarter million reservists, increased draft calls, and the extension of terms of service for many already in uniform—altogether, the addition of 511,000 to the active duty armed forces by June 30, 1969. This was the war mobiliza-tion long sought by the military and thus far assiduously avoided by John-son. The overall program would cost $2.5 billion in fiscal year 1968 and $10 billion in fiscal year 1969, raising the annual cost of the war by roughly 40 percent. The adverse impact on the balance of payments was projected to be $500 million.[94] Moreover, all such costs were *additions* to a basic defense budget whose projections for fiscal year 1970 had already been labeled "a shock" by Budget Director Charles Zwick.[95] "Now this on top of the already enormous burden we were carrying," Clifford subsequently recalled, "the dollar had gone through a period of vulnerability in the early part of '68, and in the spring this would put a lot more pressure on it, put a lot more pressure upon our balance-of-payments problem, which was already acute, so that all these matters began to come in that day by day caused me growing concern."[96]

Other top policymakers shared Clifford's anxiety about the economic cost of the war. Before leaving office, his predecessor, Robert McNamara, had noted the importance of doing "whatever we can to prevent the financial requirements [of any proposal for post-Tet Vietnam reinforcements] from ruining us in foreign exchange in our domestic economic situation [sic]."[97] Secretary of State Dean Rusk cautioned, "We have . . . got to think of what this troop increase would mean in terms of increased taxes, the balance of pay-ments picture, inflation, gold, and the general economic picture."[98] Treasury Secretary Fowler observed that events in Vietnam and developments in "the international financial picture" were "interacting," and warned that the troop increase would hurt both the economy and the dollar and likely necessitate further cuts in Great Society programs, especially those dealing with poverty and urban problems.[99] Even LBJ's resolutely hawkish national security adviser, Walt Rostow, admitted that without a tax increase, the proposed Vietnam buildup "may be very tough on the dollar."[100] U.S. policymakers clearly recog-nized a connection between the future prosecution of the war in Southeast Asia and the economic crisis that had emerged in the early months of 1968.

As word of the troop request leaked out to the press, observers outside government made the connection as well. "The gold crisis . . . and a continuing threat to the dollar," wrote Hobart Rowen in the *Washington Post*, "are bringing President Johnson face to face with basic questions on Vietnam war policy. It is now clear that there are real limits to our financial resources." Writing in the *New Republic* that the sending of more troops to Vietnam would risk "a collapse . . . of the international monetary system," Edwin Dale announced: "Someone had better tell the President, in so many words, that if he puts into Vietnam the number of troops that now seem required to restore and improve the situation there, he may throw away the fruits of a generation of brilliant economic progress."[101]

Johnson received just that message on a number of occasions in March when he went outside the ranks of his immediate advisers to seek advice on the troop request and related Vietnam issues. When the president sent Clifford and Wheeler to canvass key congressional leaders, they found little support for either a major troop commitment or a large reserve call-up.[102] Both hawks and doves feared the economic consequences of an escalation. Clifford subsequently reported to the Tuesday cabinet that Stuart Symington, a Democratic senator from Missouri and Cold War stalwart, "thinks we should get out. He thinks the dollar will depreciate."[103] Johnson's successor as Senate majority leader, the dovish Mike Mansfield of Montana, explained in a memo forwarded to the president that expanding the U.S. role in Vietnam would mean "more inflation, more balance-of-payments complication, and possibly financial panic and collapse."[104]

Still casting about for advice in late March, Johnson convened a group of elder statesmen known as the "Wise Men." The members of the group constituted a virtual "who's who" of the foreign policy establishment. They had advised him before on the war (with "hawkish" results), and he turned to them again to gauge just how much opinion had changed in the wake of recent events. One key member was McGeorge Bundy, former national security adviser to both Kennedy and Johnson. Bundy, too, recognized the connection between the economic and the political. "I now understand," he wrote to Johnson, "that the really tough problem you have is the interlock between the bad turn in the war, the critical need for a tax increase, and the crisis of public confidence at home."[105] The most imposing, and imperious, of the Wise Men, Dean Acheson, conveyed a similar opinion personally to Johnson in mid-March and spoke forcefully when the Wise Men met with the president on March 26. The United States, Acheson asserted, could not prevail in Vietnam in a reasonable time with the means available. That fact, he reasoned, "together with our broader interests in SEA [Southeast Asia], Europe, and in connection with the dollar crisis, requires a decision now to disengage within a limited time."[106] For Acheson, as for others, the matter of resources and limits had now become critical. "The gold crisis," the former secretary of state wrote a friend, "has dampened expansionist ideas. The town is in an atmosphere of crisis."[107] Clifford subsequently observed, "Speaking almost *ex officio* as the leader of the foreign policy establishment, and with his customary authority, Acheson had an unquestionable impact on the President."[108]

In the end, the decision on the troop request was Lyndon Johnson's to make. And, for LBJ, the economic context of Vietnam decision-making proved inescapable and mattered greatly: "We were struggling with one of the most serious financial crises of recent years," he later wrote. "These monetary and budgetary problems were constantly before us as we considered whether we should or could do more in Vietnam. It was clear that calling up a large number of troops, sending additional men overseas, and increasing military expenditures would complicate our problems and put greater pressure on the dollar."[109] Mindful of such economic concerns, an improving military situation in Vietnam, and the declining political support at home for both the war and his presidency, Johnson decided in a tentative and halting fashion over the course of March to scale back dramatically any deployment of additional forces to Vietnam or mobilization of reserves.[110]

By the time Johnson met with Rusk and Generals Wheeler and Creighton Abrams (who was soon to replace Westmoreland as U.S. commander in Vietnam) on March 26, the basic decisions for a reorientation of U.S. war policy had been made, and the tone of the meeting was elegiac. Their common endeavor was about to take a new turn, and Johnson seemed to need to explain to his generals why he had not met the military's request for a dramatic escalation of the war. He also sought to assure them that the new course had been forced on him by dastardly enemies and large, impersonal forces, rather than by his past mistakes or theirs. "It is the civilians [in the Pentagon]," he told Wheeler, Abrams, and Rusk, "that are cutting our guts out." Press leakers and Georgetown liberals, the *New York Times* and the *Washington Post*, Edward and Robert Kennedy, an uncooperative Congress—all suffered the president's opprobrium. But in a revealing lament, Johnson laid bare the larger forces dictating so fundamental a shift in his Vietnam policy.

The political economy of the war, Johnson told his generals, had turned against them. "Our fiscal situation is abominable," he reported. The fate of

the tax bill remained uncertain, and the administration faced a possible deficit of over $30 billion. Such a large shortfall would force interest rates up
and endanger both the British pound and the dollar. "Unless we get a tax bill
. . . [the situation] will be unthinkable." But LBJ's predicament did not end
there. The price of congressional approval for his tax increase would likely
be the sort of concomitant spending cuts demanded by Mills. Johnson
expected to be forced to make half the cuts in non-Vietnam defense expenditures. "That will cause hell with Russell [Senator Richard Russell, chairman of the Senate Armed Services Committee]. If we don't do that we will
have hell. What happens when you cut poverty, housing and education?"
Every way Johnson turned, his choices looked grim.[111]

The request for Vietnam reinforcements and a large-scale mobilization
only exacerbated the administration's plight. "That would cost $15 billion.
That would hurt the dollar and the gold sic," Johnson explained. "How can
we get the job done?" he asked plaintively. "We need more money in an
election year, more taxes in an election year, more troops in an election year
and more cuts in an election year." There was, he added pointedly, "no support for the war."[112]

Johnson concluded the meeting with his military leaders by asserting, "I
would give Westmoreland 206,000 men if he said he needed them [to stave
off a disastrous defeat] and if we could get them."[113] But Westmoreland
could not honestly couch his request in such terms. And the president realized that to fulfill such a request would be to risk further disasters, both economic and political. In the end, the lessening of the immediate military
pressure in Vietnam as the communist gains of the Tet Offensive were
rolled back, the difficulty in envisioning a likely scenario for American military victory by doing "more of the same," the erosion of popular support
for the war, and the realization that the costs of further escalation were
unacceptable at a time when the economy's performance and institutional
underpinnings were already overstrained all came together to seal LBJ's
decision to try a new tack in Vietnam.

On March 31, 1968, Johnson announced that the new troop commitment
to Vietnam would be limited to 13,500 additional support troops to bolster
the 11,000 combat troops airlifted to Vietnam immediately after the Tet
attack.[114] Johnson also reported that new emphasis would be placed on
expanding South Vietnam's role in its own defense. To help secure a political resolution of the war, he named a new peace ambassador, Averell Harri-
man, and ordered a bombing halt over most of North Vietnam. Although
American forces would remain in combat in Vietnam for nearly five more

years, the long, gradual escalation of U.S. involvement was at last capped. Henceforth, emphasis would shift from prosecution of the war to extrication from it. The decision to halt the escalation of the war was as much economic as it was political or military.[115]

The economic crisis of 1968 also directly influenced developments at home. As he moved to cap the escalation of the war in Southeast Asia, Johnson came under increasing pressure to throttle back his domestic reforms as well. On the Saturday morning in mid-March when central bankers from the gold pool nations gathered at the Federal Reserve Building in Washington to salvage the international monetary regime, the president spoke to a meeting of business leaders across town at the Sheraton Park Hotel: "We must tighten our belts. We must adopt an austere program. . . . Hard choices are going to have to be made in the next few days. Some desirable programs of lesser priority and urgency are going to have to be deferred."[116] The continuing failure to resolve the nation's fiscal impasse and the threatened collapse of the international monetary order forced on the administration exactly the sort of "discipline of stringency" that LBJ's guns-and-butter policy had sought to avoid.

Admittedly, economic woes were not the only impediment to the expansion of the Great Society in early 1968. Administrative difficulties, hardening racial attitudes on all sides, and the apparent intractability of problems such as poverty all contributed to the slowing of the administration's reform surge. The War on Poverty had proven to be politically divisive even among old-line Democrats, and Johnson's own reform ardor sometimes showed signs of flagging. He was convinced that the poverty warriors of the Office of Economic Opportunity were personally disloyal.[117] Moreover, in the spring of 1968 the president occasionally voiced bitter disappointment at the disaffection (and by implication, the ingratitude) of blacks and the young, two groups he felt had benefited most from his reform efforts in civil rights, poverty, and education.[118]

Personal pique notwithstanding, however, Johnson remained committed, in both word and deed, to his Great Society vision. In late 1967, he told reporters that he wanted to leave as his legacy "a social consciousness in concrete." He had not enjoyed complete success in moving his programs through Congress, he admitted, but "It's only half-time now; there is still another session of the 90th Congress to go."[119] As 1968 began, Johnson continued to press, in the words of a key aide, "almost frenetically" for further reform. During the first two months of 1968 he sent to the Hill the largest manpower program and most ambitious housing bill in U.S. history. He asked for a $290 million increase in appropriations for the OEO's poverty program, and in April signed into law the fair housing legislation he had been seeking since 1966.[120] The pace of reform, although no longer dizzying, remained substantial.

The face and substance of reform were changing, however, as financial exigency chipped away at the administration's reformist resolve even before economic events reached crisis proportions in March 1968. In formally requesting his tax surcharge from Congress in August 1967, Johnson had tried to sweeten the deal by promising to make spending cuts. Britain's devaluation in November increased the pressure on the administration to trim expenditures. At a special meeting called to assess the devaluation, Johnson told his cabinet, "This weekend has made it even more obvious that we must try to slash and stick with reductions in the Budget if we are to save the Great Society and try to get a Tax Bill . . . if we are not to suffer seriously." Speaking of "a new era of economic challenge," he exhorted his department heads to "sharpen your pencils and be prepared."[121] Califano urged the president to emphasize to the cabinet that "this program of cuts is designed to *preserve* the Great Society programs" from those who would use the failure to reach a compromise on the tax bill as an excuse to roll back LBJ's earlier Great Society triumphs entirely.[122] In short, the administration remained committed to reform, but under the pressure of a variety of forces, not the least of them economic, the definition of that commitment shifted increasingly from expanding reform to preserving it.

The reorientation from expansion to preservation was halting and uncertain. Sometimes Johnson talked as though the two goals were interchangeable, but when on occasion he paid lip service to both in the same breath, the tension between them became self-evident. "There is a philosophy in the Congress," Johnson told his cabinet in December 1967, "that we have done enough . . . that we should slow down and tighten up what we have done rather than undertake any new legislation. . . . I don't agree." But he added immediately, "Whatever else we do, we have got to have a price tag on everything we come up with. . . . We have got to know what every new proposal costs and who will pay for it. . . . All of you have got to ask that question. We are all good at saying what we need but we don't know who will pay for it."[123]

The pressure to control social spending increased as the administration's economic problems worsened in early 1968. Less than twenty-four hours before representing the United States at the emergency meeting of the gold pool nations over the weekend of March 16–17, Fed chairman Martin told a

Detroit audience, "It is time to stop pussyfooting, and get our accounts in order. It is time to stop talking of guns and butter. We must face up to the fact that this is a war economy."[124] "If I were dictator," Johnson mused in May 1968, near the end of the bruising tax hike struggle, "I wouldn't be cutting expenditures, I would raise them."[125] But he was not dictator, and in the winter and spring of 1968 threatening economic developments forced Johnson to accept spending cuts as the price for congressional approval of the tax increase he believed the nation needed to stave off economic ruin.

The shift from expanding the Great Society to fighting to preserve it touched off a season of political contention for the administration and its liberal constituency. The issuance in February 1968 of the National Advisory Commission on Civil Disorders report on the urban riots of the previous summer constituted an opening round. The commission, headed by Governor Otto Kerner of Illinois, called for a massive expansion of the governmental programs to deal with the ravages of white racism; its report made over 150 recommendations, which Johnson estimated privately would add between $75 and $100 billion to the federal budget over several years.[126] The commission's implicit indictment of previous efforts stung Johnson, and he instructed Califano to pass the word that the report was "destroying the President's interest in things like this."[127] Johnson's pique was familiar to those who worked with him, an emotion to which he often succumbed and which he also often overcame. More daunting were the fiscal realities the president now confronted. "I am more practical," he told a delegation of black editors and publishers, "than some of those who wrote the report and some of the staff who sent it to me. First thing we have got to do is find the money. They didn't touch upon that problem. It's like saying we need sirloin steaks three nights a week, but only have the money to pay for two steaks." "I will never understand," he wrote later, "how the commission expected me to get this same Congress to turn 180 degrees overnight and appropriate an additional $30 billion for the same programs that it was demanding I cut by $6 billion."[128]

Organized labor pressed Johnson in a similar fashion. The American Federation of Labor cautioned against any "moratorium on domestic progress" and called instead for "a resurgence of a national determination to create an ever-better society in America." The AFL-CIO program for 1968 included legislation to make the federal government the employer of last resort and denounced the very idea of cuts in social spending. Nor was the AFL-CIO leadership sympathetic to the administration's fears regarding the international economy. Califano reported to Johnson that AFL-CIO president George Meany and his staff "believe the worst [consequence of] separating the dollar from gold would be to shake up international trade for a year or two without any serious repercussions here at home."[129] In the end, the AFL-CIO agreed that the need for a tax increase was overwhelming, and it therefore grudgingly and silently acquiesced in the $6 billion spending cut demanded by Mills and others as the quid pro quo for congressional action.[130]

Liberals carried the fight to the administration's inner councils. Califano kept up a steady drumbeat, urging Johnson to "fight both the Congress and [Treasury Secretary] Fowler on anything like a $6 billion expenditure cut."[131] Johnson's legislative liaison, Barefoot Sanders, shaken by the assassination of Martin Luther King Jr. and the rioting that followed in early April, warned the president, "If, in the face of *more numerous and more vocal calls* for additional government action, the government appears to do less, by cutting appropriations in order to solve the financial crisis, we run the risk of leaving these people who want more done without any hope for accomplishing their programs within either the Democratic or Republican parties."[132] Following Sanders's lead, Califano promptly took the offensive by suggesting that any budget cuts come from such "low priority areas" as the supersonic transport airplane program, the Apollo moon-shot program, and federal highway expenditures. He implored Johnson to ask for an even greater tax hike and to direct an additional $3 to $5 billion to "relatively quick impact [social] programs." "The argument against [such a course]," he admitted, "is the balance of payments, the tax bill and Wilbur Mills." But perhaps the conventional wisdom of the Treasury Department regarding the relationship among the balance of payments, fiscal policy, and domestic priorities was based on false assumptions that had over time hardened into a "mythology" opposed to social welfare. Califano suggested that LBJ undertake "a thorough reassessment in the balance of payments and domestic priorities area—a reassessment of the same magnitude you have gone through with respect to Vietnam."[133] But Johnson's angry marginal comments on Califano's memo were unambiguous: "No!" "I don't agree." "Tell him to forget it—" "Ha!Ha!" "Forget it."[134]

In the end, Califano and his fellow Great Society all-outers lost the battle for LBJ's mind on the issue of domestic priorities. Frightened by the March gold crisis, Johnson decided that the tax surcharge was "the most urgent issue facing the country" next to Vietnam. "I knew," he later wrote, "that any call for increased spending would give my opponents the excuse they sought to call me a reckless spender and kill the tax bill. If that happened, it could bring on an uncontrollable world monetary crisis of 1931 proportions and consequences."[135] Moreover, the president realized that any such crisis would incite conservatives to destroy the Great Society rather than merely contain it. As Okun advised, "If a moderate expenditure cutback can achieve the tax bill, it would offer the best possible protection for our social programs."[136]

Johnson thus found himself fighting a two-front war. As he struggled against a recalcitrant Congress to minimize the expenditure reductions demanded for the passage of the tax hike, he also fought to gain the support of liberals for whatever expenditure reduction deal he would finally strike. In both campaigns, Johnson used what Califano characterized as "Okun's Chamber of Horrors" approach.[137] Importuning Mills to agree to a compromise spending limitation, Johnson told the Ways and Means chairman that "whether he realized it or not, the country's economy was about to go down the drain and we had to write a tax bill that we could both live with."[138]

Johnson carried the same message to his friends. In mid-May, he exposed the liberals in his cabinet to a dire analysis by the chairman of the CEA. "If the political realities are a tax bill with a $6 billion cut or no tax bill," Okun told them, "if that is the choice . . . I am ready to say by a definite margin that our economy is much better off with this overdose of fiscal restraint than none at all." He drew heavily on the recent crisis experience to drive home his point: "The international consequences of a tax bill failure would be very great indeed. It could be a calamity. We could have a sharp rise in speculation in the American dollar and another gold run." The bitter choice then, Okun warned, might be between suspending the convertibility of the dollar or increasing the price of gold. "We could get a real explosion in the world financial community. . . . It may undermine all our gains and jeopardize the complete world political situation." Okun's conclusion was self-evident, but Johnson drew him out even further. "Therefore?" asked the president. Okun answered, "Take a tax bill with the $6 billion cutback. It's hard advice to give but I think it's the best advice. It is the only advice I can give." Swallowing hard, Johnson and the liberals took it.[139]

The Revenue and Expenditure Control Act of 1968 forced on the administration's domestic agenda a discipline of stringency not unlike that already visited upon the administration's war policy. Wilbur Mills took satisfaction in what he perceived to be "the anguished cries of Federal administrators who are feeling the sharp bite of these legislative incisors."[140] Yet the outcome was more complicated than Mills's crowing allowed. The administration worked hard to shield its most critical social programs from budget cuts; Congress could agree to trim only slightly less than $4 billion from fiscal 1969 expenditures, and the president refused to make further reductions on his own.[141] Indeed, aggregate social welfare spending continued to rise, in 1969 and throughout the Nixon years. But the 1968 episode did constitute a sea change, because it shifted the emphasis from an expansion of the Great Society to its preservation. In fiscal year 1969, federal social welfare expenditures (in constant dollars) grew at a rate less than half that of 1965.[142] As the historians Irwin and Debi Unger have written, "In June 1968 the Great Society, already badly wounded at the hands of its friends and enemies alike, lost its forward movement and its inner spirit." What was left was not the powerful reform surge of mid-decade but only its inertia.[143]

In its aftershocks, the economic crisis of 1968 left a deep imprint on both foreign affairs and domestic policy, on the history of a momentous year and a remarkable historical era. Growth liberalism—the interpenetration of liberal politics and growth economics—was a defining feature of the 1960s and the apotheosis of the postwar optimism that undergirded the notion of an American Century. In 1968 growth liberalism came a cropper and the American Century came to an end. The forces at work were many, the configuration of causation complex. But matters of political economy were central. The experience and consequences of the economic crisis of 1968 remind us that the history of the 1960s was not written entirely in the streets.

4

Richard Nixon's Whig
Growthmanship

The eclipse of growth liberalism signaled the end of both the distinctive era of the 1960s and America's postwar boom. The economic stagnation, stubborn inflation, and widespread pessimism that marked the 1970s contrasted sharply with the prosperity and confidence of the earlier postwar years. The loss of optimism was manifested in a growing distrust of established institutions and a widespread loss of faith in the curative powers of economic growth.[1] The uncertainty and ambivalence about growth that had earlier appeared as an undercurrent took on a new scope and stridency in the 1970s, causing many to doubt whether future growth was either possible or desirable.

The retreat from growth was gradual, uneven, and incomplete, but it was also unmistakable. At the outset, the shift was intimated by both small revelations and large events. In the year 1970, President Richard Nixon, the celebrators of the first Earth Day, and several of the nation's top economists variously provided glimpses of a nation poised delicately between the collapse of 1960s-style growth liberalism and the rise of a new regime of balance and scarcity.

Nixon's State of the Union address in January 1970 illustrated both how far ambivalence about growth had advanced over the course of the 1960s and how strong the hold of growth remained. "Never," Nixon commented, "has a nation seemed to have had more and enjoyed it less." Noting that the GNP would increase by $500 billion over the next decade—an increase greater than the total growth of the U.S. economy from 1790 to 1950—the president asserted that the critical question was "not whether we will grow but how we will use that growth." Speaking of the nation's need for "the lift of a driving dream," he proposed that "the time has come for a new quest— a quest not for greater quantity of what we have but for a new quality of life in America." Nixon neither embraced the cult of production nor dismissed it. Instead, as had the growth liberals who preceded him, he sought a way to use growth to transcend growth, to shift society's focus from quantity to quality. The task, he declared, "is not to abandon growth but to redirect it." Growth would be a means rather than an end in itself, a way to achieve the conservative societal rejuvenation that Nixon, ever the utopian opportunist, worked hard to achieve.[2]

For an increasing number of Americans, however, Nixon's dream was the stuff of nightmares. The emergent environmental movement gave strong voice to this alternative view, and the celebration in late April 1970 of the first Earth Day—a national environmental "teach-in" modeled after the anti-Vietnam War consciousness-raising sessions common on university campuses in the mid-1960s—focused and amplified the sentiment. "A whole society is coming to realize that it must drastically change course," observed Denis Hayes, the national head of Environmental Action, the group coordinating Earth Day activities around the country.[3] The new tack was clear in outline, if not always in detail: The new environmental interest group Friends of the Earth urged Earth Day participants to demonstrate "ceaselessly" that continuous economic growth was "no longer healthy, but a cancer"; the dangers posed by "the runaway U.S. growth economy" justified "a thorough reassessment and reversal [sic] of unlimited economic growth as a national goal."[4] Senator Edmund Muskie, the Democratic vice presidential candidate in 1968 and the presumed front-runner for the presidential nod in 1972, gave the new direction an air of legitimacy when he told an Earth Day crowd at the University of Pennsylvania: "If progress means technology that produces more kinds of things than we really want, more kinds of things than we really need and more kinds of things than we can live with, we had better redefine progress."[5]

The first Earth Day celebrations did not create antigrowth ideas so much as crystallize an animus that was already in the air and spreading quickly. By the end of 1970, when the National Bureau of Economic Research sponsored a nationwide series of colloquia to celebrate its fiftieth anniversary, the Yale economists James Tobin and William Nordhaus titled their featured paper "Is Growth Obsolete?" Reflecting their firsthand knowledge as veterans of the CEA, they recalled that in the 1960s growth had been "the reigning fashion of political economy." But the climate of opinion had "changed dramatically": "Disillusioned critics," the economists reported, "indict both economic science and economic policy for blind obeisance to aggregate material 'progress.'"[6]

The public debate about growth that took shape in 1970 continued through the rest of the decade and constituted one of a number of changes that, taken together, appeared to announce a decisive break with the past. The dashing of liberal hopes at home, frustration and then defeat in Southeast Asia, the rise of the Soviet Union to nuclear parity, the loss of U.S. economic independence and world economic dominance, the stagnation of the vaunted American standard of living as the postwar economic boom came decisively to an end—the pattern bespoke a new era of limits. Some saw in that prospect an opportunity to save the fragile ecosystem and perhaps the soul of the nation as well. But most Americans, truly the people of plenty and the children of more, found the prospect of limits disquieting. In the face of such fundamental, reverberating change, American society suffered a palpable loss of confidence and optimism. The idea of limits seemed to contravene the psychic, as well as the material, dynamic of the postwar experience.

Dealing with this new reality—the problems it presented, the anxieties it generated, the possibilities it opened up, and the options it foreclosed— constituted the most fundamental challenge to the nation's political leadership in the 1970s. By the end of the decade, President Jimmy Carter, in his most famous public address, would speak to a national television audience about America's "crisis of confidence" and the "paralysis and stagnation and drift" abroad in the land. (Commentators summed up the president's portrait of woe with the word "malaise," which stuck in the public memory despite the fact that Carter himself never invoked the term.) Poignantly, Carter reminded his audience that "we ourselves are the same Americans who just 10 years ago put a man on the moon."[7] But those ten years represented more than a mere decade; the ten years after 1969 were, for the United States, a time of diminished confidence and capabilities.

I. Nixon: An American Whig in a Time of Change

It fell to Richard Nixon to preside over the transition from the foreshortened American Century to the new age of limits. The endeavor dominated his presidency, giving it a character that is obscured if one focuses exclusively or too tightly on Nixon the diplomatist or Nixon the Watergate protagonist.

One keen observer, the aged Walter Lippmann, drew attention at the time to this larger historical canvas. At the height of Nixon's presidency, after his landslide reelection and the signing of the agreement ending America's long Vietnam trauma, Lippmann characterized Nixon's historical role as having "to liquidate, defuse, deflate the exaggerations of the romantic period of American imperialism and American inflation. Inflation of promises, inflation of hopes, the Great Society, American supremacy—all that had to be deflated because it was all beyond our power and beyond the nature of things." The president had, Lippmann concluded (somewhat prematurely), "done pretty well" in a "very disagreeable role . . . imposed upon him by historical necessity." When Nixon read Lippmann's remarks in his daily news summary, he noted in the margin, "Buchanan—a wise observation."[8]

Nixon never managed to convey to the public the essential accuracy of Lippmann's elevated conception of his historical role, but others around the president saw their joint undertaking in similar terms. Henry Kissinger, Nixon's national security adviser and, in the second term, secretary of state, has recalled:

I reached high office unexpectedly at a particularly complex period of our national life. In the life of nations, as of human beings, a point is often reached when the seemingly limitless possibilities of youth suddenly narrow and one must come to grips with the fact that not every option is open any longer. . . . The process of coming to grips with one's limits is never easy.[9]

Elliot Richardson, who headed the Departments of Defense and HEW and also served as attorney general, has observed that "Nixon saw with . . . clarity that the United States needed to adapt itself, and quite rapidly, to the end of the era in which our margin of military and economic superiority was so great that we could afford to neglect the careful delineation of U.S. interests . . . and the husbanding of U.S. resources."[10] As a result, the synchronization of aims and capabilities in a changing world became a central concern of the Nixon presidency, both at home and abroad. The discipline of stringency, visited so abruptly upon Johnson and the growth liberals in 1968, was for Nixon a defining fact of life. The historical role perceived so clearly by Lippmann gave Nixon's leadership a significance that has been all but lost in the swirl of scandal and controversy surrounding a leader still remembered, not entirely unfairly, as Tricky Dick.

The character of the Nixon presidency derived further from the often discounted attitudes, the rudimentary ideology, that he brought to his historical role. Arthur M. Schlesinger Jr. expressed the conventional wisdom of liberals when he wrote in 1960 that Richard Nixon stood for "almost nothing," and William Rusher of the conservative *National Review* later agreed that "to Nixon, it's all a game of grub."[11] But the conventional wisdom of both left and right about Nixon was, on this score, simply wrong. True, throughout his long public career the Californian remained supremely pragmatic and opportunistic. As Lippmann put it, "He will do anything he thinks is expedient. . . . He's very cunning." But there was a pattern to Nixon's expediency. He inclined toward an identifiable set of core beliefs and predilections. From Nixon's arrival in the White House, John Ehrlichman recalled, the president "had a pretty well articulated sense of direction, on the domestic side as well as the foreign policy side."[12]

Nixon's sense of direction hearkened back to the Whig ideology of mid-nineteenth-century U.S. politics.[13] The antebellum Whig Party was a loose political coalition built around Henry Clay, Daniel Webster, and John C. Calhoun. The Whigs championed national economic development, hoping, as one historian has written, to use "the public promotion of economic growth" to build "a material foundation for the maintenance of public virtue."[14] They thus worked to square the circle by wedding progress to stability and order. On the societal level, the Whigs championed Henry Clay's famous "American System," a program that called for a protective tariff, federally funded internal improvements, a strong national bank dedicated to a stable currency, and a system for sharing federal revenue with the states for specified purposes. On the individual level, they were preoccupied with self-control, industriousness, and the cult of the "self-made man."[15]

Certainly few American leaders have embodied the Whig personality type as thoroughly as Richard Nixon. He was the archetypal self-made man who can never stop striving; who, pitted always against weakness within and adversity without, re-creates himself each day by dint of struggle. The effort was constant and endless; the emphasis, as Garry Wills acutely observed, always on "the process, not the destination; the rising, not having risen."[16] "Struggle," Nixon wrote revealingly, "is what makes us human instead of animals."[17]

Nixon was not merely an exemplar of the Whig personality type—he was its avowed champion as well. The self-made man was at once a phenomenon of individual psychology—the result of some powerful combination of nature and nurture—*and* a social creation, and Nixon worked hard to encourage and celebrate his own traits in others. From the Checkers speech in 1952 to his acceptance address at the Republican national convention in Miami in 1968, Nixon spoke to, and for, "the great majority of Americans, the forgotten Americans" who had succeeded to the American Dream his way—by hard work rather than by native genius, social connections, or family wealth.[18]

Nixon's Whig orientation manifested itself in his policy as well as his personality. It colored his presidency in ways that confused people at the time and have continued to confound commentators ever since. There was about the Nixon presidency, the economic adviser Herbert Stein has noted, a "general schizophrenia."[19] "His heart was on the right," the speech writer William Safire observed, "and his head was, with FDR, 'slightly left of center.'"[20] Drawing a bead on the "real" Nixon was no easy task, then or now.

The real Nixon was the Whig Nixon, whose views and policies embodied all the considerable tensions and ambiguities, as well as the essential purposes, of the Whig tradition. He entered the White House, he claimed in his memoirs, "determined to be an activist President in domestic affairs," but critics have had difficulty crediting such avowals. Most have seen only Nixon's genuinely conservative instincts and intentions, emphasizing his unmistakable antipathy toward the Great Society and what one historian has called his desire to "turn the country away from the New Deal traditions."[21] But Nixon was complicated in this as in so many other regards: his conservative, anti-New Deal instincts coexisted with a genuine activist bent. "He wanted to use the power of the presidency," Herbert Stein has observed. "He just didn't believe that those other two million people in the federal government were capable of doing anything, or would do it if he told them." The result was a curious ambivalence: Nixon believed in minimal federal intervention in the economy, but also thought, in Stein's words, that "great presidents were activist presidents."[22]

Whig principles allowed Nixon to reconcile such opposing impulses, to be "modern" while championing traditional virtues, to pursue both progress and order. Nixon could never bring himself simply to endorse the status quo. "That," he told reporters, "is completely contrary to the American tradition." The United States was "a 'go-ahead,' not a 'stand-still,' country." Americans wanted "change that works, not radical change, not destructive change, but change that builds rather than destroys."[23]

In pursuing sensible change, Nixon identified with a historical figure who, like himself, defied easy categorization—Benjamin Disraeli. When domestic affairs adviser Daniel Patrick Moynihan recommended that the president read Robert Blake's newly published biography of the nineteenth-century British prime minister (which, at nearly eight hundred pages in length, Moynihan himself had not finished, or so the story goes), Nixon found inspiration. "Tory men and liberal policies are what have changed the world," he enthusiastically told Moynihan.[24] Thereafter, Nixon would occasionally recommend the book to those who, in Elliot Richardson's words, "wished to understand him and his purposes."[25] And it was the lesson of Disraeli that Nixon took with him on his dramatic trip to China in 1972: "In America, at least at this time," he told Mao Tse-tung, "those on the right can do what those on the left can only talk about."[26]

The inspiration that Disraeli provided on the historical front, John Connally provided in the flesh. Nixon engineered the sort of tactical surprise he relished when in December 1970 he tapped the nominal Democrat to be his treasury secretary. Nixon's aides spoke mockingly of their boss's "infatuation" with the four-time governor of Texas. The relationship undoubtedly had a significant personal dimension. Connally's "swaggering self-assurance," Henry Kissinger has written, was "Nixon's Walter Mitty image of himself."[27] Connally was indeed what Nixon could only wish to be: physically prepossessing, personally charming, at ease with others and with himself. The president also respected the Texan's feel for power and willingness to think big thoughts and take big chances. When Nixon was not recommending Blake's *Disraeli* to those who wanted to understand him better, he would (according to speech writer William Safire) occasionally comment, "Talk to Connally. He understands me."[28] Their relationship rested on more than personal rapport, however.

Connally shared Nixon's Whig orientation. A self-labeled "conservative who believed in an active government," Connally had worked energetically as governor to develop the Texas economy by bolstering higher education and courting high-tech industry.[29] Thus, affinities both psychological *and* philosophical caused Nixon to see Connally as "the only man [of his acquaintances] who could be President."[30] Nixon often discussed how best to set up the Texan as his successor. And both he and Connally entertained the thought of creating a new, distinctly Whiggish party, which the president wanted to call the "Independent Conservative Party."[31]

Nixon's progressive conservatism gave his administration's policies a distinctive cast that defied easy categorization. Nixon worked hard to find a middle ground between the hyperactivism of the growth liberals JFK and LBJ and the sort of minimalist government championed by Barry Goldwater and the Republican right. Driven by his own predilections and by the object lesson of growth liberalism's implosion, Nixon moved as president to scale back government undertakings abroad and at home while still honoring basic international and domestic commitments.

On the world stage, Nixon and his advisers perceived that America's capacity for action was distinctly limited. As Kissinger later expressed it, "Our resources were no longer infinite in relation to our problems; instead we had to set priorities, both intellectual and material."[32] What Nixon's national security adviser and secretary of state expressed with characteristic eloquence, Treasury Secretary Connally expressed more brusquely when he reminded America's allies that "no longer does the U.S. economy dominate the free world." It followed, therefore, that aspirations and commitments would henceforth have to be more closely articulated with capabilities.[33]

The administration moved on several fronts to bring U.S. commitments in line with its chastened view of U.S. capabilities. In national security policy, the scaling back began immediately. At his first presidential press conference, in January 1969, Nixon retreated from his campaign pledge to regain U.S. nuclear *superiority* and adopted instead the goal of nuclear *sufficiency*.[34] The SALT I agreement that Nixon negotiated with the Soviets in effect implemented this conceptual shift. In the area of conventional forces, U.S. planners returned their contingency planning to the 1 1/2-war standard that had defined military readiness in an earlier day. Meanwhile, the administration trimmed military spending substantially, making the largest cuts since the United States had begun rearming for the Cold War in 1950.

Part of the conventional drawdown resulted from the U.S. disengagement from Vietnam, but the cutting went beyond that required by the gradual termination of the Asian conflict: overall defense spending, measured in constant dollars, fell 32 percent between fiscal year 1969 and fiscal year 1975, and military expenditures for purposes unrelated to Southeast Asia fell by about 10 percent.[35] Because the administration's cuts could never keep pace with the demands of antimilitary critics and because the administration opposed more vigorous efforts, such as those of Senate majority leader Mike Mansfield to cut U.S. forces in Europe by half, Nixon seldom got credit for the genuine progress he made in containing military spending.

As Nixon trimmed U.S. military capability, he simultaneously worked to scale back America's international commitments. While on a round-the-world trip in the summer of 1969, Nixon paused to welcome back to earth the Apollo astronauts splashing down in the mid-Pacific from the first moon landing, and at an informal press briefing at an officers' club on Guam he enunciated what quickly became known as the Nixon Doctrine: henceforth, the United States would give its allies the protection of its nuclear umbrella against threats coming from nuclear superpower adversaries and would fulfill existing treaty obligations to furnish military and economic aid in the face of lesser threats, but the manpower to meet non-nuclear aggression would be the responsibility of the nation directly threatened. There would be no more Vietnams. "Neither the defense nor the development of other nations can be exclusively or primarily an American undertaking," he elaborated. "We shall be faithful to our treaty commitments, but we shall reduce our involvement and our presence in other nations' affairs."[36] The Nixon Doctrine was, in the words of a prominent student of foreign affairs, "essentially a rationale for retrenchment."[37]

Nixon and Kissinger also developed the concept of "linkage" to ensure that whatever actions the United States did take in world affairs would have the maximum possible results. The president and his national security adviser believed that "the great issues are fundamentally interrelated" and that progress in any one area of contention needed to be tied to progress on other political, economic, or military issues. Linkage reflected both the perceived complexity and interrelatedness of world affairs and the need, as Kissinger later explained, "to free our foreign policy from oscillations between overextension and isolation and to ground it in a firm conception of the national interest."[38] Viewed by opponents at the time as a risky device that would inevitably encourage foot-dragging by a hard-line anti-communist administration, linkage was in reality an economic calculus for a new regime of limits, an attempt to avoid overextension by leveraging discrete diplomatic (and ultimately economic) inputs into broad payoffs.[39]

In time, the administration placed both the Nixon Doctrine and the concept of linkage in the service of its grandest strategic conception: détente. Nixon and Kissinger sought a relaxation of tension with America's superpower adversaries, the Soviet Union and the People's Republic of China, for a multitude of reasons; not least among them was the need to adjust to a new epoch. As Kissinger explained in mid-1970, "We are doing what we are doing because we believe that if America is to remain related to the world it must define a relationship that we can sustain over an indefinite period."[40] Détente constituted a return to an asymmetrical formulation of containment. It reflected Kissinger's insight that "no country can act wisely simultaneously in every part of the globe at every moment of time" and accepted the hard reality of limits made so unmistakably evident by the Vietnam debacle.[41] The logic of détente implicitly admitted that the resources even of the United States were finite. Nixon and Kissinger never intended détente to end or supersede the Cold War, but rather they believed that the strategy would enable the United States to continue its Cold War mastery with less danger and at lower and more easily sustained economic and political costs. Détente aimed, in the words of one analyst, "to manage the retreat of the United States from its lonely pre-eminence in world affairs back to a status more like first among equals."[42]

Nixon pursued an analogous course at home. "I wanted to be an activist President in domestic policy," he later wrote, "but I wanted to be certain that the things we did had a chance of working." Domestically as well as internationally, the Republican administration worked to bring commitments in line with capabilities, especially in the wake of what Nixon viewed as growth liberalism's "misguided crash program" under JFK and LBJ.[43] The Nixon Doctrine, the president suggested to the journalist Theodore White in early 1973, had a domestic counterpart in the administration's program of revenue sharing.[44] A key element in the domestic agenda Nixon labeled the "New Federalism," revenue sharing returned federal tax revenues to state and local governments for use as they saw fit: general revenue sharing provided no-strings federal grants, and special revenue sharing provided federal funds in the form of block grants for state and local projects in specified areas, including job training and community development. Like the Nixon Doctrine abroad, revenue sharing addressed the problem of seemingly excessive commitments by means of devolution, the shifting of important responsibility away from the center to the locality.

The other components of Nixon's New Federalism complemented revenue sharing. The administration's various attempts at federal government reorganization and its revolutionary proposal of a guaranteed annual income were intended, Nixon said, to "close the gap between promise and performance" and "make government run better at less cost."[45] The start-up costs of such reforms would be considerable, the president admitted, but the projected cost of continuing the present system into the 1970s was "staggering."[46] At bottom, Nixon's domestic reforms sought to rationalize government—and, if successful, the effort would prove a bargain.

The uneven results of Nixon's New Federalism agenda have made it difficult to take the measure of his domestic record, either at the time or since. Several key legislative initiatives failed to pass. Welfare reform died a lingering death at the hands of an unusual coalition of antiwelfare conservatives and anti-Nixon liberals. The administration won approval of general revenue sharing, but failed to gain approval of special revenue sharing in a number of controversial areas. Government reorganization became the stuff of endless dispute. When, in the face of legislative frustration, Nixon tried to rationalize government unilaterally through administrative means, he contributed to a battle over executive power that culminated in the Watergate affair and his own political destruction. Moreover, the reforms of the New Federalism often ran in contradictory directions: Some changes, notably revenue sharing, strengthened state and local government, but other initiatives, especially in environmental policy, augmented the federal government dramatically. Although the avowed purpose of rationalizing government was to do more with less, spending for domestic purposes continued to grow rapidly. Entitlement spending increased 76 percent (in constant dollars) between 1969 and 1974, and spending for means-tested programs (such as food stamps, Medicaid, and Supplementary Security Income under Social Security) grew even faster.[47] Accordingly, subsequent scholarship has played down the widespread contemporary fear that Nixon was out to emasculate government or dismantle the modern welfare state.[48] A recent study by the Brookings Institution concludes that the New Federalism "partly shared and partly accommodated itself to the prevailing political culture of modern liberalism," seeking "to restrain—but not halt—the unbridled growth of public programs."[49] Both at home and abroad, the Nixon administration honored old commitments while subjecting means and ends to a new scrutiny and discipline, albeit with mixed success.

The approach underlying the Nixon Doctrine and the New Federalism was the product of instinct and reflex, and of a kind of calculation that can properly be called farsighted. It embodied Nixon's innate, Whiggish preference for carefully modulated, orderly progress. It was also a reflexive response to the apparent lesson of the late 1960s, expressing a determination to avoid the costly consequences, to both the nation and its political leadership, of further overreach. But the approach had another aspect as well, which Nixon's critics have had difficulty in discerning: retrenchment and rationalization looked forward as well as backward. Indeed, in their broad outlines, Nixon's policies were shaped as much by expectations of the future as by inspirations and lessons from the past. In his most thoughtful moments, Nixon sought to use the policy of retrenchment abroad and rationalization at home to reposition the United States for what he believed was a newly emerging post–Cold War era.

Nixon spelled out his view of the future most clearly in a briefing for media executives in Kansas City in July 1971. His remarks, largely overlooked in the standard treatments of the Nixon presidency, were his own, based on notes handwritten in advance on a yellow legal pad, as was his practice. The briefing began with a discussion of domestic policy by other administration figures, and the president followed with an explanation of how his domestic and foreign policies fitted together in a larger frame. Nixon asserted that the national fixation on Vietnam had obscured the "very significant changes that have occurred in the world over the past 25 years . . . [and] even more dramatically, perhaps, over the past 5 to 10 years." The United States had dominated the world economically and militarily since the end of the Second World War, but was entering a new epoch "no longer . . . in the position of complete preeminence or predominance." There were now, or soon would be, five "great power centers" in the world, measured "in economic terms and economic potentialities": the United States, Western Europe, Japan, the Soviet Union, and China. Those five superpowers, he explained, "will determine the economic future and, because economic power will be the key to other kinds of power, the future of the world in other ways in the last third of this century." Thus, the Cold War, in part because of Nixon's own efforts to nudge the chief adversaries from confrontation to negotiation by means of détente, would give way to a new contest of global economic competition among nominal friends and allies and erstwhile foes. "Success on the negotiation front . . . simply means," he observed, "that the competition changes and becomes much more challenging in the economic area than it has been previously."[50]

Nixon presented his foreign and domestic initiatives as preparation for the new global economic competition. The struggle would be fierce, the outcome was not guaranteed, but the goal was continued U.S. preeminence. The United States needed, in Nixon's words, "to run this race economically and run it effectively and maintain the position of world leadership." Détente and the Nixon Doctrine would contribute by lessening the likelihood of catastrophic, Vietnam-style embroilments abroad. But the prospect of global economic competition also dictated that "America now cannot be satisfied domestically." Accordingly, the New Federalism was needed to "thin down" the federal government in order "to get it ready for the race."[51] Soon Nixon would put macroeconomic policy to work in the same cause, casting economic growth into a new role as the engine of victory in a competition that would both guarantee continued world leadership and provide the challenge required for the spiritual rejuvenation of the American people.

II. Whig Growthmanship

In the months following his Kansas City speech, Nixon moved dramatically to incorporate a policy of robust economic growth into his preparation for the new global economy. His initiatives included powerful stimulative actions, the termination of the Bretton Woods international monetary regime, and the first imposition of peacetime wage and price controls in U.S. history. Nixon touted the changes as "the most comprehensive new economic policy" since FDR's early New Deal measures, and the characterization was a fair one.[52] In a burst of public relations enthusiasm, the administration labeled its program the New Economic Policy, unmindful that Lenin had already appropriated that phrase for *his* economic reforms in the Soviet Union in the 1920s. Nixon's New Economic Policy called for action on a variety of fronts, but at bottom the initiatives were driven by the administration's pursuit of growth. For reasons of both short-term political advantage and long-term strategic vision, Nixon reconfigured the political economy of growth by taking elements of the defunct growth liberalism of the 1960s and imbuing them with key values from his own Whig persuasion. In effect, Nixon brought growthmanship into the bipartisan mainstream. Ironically, he did so at the historical moment when the heyday of rapid and relatively easy growth was coming to a close. In the end, the emergent global economy, which Nixon foresaw presciently if imperfectly, proved a more treacherous environment for both his presidency and the nation than he had envisioned.

Nixon's redefinition of growthmanship resolved a long-running debate within the administration about the role and priority of economic growth. The administration's initial attitude toward growth was at once optimistic and subdued. On the one hand, policymakers believed that despite the problems besetting the U.S. economy at the end of the 1960s, growth would remain a constant in American life well into the future. In an inaugural address that mentioned economic affairs only in passing, Nixon observed, "We have learned at last to manage a modern economy to assure its continued growth." Nixon's first chair of the Council of Economic Advisers, Paul McCracken, predicted in late 1969 that the decade of the 1970s would bring "unusually rapid basic economic growth." While the immediate challenge required a "preoccupation with the disorderly inflation that we inherited," McCracken told the president that the larger challenge was to "keep the economy moving as smoothly along that basic [rapid growth] path as possible."[53]

On the other hand, however, the administration held a chastened view of what growth made possible. Not even the rapid growth predicted by McCracken could obviate the necessity for hard choices. "With or without Vietnam," the CEA reported, "we confront powerful claims upon the national output which exceed its potential size."[54] "Despite prospective rapid growth of output," the president's economic report to Congress in February 1970 observed, "a decision to satisfy an existing claim on a larger scale or to satisfy a new claim will require giving up something on which people are already counting."[55] The heady we-can-have-it-all days of the 1960s were past—America had become a zero-sum society.

Beyond the sense that growth was assured but its promise limited, Nixon and his staff initially were uncertain as to what role growth ought to play in the administration's economic program. William Safire, a presidential speech writer who dabbled in economic themes, touched off an extensive debate in Nixon's first year when he suggested that the administration adopt and publicize as its economic philosophy what he called "growth economics."[56] Safire never explained just what he meant by growth economics, but he assured Nixon that such a policy was "cool, rational and responsible— but . . . also newsworthy and exciting and creative." Safire's suggestion was, in reality, more a plan for a public relations campaign than it was a substantive prescription for public policy. Nevertheless, the administration was constantly casting about for politically salable themes and Safire's proposal impressed Nixon. "An excellent idea—one of the best I've seen in the Administration," the president noted in the margin of Safire's memorandum. "We need more like this. I believe we should follow thru."[57]

When Haldeman circulated Safire's memo to those responsible for economic policy, the choice of growth as the administration's keynote quickly sparked controversy. In typical bureaucratic fashion, virtually everyone agreed that there was great merit in identifying and "selling" the economic philosophy of the Nixon presidency, but differed sharply over what that philosophy was or should be. Murray Weidenbaum of the Treasury Department suggested that growth would be an acceptable theme if it were coupled with "progress," in order to indicate the administration's "commitment to economic expansion . . . with maximum reliance on the private sector and on state and local governments."[58] Others had stronger reservations. CEA member Herbert Stein opposed any emphasis on growth, privately telling his boss, CEA chairman Paul McCracken, that Safire's focus was "a cliché and wrong." Growth was "not the Administration's main concern and . . . not the country's main concern." "We are rich," Stein argued, "we will almost inevitably become richer; and there is not much we can do to affect the rate at which we become richer within eight years."[59] The CEA couched its formal, collective objections in softer language, telling the president that Safire's concept of growth economics was "too specific and . . . gives the wrong emphasis." Growth was an objective, but "not the only or most important" one. A more appropriate theme, the CEA suggested, was the "goal-directed" nature of administration policy—the willingness and ability to choose, "balancing alternatives against each other and recognizing the limits of our total resources."[60] In the face of such ambivalence and opposition, Safire's idea went nowhere.

Ironically, the passage of time proved Safire more premature than wrong, however. In the years that followed, the press of events combined with Nixon's personality, philosophy, strategic vision, and political calculation to incline the administration's economic policy increasingly toward a growth orientation. The movement was slow at first, then stunningly swift. At the outset, the administration saw the Vietnam inflation as its major problem. McCracken alerted the cabinet in March 1969 that "skepticism and growing inflation-mindedness are disorganizing the economy. The problem was inherited, but responsibility for a solution is now ours."[61] Accordingly, the administration devised an economic "game plan" that sought, McCracken told Congress, to "slow down the growth of total demand gradually."[62] The policy of "gradualism" relied on the traditional weapons of fiscal and monetary restraint to slow the economy and curb inflation. The existing 10 percent income tax surcharge was extended and the investment tax credit was repealed; growth in the money supply slowed from 7.9 percent in the second half of 1968 to less than 5 percent in mid-1969.[63]

Gradualism proved to be a delicate policy. The trick, of course, was to throttle back the economy just enough to stifle inflation, but not so much or so fast as to create an economically and politically painful recession. Although he was neither very interested nor particularly well versed in economics, Nixon had several bedrock beliefs; chief among them was what Herb Stein has called "a phobia about unemployment."[64] Nixon especially feared the electoral consequences of rising joblessness. His view derived in part from his conviction that rising unemployment during the recessions of 1954 and 1958 had hurt the Republicans badly in congressional races and that increased joblessness during his 1960 presidential campaign against John F. Kennedy had cost him the White House.[65] The lesson seemed to be that inflation was bad but unemployment was worse. As Nixon explained to his Cabinet Committee on Economic Policy (playfully dubbed the CABCOM-MECOPOL by William Safire), "When you start talking about inflation in the abstract, it is hard to make people understand. But when unemployment goes up one-half of one percent, that's dynamite." "We'll take inflation if necessary," he told his domestic adviser John Ehrlichman, "but we can't take unemployment."[66] Moreover, Nixon's partisan concern was reinforced by the dire analysis of his domestic adviser Daniel Patrick Moynihan, who warned in February 1970: "If a serious economic recession were to come along to compound the controversies of race, Vietnam, and cultural alienation, the nation could indeed approach instability."[67]

Gradualism chaffed in other ways as well. It seemed stodgy. As McCracken told a meeting of top economic policymakers at the end of Nixon's first year in office, "Policies have tightened, but results have moved into the picture with glacial speed." For Nixon, gradualism was the economic equivalent of the gridiron strategy of "three yards and a cloud of dust"—and he was at heart a devotee of the long bomb in both football and public policy.[68]

In the end, despite close monitoring by Nixon's economic advisers, gradualism's combination of fiscal austerity and monetary restraint overshot the mark and helped nudge the economy into a mild recession. In February 1970, McCracken reported, "The economy is now beginning to show visible results from earlier policies of restraint. Skepticism as to whether the policies would ever really bite is now giving way to worry about 'overdoing it.'" Soon the economy was mired in a new condition—"stagflation"—which combined the problem of inflation with sluggish output and rising unemployment. In May, McCracken reported to the cabinet, "The economy has had its disappointing developments this year. It has been weaker than we had expected. Unemployment has risen more sharply. Price developments have been more stubborn." In July 1970, Nixon met with top economic advisers and concluded that the "major battle is recession, not inflation."[69]

Confronting an increasingly challenging (and politically threatening) economic situation, the administration abandoned gradualism—gradually. By late August, McCracken told the president that "we have reached at least a 'review point' if not a decision point. . . . This phase has worked out about as well as such a distasteful episode can." The task now, he continued, was to decide what constituted an "optimum" path for the economy in the year ahead and how that path could be achieved.[70]

In the final months of 1970, Nixon and his advisers decided to move aggressively to stimulate the economy. In part, the turn in policy was dictated by the state of economic affairs: the recession Nixon had feared was now a well-established reality. In part, the change in strategy also constituted a political response to the unexpectedly strong Democratic gains in the November 1970 off-year congressional elections and to what Stein delicately referred to as the growing "gap between where we'll probably be and where we would like to be in [the presidential election year] 1972."[71] Finally, the shift in policy also reflected Nixon's temperamental and philosophical preference for the modern, innovative, and dramatic over the conventional. For all these reasons, the president announced to the National Association of Manufacturers on December 4, 1970, that the time had come to move to "the next phase of our economic plan" in order to "help move our economy up to its full potential of growth and employment."[72]

The new expansionist approach brought movement on several fronts. First came the naming of John Connally as treasury secretary in mid-December 1970. Henry Kissinger, no shrinking violet himself, believed the Texas Democrat to be "the most formidable personality in the Cabinet."[73] Connally was no expert in economics, but he brought to the reformulation of Nixonomics an audacity that in the coming months would reinforce the president's own daring. Just one day after being publicly nominated for the treasury position, Connally lectured Nixon and his aides in a top-level discussion of the administration's overall domestic program: "I say let's run the risk [of thinking big]. If you lose, you lose big—but what's the sense in losing small?"[74] Nixon wanted both the appearance and reality of dramatic change. Connally seemed made-to-order to provide both. Not surprisingly, Kissinger found the president filled with "self-congratulatory pride for weeks" after Connally's appointment.[75]

Connally set to work immediately, although he was not officially sworn in until mid-February 1971. His flair for the exercise of power, together with his obvious standing with the president, catapulted him to the front rank of Nixon's advisers. Whereas the so-called quadriad of economic advisers (which included the chair of the CEA, director of the OMB, chair of the Federal Reserve, and secretary of the treasury) had been meeting regularly over lunch at CEA chairman Paul McCracken's Cosmos Club near Dupont Circle in the capital, Connally quickly engineered a change of venue to the secretary's private dining room in the Treasury Building. To John Connally, the symbolism of power was itself power. In June 1971, Nixon confirmed Connally's influence by publicly anointing him the administration's sole authoritative spokesman on economic issues.

With Connally ensconced at Treasury, Nixon took a second step away from gradualism by unleashing the administration's monetary and fiscal policy. Nixon had already, throughout 1970, been pressing the new chairman of the Federal Reserve, his longtime adviser Arthur Burns, to ease off the monetary reins, sometimes losing his temper when Burns seemed unable to hear or unwilling to heed the administration's stage-whispered directives: "He'll get it right in the chops," an exasperated Nixon told aides in November 1970. On the heels of the Connally nomination, Nixon repeated the message to the Fed chairman: "Domestically we should err on the side of a too-liberal monetary policy, Arthur. We should risk some inflation."[76] As a result of such prompting and its own independent assessment, the Fed increased the stock of money at an annual rate of almost 6 percent in the first half of 1970, nearly 5 percent in the second half, and roughly 10 percent in the first six months of 1971.[77]

Nixon opened up the administration's fiscal policy as well. He used the occasion of his January 1971 State of the Union address to announce an expansionary budget for the next fiscal year, and highlighted the concept of a full employment budget "designed to be in balance if the economy were operating at its peak potential." Since the economy was in fact mired in a recession, such a budget guaranteed an expansionary deficit. "By spending as if we were *at* full employment," the president oversimplified, "we will help to *bring about* full employment."[78] Submitting his full employment budget to Congress a week later, he reaffirmed his determination "to take an activist role in bringing about . . . prosperity . . . [and] creating the climate that will lead to steady economic growth with improving productivity and job stability."[79] All over America, jaws dropped when Nixon told the press, "Now I am Keynesian, as I have duly noted."[80]

In order to guide policy during the expansion, the administration in January 1971 predicted a GNP of $1,065 billion for the calendar year. It was a very good scenario, indeed. While Stein privately described the estimate as "desirable," "feasible," and "probable," McCracken admitted to the president that "this $1,065 is ambitious."[81] The $1,065 billion figure entailed a 9 percent jump in GNP over 1970, at a time when most private projections foresaw an increase of only 7 to 8 percent. The economist Paul Samuelson called the administration's forecast "poppycock," and Arthur Okun reported that the $1,065 figure "startled and puzzled the profession."[82] The explanation for the optimism of the official figure was simple if not self-evident: the administration viewed the $1,065 figure as a target as well as a prediction, a goal whose very existence would discipline policy and convey forcefully to the Fed the necessity for an expansive monetary policy. "Now that we are all agreed that $1065 billion is our target and that it can be achieved," wrote Stein, "all that is required is to do it."[83]

Just "doing it" proved difficult, however. The move away from gradualism became itself too gradual, as the economic recovery proceeded at a distressingly slow pace. As Nixon subsequently recalled:

The economy remained sluggish in the early months of 1971. There were signs of improvement ahead, but patience had worn thin and we ran out of time. Demands for action poured down on the White House from all sides. Media criticism of our policies became intense. Republicans as well as Democrats reflected the pressure they were receiving from their constituents and vociferously called for new policies.[84]

The drumbeat of concern was constant. In early March, McCracken warned Nixon that the pace of expansion "must soon start to quicken if we are to achieve the economic goals laid out."[85] In mid-June he reported that the economy was "obviously well below the path that would have yielded $1065 billion." Asserting that the administration now faced "the necessity for a clean-cut decision," he asked: "Do we now accept the probability of a significantly lower path for the economy than we once contemplated, or do we adopt new policies to stimulate the economy?"[86]

McCracken's phrasing of the question made the choice seem obvious, but the matter was, in fact, more complicated than that. A more aggressive pursuit of growth threatened to exacerbate other problems. For example, further stimulation might well reignite inflation, which remained worrisomely high despite the nearly year-long recession. Nixon was already under pressure to adopt some sort of incomes policy. He vehemently opposed wage and price controls, on the basis of both conservative principle and his own unhappy experience as a junior lawyer in the Office of Price Administration during the early months of World War II. In August 1970, the Democratic Congress had put Nixon on the defensive by giving the president the authority to impose sweeping wage and price controls, thereby saddling the administration with the appearance of holding back in the struggle against inflation.

Thereafter, Fed chairman Arthur Burns incurred Nixon's wrath by asserting publicly that some sort of incomes policy, perhaps a wage-price review board, might be a necessary accompaniment to the emerging emphasis on economic expansion. "The stimulative thrust of present monetary and fiscal policies," he told the Joint Economic Committee in February 1971, "is needed to assure the resumption of economic growth and a reduction of unemployment. But unless we find ways to curb the advances of costs and prices, policies that stimulate aggregate demand run the grave risk of releasing fresh forces of inflation."[87] Again in late May 1971, Burns warned the president and his chief economic advisers privately of the danger of inflation speeding up, and he urged Nixon to keep an open mind about possible wage-price controls.[88]

A second problem militating against a stronger stimulative program was the precarious international standing of the dollar. By risking further inflation, stimulative fiscal and monetary policies might unsettle the international economy by creating doubt as to whether the United States was disciplined enough to undertake the deflationary course its balance-of-payments deficit seemed to call for. The problem had lain dormant during Nixon's first two years in the White House; in 1969 and 1970, the pressure on the dollar had abated as the exchange markets focused their speculative energies on the franc and mark. Nixon's initial economic policy of gradualism had used monetary restraint to combat inflation and had resulted in interest rates high enough to attract a large inflow of Eurodollars. That influx drained off the dollar reserves of foreign central banks and relieved the pressure on the U.S. gold stock.[89]

By the end of 1970, however, the Bretton Woods international monetary regime was again impinging on the autonomy of U.S. domestic economic policy. In mid-December, Burns informed Nixon that the president's numerous entreaties for a looser monetary policy had been answered, with interest rates falling accordingly. But, he added, "we may have an international crisis." With both France and Germany requesting large gold purchases for dollars from the U.S. Treasury, Burns suggested that the administration "give serious thought . . . to increasing the price of gold or embargoing its sale." "We have to manage economic policies," McCracken observed, "in a way that keeps an eye on our balance of payments and another on our domestic economy."[90]

Pressure on the dollar increased in the spring of 1971. Dollars left the United States as domestic interest rates dropped; investors sought higher rates elsewhere, and speculators began to anticipate a devaluation of the dollar. The announcement in May that the U.S. merchandise trade balance had shifted from a small export surplus to an import surplus underscored the dollar's vulnerability. (In 1971 the United States would suffer its first yearly merchandise trade deficit since 1893.)[91] Also in May, the Treasury Department's Office of Financial Analysis concluded privately that the dollar was overvalued by between 10 and 15 percent. In the face of such developments, Paul Volcker, treasury under secretary for monetary affairs, and John R. Petty, assistant secretary for international affairs, began contingency planning for the suspension of dollar-gold convertibility.[92]

Once again, as in 1968, growth economics was on a collision course with the imperatives of the international system. But this time the United States had run out of expedients that might allow a last-minute escape. As the

political scientist Joanne Gowa has written, "Officials in the Nixon administration confronted a stark choice. They could preserve U.S. autonomy in
making domestic economic policy or they could try to preserve an established network of economic relationships that had returned substantial,
albeit diminishing, benefits to the United States."[93]

Nixon and his advisers saw their predicament clearly. In the president's
1973 *Economic Report,* they explained:

The combination of problems created a dilemma for economic policy. A rate of
expansion and a level of unemployment less favorable than policy had projected
could have been remedied by more expansive fiscal and monetary measures. But this
remedy would have made the other problems worse. It would have stimulated the
still lively expectations of continuing or even accelerating inflation and it would have
speeded up the flight from the dollar.

There seemed to be only one solution to the administration's quandary: as
the *Economic Report* observed in retrospect, "The problems had to be dealt
with simultaneously."[94]

Nixon's New Economic Policy, announced in mid-August 1971, was the
landmark attempt to deal with all of the nation's chief economic woes at
once. The NEP took its final shape in an atmosphere charged with intrigue
and drama. On Friday, August 13, Nixon's top economic advisers slipped quietly out of Washington for a secret weekend meeting at Camp David. To
avoid detection by the press, they traveled in several helicopters from different helipads, informing neither families nor office staffs of their actual destination. Upon arrival, Nixon instructed them that "no calls are to be made
out of here except to get information."[95]

Once assembled, the group self-consciously noted the historic nature of
their gathering by signing the Camp David guest book. Nixon's chief economic advisers headed the list: John Connally (secretary of the treasury),
George Shultz (director of the Office of Management and Budget), Arthur
F. Burns (chairman of the Federal Reserve), and Paul McCracken (chair of
the Council of Economic Advisers). Other top experts in attendance
included Paul Volcker (treasury under secretary for monetary affairs), Peter
Peterson (head of the Council on International Economic Policy), and Herbert Stein (a member of the CEA). White House chief of staff H. R. Haldeman, domestic adviser John Ehrlichman, and speech writer William Safire
rounded out the list of principals.

The purpose of the meeting initially puzzled the speech writer Safire,
who traveled to Camp David with Stein and asked him, en route, what was

afoot. "This could be the most important weekend in the history of economics since March 4, 1933," the avuncular economist replied. It had something to do, he elaborated, with "closing the gold window," a phrase that held little meaning for a speech writer who had never taken economics in college. When Safire repeated his newly acquired nugget of information to a treasury official seated beside him, the latter pitched forward with his face in his hands and whispered, "My God!" At that, even Safire realized something big was in the offing.[96]

Others came to the Camp David meeting with a clearer conception of why they were there. Nixon and Connally had for several months been discussing how to expand the domestic economy while simultaneously addressing the related problems of inflation and the international standing of the dollar. A further spur to action came in mid-July when Nixon held a congressional briefing to discuss his upcoming trip to China, only to find, he later recounted, that "for every one who expressed support of that dramatic foreign initiative, at least twice as many used the opportunity to express concern about our domestic economic policies and to urge new actions to deal with the problems of unemployment and inflation."[97] As the congressional leaders left, Nixon asked Connally to consult privately with other senior economic advisers and formulate a new action program.

Connally fulfilled his assignment in a fashion that fully justified Nixon's faith in him as a "big play" man. On August 2, the two men discussed Connally's tentative plan, which included an investment tax credit to stimulate the economy, a wage and price freeze to stem inflation, an import tax to help the balance of payments, and the termination of dollar-gold convertibility to protect the dollar. In his diary entry for the day, Haldeman called the proposal "a huge economic breakthrough" and "a rather momentous decision." Nixon later described Connally's plan as "in effect, total war on all economic fronts." Recognizing the sweeping nature of his proposal, Connally told the president, "I am not sure this program will work. But I *am* sure that anything less will not work."[98]

The president and his advisers agreed to mull over the plan, but events soon forced their hand. In early August, the dollar came under increasing pressure in the European exchange markets and the price of gold rose to nearly $44 an ounce, its highest level since the introduction of the two-tier system in 1968. Reports that the British were requesting the conversion of $3 billion into gold added to a growing sense of crisis. (In fact, the British asked not for conversion but for a guarantee of their dollars against loss in case the United States devalued.) On August 12, Connally cut short a Texas vacation and returned to Washington to warn Nixon that the situation was deteriorating daily. That evening, the two men agreed to hammer out a final program with key advisers and announce the result immediately. "We'll cover the whole thing when we do it," Haldeman noted in his diary that night, "so it's going to be quite an earthshaking operation."[99]

The discussions at Camp David began Friday afternoon, August 13, and lasted until the next evening. The matter of greatest controversy was the question of whether to close the gold window. Burns argued strenuously against ending convertibility, contending that such a fundamental alteration of the Bretton Woods system would pose grave political and economic risks. Politically, the Communist world would gain a propaganda victory— the weakness of world capitalism revealed!—and Nixon's partisan adversaries at home would attack him for abandoning a gold exchange system that enjoyed almost religious standing among conservatives. Burns also warned against the unpredictability of the economic results that might follow: "We are releasing forces that we need not release." But the decision went against the Fed chairman when, in the end, Nixon sided with those who believed, as George Shultz had told him earlier, "that, while we will be cooperative in international problems, *our domestic economy* and its *orderly expansion come first.*"[100]

The package finally agreed upon committed the administration to action on three related fronts. First, to grow the economy—the goal that had brought affairs to this pass—the New Economic Policy included a 10 percent investment tax credit, a repeal of the existing 7 percent federal excise tax on automobiles, and the early implementation of a previously scheduled increase in personal income tax exemptions. The CEA estimated that the NEP would through these policies raise the 1972 GNP by $15 billion, equal to 1.3 percent of GNP for 1972 operating at full employment, and would reduce the unemployment rate for 1972 by approximately 0.4 percent.[101] Second, to offset the inflationary potential of such stimulative actions, the NEP included a $4.7 billion cut in federal spending and a temporary postponement of the administration's revenue sharing and welfare reform initiatives, as well as an executive order freezing all wages and prices for a period of ninety days, with the promise of further action to ensure wage and price stability thereafter. Third, the NEP took steps to protect the dollar, both in the face of market forces arrayed against it and in the wake of the NEP's other changes. These included the termination of dollar-gold convertibility and a commitment to press for a new international monetary system. In addition, there would be a temporary 10 percent tax on imports, which the administration believed would contribute on all fronts. Overall,

McCracken observed privately to the president, the NEP dealt "in an integrated way with the three major policy problems of the U.S. economy—inflation; unemployment and economic slack; and an imbalance in our external economic position."[102]

With the final outline of the NEP in hand, Nixon hurried to make the program public in order to head off leaks and speculation of either a journalistic or financial nature. On Sunday evening, the president told a national television audience that "the time has come for a new economic policy for the United States." "We are going to take . . . action," he promised in an understatement, "not timidly, not halfheartedly, and not in piecemeal fashion." In conveying his own rough draft of the address to Safire for polishing, Nixon had instructed his speech writer to downplay "the gobbledygook about [a] crisis of international monetary affairs" and concentrate on "emotional feel, lift." Accordingly, the president concluded his live broadcast by calling for Americans to use the departure of the NEP "to help us snap out of the self-doubt . . . [and] self-disparagement that saps our energy and erodes our confidence." By using the NEP to meet the challenge of global economic competition, the United States could ensure that "our best days lie ahead."[103]

In the campaign to "sell" the NEP that followed, Nixon emphasized the theme of national renewal. Briefing administration officials the very next day, he invoked the message of his earlier Kansas City Doctrine: Americans could no longer "just assume" economic preeminence. "We must recognize that this is a period of peaceful challenge for peaceful competition [*sic*] and that American industry . . . labor . . . [and] government . . . must find ways to be more efficient, more productive, if we are going to maintain our position." The United States needed to succeed in the new global economy in order to "play the role we were destined to play of being the strongest nation in the world" and because "whenever a person or a nation quits trying to do its best, quits trying to be number one, something goes out of that person or . . . nation."[104]

Having rallied his own troops, Nixon embarked on a whirlwind cross-country tour to drum up popular support for the NEP. In New York City, he asked an international gathering of the Knights of Columbus, "Do we have the character, the richness in spirit, and the strength in spirit that a nation needs?" The answer, he suggested, would come in "what we do with the challenge of peaceful competition, [and] what we fail to do." Traveling to Springfield, Illinois, he invoked the spirit of Lincoln, calling on Americans to "revitalize in ourselves" Lincoln's sense of destiny and strong competitive spirit. Stopping at Idaho Falls, Idaho, the president spoke of "a new era of competition with other nations" and promised, "We are going to make America strong. We are going to make it grow." To the Veterans of Foreign Wars convention in Dallas: "The new prosperity we seek is in no sense a cushion of a self-indulgent old age in this Republic; rather, it will serve as a launching pad for new greatness in America's third century." Even after the trip ended, Nixon continued to sound the same themes. The dedication of the Air Force Museum in Dayton, Ohio, in early September occasioned remarks about a new era of international competition in aviation and "all areas"; on Labor Day the traditional presidential remarks focused on the singular importance of increasing productivity, lest the United States "relax . . . and fall behind" in the emerging economic contest. "America," Nixon told a joint session of Congress in a nationally televised address on the NEP on September 9, "can be her true self only when she is engaged in a great enterprise." The new global competition would provide that enterprise.[105]

It is tempting to dismiss Nixon's rhetoric as nothing more than a huckster's pitch, but to do that cheats us of a full appreciation both of the motivation behind the NEP and of the larger dimensions of Nixon's growthmanship. As we have seen, although the wage-price freeze and the closing of the gold window were the most discussed (and probably the most remembered) aspects of the NEP, the basic impetus behind those moves was the desire to spur the growth of the domestic economy. And what of the turn to growth itself? What drove it? Here we might profitably invoke a distinction Nixon himself drew in his memoirs between the *economics* of economics and the *politics* of economics.[106]

As a matter of economics, Nixon's pursuit of growth was a straightforward response to a prosaic problem: the recession of 1969-70 and the economy's subsequent sluggish recovery. At the same time, the turn to growth was an exercise in the politics of economics. Nixon was acutely conscious of the political danger posed by rising unemployment. "All the speeches, television broadcasts, and precinct work in the world could not counteract" the negative political impact of an economic downturn, he had written in 1962.[107] Moreover, Nixon and his advisers wanted to pump up the economy in order to position the Republicans for the 1972 election. Meeting with Haldeman, Ehrlichman, and Shultz in late 1970, Nixon insisted, "The trend must be *improving* in '72." White House aide Patrick Buchanan has recalled that the administration was "anxious not to enter a presidential year with the economy running at less than breakneck speed."[108] Thus, Nixon's turn to growth beginning in late 1970 represented both competent leadership and political cunning. In addition, it expressed his temperamental preference for the surprising, the daring, the innovative—for the long bomb. But the campaign to sell the NEP suggests other, deeper motives at work as well.

Nixon saw growth as a key element in two overlapping crusades. One was the effort to salvage American leadership in a world defined increasingly by what Peter G. Peterson, Nixon's chief adviser for international economic affairs, called variously "the new world economy" or the new era of "economic co-equality." Growth was a sine qua non for success in the ferocious global economic competition now under way. As Peterson observed, "Our own requirements are clear: we must return our economy to a rate of balanced, sustained growth in order to maintain advances in productivity and to ensure that our economy remains competitive. . . . We must do this to meet the needs and desires of our society at home, and to preserve a strong position in the world as well."[109] Peterson's ideas helped inspire Nixon's Kansas City Doctrine and the president's geopolitical formulation of those ideas in turn informed the NEP. By redefining growth as both a requirement for and reward of successful competition, Nixon infused growth with Whiggish values (bourgeois striving) and put it in the service of Whiggish ends (national development). By pursuing growth in the name of competition, America would, Nixon promised, "find the roots of our national greatness once again." The self-made nation remade—"an America proud and strong, as vigorous in its maturity as it was in its youth"— would prevail in the new era.[110]

Growth *qua* competition figured in a second grand crusade as well—the attempt to make over the American people, to resolve what Nixon in his first inaugural address described as America's "crisis of the spirit."[111] Nixon believed that moral rot had set in virtually everywhere—politics, the business world, religion, the arts, and academe. The symptoms were unbridled negativism, an immobilizing loss of self-confidence, an estrangement from traditional values, and the demise of patriotism.[112] He was particularly distressed that the malaise seemed farthest advanced among society's most favored and successful elements. Dining on the presidential yacht *Sequoia* with the Rev. Billy Graham, Kissinger, and several close aides a week before launching the NEP, Nixon spoke at length about what Haldeman in his diary labeled the president's "leadership decadence theory." The problem was not the alienation of youth or the rebellion of the hippies, but "rather our leadership class, the ministers (except for the Billy Graham-type fundamentalists), the college professors and other teachers . . ., the business leadership class, etc., where . . . they have all really let down and become soft."

Graham agreed, Haldeman recorded, "but expanded that what this country needs from the P [president] is a very strong challenge." The times required "a call to the people that taxes them and requires them to sacrifice and work, such as Kennedy did rhetorically but never . . . substantively."[113]

Graham's suggestion that the president issue a Kennedyesque call to duty and greatness fell on receptive ears, for Nixon, to a degree that often astonished and infuriated his critics, fancied himself a moral leader. "The primary contribution a President can make," he had written earlier, "is a Spiritual uplift"; hence Nixon's repeated mention—in the speech that kicked off his 1968 campaign for the presidency in New Hampshire and in two subsequent State of the Union addresses—of the nation's need for "the lift of a driving dream."[114] Nixon prepared his Kansas City Doctrine with that need in mind. As his notes for that briefing make clear, he believed the "National spirit" was "most important"; Americans needed "confidence in selves," "faith in our principles," and what Nixon called "the Spirit of Vigor," which included "courage . . . stamina . . . [and the] character which [the] nation had in youth."[115] The NEP translated Nixon's vision of the post–Cold War order into policy; it was intended both to position the United States for the coming economic struggle and, no less important, at the same time to fire the American spirit anew.

Spiritual considerations were much on Nixon's mind as he and his staff devised the NEP at Camp David. On the Saturday evening after the hard decisions had been made, Haldeman, Ehrlichman, and Weinberger visited the president's quarters in the Aspen lodge and found Nixon in what Haldeman described in his diary as "one of his sort of mystic moods," in his study with the lights off and a fire roaring despite the late summer heat outside. Nixon told his visitors that this was where he made all his big decisions. "We're at a time where we're ending a period where we were saying that the government should do everything," he explained. "Now all of this will fall unless people respond. We've got to change the spirit. . . . You must have a goal greater than self, either a nation or a person, or you can't be great."[116] The same day, Nixon told Safire privately that "all Americans, not just our government but our people should welcome the . . . necessity, the opportunity, the excitement of meeting the challenge of competition."[117] Through such an undertaking, the American people, led by a self-made man, would remake themselves.

The contest would build character, both individual and national. Critics might complain that, as driving dreams go, this was pretty thin gruel, but Nixon's blending of the material and the spiritual demonstrated forcefully how malleable the concept of growth could be: just as growth liberals in the 1960s had promised world hegemony and the social reconstruction of America to liberal specifications, now Richard Nixon promised continued world leadership and the moral rejuvenation of the American people according to conservative lights. And there was one other similarity that Nixon's Whig growthmanship shared with the growth liberalism that preceded—it, too, failed.

III. The Fate of Nixonomics

The Watergate affair brought down the Nixon presidency almost exactly three years after the launching of the NEP, but by then the administration's growth strategy already lay in ruins. Economic stimulation paid substantial, short-run political dividends in Nixon's drive for reelection in 1972, but the ultimate price of those short-term gains proved high indeed. An economic initiative, a geopolitical stratagem, a spiritual crusade—Whig growthmanship foundered on every count.

The economic consequences of Nixon's Whig growthmanship were more negative than positive, largely because in the end the administration spurred the economy too hard. Soon after unveiling the NEP, policymakers began to worry that its stimulative impact would fall short of what was needed to rachet the economy onto an acceptably robust growth path. In mid-October 1971, McCracken warned that the economy remained on a "path of sluggish expansion," and his replacement as CEA chairman, Herbert Stein, advised Nixon at the end of the year to look "for ways to pump up the economy more rapidly." At the same time, the initial success of the NEP's wage and price controls lulled policymakers into thinking that the economy could easily accommodate more stimulus without reigniting inflation. As Stein later observed ruefully, "We did not foresee that the initial apparent success of the controls would seduce us into excessively expansionary fiscal and monetary policy."[118]

Falsely reassured, the administration pulled out all the stops in early 1972. "We should push forward," Stein exhorted, "with the fiscal and monetary expansion on which the rise of the economy is predicated."[119] At the Fed, Arthur Burns agreed, although sometimes grudgingly, and in the deliberations of the Federal Open Market Committee he advocated a more aggressive policy of monetary expansion.[120] During calendar 1972, the money supply (M-1, consisting of currency and demand deposits) increased

9 percent, compared with an average annual increase of just over 5 percent for the 1965–70 period.[121] On the fiscal front, Stein later recounted that the administration went "all out for increasing expenditures in the first six months of calendar 1972." Nixon urged the cabinet to "spend their budgets" and the Department of Defense followed orders in exemplary fashion, buying a two-year supply of toilet paper and enough trucks to meet transportation procurement needs for several years. Such efforts caused federal spending for calendar 1972 to rise nearly 11 percent, buoyed further by a stunning 20 percent increase in Social Security benefits that took effect just days before the November presidential election. Overall, the economist Alan Blinder, in a careful analysis, has characterized federal fiscal policy for 1971-72 as "tremendously expansionary" and the money growth rate for the same span as "extraordinarily exuberant . . . by historical standards."[122]

It is commonly (and powerfully) argued that the accelerated stimulation of 1972 was a simple matter of buying the presidential election. To be sure, a strong element of political calculation ran through all of the administration's actions, from the economy to civil rights to Vietnam. To reduce the administration's economic policies wholly to that influence, however, understates the difficulty of framing policy at a volatile moment when the business cycle intertwined with an elemental secular transformation of the national and world economies in ways that were, at the time, difficult to discern. As we have seen, the administration's pursuit of growth sprang from a variety of motives and intentions. Moreover, administration policymakers were hardly alone in underestimating the inflationary dangers still alive in 1972, or in overestimating the economy's growth potential. Nixon's partisan opponents called loudly for even more expansionary policies in the months leading up to the 1972 election, accusing the administration of acting so cautiously as to risk prematurely snuffing out the expansion then under way. When the president proposed a spending ceiling in July 1972, Walter Heller and John Kenneth Galbraith echoed Paul Samuelson's complaint to the Joint Economic Committee that the administration "can stand everything but success. In the summer of our healthy advance, they look forward to the winter of our excess." In this instance, human fallibility probably explains at least as much as political wickedness.[123]

If the intentions behind the excessive stimulation of 1972 are debatable, the result was not: economic disaster. Warnings that trouble was brewing came from within the government and without. Stein reported to Nixon in February 1972 that "grumbling is beginning to be heard from the financial community, at home and abroad, about our expansive fiscal and monetary policy," but he characterized the complaints as "mild" and concluded, "We should not allow it to deter us from our chosen course." Soon, however, rumblings surfaced from sources other than the self-interested bond market. Milton Friedman told Stein privately that he was "appalled" at the thrust of public policy: "I can see very little chance of avoiding major disaster in 1973 or perhaps early 1974. Whether you emphasize fiscal effects or monetary effects, we are turning the heat up under the pot very high indeed." In April 1972 OMB director George Shultz warned Nixon that the fiscal situation was "close to being out of hand." But Stein still plumped for growth: in the same month, he told the president that the real danger was "that we will be short of the targets [for GNP and unemployment], and we should be leaning on the side of more stimulus." Events soon proved the Cassandras right, however, and by early 1973 the U.S. economy was, as Stein later admitted, "in the grip of a classical demand-pull inflation against which the controls were powerless."[124]

Meanwhile, a series of supply-side shocks rocked the U.S. economy, exacerbating the already bad situation. A disastrous drought forced the Soviet Union (and other nations) to buy massive amounts of U.S. grain in 1972, putting upward pressure on retail food prices soon thereafter. Even more damaging was the energy shock that came in the wake of the Arab-Israeli Yom Kippur War of October 1973. At first, the Arab oil-producing states cut production 10 percent to put pressure on Israel's chief ally, the United States; when Nixon responded to early Israeli military reverses and massive Soviet aid to the Arab forces by providing a crucial U.S. airlift of arms to the Israelis, the Arab oil producers punished the administration by declaring a total embargo on oil exports to the United States, which remained in effect for five months. At the same time, the Organization of Petroleum Exporting Countries (OPEC) engineered a 400 percent increase in the price of oil. The combination of the temporary embargo and the permanent (or so it seemed) price hike threw American motorists into a tizzy and the economy into a tailspin.

A vicious downward economic spiral followed. The combination of demand-side overstimulation and supply-side disruptions drove the consumer price index up 8.8 percent in 1973 and 12.2 percent in 1974, with wholesale prices rising even faster at 18.3 and 21.3 percent for the same years. The termination of the administration's wage and price control experiment, parts of which lasted for two and a half years, unleashed further inflationary pressure, and in 1974 the United States experienced its worst inflation in over half a century. The economist Robert Gordon has since estimated that of the

12 percent inflation rate, 5 percent represented underlying inflation, 3 percent the effect of energy and food supply shocks, 2 percent the result of removing controls, and 2 percent the delayed result of excessive demand growth.[125] Clearly administration policies had made a bad inflation problem worse.

Meanwhile, in late 1973 business activity turned down and the economy gradually settled into the worst recession since the 1930s. As 1973 came to an end, Stein told Nixon, "The economic prospect at this point is as complicated and uncertain as at any time in the past five years. . . . The range of possibilities for next year . . . includes a very bad combination of unemployment and inflation." Having suffered a foretaste of stagflation earlier, the administration now experienced the malady in its pure form. When, in early 1974, Stein privately characterized the economy as "beleaguered," he spoke in measured understatement.[126]

To deal with these catastrophic developments, the administration and the Fed retreated to what Stein has called "the old-time religion": tight fiscal and monetary policy would have to be used, despite the painful costs. Nixon put the clamps on federal spending in 1973, trimming his own budget recommendations and impounding (i.e., refusing to spend) billions of dollars appropriated by Congress against his wishes. At the same time, the Fed drove up interest rates to record levels. "The requirements for full economic recovery may sound like harsh medicine," Nixon told the nation in May 1974, "but there is no alternative if we want to keep down the cost of living. I wish I could tell you there is a way out of the present inflation without such measures, but there is not. We cannot spend our way to prosperity." In the last public address of his presidency, as the Watergate crisis engulfed him in late July 1974, Nixon asserted, "Our strategy must have two elements—mainly restraining demand in the short run and expanding supply in the long run." But, for Nixon, there would be no long run; two weeks later, with the economy in shambles, Watergate brought his presidency to an end.[127]

There is little doubt that the throes of the Watergate scandal inhibited Nixon's response to the collapse of his economic game plan. Nixon himself warned in August 1973 that "a backward-looking obsession with Watergate" was causing the nation "to neglect matters of far greater importance to all of the American people." Although the self-serving quality of Nixon's contention is obvious, his biographer Stephen Ambrose has estimated that by mid-1973 the president was spending fully three-quarters of his working time on matters related to Watergate. Nixon, Henry Kissinger has written, "lived in the stunned lethargy of a man whose nightmares have come true."[128] Inevitably, the torpor of despair affected Nixon's personal performance. When Washington put U.S. forces on nuclear alert during the Yom Kippur War, reawakening memories of the Cuban Missile Crisis, Nixon was largely out of the decision-making loop; in November 1973, former Colorado governor John Love, Nixon's emergency energy adviser, resigned, complaining that it had become difficult "even to get the attention of the President"; in early 1974, OMB director Roy Ash flew to the California White House to go over the budget, only to find himself unable to see the beleaguered president, who was in a Watergate-induced seclusion.[129]

By the end, Watergate left Nixon dazed and thoroughly distracted. The day after Nixon's final public address (on the economy to a business audience in Los Angeles), Kissinger brought a foreign dignitary to meet the leader of the Western world: Although the president appeared calm, the secretary of state later recounted that "it clearly took every ounce of his energy to conduct a serious conversation. He sat on the sofa in his office looking over the Pacific, his gaze and thought focused on some distant prospect eclipsing the issues we were bringing before him."[130]

Nixon's chief speech writer, Ray Price, has contended that the Watergate trauma "came close to wrecking the economy," but that view errs in implying that, but for Watergate, Nixonomics would have succeeded.[131] The claim is wrong on several counts. First, the administration's growth offensive had itself contributed significantly to the problems befalling the U.S. economy: excessive fiscal and monetary stimulation had overheated the economy; the wage and price controls originally designed to facilitate that stimulation had proven dangerously seductive in the short run and politically untenable in the long, and their ultimate removal added a catch-up burst of inflation at just the wrong time; and the dollar devaluations of 1971 and 1973 that followed the abrogation of Bretton Woods further exacerbated the inflation of the period.[132]

It is questionable whether wiser policies could have avoided completely a major economic trauma in the early and mid-1970s, even without Watergate. The secular forces confronting any U.S. policy were formidable indeed. The postwar "golden age" of unprecedented worldwide economic growth ended in 1973.[133] Falling commodity prices, a large infusion of technology, institutional stability in the world economy, and a self-conscious commitment by policymakers everywhere to high levels of employment and output had together driven a great postwar boom, but in 1973 national economies everywhere except in Asia faltered. Supply shocks drove up prices, productivity sputtered, and institutional structures strained. Neither economists nor policymakers seemed able to explain, much less reverse, the unhappy conjunction of soaring prices, low capacity operation, and rising unemployment.

Moreover, American policymakers struggled with several problems unique to the U.S. economy. The entry into the job market at this time of the baby boomers, born after World War II and now seeking employment in massive numbers, swelled the U.S. labor force by 40 percent over the 1965-80 period. The economy had to create an unprecedented number of new jobs merely to keep pace with the demographic onslaught.[134] The influx of young workers, together with the entry of large numbers of relatively inexperienced women into the workforce beginning in the late 1960s, also contributed to a significant drop-off in the economy's rate of productivity increase. Other developments, including falling capital investment rates, reduced research and development spending (as a percentage of GNP), and increasing government regulation, compounded the productivity problem. The discernible secular shift in national output away from goods and toward services, where productivity increases were more difficult to realize, also hurt. The end result was an economy whose gains in efficiency were, for a variety of reasons, slowing notably.[135]

At the same time, resurgent international competition was bringing heavy pressure to bear on U.S. firms. Although the United States still generated 30 percent of the world's total GNP in 1970, America's traditional competitors in Europe and Japan, temporarily laid low by the devastation of World War II, were returning to the economic fray armed with modern plants and equipment and unencumbered by the heavy military burdens shouldered by the superpowers. The so-called NICs (newly industrializing countries) such as South Korea, Taiwan, and Brazil also made inroads into the foreign and domestic markets of the U.S. firms. Between 1969 and 1979, the value of imports to the United States nearly doubled, and American exporters found themselves engaged in ferocious competition in many sectors that they had previously dominated.[136] Although Nixon and his advisers had correctly predicted the coming of the global economy, just how difficult the transition to that new order would be surprised them—and most other Americans as well. While it is indisputably correct to fault Nixon's NEP for its contribution to the powerful negative currents running through both the world and domestic economies in the early 1970s, it is hard, even after the fact, to envision a hypothetical approach that could have guaranteed a smooth path for the U.S. economy as it moved from hegemony during a golden age to mere equality in a time of troubles.

A failure as economic policy, Whig growthmanship fared no better as a moral crusade. Nixon's hopes for a conservative renaissance based on the moral equivalent of war in the global economy never took wing. Predictably, it proved difficult from the outset to rouse the nation with a materialist battle cry for an economic competition whose shape was still largely invisible to most Americans, especially after a decade of exhausting struggle and contention over causes that marched under the rather more compelling banners of peace and freedom. In addition, the Watergate debacle impeded any moral crusading whatsoever by an administration whose leaders were increasingly preoccupied with staying out of jail. Finally, any chance for success that Nixon's campaign for spiritual rejuvenation through economic competition might have had, absent Watergate, was seriously weakened by the dramatic change in popular attitudes regarding growth that crested just as the administration embarked on the great enterprise that Nixon hoped could make Americans good once again. Of a sudden, or so it seemed, economic growth fell out of style.

5

The Retreat from Growth
in the 1970s

In politics as in everyday life, timing is all-important. In launching a moral crusade based on economic growth and competition in the early 1970s, Richard Nixon ran afoul of some of the most powerful trends of the day. His efforts coincided with the most vigorous challenge to growth of the entire postwar period. As we have seen, growth had never been an exclusive goal and had never been wholly immune from criticism.

Critics of growth prospered even in the heyday of growthmanship. When John Kenneth Galbraith in the late 1950s described how "the paramount position of production" was upsetting the desired balance of the U.S. economy as between public and private goods and services, his book *The Affluent Society* rose to second place on the *New York Times* best-seller list and his name became a byword among the cosmopolitans who shared his disdain for what he memorably labeled "the conventional wisdom." Nevertheless, Galbraith had claimed (in his inimitable self-effacing way) that his was a singular, prophetic voice, and had maintained that in bravely attacking "the cult of production" he was challenging "a phenomenon . . . still of heroic proportions."[1] But by the end of Nixon's first term, growth liberalism was in tatters and its Whiggish epigone was in the process of self-destruction. Part cause and part effect, the critique of growth now became more widespread, thoroughgoing, and strident than ever before.

I. Sources of Discontent

The attack on growth came from far and near. A surprisingly influential source of discontent was Britain, where ambivalence about growth had for over a century contributed to the economic stagnation that lately went by the name "the English disease."[2] In 1967, Ezra J. Mishan, an instructor at the London School of Economics, extended Galbraith's analysis into an unrelenting attack on what he characterized as "growthmania." Whereas the American economist had held out the hope that a better allocation of resources could make growth into a positive force, Mishan warned his readers that "no sign of any such optimism about the future will be found lurking in any corner of this essay." Instead, he argued that continued economic growth was "more likely on balance to reduce rather than increase social welfare."[3]

Nostalgia for a simpler past suffused Mishan's analysis and was, indeed, characteristic of the British critique of growth. The "promised land of Newfanglia" had yielded mainly despoilers and polluters—the modern airliner and automobile stood out—and Mishan longed for "the rich local life centered on township, parish and village" that had long since been "uprooted and blown away by the winds of change." A similar wistfulness constituted the major theme of Peter Laslett's evocatively titled *The World We Have Lost*, a well-received historical reconstruction of everyday life in preindustrial Britain. Before the industrial revolution enshrined "progress," Laslett wrote, "the whole of life went forward in the family, in a circle of loved, familiar faces, known and fondled objects, all to human size." The story since, he implied strongly, had been one of declension, in the quality of life if not the quantity of things. Laslett's glowing description of "the tiny scale of life" in preindustrial times was followed in 1973 by a vastly influential prescription for the future based on the same conceit. In *Small Is Beautiful*, a best-seller on both sides of the Atlantic, the British economist E. F. Schumacher called upon humankind to develop "technology with a human face" that would aim to achieve "health, beauty and permanence" rather than mere productivity. The goal of Schumacher's self-proclaimed "Buddhist economics" was "the maximum of well-being with the minimum of consumption." In introducing the U.S. edition of *Small Is Beautiful* to the American audience, Theodore Roszak, who a few years earlier had helped explain the 1960s counterculture to confused readers, lashed out at Schumacher's ultimate target: the reigning "growthmania" that could rightfully only be considered "childish nonsense" or "criminal prodigality."[4]

Roszak's part in introducing *Small Is Beautiful* to American readers bespoke the powerful influences closer to home that were contributing to the critique of growth. The 1960s counterculture, of which Roszak had been both chronicler and champion, gave new life to the American antimaterialist tradition and in so doing prepared the way for a positive reception of Schumacher's ideas.[5] The counterculture's complaint against the established order was primarily psychological and moral: American capitalism, with its fixation on material growth, left people neither happy nor fulfilled. Hippies sought the sort of salvation not guaranteed by a rising GNP. As one counterculturalist put it, the true hippie "sees a madness in the constant fight to sell more washing machines, cars, toilet paper, girdles, and gadgets than the other fellow."[6] Alienated from the culture of capitalism, yet deeply suspicious of traditional political radicalism, members of the counterculture sought fulfillment in personal reconstruction and, often, in the creation of alternative communities of the like-minded, such as San Francisco's Haight-Ashbury, New York City's East Village, or the host of rural communes that flickered into life in the late 1960s and early 1970s. When Schumacher concluded *Small Is Beautiful* by exhorting people everywhere to "work to put our own inner house in order," the prescription had a strong resonance for an American audience already familiar with the counterculture's often inchoate but essentially similar urgings.[7]

The enthusiastic welcome afforded Schumacher when he visited the United States on a speaking tour in 1977 reflected more than the influence of the counterculture, however. Schumacher found himself invited to the White House by a president who had actually read his book and lionized by public figures ranging from Ralph Nader and Jerry Brown to Elliot Richardson and Gary Hart.[8] Such attention resulted not simply from the rippling influence of counterculture ideas but also from a broader alteration in mainstream values that was the culmination of a deep-running trend in the economy and society. As the 1960s ended, values were shifting away from the work orientation, self-discipline, restraint, delayed gratification, and respect for external authority and objective standards that together constituted a producer ethic, and were moving instead toward a new emphasis on self-fulfillment. The change had been under way since the emergence of the modern consumer economy and its accompanying therapeutic culture in the early decades of the twentieth century, but now at the beginning of the 1970s the shift seemed to reach a peak. So large was the reorientation of values that we have not yet, a generation later, been able to describe it fully, much less explain it or grapple with its implications.

Contemporary observers attempted to capture the reorientation with a variety of labels. Ronald Inglehart wrote in the mid-1970s of the rise of a "post-materialist" mind-set: "a shift from overwhelming emphasis on material consumption and security toward greater concern with the quality of life," which he saw unfolding gradually but irresistibly throughout the industrialized West. David Reisman observed that "post-industrial attitudes" were now "widely prevalent." According to Daniel Bell, Western society was witnessing "the end of the bourgeois idea." One result of its demise, Bell wrote in a brilliant social commentary, was a growing gulf between the techno-economic order and the national culture—the former ruled by considerations of efficiency, functional rationality, and the "organization of production through the ordering of things, including men as things," the latter increasingly opposed to the bourgeois values of an earlier age and dedicated to the self as the measure of worth and touchstone of excellence.[9]

The shift in values may profitably be observed by comparing two of the most celebrated analyses of postwar social science, one dating from the 1950s, the other from the 1980s; taken together, the two studies frame the process of change, capturing it in mid-course if not quite explaining its entirety. In 1950, David Reisman published *The Lonely Crowd* to immediate and lasting acclaim. Reflecting the fear of mass culture and mass society and the conformity they were thought to breed, Reisman examined the characterlogical mechanisms that various types of societies throughout history had developed to ensure conformity: premodern societies used shame to create a tradition-directed social character or mode of conformity; industrial societies such as nineteenth-century America used guilt to motivate an inner-directed social character; and modern America had, by mid-century, witnessed the emergence of an other-oriented mode of conformity based on anxiety. While all three character formations had particular strengths and virtues, all had, in Reisman's analysis, deep flaws as well. Hope for the future, he argued, lay in the emergence of yet another type of character orientation: genuine autonomy. Only the autonomous, Reisman argued, were "in their character capable of freedom." But as of 1950, Reisman's discussion of autonomy was less descriptive of an existing reality than it was hopeful "of finding ways in which a more autonomous type of social character might develop."[10]

A scant generation later, in the mid-1980s, the sociologist Robert Bellah and a team of coworkers reported that Reisman's hope had in fact been fulfilled, but with unhappy consequences. In *Habits of the Heart: Individualism and Commitment in American Life*, Bellah reported that the central problem facing American culture had shifted dramatically since mid-century. Americans were no longer endangered by the press of conformity, but rather by an excess of "expressive individualism" that emphasized self-expression to the detriment of communal concerns and responsibilities.[11] The danger of centripetal implosion had been replaced by the fear of centrifugal atomization. The shift captured by these bookend masterworks was the triumph of the postindustrial, postmaterialist mind-set chronicled by others.

As it unfolded, the reorientation of fundamental values found both champions and detractors. In a particularly loopy but strangely intuitive and surprisingly influential essay, Yale University law professor Charles Reich in 1970 claimed that the new value system, which he labeled Consciousness III, was transforming the nation's culture and saving its soul. Writing later and with somewhat greater emotional distance, Peter Clecak characterized "the quest for fulfillment" as the "central, energizing thrust of American culture" in the 1960s and 1970s; he, too, found the quest, on balance, honorable in intention and beneficent in outcome. Others took a more jaundiced view, perhaps most memorably captured in Tom Wolfe's famous characterization of the 1970s as the Me Decade. In 1975, Peter Marin lashed out at what he called "the New Narcissism" of the day, while the social critic and historian Christopher Lasch developed the same theme to the point of exaggeration in a relentless jeremiad entitled *The Culture of Narcissism: American Life in an Age of Diminishing Expectations*. Attacking from that point on the American political spectrum where the populist left seemed, momentarily at least, to converge with the anti-elitist right, Lasch tracked the cult of the self into every nook and cranny of contemporary culture and smote ferociously its every manifestation, no matter how trivial. Daniel Yankelovich provided a more balanced analysis of the new cultural tide, both its dangers and its possibilities, in a book tellingly entitled *New Rules*. But a precise assessment of the shift in values is less important for our purposes than the widespread agreement that a significant change in values was becoming evident in the 1970s and that its basic direction was one hardly favorable either to Nixon's Whig growthmanship or to any other pro-growth endeavor.[12]

Both the highly visible 1960s counterculture (and its spillover) and the tectonic shift in mainstream values helped prepare the way for a third development antithetical to growth: the explosive arrival on the political scene of a new environmental movement that at first augmented and then gradually replaced the earlier conservation movement's producerist emphasis on efficiency with a consumer-oriented dedication to the preservation of natural environments and concern about air and water pollution.[13] Many date the emergence of the new environmental movement from the publication in 1962 of Rachel Carson's antipesticide exposé, *Silent Spring*. Carson gathered the concerns and research of other naturalists into a masterpiece of popularization. The volume's selection by the Book of the Month Club and the publicity generated by the chemical industry's predictable but ham-fisted counteroffensive combined to make the book a commercial block-buster; Carson's compelling argument and arresting metaphor—spring without the sounds of nature's fragile creatures—had a powerful impact on the national consciousness.

Thereafter, a string of ecological disasters in the late 1960s seemed to confirm Carson's point about the fragility of the ecosystem, as smog regularly enveloped Los Angeles, fish kills made the condition of Lake Erie a national scandal, and Cleveland's Cuyahoga River became so polluted with industrial waste that it caught on fire. In 1967 the supertanker *Torrey Canyon* broke apart off the coast of England, in time polluting beaches as far away as Cape Cod. The earth seemed very small and vulnerable, indeed. In January 1969, a Union Oil Company oil-drilling rig in the Santa Barbara Channel off the California coast malfunctioned, creating an oil slick that at one point covered 500 square miles and turned several California beaches into disaster zones. The Santa Barbara spill was, Nixon's chief environmental adviser has written, "comparable to tossing a match into a gasoline tank: it exploded into the environmental revolution."[14]

The rise of the environmental movement brought ecological issues to the fore in the late 1960s and early 1970s with what one public opinion analyst called "unprecedented speed and urgency." Before 1965, the Opinion Research Corporation did not even ask questions regarding pollution, but within two years the firm found a majority of the respondents in its national poll reporting "serious" concern over air and water pollution.[15] The press reacted quickly to public concern and in so doing amplified it; in the early 1970s leading newspapers made the environment the chief domestic topic of editorial expression.[16] The attention paid to environmental issues in turn excited a flurry of organizational activity by environmentalists intent on increasing their influence. Between 1967 and 1972 a host of new organizations appeared, among them the Environmental Defense Fund, the National Resources Defense Council, Friends of the Earth, Environmental Action, and the Environmental Policy Institute. Equally impressive, new members flooded into established institutions, swelling their rolls to record levels: the Sierra Club membership increased from 15 million in 1960 to 83 million in 1969 and 136 million in 1972; membership in the Audubon Society rose from 32 million to 120 million to 232 million over the same years.[17] Inevitably, such developments registered on the nation's political leadership. In his State of the Union address in January 1970, Richard Nixon predicted that, second only to the desire for peace, the environment would be "the major concern of the American people in the decade of the seventies."[18] Thus, the celebration of the first Earth Day in April 1970 marked the coming of age of the new environmental movement rather than its birth, a culmination rather than a beginning; the attention generated by the Earth Day festivities provided still more impetus, but to a movement already enjoying remarkable momentum.

The impact of these developments on popular attitudes has been a matter of debate. Critics have cast the environmental movement as fundamentally opposed to technology and have accused environmentalists of wanting to replace modern science with their own "unregenerate obscurantism."[19] However, the historian Samuel P. Hays has argued that the environmentalists of the day constantly urged that science and technology be pushed harder to develop solutions to existing problems that "the system" considered intractable or insolvable. In truth, both sides in the argument make reasonable points. The attitudes of environmentalists toward science and technology were complex and often ambivalent. Consequently, although public opinion polls indicated a growing uneasiness about technological development, notably among the young and those most concerned about the environment, the wholesale repudiation of science and technology feared by some critics of environmentalism never materialized.[20]

The environmental movement did, however, sanction a significant attitudinal change of a related sort: dissent from growth was integral to the ecological complaint, often implicitly so, sometimes explicitly. Some arrived at the antigrowth conclusion circuitously. For example, Professor Barry Commoner of Washington University in St. Louis, who was immortalized on a 1970 *Time* cover as ecology's Paul Revere, took pains in his influential call to arms to distance himself from an attack on economic growth per se: "What happens to the environment," he wrote in his best-selling book *The Closing Circle*, "depends on *how* the growth was achieved." For Commoner, the true villain was "environmentally intense technology." But the distinction he drew so carefully seemed to blur when he sketched out "the economic meaning of ecology": under capitalism, he wrote, "pollution is an unintended concomitant of the *natural drive* [emphasis added] of the economic system to introduce new technologies that increase productivity." "There appears," he concluded, "to be a basic conflict between pollution control and what is often regarded as a fundamental requirement of the private enterprise system—the continued maximization of productivity." Growth, it turned out, *was* the villain after all, at least under capitalism.[21]

Kenneth Boulding, an economist and a thoughtful environmental spokesman, reached the same conclusion without Commoner's obfuscation.

He distinguished between the existing "cowboy economy" that regarded production and consumption as good things and the emergent "spaceman economy," in which "the earth has become a single spaceship, without unlimited reservoirs of anything, either for extraction or for pollution." On the coming spaceship earth, production and consumption would be regarded as "something to be minimized rather than maximized." Less prominent environmentalists echoed the sentiment. As one student journalist wrote in her campus newspaper, the ecology movement needed to demand not "an improved environment" but a "radically altered" one: "This society has already 'expanded' to the hilt—it is that expansion which is killing us, population-wise, technologically, industrially. The thrust now must be to cut back." In early 1972, that view took center stage as the Anglo-pessimism of the British, the counterculture complaint, postmaterialist value change, and environmental consciousness combined to generate the loudest debate yet over the possibility and desirability of continued economic growth.[22]

II. The Limits to Growth Debate

The most direct attack on growth of the postwar period began in January 1972 with the publication in Britain's *Ecologist* magazine of a lengthy statement by thirty-three distinguished scientists and philosophers, including the biologist Sir Julian Huxley, the geneticist C. H. Waddington, and the naturalist Peter Scott. They averred that unrestricted population and industrial growth threatened to destroy "society and . . . the life support systems on this planet, possibly by the end of this century and certainly within the lifetimes of our children." Only the achievement of a steady-state economy could prevent "a succession of famines, epidemics, social crises, and wars."[23]

Almost simultaneously, advanced word appeared in the U.S. press of a new study entitled *The Limits to Growth*, produced by a team of researchers from the Massachusetts Institute of Technology and sponsored by, as *Time* put it in a burst of legitimacy-by-association hyperbole, "the . . . eminently respectable members of the prestigious Club of Rome."[24] The Club of Rome had been founded four years earlier by Aurelio Peccei, an Italian business consultant who was a member of the management committee of Fiat and former chief executive officer of the Olivetti Company. In 1972 its members included approximately seventy eminent scientists, business executives, educators, and technocrats from twenty-five nations. The Club consciously excluded political officeholders from membership, the only exception being the U.S. senator Claiborne Pell, a Rhode Island Democrat. The group met only irregularly (three times between 1968 and 1972) but funneled large amounts of money from the Agnelli Foundation (Giovanni Agnelli was the chairman of Fiat) and the Volkswagen Foundation into efforts to address what Peccei called the "world *problématique*"—the complex of intermeshing problems whose scale, scope, and intricacy spilled over national boundaries and defied the normal channels and mechanisms of problem-solving. The press of economic and population growth against a finite world constituted the Club's first point of attack.[25]

The Club's examination of growth, labeled the Project on the Predicament of Mankind, began in 1970. In meetings at Bern, Switzerland, and Cambridge, Massachusetts, Jay Wright Forrester, formerly the director of MIT's Digital Computer Laboratory and at the time a professor of management at MIT's Sloan School, outlined a computer simulation model of the global system that enabled researchers to study the interaction of several components of the *problématique*. Most promising, Forrester's "system dynamics" approach seemed to offer the analytical rigor necessary to track interrelated variables through time while taking into account delayed reactions and complicated feedback loops among the various factors. Having sold the Club on his basic technique, Forrester then turned over the tasks of tweaking and applying his model to an MIT team of seventeen researchers from six nations, headed by his twenty-eight-year-old protégé Dennis Meadows.

The MIT team ran computer simulations of the interaction of five variables: population growth, food supply, capital investment and industrial output, nonrenewable resource depletion, and pollution. Using a variety of scenarios based on differing assumptions, some more optimistic than others, the exponential growth of population and capital/output repeatedly ran into the limits imposed by either resource depletion or pollution, or both. The most benign outcome was the catastrophic collapse of the world system by the year 2100.[26] Real-world resource and pollution problems, the report suggested, could be kept manageable only if population growth and capital investment/output were quickly stabilized and held steady. The choice, to the extent that one existed, was between a self-imposed limitation on growth or disaster.[27]

To drive home the need for swift action, the MIT team added to their myriad charts and diagrams a telling discussion of the most striking characteristic of the exponential pattern of growth exhibited by population and industrial production: the suddenness with which it reaches an outer limit. "Suppose," they wrote, you own a pond on which a water lily is growing: The lily plant doubles in size each day. If the lily were allowed to grow unchecked, it would completely cover the pond in 30 days, choking off the other forms of life in the water. For a long time the lily plant seems small, and so you decide not to worry about cutting it back until it covers half the pond. On what day will that be? On the twenty-ninth day, of course. You have one day to save your pond.[28]

The message was clear: only prompt action could prevent catastrophe.

The actual publication of the MIT team's report to the Club of Rome was accompanied by a public relations blitz that would have made General Motors proud. The U.S. publisher of the MIT/Club of Rome study arranged to launch a popularly priced book version—without accompanying technical apparatus—at a symposium sponsored by Washington's prestigious Woodrow Wilson Center for Scholars. A Washington public relations firm, Calvin Kytle Associates, coordinated the release of publicity and managed to excite great interest. The first copies of *The Limits to Growth* hit the bookstands on the day that the Wilson Center symposium took place in the imposing Great Hall of the Smithsonian Institution. The Club of Rome's handiwork quickly became the intellectual sensation of the season. And more: by the end of the 1970s, 4 million copies of *The Limits to Growth* were in print in thirty languages. Peccei noted proudly that what had originally been undertaken as "a commando operation" against "stagnant, wishful thinking" quickly resulted in "a new kind of discourse . . . under way in practically every part of the world."[29]

The critical response to *The Limits to Growth* proved less easy to manipulate than its initial publicity. The reviews were decidedly mixed. For some admirers, the Club of Rome heralded "the demise of the Rostowian metaphysic." The computer's logic seemed irrefutable. As an essayist for *Time* observed, "Only a superoptimist would insist that growth could continue forever; that would presuppose that resources are literally infinite." Kenneth Boulding commented that anyone who believed that exponential growth could go on forever in a finite world was either a madman or an economist. The Club's fundamental point impressed supporters as so self-evident as to be truistic.[30]

Others doubted that a cliché could serve as a useful guide to action. Were the outside limits near enough to justify the Copernican revolution in thought and deed called for by the Club? In order to resolve that question, commentators scrutinized the Club's argument and found much to question. The report's data, methodology, analysis, and conclusions all drew fire, and the critics scored heavily on several counts.[31] At the most concrete level, did the report's database constitute a sufficiently strong foundation for such dire projections and sweeping prescriptions? Critics charged that the very weakness of the report's statistical base had in turn necessitated such a high level of aggregation that plausible regional distinctions—as between rich and poor, or developed and undeveloped areas—became impossible to make. Other methodological sins further weakened the study. Skeptics pounced with relish on the dangers of extrapolating current trends exponentially into the future: such predictions in the 1870s, they noted gleefully, would have predicted cities a century later buried under horse manure.

The most damning criticism zeroed in on the report's analysis. The economist Carl Kaysen pointed out the absence of any adjustment mechanisms in the MIT model. The authors of *The Limits to Growth* provided little hope for any mitigation or avoidance of the disasters they foresaw; the MIT model allowed no role for human agency or technological innovation or market mediation. "Prices play no significant role in the basic logical structure that supports the argument of 'Limits,'" Kaysen complained, "although it is precisely their function to make smooth transitions possible as scarcities and demands change."[32]

Particularly galling to critics was the fact that such analytical flaws seemed to be obscured from public view by the technological romance and putative rigor of the computer. "Computer fetishism," sniffed the highly regarded Science Policy Research Unit at the University of Sussex in a collective critique. The old GIGO syndrome well known to the computer literate—"garbage in, garbage out"—had in the hands of the MIT team become Malthus in, Malthus out, with the computer merely regurgitating the flawed assumptions of its programmers.[33] The Club of Rome report, the economist Henry Wallach observed, had treated "a calculating machine" as "an oracle" in order to hype its predetermined hypothesis.[34]

Moreover, critics contended, the use of computer modeling endowed *The Limits to Growth* with "the surface appearance of scientific neutrality and objectivity," whereas in reality the MIT researchers conveyed a message "which can only be fully understood in the context of their own beliefs, values, assumptions and goals." To some that message reeked of technocracy, a guiding principle of which held that dramatically simple (albeit elaborate) technical answers can be found for the most daunting and complex of human problems, even (or especially) if those problems have deep social, political, and cultural roots. The authors of the Club of Rome report seemed also to betray the vaguely authoritarian impatience with the temporizing and compromise inherent in the democratic process that was another hallmark of technocracy. Meanwhiie, the draconian nature of the Club's proposed solution—a shift to no growth virtually overnight—diverted attention from less totalistic but still critical questions regarding the composition and distribution of economic growth: what kind of growth and for whom?[35] In the face of this barrage of criticism, the Club of Rome took a quick step backward, specifying publicly that *The Limits to Growth* was a report *to* the Club, not *by* the Club, and emphasizing the necessarily tentative nature of this "first hesitant step towards a new understanding of the world."[36]

But more striking in retrospect was the fact that the highly critical discussion of the report never fully offset the dramatic impact of its highly publicized launch or the power of its most fundamental point. The Club may have lost the battle of words, but it could still claim victory in the larger war of public perceptions. As Peccei proudly told an interviewer in 1974, "No critic has yet disproved the existence of a fundamental mismatch between headlong human proliferation and insatiability, which are dominant traits of present-day society, and our planet's limited, vulnerable carrying capacity." Even *Business Week*, no friend of the Club's analysis, commented, "For all the criticism, practically everyone agrees that on a finite planet, growth must end sooner or later."[37] Critics discovered that it was, indeed, hard to argue with a platitude. Leonard Silk, who covered the *Limits* controversy for the *New York Times*, was a devastating critic, but nevertheless concluded:

This industrial society is getting dangerously crowded, complex and putrid. We urgently need a change in social values—a shift in our goals from increasing the quantity of production to improving the quality of life. Almost the whole of our society and its institutions, business and governmental, are geared to growth of the old kind; the shift can occur only if we have what the M.I.T. group correctly calls a Copernican Revolution of the mind.[38]

Economists favorably disposed toward growth found themselves conceding significant ground despite their strong substantive reservations. Nobel laureate Paul Samuelson called the report "surprisingly superficial on the factual side" but admitted that "an affluent society uses up irreplaceable resources at a tremendous rate. . . . If not in the year 2000 or in the year 2073, nonetheless, sometime ahead catastrophic problems will descend upon humanity unless we use our conscious intelligence to do something about it."[39] Even such a guru of growth liberalism as Walt Rostow agreed that the Club of Rome report had had an important, positive impact, despite its "technical inadequacies and the lack of data to fill the terms of its equations." He refused to join in criticism of *The Limits to Growth* because he believed the study had contributed to the sort of "profound adjustments in the way men and governments act and think" that were necessary in order to "find the way to some more or less stable but dynamic equilibrium between man and his physical environment." After "two centuries of relatively uninhibited expansion in population and production, with all of the habits of mind and action that experience carried with it," international cooperation to reach such a dynamic equilibrium was imperative; the alternative, Rostow feared, might be yet another "grandiose cycle" that could well "disintegrate the industrial civilizations we have built."[40]

Thus, despite the assaults on *The Limits to Growth* by critics, the study's essential contention had a significant impact: there *were* limits and some accommodation, however belated and grudging, had to be made to that reality. It was a message that found a public already made receptive by the counterculture's highly visible rebellion against mainstream materialism, by the less dramatic but perhaps more powerful influence of postmaterialist values throughout Western industrial societies, and by the warnings of the emergent environmental movement. The combined weight of these developments, together with adverse economic developments, policy errors, and political misdeeds, doomed Nixon's hopes for a geopolitical and moral crusade based on the twin engines of economic growth and competition.

In early 1973, the president complained of "a certain tendency to despair" and "doomsday mentality" that held continued economic growth and environmental protection to be mutually exclusive. Reverting to language that he used probably less because it persuaded others than because it expressed his true Whiggish self, Nixon urged Americans to "convert the so-called crisis of the environment into an opportunity for unprecedented progress." "Now," he urged, "is the time to stop the handwringing and roll up our sleeves and get on with the job." But even Nixon retreated a bit. "I believe," he said, "there is always a sensible middle ground between the Cassandras and the Pollyannas. We must take our stand upon that ground."[41] He tried to articulate such a position in his commencement address at Florida Technological University in June 1973. Nixon included in his speech an unexceptional denunciation of "Malthusian pessimism about the future," but made a notable concession when he trotted out his rhetorical chestnut about no nation being its true self unless engaged in a great enterprise. Building world peace, he told the graduates, was one such endeavor; creating prosperity without the spur of war or the threat of inflation was another. And, he continued, building a better environment was a third. The addition of this new element to his by-now-familiar homily testified to Nixon's recognition of a change in values that would influence public discourse for the remainder of the 1970s.[42]

Where the main channel of that discourse would run was made clearer by the publication of the Club of Rome's often-overlooked follow-up study to *The Limits to Growth*. In August 1974, the month of Nixon's resignation from office, Professors Mihajlo Mesarovic of Case Western Reserve University and Eduard Pestel of Germany's Hannover University put the finishing touches on *Mankind at the Turning Point*. This second Club of Rome study trod familiar ground but took into account several of the most damaging criticisms of its predecessor. Growth was still at the heart of the *"problématique humaine,"* but the danger was now specified much more carefully. A disaggregated model of the world economy allowed for crucial regional distinctions to be made. Undifferentiated growth—"growth for growth's sake in the sense of ever increasing numbers and larger size"—was bad, but the answer was not the stark and simple alternative of no growth. Humanity needed, rather, to aim for "organic growth," that is, balanced, differentiated growth that would allow poor regions still to develop while causing the growth of rich regions to taper off dramatically. Whereas a continuation of undifferentiated growth guaranteed a doomsday scenario of inevitable, catastrophic collapse, organic growth held out the possibility of an escape— not *from* growth but rather *through* growth. Much of the discussion of growth for the remainder of the 1970s would reflect a similar attempt to subordinate and otherwise hedge growth without forgoing it completely.[43]

III. The Rhetoric of Balance

Throughout the 1970s, the concept of balance constituted a central theme in discussions about growth. Nearly everyone seemed to agree that growth needed to be balanced in order to be economically sustainable and politically viable as a national goal. Indeed, it became difficult to find dissent regarding the value of balance. Even the Edison Electric Institute, the trade association of America's electric utilities and, in the eyes of environmentalists and antigrowth advocates, the antichrist of economic development, admitted publicly in early 1978 that "it's clear to most of us that economic growth cannot continue as before." The nation needed to reach "a compromise that involves *some* growth . . . [and] provides a balance of economic and environmental priorities."[44]

Balance was the key, but just what balance meant remained uncertain. Was it a substantive concept or a public relations buzzword? The Nixon administration wrestled with the issue at a time when support for growth still ran strong. In mid-1969, Richard Nixon created a National Goals Research Staff (NGRS) within the White House and charged it with identifying "the key choices open to us" and examining "the consequences of those choices."[45] Leonard Garment headed the effort and Daniel Patrick Moynihan oversaw it in his capacity as the president's counselor and domestic adviser and the administration's intellectual-in-residence. On July 4, 1970, the National Goals group issued its first—and only—report, entitled *Toward Balanced Growth: Quantity with Quality.*[46]

The extraordinary balancing act of the report's title—balance and growth, equilibrium and dynamism, quantity and quality, optimism and anxiety—seemed to express, depending on the reader's own predilections, either subtlety or evasiveness. Still, no previous state paper had spoken so thoughtfully about America's postwar growth. The authors proceeded from the basis provided by the president's forecast in his 1970 State of the Union address that in the next decade the U.S. economy would grow by 50 percent, an increment larger in absolute size than the entire growth of the national economy from 1790 to 1950. Such growth was, they contended, a positive force in American life: it provided jobs, raised the standard of living, reduced poverty, and played "a great stabilizing role" by enabling the less-well-off to improve their lot without having to take wealth away from others. Accordingly, Americans had come to place a high value on continued growth, although never committing the nation to a single-minded pursuit of "growth only for its own sake" as critics sometimes charged.

Nevertheless, the NGRS reported, "today there is an explicit challenge to the view that we can or should continue to encourage or permit the unfettered growth of our economy." Vietnam had taught that resources were not infinite and that priorities were essential; environmental concerns raised tough questions about the limits imposed by nature; the movement for technology assessment demanded a new, more rigorous look at the costs and unintended consequences of technological change. Perhaps most significant, Americans were in the process of developing a new value system that caused them to view growth in a new light. The values of the 1930s were giving way to a new sensibility. "During those [earlier] years," Nixon's brainstormers wrote, "smoke billowing from a factory chimney was a reas-suring sight. However, it now seems evident that we pursued too narrow a set of objectives far too long." As American culture took a postmaterialist turn, quantitative concerns were giving way to a new focus on the quality of life.

The task now, the NGRS concluded, was to "ensure continued economic growth while directing our resources more deliberately to filling our new values." Trade-offs needed to be made and new compromises needed to be struck. But if growth was an important part of the problem, it was also a crucial part of the solution. The answer was "not to stop growth, but to redirect it." By implementing an "explicit growth policy," government could make the adjustments necessary in order to sustain growth into the future. "The new qualitative goals being proposed and the old goals yet unmet can be achieved," the National Goals group concluded, but "only if we have continued economic growth." Balance and guidance would make possible the continued growth that was necessary.

Moynihan considered such prescriptions "essentially undemanding," but they proved to be too much for Nixon's inner circle of advisers. "From the outset the White House has treated [the project] . . . as some crazy socialist scheme," Moynihan complained to Ehrlichman and Haldeman, calling the experience "rather too painful." Although the NGRS in the end plumped for growth, its hedging of the concept troubled an administration that would soon embark on its own growth crusade. Herbert Stein expressed the administration's ambivalence in a witty poem he sent to the exasperated Moynihan:

> Haiku
> The quality of life
> Is a national goal,
> But fifty-two points on the Dow Jones
> Is a girl's best friend.[47]

Attitudes regarding balance proved no less uncertain outside govern-ment. In late 1973, Nelson A. Rockefeller organized a private-sector investi-gation of the problems and choices confronting American society. The Commission on Critical Choices for Americans aimed to set the public agenda in the fashion of its family progenitor, the Rockefeller Brothers Fund Special Studies Project of the late 1950s. Forty-two prominent Ameri-cans, including political figures, labor leaders, educators, technocrats, and business luminaries, worked with over one hundred specialists to produce fourteen volumes of findings. When Rockefeller left the undertaking to become Gerald Ford's vice president, William J. Ronan, the head of the New York and New Jersey Port Authority, replaced him as chairman of the commission.

Critical choices about growth stood high on the commission's agenda. "For the first time in our history," Rockefeller declared, "there is significant opposition to the concept of continued economic growth and the actual development of resources to that end." Since the United States had been "synonymous with growth," the challenge struck at the heart of American life. A no-growth America would have to forswear "the increased production, jobs, and income" that historically held social and economic tensions in check while amalgamating "the varied parts into a greater whole as a nation"; a "static or shrinking pie," Rockefeller warned, would perforce divide Americans and exacerbate tensions. Moreover, he feared that the imposition of a no-growth regime would require "far more regulation and regimentation than has ever pertained here in peacetime." As devoted to economic growth as any public figure of his day, Rockefeller clearly worried about the consequences and implications of the emerging challenge to growth.[48]

Despite Rockefeller's preference for growth, the commission in the end moved slowly and clumsily, like a huge, unwieldy supertanker of introspection and ideas, in the direction of balance. Perhaps, it admitted, the United States (and a large part of the industrialized West as well) had been off on a materialistic spree, but it was possible that Americans were now entering a new maturity that would enable them to "move beyond consumption to find fulfillment." Such a step "may present the biggest choice of all." "We do not want to see growth abandoned," acting chairman Ronan cautioned: "It is a question of how we grow—and harmonization may be the key."[49]

Balance, adjustment, harmonization—concepts central to what Ronan called the "new values for growth"—all promised concordance but yielded conflict and confusion.[50] The need for balance became increasingly unexceptionable, but defining balance proved to be intellectually difficult and politically tricky. The 1978 White House Conference on Balanced National Growth and Economic Development illustrated just how difficult and tricky. The conference was first proposed in 1976 by the Senate Environment and Public Works Committee, chaired by Democrat Jennings Randolph of West Virginia. Carter's Commerce Department organized the gathering, with West Virginia's governor John D. Rockefeller IV acting as chairman and Michael S. Koleda, a vice president of the National Planning Association with a Ph.D. in economics from Brown University, serving as conference director. For five days at the end of January and beginning of February 1978, five hundred official delegates and countless observers and hangers-on descended on Washington to conduct what the press characterized as "the nation's first town meeting on growth."[51]

The conference organizers sought to update the nation's postwar commitment to growth and high employment for "the changed circumstances and new realities of the 1970s and 1980s." Much had indeed changed. There were new constraints on growth in the form of resource shortages; new doubts about the efficacy of macroeconomic policy to achieve satisfactory growth; and new objectives—equality of opportunity, environmental protection, resource conservation, quality of life—added to the national agenda, objectives "which must be integrated with and often balanced against efforts to stimulate growth and employment."[52] But, the conference organizers admitted, because the nation's "social, economic, environmental and physical aspirations may sometimes be in conflict," balance often proved difficult to achieve.[53] As Commerce Secretary Juanita Kreps observed, "The phrase 'trade-offs' has become part of every decisionmaker's vocabulary."[54]

In that likelihood of conflict lay the trap for policymakers. Balance suggested harmony—until you asked people to define it. Economic growth had hardly ended conflict in American life—witness the 1960s—but it had enabled Americans to avoid some of the conflict over wealth, status, and power likely in a highly individualistic, highly unequal society. To call for balanced growth opened new realms to contestation; to balance competing values and debate trade-offs threatened to reawaken and exacerbate conflicts that growth, for both better and worse, had allowed Americans for a generation to avoid or mute.

"Within hours of the opening of the conference's first sessions," reported Thomas Oliphant of the Boston Globe, "it was apparent that one person's balance is another's cause for grief."[55] The White House Conference on Balanced Growth illuminated brightly what its chairman, Rockefeller of West Virginia, described as "the incredible array of tensions involved with growth."[56] Predictably, there was conflict over competing national priorities. The auto magnate Henry Ford II complained that "balanced growth" was simply a euphemism for Luddite stagnation, a term wielded by those who would sacrifice industrial progress on the altar of environmental purity. Others talked of the tension between the goals of full employment and price stability. A second kind of conflict focused on the issue of equity, with balance in that case referring to how fully various groups shared in the fruits of growth. For example, the National Conference of Puerto Rican Women informed conference director Koleda that its membership considered economic growth important but "would rather have slower growth and insure participation of Hispanics in the economy."[57]

A third kind of conflict was locational. By the mid-1970s, open warfare had broken out between the champions of the still-dynamic Sunbelt and the representatives of the becalmed Frostbelt (or Rustbelt; the label varied but generally designated the Upper Midwest and Northeast, where so much of America's industrial development had occurred).[58] Any meaningful concept of balanced growth needed somehow to address the differing trajectories of these sections under the new regime of limits. Despite an attempt by New York senator Daniel Patrick Moynihan and Georgia governor George Busbee to lower the temperature of the regional debate, tensions between northern and southern delegates to the conference remained palpable.[59] Divisions among urban, suburban, and rural interests were perceptible as well. Commerce Secretary Kreps had warned the delegates at the outset of the conference against "the tyranny . . . of seeing ourselves as Easterners or Westerners, whites or non-whites, environmentalists or developers." "We seem to have forgotten," she lamented, "that we are all citizens of the same country, that our lives are interdependent, more interdependent now than ever before in history."[60] In a world of balance, trade-offs, and tough choices, interdependence could be the stuff of division perhaps more easily than the basis for cooperation.

The conference's reviews varied wildly. A syndicated columnist for *Newsday* called the meeting a "watershed event in American governance" and likened it to the Constitutional Convention of 1787.[61] Others differed. When President Carter asked Tom Hayden, who had come as a delegate from California, what he thought of the affair, Hayden asked, "Do you want my frank opinion?" The president nodded. "The test of good government," opined the 1960s radical, "would be if you could abolish such conferences."[62]

Hayden's comment could not have pleased Carter. Clearly, the conference had failed to create a national consensus on balance. The outcome was all the more disappointing because the administration had organized the conference with several objectives firmly in mind. First, it had wanted to soften the conflict that the transition to an era of limits inevitably excited. To that end, the conference organizers had officially titled the session on regional relations "Beyond Sunbelt-Frostbelt," hoping to encourage a positive discussion that would move beyond accusations of federal favoritism toward one region or another. The conference succeeded in muting for the moment the most vociferous conflicts attending the issue of balanced growth, but the conflicts themselves would not go away.

The administration's second objective for the conference was to ease the political pressure on the president to do more on the growth front. By the time of the conference, policymakers had come to recognize the limited efficacy of traditional macroeconomic policy for generating growth without inviting dangerous inflation; meanwhile, playing the role of arbiter among the various interests competing for portions of a stable or even shrinking pie left the White House in an unenviable political position. To deal with these related problems, the Carter administration sought to decentralize the responsibility for growth policy by emphasizing what state and local governments and regional agencies might do to boost and balance economic growth and development. Hoping to encourage non-Washington answers to the problem of balanced growth in an age of limits, the administration invited a large number of mayors and governors to serve as conference delegates and gave state governors the power to name 375 of the 500 official delegates. "We have to pull away from this notion that everything has to fall squarely into the lap of the federal government," said White House aide for intergovernmental affairs Jack H. Watson Jr., who served as Carter's White House point man in planning for the conference.[63]

The administration's hope for decentralization was only partially realized. Press accounts of the proceedings emphasized the theme that localities, states, and regions all had larger roles to play in matters related to growth.[64] But there was a significant ambiguity in the clamor for decentralization, which Carter recognized immediately. In his farewell comments to the conferees, the president expressed his support for the principle of decentralization: "I agree completely with that concept." But he noted that while he had heard "a great deal of applause at the mention that we shift the financial burden to Washington and shift responsibility from Washington," he had not heard "any applause for the other side" of that formulation. Carter, of course, wanted to shift both responsibility *and* burden away from the federal government. "But we're all in it together," he added equivocally.[65]

Later evaluations of the conference further attenuated even this weak commitment to decentralization. When the conference advisory committee headed by West Virginia governor Rockefeller reported in May, it called for greater decentralization within the federal system but also suggested that the federal government free up states and localities to play a more vigorous role in growth issues by picking up their existing share of the cost of welfare and Medicaid. Moreover, the advisory committee reported that "the clearest and most important" message of the conference had been a general agreement that the federal government needed to upgrade *its* capacity to deal with growth and its consequences. The nation required a "national growth policy process" to clarify national goals, identify trade-offs, and resolve conflicts; and the president needed "a federal growth policy unit" to advise him on growth-related issues.[66] Clearly, this was not the sort of evasive decentralization the administration had originally sought. Koleda added to the confusion when, in reporting on the conference to outside groups, he identified decentralized growth with a bygone era of plenty, which was giving way, he claimed, to a new effort to conserve both energy and infrastructure by "recentralizing" economic activity.[67]

In the end, the White House Conference on Balanced Growth and Economic Development justified Tom Hayden's cynicism. Little was achieved, and even that was shrouded in ambiguity. The hope that such a national town meeting on growth could breathe clear meaning into the concept of balanced growth was dashed by the comment of Senator Randolph, the progenitor of the event, in the conference's final report: "We know in our hearts what we mean by balanced growth."[68] Perhaps the only thing made clear by the conference was the fact that nearly a decade of discussion about balance had left the concept murkier than before.

IV. Growth Subordinate: The Political Economy of Stagflation

As Americans debated whether they wanted growth and what it meant when they did, policymakers in Washington were finding growth an increasingly elusive goal for economic reasons as well. During the mid- and late 1970s, the United States confronted the most trying economic circumstances since the end of the Second World War, and policymakers' efforts to deal with the nation's economic woes contributed in a concrete way to the subordination of growth as a societal goal. Although concern over the simultaneous appearance of both inflation and stagnant output had been voiced earlier, the ten-year period beginning in 1973 brought stagflation of a new, more virulent sort. Policymakers throughout the Western, industrialized world wrestled with the new predicament at a time when rising international competition and the emergence of a truly global economy increasingly limited their freedom of action. In this new environment, the growth orientation that had, in its several earlier guises, figured so prominently in economic policymaking no longer seemed relevant. In a world

beset by stagflation, the primary goals became damping inflation and cushioning recession; the watchword in this new environment was not growth
but stability, especially price stability.

When Gerald Ford became president upon Nixon's resignation from
office in early August 1974, he found the world economy in disarray. In late
July, the Organization for Economic Development (OECD) reported that the
industrialized West had suffered a deceleration of growth of record proportions; shortly after Ford took the oath of office, the International Monetary
Fund reported that inflation was surging in economies all around the globe.
The combination proved disastrous. In the United States, wholesale prices
rose 3.7 percent in July and consumer prices 1.3 percent in August, both near
records. A Gallup poll reported in mid-July that Americans believed inflation
to be, far and away, the nation's most important domestic problem. It surprised few observers, then, when the new president used the occasion of his
first national address to rally his television and radio audience for a struggle
against inflation as "domestic public enemy number one."[69]

Ford continued his emphasis on inflation long after it had become clear
to others that rapidly rising prices constituted only one part, although
admittedly an important one, of a larger problem facing the economy. At
congressional urging, the president convened a "domestic summit meeting" in order to clarify the economic situation. A series of twelve mini-con-
ferences held around the country throughout the month of September
paved the way for a culminating two-day summit conference at the end of
the month. The first such mini-conference brought twenty-eight top academic and business economists to the East Room of the White House, where
the president called upon them to "draw up . . . a battle plan against a common enemy, inflation . . . our domestic enemy Number 1." George Shultz,
only recently returned to private life after serving as Nixon's secretary of
labor, director of the OMB, and secretary of the treasury, brought down the
house by observing, "Well, the economy is in terrible shape, and I wish you
guys in government would do something about it." In summarizing the
economists' deliberations for the president, Shultz maintained that the fore-
casts advanced by the various participants "were not all that different from
one another; you could throw your hat over all of them."[70] In reality, however, a significant division had developed.

Many of the economists gathered at the White House were beginning
to wonder whether inflation was indeed the number one enemy. Shultz
spoke for a numerical majority of those present who saw the problem as
more complicated than that: "We continue to identify the major risk as the

risk of inflation," he agreed, "but at the same time . . . there has been a growing sense of a risk on the unemployment and recession side." Two notable dissenters spoke against any concessions to the fear of an economic slowdown, however. John Kenneth Galbraith urged a thoroughly traditional (almost Republican) approach: increase taxes and keep monetary policy tight in order to stifle the inflation "which is, after all, the source of a great deal of suffering at the present time." "Let us not," he pleaded, "be beguiled by the fear of recession and have that fear keep us from attacking inflation." Milton Friedman, popularly viewed as Galbraith's ideological archfoe, expressed surprise at his agreement with his liberal adversary but echoed Galbraith's fundamental point: "The sooner we bite the bullet and take the cure, the better."[71] Significantly, Ford heeded the minority view, partly because it accorded with his own judgment and partly because the economic situation was in flux and was therefore sufficiently ambiguous as to discourage an abrupt, highly public, and politically embarrassing about-face. Gerald Ford would not eat crow unless and until he absolutely had to.

Ford held fast to his war on inflation even as the economy eased slowly into the most severe postwar recession yet. In late September, 800 invited delegates and perhaps another 1,200 onlookers and newspeople jammed into the International Ballroom of Washington's Hilton Hotel amid the sort of spectacle and media attention traditionally reserved for summit meetings of the Cold War variety. The administration formally labeled the summit a "conference on inflation" and in his welcoming remarks Ford dwelled again on the acute threat posed by inflation, but the economists in attendance responded more forcefully than before that the economic prospect was more complicated (and daunting) than the president allowed. "The number one thing that is wrong about most discussions is the statement that our number one problem is inflation," Paul Samuelson observed pointedly. The real problem, he maintained, was stagflation. The enemy, Walter Heller explained, was the vicious combination of "stubborn inflation" and "menacing recession" now confronting the nation. Once again, George Shultz gave the judgment a bipartisan imprint: "I think it is pretty clear that there is practically no dissent, that the reality . . . is stagflation . . . [and] while inflation is public enemy number one, there are other problems to be attended to as we attend . . . inflation."[72] But when Ford presented his economic policy recommendations to Congress a week later, they reflected his own preconceptions rather than the consensus of economists at the summit: a temporary tax surcharge, a ceiling on spending, and an ill-fated voluntaristic campaign to Whip Inflation Now (WIN). As Senator Bob Dole observed, Ford was a less complicated political animal than Nixon: "Ford's objective was more simple. He aimed to be a good Republican president, moving within the traditional Republican philosophy." The struggle against inflation, Ford commented in a 1978 interview, "provided the basic theme of my administration."[73]

The fear of inflation shaped policy even after the administration finally admitted publicly that the economy had fallen into a serious recession. In mid-December 1974, Ford told the Business Council what his audience undoubtedly already knew: "We are in a recession. Production is declining, and unemployment, unfortunately, is rising. We are also faced with continued high rates of inflation greater than can be tolerated over an extended period of time."[74] With unemployment rising to 7.2 percent in December, the GNP dropping 7.5 percent (in constant dollars) in the fourth quarter, and inflation remaining distressingly high (in double digits for the year), stagflation had indeed taken hold of the U.S. economy. The presumably automatic trade-off between inflation and unemployment no longer worked. "I have been a student of the business cycle for a long time," Fed chairman Arthur Burns told the Joint Economic Committee, "and I know of no precedent for it in history."[75]

The Federal Reserve and the administration tried to rachet down the unemployment caused by the 1974–75 recession, but sought to do so gradually in order not to reignite the lingering inflation. Fed chairman Burns, CEA chairman Alan Greenspan, and Ford remained fearful that overly expansive antirecession measures would exacerbate the more deeply rooted problem of inflation. "Recession is the number-one problem in the short run," Burns told a reporter, "but inflation is the number one in the longer run." As Greenspan later recalled, the administration sought "to simmer down the deficit, the rate of inflation, and eventually get to a stable, balanced economy. . . . I thought that if the short-term policy became expansionary at this stage, it would prove eventually counterproductive." A gradualist approach to combating the recession left the administration open to charges of hard-hearted inaction, but Ford believed that the long-run economic risk of inflation justified his policy. "Unemployment is the biggest concern of the 8.2 percent of American workers temporarily out of work," he admitted as the recession worsened in 1975, "but inflation is the universal enemy of 100 percent of our people."[76]

Under pressure, the administration did act to cushion the recessionary blow, but always with an eye on long-term price stability. As unemployment rose in 1975, Ford twice called for tax reductions (first in the form of temporary rebates, later permanent reductions), but he always coupled such moves with demands for expenditure cuts and spending limits. When the Democratic Congress proved more amenable to cutting taxes than slashing spending, Ford invoked a veto strategy to turn back measures that threatened a budget overrun. Stability remained the primary focus, and Ford proved his devotion to that cause by refusing to pump up the economy in the approach to the 1976 presidential election.

The accidental president, an object of much scorn and derision as a man wholly unequal to his job, sacrificed himself on the altar of price stability. As Ford himself later recalled,

I never in any serious way considered increasing spending in 1976. For one thing, I was not sure that any great increase in spending would produce a significant reduction of unemployment. More important, I had concern that any wild increase in spending, even if it won the election, would regenerate inflation, which would not lead to a very happy outcome for the country. Basically, I believed that a balanced, responsible economic policy would lead to success in the election. It almost worked.

Ford's reticence was matched by Arthur Burns's hesitancy at the Fed: the charge that he had conspired to swing the 1972 election to Nixon by means of a dangerously expansive monetary policy had stung Burns badly, and he was determined to act cautiously in 1976. Ford and Burns acted both out of principle and in the optimistic expectation that the economic recovery from the 1974–75 recession already under way would continue unabated through the election season. But in the summer of 1976 the economy faltered; Ford promised another tax cut with sufficient spending cuts to leave the budget in balance, but the time for effective stimulative action had passed. The pause in the economic recovery was only temporary, but it helped swing a close election to Jimmy Carter.[77]

Carter came to the presidency on the wings of a Kennedyesque promise to recapture the economic momentum of the 1960s. In his first head-to-head debate with President Ford, the former Georgia governor savaged the administration for accepting sub-par economic performance; establishing a vivid contrast between himself and the incumbent, Carter emphasized the need to reduce unemployment and minimized the danger of inflation in an economy utilizing less than 75 percent of its existing productive capacity. "A growth in our national economy equal to what was experienced under Kennedy, Johnson, before the Vietnam War"—5 to 5.5 percent—would, Carter promised, make it possible by 1981 to achieve full employment, reduce inflation, and produce both a balanced budget and a $60 billion surplus that could be used to fund "the programs that I promised the American people."[78] Carter's faith in growth and playing down of inflation during the campaign reflected the influence of his early advisers, who were, in the words of one economic historian, "the old gang" of Keynesians who had clustered around JFK and LBJ.[79]

Once in office, the Georgian followed through on his early commitments by quickly presenting an economic stimulus package to Congress. "We are," he declared, "in the middle of the worst economic slowdown of the last 40 years." To attack the problem, he proposed a $31 billion (over two years) program of $50 per capita tax rebates, a small permanent business tax reduction, increased public works spending, and an expansion of public service employment.[80] For a fleeting moment, it appeared to many liberal Democrats that their hope for a revival of 1960s-style growth liberalism was about to be fulfilled.

Carter was not *that* kind of liberal, however, and the economic circumstances he confronted in the mid-1970s were quite different from those faced by the policymakers of the New Frontier and Great Society. Carter was what Robert Kuttner has called a minimalist liberal. The anonymous Washington insider who quipped, "I don't know if he's Franklin Roosevelt or Richard Nixon," perhaps overstated, but he spoke for many who discovered that Carter's politics defied easy categorization. With time, it became clear that Carter's social and racial liberalism was closely balanced by a deep fiscal conservatism and an abiding concern for managerial efficiency. The ideological mix was sufficiently removed from the New Deal tradition to cause Carter's chief domestic adviser, Stuart Eizenstat, to characterize his boss as "the first neoliberal Democratic president, fiscally moderate, socially progressive, and liberal on foreign policy issues."[81]

Among the qualities that distinguished Carter from his immediate Democratic predecessors was his appreciation that the United States had indeed left behind the exuberant growth of the immediate postwar years and entered a new season of limits. One reason for this different perspective was the mounting evidence pointing to such a conclusion that had become available in the 1970s. A second reason was the fact that what the historian Leo Ribuffo has called Carter's "visceral puritanism" predisposed the Georgian to focus on the proof and implications of decline. Nixon before him had perceived the existence of limits, but thought that creative leadership could salvage U.S. preeminence; Carter, on the other hand, believed that such limits constituted a new reality that could be accommodated but not transcended.

"Dealing with limits," Carter recalled after leaving office, had been "the subliminal theme" of his presidency. He warned Americans in his inaugural address that *"more* is not necessarily *better*, . . . even our great nation has its recognized limits, and . . . we can neither answer all questions nor solve all problems. We cannot afford to do everything." And he reiterated that theme toward the end, speaking at the dedication of the John F. Kennedy Presidential Library in Boston in late 1979:

President Kennedy was right: Change is the law of life. The world of 1980 is as different from what it was in 1960 as the world of 1960 was from that of 1940. . . . After a decade of high inflation and growing oil imports, our economic cup no longer overflows. . . . We can no longer rely on a rising economic tide to lift the boats of the poorest in our society. . . . We have a keener appreciation of limits now—the limits of government, limits on the use of military power abroad; the limits on manipulating, without harm to ourselves, a delicate and a balanced natural environment. We are struggling with a profound transition from a time of abundance to a time of growing scarcity in energy.[82]

It is not entirely surprising, therefore, that once elected, Carter began to draw back from the growth rhetoric of his campaign and from his own initial stimulus package in particular. An aide later recalled, "The President's first instincts were not to go the route on the stimulus. That was his own gut instinct."[83] Carter's Keynesian advisers prevailed for a time, but even in the early stages, CEA chairman Charles Schultze later recalled, "the need, the perceived need, both politically and economically, for economic stimulus ran against the grain of his fiscal conservatism."[84] By April 1977, the combination of an upturn in economic activity, worry about the $66 billion deficit inherited from the Ford administration, and renewed concern about building inflationary pressures produced what Carter has called "a major fiscal and political problem—a turning point." The $50 tax rebate proposal was still pending in Congress, but Budget Director Bert Lance and Treasury Secretary Michael Blumenthal agreed with the president that the rebate "now seemed not only unnecessary but likely to spur inflation, a growing threat we had ignored too long." Other advisers warned that to reverse field now would be taken as a sign of confusion or indecision, but Carter made up his mind "to bite the bullet." The decision was a defining one: "From then on," he later wrote, "the basic course was set. . . . I knew I had made the correct decision; for more than three and a half years, my major economic battle would be against inflation, and I would stay on the side of fiscal prudence, restricted budgets, and lower deficits." "One failure could cause the downfall of this administration," he told a cabinet member at midterm, "Inflation. Almost everything is subservient to it in political terms."[85]

Carter's nomination of Paul Volcker to the chairmanship of the Federal Reserve in 1979 demonstrated how far his commitment to restraint would carry. Volcker promptly led the Fed into a vigorous anti-inflation campaign that relied on the management of the money supply rather than the less aggressive manipulation of interest rates. Now determined by economic conditions, interest rates soon shot through the roof and helped slow the economy into an election-year slump. In March 1980, Carter made his own contribution to the slowdown by presenting a balanced budget for fiscal year 1982 and threatening to veto any bills that endangered that goal. At the same time, he requested the Fed to impose selective restraints on consumer credit, causing consumer spending to collapse with unforeseen speed and disastrous consequences.[86]

Carter's desperate mix of halfhearted attempts at economic expansion to deal with the pain of unemployment and the threat of recession, alternating with determined attempts at retrenchment to attack the omnipresent danger of inflation, ultimately failed on both counts. To be sure, Carter had inherited a set of intertwined problems that seemed nearly intractable, and they worsened over time. The decline in productivity continued, and the stoppage of Iranian oil production because of revolutionary turmoil touched off yet another round of OPEC price hikes that nearly tripled the price of oil between 1979 and 1981. By 1980, the economy was in a recession, with unemployment rising to 7.8 percent; inflation raged out of control, as consumer prices skyrocketed (at an annualized rate of 15.9 percent in March); and interest rates reached postwar highs, as the federal funds rate (which governs interbank borrowing of reserve funds) jumped to 19.4 percent by the end of March and the prime rate reached 18.5 percent a month later. The stagflation that had gripped the U.S. economy at mid-decade seemed now, four years later, all the stronger and more debilitating.[87]

As the presidential election of 1980 loomed, Carter came under increasing pressure to pump up the economy in answer to Reagan's rousing call for massive tax cuts to "stimulate . . . [the] economy, increase productivity, and put America back to work."[88] On the president's left flank, organized labor and the forces aligned with Massachusetts senator Ted Kennedy called for an all-out fiscal and monetary attack on unemployment and economic slack. During the 1980 campaign, Carter's own advisers, the president noted in his diary, were "unanimous in asking me to approve a tax reduction and a moderate spending program to assuage Kennedy and to stimulate the economy. I was adamantly against it and, after considerable discussion, prevailed."[89] In the end, the administration did put forth a modest program of spending increases and tax cuts, the latter to take effect in 1981. Carter told his advisers that the last-minute economic revival plan "rubs me [the] wrong way," but admitted that "we need to do it to keep from being savaged politically."[90] As was often the case during the Carter presidency, such temporizing did not represent a departure from fiscal conservatism so much as add to it the appearance of desperate pandering. The failure to avoid recession and control inflation proved fatal in the end, combining with the Iranian hostage debacle and Reagan's disarming personal charisma to seal Carter's overwhelming defeat.[91] In the economic environment of the 1970s, the politics of stabilization and retrenchment proved fully as treacherous for Ford and Carter as had the economics of growth for their liberal predecessors.

The retreat from growth and confrontation with stagflation cost the Democrats more than just the White House in 1980. The party fell into disarray in the late 1970s as Americans entertained new doubts about growth and as stagflation imposed an unfamiliar discipline upon Democratic policymakers maneuvering uncertainly in a time of limits. The difficult conditions of the 1970s presented the party of the New Deal and Great Society with a fundamental identity crisis. The political apparatus whose driving force had, for over a quarter century, been an identification with and reliance on economic growth had difficulty redefining and repositioning itself for a time of slow or no growth and constant inflationary pressure. The fact that the economic policies needed to fight inflation worked against growth and proved incompatible with the political needs of the Democratic coalition further complicated matters.

Carter's fiscal conservatism, partly instinctual and partly situational, brought him into conflict with his party's constituency groups from the outset of his presidency. The American Federation of Labor attacked the administration's initial January 1977 stimulus plan for emphasizing tax cuts over job creation, and organized labor continued to hammer Carter thereafter for devoting too much attention to the battle against inflation and not enough to the achievement of full employment.[92] Black leaders sniped at the administration—the Congressional Black Caucus was especially outspoken—for its failure to embrace the Humphrey-Hawkins bill, which, in its original form, would have made the federal government the economy's employer of last resort in the drive for full employment.[93]

On their part, administration policymakers grew exasperated with the inability of their party cohorts to recognize the imperatives of the new economic circumstances. Carter subsequently recalled that "even in . . . the spring of '77, I was already getting strong opposition from my Democratic leadership in dealing with economics. All they knew about it was stimulus and Great Society programs."[94] As a result, the president confided to his diary early in 1978, "in many cases I feel more at home with the conservative Democratic and Republican members of Congress than I do with the . . . liberals."[95] OMB director James McIntyre complained that the party's constituency groups were impossible to please: "Every time we added money to those constituency programs, the constituents were not satisfied. They always wanted more." "We are giving them 90 percent of their agenda," commented White House media adviser Gerald Rafshoon, "and all they talked about was the 10 percent they were not getting."[96]

Party liberals battled Carter over budgetary restraints from both within and without. At HEW, Secretary Joseph Califano bridled at being told to reform welfare only to have the White House back away when the changes he proposed appeared too costly.[97] Rallying the forces of the old-style liberalism, Senator Kennedy called for an expansive, expensive national health insurance system at the same time Carter was postponing his own promised health insurance legislation for fiscal reasons and telling Americans that they "must face a time of national austerity" and make "hard choices . . . if we want to avoid consequences that are even worse." By the time Democrats met at their midterm party conference in Memphis in 1978, the liberal rebellion against the president's fiscal conservatism was at full tilt, with Kennedy and United Auto Workers president Douglas Fraser leading the charge.[98]

The liberal rebellion culminated in Kennedy's challenge for the 1980 Democratic nomination. Carter vowed to "whip his ass" if Kennedy entered the primaries against him, and the incumbent went into the New York City convention with a decisive lead in delegates. The Kennedy forces rallied for a final battle on behalf of economic expansion. They demanded wage and price controls, a $12 billion jobs-creation program, a formal renunciation of any action that would significantly increase unemployment, and a prohibition against using high interest rates and unemployment to fight inflation. Realizing that such commitments would, if taken seriously, hamstring meaningful action against inflation, the administration fought back. Domestic adviser Stu Eizenstat worked the convention floor to urge their defeat, only to be shouted down by angry delegates. Kennedy agreed to withdraw the call for wage and price controls, but his forces prevailed on the other economic proposals. Carter refused to endorse the remaining planks but agreed to support their intent. "It is hard to think of another recent occasion," Eizenstat later commented bitterly, "on which a major political party so explicitly acted in ways contrary to common sense, good economics, and the national mood. The convention portrayed a party that had lost touch with economic and political reality." "It was clear to me then," he recalled, "that the party was over, both literally and figuratively."[99]

The Democrats found themselves immobilized as the 1970s ended. The tattered remnants of growth liberalism had appeal but little relevance in a time of limits; the struggle against inflation required a regimen of restraint, sacrifice, and pain that a party coalition nurtured on economic growth and programmatic largess appeared incapable of providing. The gap between the allure of expansive government activism and the reality of fiscal responsibility constituted, according to the historian Steven Gillon, "the central problem facing the modern Democratic party." In October 1980, Vice President Walter Mondale called upon progressives to "adjust the liberal values of social justice and compassion to a new age of limited resources."[100] The failure of the Democrats to achieve such a redefinition in the 1970s left the party adrift without a compelling guiding theme.

V. The Legacy of Ambivalence

The Democrats were not the only ones confounded by the many-sided retreat from growth in the 1970s. A decade of challenges to growth, both rhetorical and real, left Americans of all political stripes disconcerted. In the late 1970s Daniel Yankelovich and Bernard Lefkowitz examined the existing polling data and found Americans "midway between an older post–World War II attitude of expanding horizons, a growing psychology of entitlement, unfettered optimism, and unqualified confidence in technology and economic growth, and a present state of mind of lowering expectations, apprehensions about the future, mistrust in institutions, and a growing psychology of limits." Researchers at the University of Michigan's Survey Research Center agreed that "the certainty and assurance which prevailed in the early postwar years has given way in the 1970s to public disorientation and confusion."[101]

Attitudes toward growth manifested a distinctly schizoid quality. On the one side, the Harris Survey reported "a deep skepticism about the nation's capacity for unlimited economic growth . . . [and] the benefits that growth is supposed to bring." Such views, Louis Harris concluded, "suggest that a quiet revolution might be taking place in our national values and aspirations."[102] But even while this skepticism was intensifying, Americans were also answering pollsters' questions in a way that bespoke a rising sense of material entitlement. Throughout the mid-1970s, the number of people agreeing that "it is permissible to buy the things I want when I want them" increased year by year.[103] While presiding over the White House Conference on Balanced Growth, West Virginia governor John D. Rockefeller IV complained that Americans evinced little inclination "to conserve or to change their lifestyles or to even dream about that particularly. . . . In fact, the ethic of 'more' seems very much to be our national standard."[104]

Carter's final attempt to set forth a national agenda reinforced the ambivalence about growth rather than dispelling or resolving it. Soon after his malaise speech of July 1979, the president brought Hedley Donovan, the former editor of *Time*, into the administration and asked him to set up a commission to examine the long-range direction of the country. "Something has changed in the national spirit," Donovan told the White House senior staff. "America is not itself when it lacks faith in the future and . . . a vision of the future." Donovan's proposed President's Commission on a National Agenda for the Eighties would provide such a vision by addressing "the present national mood and . . . the very broad question of how some sense of common purpose and optimism might be resolved."[105]

At Donovan's urging, William J. McGill, the president of Columbia University, took over as the commission's chairman and set about to model the enterprise after President Dwight D. Eisenhower's 1960 Commission on National Goals. After 15 months, McGill and his 45 commissioners had expended $2.8 million, invested over 5,000 hours of work, and produced a total of 1,236 pages of published findings and recommendations—but the result differed fundamentally from the Eisenhower model.[106] As McGill and his colleagues noted in the opening passages of their final report, America had "changed significantly in the past two decades." The optimistic mood of the 1960s—"the generally accepted view . . . that there were no inherent limitations"—was gone, likely forever. "A new constellation of factors" now required the United States "to make some fundamental choices." The reality of limits required "that we set priorities, that we choose among many good and decent ends." And merely choosing did not guarantee success: "Whatever decisions are made," the commissioners concluded, "we as a nation shall not painlessly achieve most of the larger goals, nor easily solve many of the difficult problems." The Commission on a National Agenda for the Eighties had as subdued a vision of America's future as did the president to whom they reported.[107]

The question of how best to respond to the new age of limits sparked a debate within the commission on the issue of economic growth. The commission's panel on "The American Economy" argued that the restoration of "substantial economic growth" constituted the nation's "highest economy priority." Admitting that a full return to the growth rates of the early postwar period might be "unrealistic" and disavowing a growth-at-any-cost approach, the panel nevertheless stressed that the restoration of growth was a necessary precondition for the achievement of both an improved standard of living and the panoply of social justice and quality-of-life objectives.[108] But the commission's panel on "The Quality of American Life" took a very different tack, urging an accommodation to "the likelihood of a continued transition to slower economic growth."

The quality-of-life panelists found the prospect of a return to higher growth rates neither undesirable nor impossible, but maintained that "the costs of such a return would be considerable—and perhaps more than the American public would be willing to pay." A key task for national leaders in the 1980s would be "to cope with the tensions between high expectations and the realities of . . . resource constraints and somewhat slower growth rates."[109] In the end, the commission resolved the differences between the two panels in favor of growth: the formal report of the commission as a whole called for "a national commitment to restoring substantial economic growth." But this, too, was hedged by an accompanying call for a "sustained and successful anti-inflation program."[110] Not even Jimmy Carter's designated visionaries, it seemed, could avoid the ambivalence about growth that by 1980 had become a central feature of public policy discourse.

The sociologist Amitai Etzioni reported to the President's Commission on an Agenda for the Eighties on precisely the matter of such ambivalence. He noted that a recent poll found that 30 percent of Americans were "progrowth," 31 percent "anti-growth," and 39 percent highly uncertain somewhere in between. The nation, Etzioni declared, was torn between its commitment to two core projects, a mass production-mass consumption society on the one hand and a quality-of-life society on the other. The result was a peculiar "social-psychic disarray" that seemed to be everywhere in evidence at decade's end. But, the sociologist predicted, such cognitive dissonance could not continue much longer. Americans would have to choose between "rededication to the industrial, mass-consumption society" or "clearer commitment to a slow-growth, quality-of-life society." "In the long run," he wrote, "high ambivalence is too stressful for societies to endure."[111] In 1980, Ronald Reagan proved Etzioni correct. In winning the presidency, the erstwhile movie actor performed one of the most striking political feats of the modern era: he stole the growth issue that had for a generation been a Democratic staple, repackaged it, and made it his own. What Richard Nixon sought to do by stealth and indirection, Reagan did with flare and fanfare. In the 1980s, Reagan used the growth issue to alter fundamentally, in ways both good and bad, intended and unintended, the political economy of modern America.

6

The Reagan Revolution and
Antistatist Growthmanship

Both good stories and strong arguments can be ruined by exaggeration, which, often as not, is driven less by an urge to deceive than by a desire to keep things simple. The temptations of neatness are especially acute for historians, who have the difficult task of making the past comprehensible without sacrificing the bewildering complexity that usually characterizes human affairs. As we have seen, many policymakers, opinion molders, and ordinary Americans appeared to give up on growth in the 1970s. Yet, even during the general retreat from growth, others continued to look to growth as a way out of the nation's apparent economic dilemma. Their efforts constituted the real beginnings, in the 1970s, of what later came to be labeled the Reagan Revolution. That conservative reorientation of public affairs began not when Ronald Reagan took the oath of office in January 1981, or even at the time of his election to the presidency several months earlier, but rather in the more obscure byways of the past, in the fumblings of the mid-1970s to somehow recapture the economic and psychological momentum of the economic golden age that had come to an effective end in 1968 and that Richard Nixon's exertions had failed to reawaken. In the 1980s Ronald Reagan built on these beginnings by appropriating economic growth in an effort to drive a stake through the heart of modern liberalism.

I. Casting about for a Policy

As Nixon's economic initiatives collapsed disastrously, along with the

rest of his presidency, in the aftermath of Watergate and the onset of stagflation, other political leaders, unwilling to participate in the retreat from
growth under way in the broad culture, cast about for ways to recapture the
economic vigor of the early, halcyon postwar years. The ensuing search
continued from Nixon's final days until the end of the decade and generated
three major approaches. From the left side of the political spectrum came a
proposal for a demand-side fiscal Keynesianism that hearkened back to the
call for full employment at the end of World War II and to the growth economics of Leon Keyserling. Others, again chiefly liberals, took a different
tack, proposing to recapture economic momentum by means of microeconomic intervention and guidance at the level of particular business sectors
and individual firms: so-called industrial policy. Meanwhile, on a third front,
conservatives suggested a dramatic departure from standard Keynesian
demand-side macroeconomic analysis, recasting their traditional preference
for reduced taxes and small government in the form of a new growth-oriented economic analysis and policy that focused on the preeminent contribution of the supply side to the task of increasing economic well-being.
Over the course of the 1970s, the struggle among these competing prescriptions for growth yielded no clear winner, but in the long run it prepared the
way for the conservative reorientation of the U.S. political economy that
distinguished the 1980s.

In June 1974, Representative Augustus F. Hawkins, a Democrat from the
congressional district around the Watts area of Los Angeles, and Representative Henry S. Reuss, a Wisconsin Democrat, introduced the Equal Opportunity and Full Employment Bill. Hawkins characterized the bill as an
attempt to "return to the original intent of the Murray-Wagner full
employment bill as introduced in 1945." Two months later, Senator Hubert
H. Humphrey introduced a counterpart version in the Senate. Commonly
called Humphrey-Hawkins, the proposed legislation was, as the historian
Wyatt C. Wells has put it, "essentially a plan to expand demand as fast as
possible."[1] The *New Republic* observed that "the only ironclad rule" in
Humphrey-Hawkins was "that from now on every administration should
be required to foster growth in the economy." Although the journal characterized Keyserling as "the father" of Humphrey-Hawkins, he had no hand
in the original drafting of the legislation. However, he played a prominent
role as Hawkins's representative when the bill was subsequently redrafted
on its way to ultimate passage (working with Jerry Jasinowski from the staff
of the Joint Economic Committee, three AFL-CIO representatives, and the
principals themselves); he also testified in support of the bill on numerous

occasions and fought energetically both privately and publicly to secure its approval. In the end, Keyserling could claim at least indirect intellectual paternity, because the bill embodied his demand-side, spending approach and his strong pro-growth orientation.[2]

Over the next several years, Humphrey-Hawkins stayed at the top of the liberals' legislative agenda. Civil rights groups and organized labor gave the bill vigorous support. Along the way to its final passage in 1978, Humphrey-Hawkins underwent considerable revision, but its fundamentals remained essentially the following: the bill recognized employment at a "decent" wage as a personal right and committed the federal government to a numerical, long-term full-employment goal; in order to achieve that goal, it called for an annual presidential Full Employment and Balanced Growth Plan to coordinate long-range fiscal and monetary policy; and it established that, in the event the private sector could not fulfill the bill's pledge of full employment, the federal government would operate as the employer of last resort and provide public service jobs for all able and willing adults.[3]

Two central premises underlay the particular provisions of Humphrey-Hawkins, and both reflected Leon Keyserling's influence. The first assumption was that the problem of stagflation in the 1970s was more a problem of stagnation than of inflation and that it needed to be addressed chiefly as a failure of demand. In Keyserling's estimation, slow growth and consequent economic stagnation resulted primarily from the inadequacy of demand brought on by a maldistribution of income. Historically, he told his fellow Democrats in 1974, productive capacity had been allowed to grow significantly faster than demand: "When this has resulted in blatant overcapacity,'" he argued, "the sharp cutbacks in business investment plus the enduring and larger deficiencies in ultimate demand have brought on stagnation and then recession."[4] The surest remedy was to strive for full employment as a way of improving income distribution and ensuring adequate demand. "More rapid expansion of private consumption and increased public outlays" would position the economy "for vigorous movement toward reasonably full resource use."[5]

The second key assumption underlying Humphrey-Hawkins was the belief that such action to bolster demand could be undertaken with little concern for inflationary dangers. Keyserling believed that the so-called Phillips curve, which proposed a trade-off between employment and inflation (when one went up, the theory had it, the other went down), was an "utter fallacy." In his view, it was the suppression of real economic growth and the acceptance of excess unemployment, often in the mistaken effort to attain price stability, rather than any boosting of demand by the federal government, that constituted the most serious source of inflationary pressure. A "stunted and repressed economy" caused a "tremendous decline in the rate of productivity gains," and this in turn resulted in higher per unit labor costs and inevitable price increases.[6]

The opponents of Humphrey-Hawkins attacked both of these assumptions. Some disputed the analysis that fixed on demand as the crucial factor. In time, their line of criticism would contribute to the emergence of a new supply-side economics, a topic discussed at length below. A much broader array of critics expressed concern over the inflationary danger in the Humphrey-Hawkins approach. The opposition from conservative economists was somewhat predictable. Milton Friedman characterized the bill as "close to a fraud" and warned that it would "very likely ignit[e] . . . a new inflationary binge."[7] More damaging was the criticism of influential Democrats, including John Kenneth Galbraith, Arthur Okun, Alice Rivlin (director of the Congressional Budget Office), Paul Samuelson, and George Schultze. Schultze, who had served in the Bureau of the Budget under Johnson and would become chairman of the CEA under Jimmy Carter, was a particularly effective critic precisely because he seemed to eschew ideological posturing. "Every time we push the rate of unemployment toward acceptably low levels, by whatever means," he warned, "we set off a new inflation. And in turn, both the political and economic consequences of inflation make it impossible to achieve full employment or, once having achieved it, to keep the economy there."[8] The nonpartisan Congressional Research Service of the Library of Congress concluded similarly that Humphrey-Hawkins would "greatly accelerate the inflationary spiral."[9]

The supporters of Humphrey-Hawkins, on the other hand, believed that the dangers of inaction were themselves considerable, justifying strong action and the taking of some risks. Speaker of the House Carl Albert (D., Okla.) warned that extended joblessness was creating "a sizable segment of our population in danger of developing an alienated way of life, of becoming a class apart, separated from the mainstream of our society and maintained by an inequitable and inadequate welfare system."[10] To Keyserling, the challenge was moral as much as it was technical. "The whole problem in the United States," he asserted in 1975, "isn't economic at all, it's moral. . . . We don't sufficiently recognize our moral obligation toward unemployed people . . . or toward the poor." Americans, he claimed, had "the capacity within 10 years to remove the conventional economic problems, and devote ourselves entirely to the higher purposes of life."[11] To the critics of

Humphrey-Hawkins, such noble intentions threatened to compound problems rather than solve them. Herbert Stein noted that the bill aimed at "achieving all kinds of good things" but that it demanded that the federal government achieve them all at once, refusing to "recognize any difficulty in achieving any of them, except lack of heart and will."[12]

In time, the weight of criticism, the force of opposition, and the lukewarm enthusiasm of President Jimmy Carter and his advisers compelled the sponsors of Humphrey-Hawkins to make significant concessions in order to win congressional approval. By the time Carter signed the Full Employment and Balanced Growth Act of 1978 into law in October, the original Humphrey-Hawkins proposal had been considerably diluted. For example, the final version eliminated the absolute, legally enforceable right to a job for all willing and able Americans, as well as the specific mechanisms for job creation by the government acting as employer of last resort. The numerical goal of a 3 percent rate of unemployment for adult Americans within four years was reduced to a slightly less demanding goal of a 3 percent adult and 4 percent overall rate of unemployment within five years. Most significant, in the final version of Humphrey-Hawkins lawmakers added to the unemployment goal a specific (albeit explicitly subordinate) goal of reducing the rate of inflation to 3 percent within five years and to zero percent by 1988, thus introducing a tension between the goals of maximum employment and absolute price stability that made it unlikely the act would be administered in the fashion originally intended. Finally, in part at Carter's urging, a number of escape clauses left open the possibility that either the president or Congress could alter the bill's numerical targets if economic circumstances justified deviation.

The changes written into the bill as it made its way through the legislative process and the fashion in which its particulars were subsequently administered dashed the original hopes of the Humphrey-Hawkins supporters. In crucial regards, the act was a dead letter from the outset. Three days before signing Humphrey-Hawkins into law, President Carter announced a new anti-inflation program, setting off a new round of budget-cutting; in January 1979, the administration followed the letter of the law by submitting to Congress an unemployment goal for 1979 and 1980 of 6.2 percent, which was actually higher than the then-current unemployment rate. When Carter and his advisers made it clear that they were willing to countenance higher unemployment in their struggle to bring inflation under control, Representative Hawkins complained that the administration was violating "the intent of the Humphrey-Hawkins Act for 1979 and 1980" and making it "utterly impossible to reach the mid-1983 goals."[13] From the vantage point of the mid-1980s, Keyserling complained bitterly but correctly, "Since 1978, neither the President nor the Congress has paid any significant attention to the large purposes of the . . . Act."[14]

In the end, the recycling of demand-side, Keynesian growth economics proved an expensive and chimerical episode for Democrats. They expended much political energy and capital to pass a law that in retrospect yielded only relatively minor procedural advances—the requirement of specific numerical targets and the requirement of regular explanations by the Federal Reserve concerning the relationship among its monetary policies, the president's targets, and the Humphrey-Hawkins goals. By any calculus, the cost was exorbitant. The actions of the Carter administration in avowing support for Humphrey-Hawkins, so long as its most egregious flaws were remedied, and then abandoning its larger purposes in the wholly defensible (but also wholly predictable) struggle against inflation smacked of disingenuous betrayal and helped complete a break between Carter and the Democratic left wing that neither could afford. To the administration, the supporters of Humphrey-Hawkins appeared to be woolly-headed idealists out of touch with the more intractable aspects of economic reality; in the eyes of the Left, Carter and his advisers stood convicted of hard-hearted perfidy.

An alternative to the traditional demand-management Keynesianism of Humphrey-Hawkins appeared simultaneously, although it would later come to be remembered more as an artifact of the 1980s: industrial policy. Whereas fiscal and monetary policies are generally macroeconomic, intended to affect broadly the entire economy, industrial policy is microeconomic, designed to influence behavior in particular sectors. The purpose is usually to cushion the decline of older industries or to encourage the rise of new technologies. Industrial policy took hold after World War II in both Europe and Japan, and seemed to many observers to account significantly for the competitive vigor of those economies in the 1970s. As the American economic system faltered, some liberal advocates of government planning borrowed inspiration from the "indicative planning" of the Europeans and the institutional wizardry of the Japanese Ministry of International Trade and Industry (MITI) and sought to duplicate their feats in the U.S. economy.[15]

One of the earliest forays into the realm of industrial policy began somewhat accidentally during the closing days of the Nixon presidency, when the beleaguered administration in 1974 created the National Commission on Supplies and Shortages, which was intended to provide guidance for dealing with the energy crunch touched off by the Arab oil embargo. Nixon stacked the group with conservatives in order to produce a moderate outcome; but Senator Hubert Humphrey later added to the commission a small unit that labored under the unwieldy title of Advisory Committee on National Growth Policy Processes, and this latter group pushed beyond Nixon's original intentions to help pioneer the idea of an American industrial policy.

The initial formulation of industrial policy reflected the deepening economic pessimism of the day. The Advisory Committee on National Growth Policy Processes reported that the historical "frontier society" had come to an end and that a new "American approach to planning" was needed to guide the nation "from a world view of limitless resources and opportunities to one in which both are limited." The "new phase of industrial and societal development" required Americans to "conserve, husband our resources, define more sharply our objectives at home, [and] use our strength more selectively abroad." Only planning, down to the level of regions and sectors, could achieve these ends. Among its recommendations, the committee called for the creation of a center for statistical policy and analysis to gather data for use by, among others, a new "sectoral economic staff" in the Executive Office of the President, which would "follow and analyze key sectors of the private economy on the President's behalf." In the end, the committee's report had little practical impact. Indeed, a close reading of the reservations expressed by the individual committee members in the report's codicil makes it clear just how controversial any proposal for the extension of government planning down to the microeconomic level of sectors and firms was. Nevertheless, from these beginnings emerged a discussion that would continue into the 1990s.[16]

Jimmy Carter moved surprisingly far in the direction of industrial policy, at first haltingly, through inadvertence, and later by design. The administration found itself initially driven to sectoral interventions by the travail of sick industries. In an effort to help a steel industry reeling under the onslaught of international competition, Carter in 1977 implemented the so-called Solomon plan (named for the under secretary of the treasury, Anthony M. Solomon, who oversaw its development), which put a price floor under foreign-made steel and called for a tripartite committee to advise on industry modernization. Similarly, when the federal government came to the aid of the ailing Chrysler Corporation in 1979, it coupled a massive infusion of fresh money with ongoing, and initially intrusive, government oversight of the auto manufacturer's performance. Meanwhile, Carter's program of partial deregulation of airlines, gas and oil prices, electric power generation, trucking, railroads, telephone equipment, and banking constituted, in an admittedly paradoxical way, yet another form of intervention into particular industrial sectors.[17]

As his term drew to a close, Carter moved more purposefully toward a sector-specific, microeconomic approach—although still in a fashion characteristically both tentative and ham-fisted. Adrift both politically and economically in 1980, the administration searched for some alternative approach to economic problems that it could, in an election season, call its own. The State Department commissioned studies of the industrial policy experiences of Japan, West Germany, France, and Sweden, while the Treasury Department undertook a historical study of America's own Reconstruction Finance Corporation in the 1930s and 1940s. Meanwhile, an interdepartmental "Economic Policy Group" debated the pros and cons of varying degrees and styles of sectoral intervention. Carter's domestic adviser, Stuart Eizenstat, wrote to the president, "I believe an initiative on an industrial policy . . . would excite . . . [blue-collar] workers and offer the nation hope that our basic industries will remain competitive." Finally, in August 1980, Carter announced a new "Economic Revitalization Program," which included a national development bank, an Economic Revitalization Board, tripartite committees for major industries, and a host of targeted policies for particular industries.[18]

In the end, nothing came of Carter's industrial policy initiative. It was, the historian Otis Graham has written, "stillborn." The press largely ignored the president's proposals, the Economic Revitalization Board never met, and Reagan's overwhelming victory in the November election ensured that industrial policy would for the foreseeable future be more talked about outside government than acted upon inside government. Even the Carter administration seemed to disown the idea that it had momentarily embraced: its final Economic Report, submitted in January 1980, included a section entitled "The Dilemma of Industrial Policy," which contended that the basic industrial policy practices of encouraging emergent industries and supporting declining ones went "beyond the legitimate needs for balance, consistency, and flexibility in Federal actions affecting individual industrial sectors."[19]

Because of such confusion and a deep national ambivalence about the wisdom and propriety of systematic state intervention in microeconomic affairs, industrial policy remained the subject of heated debate into the 1990s. When the approach seemed to lose its allure, some of its champions linked it to economic globalization and repackaged it as strategic trade policy. Increasingly, the boosters of industrial policy promised a return to the fast growth track. Calling for "the reindustrialization of America," *Business Week,* a staunch champion of industrial policy, proposed a "new social contract" as the basis for economic reinvigoration. Americans needed to pull together, the editors of that business journal declared in June 1980: All social groups needed to acknowledge "their [overriding] common interest in returning the country to . . . strong economic growth." "Indicative planning involving government participation" would make an important contribution to renewed growth.[20]

But industrial policy never recovered from its shaky start in the 1970s. Was such planning designed to achieve growth or—shades of the New Deal's NRA!—to administer limits? And could government microeconomic fine-tuning realistically be expected to succeed at either task when macroeconomic fine-tuning had so clearly failed? Although the merits of industrial policy would continue to be debated, the attention of policymakers had by the end of the 1970s already shifted to an alternative approach that had emerged alongside the demand-side Keynesianism of Humphrey-Hawkins and the planning impulse of industrial policy: supply-side economics. In the end, this third approach would guide the pursuit of growth in the era of Ronald Reagan.

The supply-side alternative took shape most clearly in the tax-cutting proposals advanced by Representative Jack Kemp, a Republican elected in 1970 from a congressional district around Buffalo, New York. Kemp was an unlikely champion of new economic ideas. He came to political economy by way of a professional football career that included two broken ankles, two broken shoulders, a broken knee, and eleven concussions along with his considerable gridiron success. A native Californian, Kemp had been an uninspired student while majoring in physical education at Occidental College; instead of excelling at academics, he channeled his considerable energy into excelling at football. He played quarterback well enough to lead small-college passers in accuracy, and in 1957 graduated into the professional game. In the mid-1960s, Kemp led the Buffalo Bills of the upstart American Football League to two league championships and won recognition as the AFL's player of the year in 1964. He also gained important experience as the elected president of the AFL Players' Association, a players' union that he helped to establish. In 1970, local Republicans recruited him to run for Congress; he won that first election in a squeaker and ultimately served eighteen years, enjoying so much support that he sometimes ran unopposed.

In Congress, Kemp marched to his own drummer. A fierce and dependable conservative on many issues, he was from the beginning what he later characterized as a "bleeding heart conservative": he opposed abortion but strongly supported the Equal Rights Amendment, and he opposed school busing to achieve integration but became one of the Republican Party's most credible champions of racial equality.[21] Most of all, Kemp loved ideas, and the idea dearest to him was economic growth.

In reality, Kemp was more an "opportunity populist" than a traditional Republican conservative, and growth appealed to him because it seemed to be the wellspring of opportunity. Growth would enable the blue-collar voters of Buffalo and its Rustbelt environs to bounce back from the ravages of stagflation. Growth would extend the ladder of opportunity to those born on the margins of American society. Growth would allow many social problems "to take care of themselves," he wrote, and would make those that remained "more manageable." Since the late 1960s, Americans had had "imprinted on the national consciousness a sense of futility about our ability to regain economic vitality." "We are asked," he complained, "to accept the idea that America's dynamism has run into the resource limitations of the earth, and [that] the kind of growth that once was a way of life for Americans is no longer possible."[22] Irrepressibly optimistic, Kemp built his political career on the effort to prove such naysaying wrong.

The Buffalo congressman seized upon tax reduction as the engine to move his growth crusade along. Tax relief was "not so much an end in itself," he claimed, as it was "a means of getting this economy moving again."[23] Thus, it was in the name of growth that Kemp sponsored the Jobs Creation Act of 1975, also known as the Kemp-McClure bill, which aimed at stimulating capital formation and investment rather than boosting demand à la Humphrey-Hawkins. The fifteen individual provisions of Kemp-McClure constituted a smorgasbord of tax relief for business: cuts in the corporate tax rate, increased investment credits, and liberalized provisions governing depreciation and the exclusion of corporate dividends and certain capital gains from taxable income.

On the surface, the debate over Kemp-McClure sounded like the familiar argument that Republicans and Democrats had been having since the end of World War II about who should be the chief beneficiaries of tax relief. Kemp defended his bill's traditional Republican trickle-down economics by arguing that after several decades of government economic policies aimed at bolstering consumption in an effort to offset what Keynesians saw as the modern economy's tendency toward excess savings, it was finally time to stimulate production directly. The initial increase in the deficit resulting from his production-enhancing tax cuts would be more than counterbalanced, he claimed, by the additional revenues generated by the growth his incentives would release.[24] To critics such as Keyserling, who at the time was fighting hard on behalf of the competing Humphrey-Hawkins approach, Kemp's proposed Jobs Creation Act was "unsound economics and erroneous social policy." Sticking to his Keynesian guns, Keyserling insisted that the problem of adequate business investment was not lack of adequate capital but rather "lack of adequate ultimate demand." Kemp's approach, he said, was "'class legislation' of the worst sort" that would "make the tax burden even more regressive . . . by shifting a larger portion of the burden to those least able to pay, especially low income people, and away from those best able to pay."[25]

The debate over revenue policy took a new twist, however, when Kemp expanded his tax-cutting effort. Kemp himself soon came to view the exclusive emphasis on business taxes in the Jobs Creation Act of 1975 as a mistake. With the help of Norman Ture, who ran a Washington consulting firm, and Paul Craig Roberts, an economist on Kemp's own legislative staff, the congressman developed a new, broader, supply-side rationale for his tax-cutting proclivities. In late September 1975, Kemp published an op-ed piece in the *Washington Star* that emphasized that tax reduction done the right way would have its chief impact not by boosting demand but rather by affecting supply-side incentives; most significant, he suggested that the broadest improvement of incentives could be obtained by reducing the marginal rates in the income tax. In the spring of 1976, Jude Wanniski, an associate editor of the *Wall Street Journal*, helped push Kemp farther down the supply-side path. The journalist reinforced the idea that the key to economic prosperity was to increase economic incentives by trimming marginal tax rates, and helped persuade Kemp that it was therefore necessary to go beyond Kemp-McClure's emphasis on tax cuts for business.[26] Later that year, Kemp told the Republican national convention that "ideas rule the world" and that it was time for the Republicans "to move the American people with our ideas once again."[27] Kemp's own formulation of a broad-based supply-side tax cut provided Republicans with the idea that would galvanize their effort throughout the rest of the decade to wrest political control of the nation from the faltering Democrats.

Kemp by now had become fascinated with the political and economic success of the famed Kennedy-Johnson tax cut of 1964–65. The *Wall Street Journal* openly likened his evolving views on economic growth through tax reduction to those of Kennedy and his advisers, and early in 1977 Kemp asked his new staff economist Bruce R. Bartlett (Roberts had departed to become minority staff economist for the House Budget Committee) to "draft a bill explicitly duplicating the Kennedy tax cut." In July 1977, Kemp joined Delaware's Republican senator William Roth in introducing the Kemp-Roth Tax Reduction Act, which called for a 30 percent reduction in personal income rates, to be phased in over three years. Where the Kennedy-Johnson tax cut had reduced the highest personal income tax rate from 91 to 70 percent, Kemp-Roth aimed to move it from 70 to 50 percent; where the earlier cut had reduced the lowest rate from 20 to 14 percent, Kemp-Roth aimed to slice that still further, from 14 to 8 percent. The Republican leadership in the House and the Republican National Committee quickly endorsed the bill, and within months Kemp-Roth emerged as the chief Republican solution to America's stagflation malaise.[28]

The response of professional economists to Kemp-Roth was divided and vehement. The critics of Kemp-Roth, chiefly liberal Democrats and fiscally conservative Republicans, were unusually outspoken in their denunciation of the bill as an irresponsible free lunch that would further stoke the flames of an already dangerous inflation. Gardner Ackley called Kemp-Roth "the most irresponsible policy proposal—seriously advanced by people who should know better—that I can recall during the nearly forty years I have been closely observing or participating in national economic policy-making." If he and his fellow Keynesians were correct that "tax cuts increase aggregate demand by much more than they raise aggregate supply," the "mammoth" reductions called for by Kemp-Roth "could produce an inflationary outburst that would dwarf anything we have seen up to now." Franco Modigliani of the Massachusetts Institute of Technology warned that the Republican program would "do irreparable damage to the United States economy." Harvard's Otto Eckstein characterized the changes sought by Kemp-Roth as simply "too large and too sudden." Walter Heller attacked the invocation of the Kennedy-Johnson cut of 1964 as precedent. The earlier cut, he insisted, "was a demand-side response (that is, stepping up consumer and business demand to take up existing slack in labor and product markets)—exactly the opposite of . . . [the] implausible supply-side theory." Even the chief economist for IBM, who argued for the desirability of some sort of tax reduction, considered Kemp-Roth so large as to be likely inflationary and therefore deemed it "unwise."[29] From among Eisenhower's top economic advisers, both Arthur Burns and Neil Jacoby opposed the proposal; the nation needed tax reduction, Jacoby noted, but it needed a balanced budget even more.[30]

A less numerous but hardly undistinguished lot of professional economists supported Kemp-Roth, but their analyses and judgments were rather more guarded and less emphatic. Alan Greenspan, Paul McCracken, and Herbert Stein—all former economic advisers to Republican presidents Nixon and Ford—supported the bill, but they characterized as speculative and extravagant the contention of some supporters that the energizing effects of the cuts would quickly offset the immediate revenue losses from cutting the income tax by a third over three years. Nevertheless, all believed that Kemp-Roth offered the best available vehicle for reining in government expenditures. As McCracken expressed it: "The primary case for Kemp-Roth is a growing conviction that Government has been allocating too much of the national income to itself, and that the time has come to change this."[31] Making the same argument in his regular *Newsweek* column, Milton Friedman wrote that "the only effective way to restrain government spending is by limiting government's explicit tax revenue—just as a limited income is the only effective restraint on any individual's or family's spending."[32] Clearly, these supporters valued what Kemp-Roth would do to the size of the public sector at the federal level as much as its vaunted ability to generate a dramatic growth spurt through heightened incentives to produce.

While the experts debated, Kemp-Roth struck a resonant chord with the general public. A 1978 Roper poll reported that the public supported a 30 percent tax cut by a two-to-one margin. The popular mood had finally caught up with Kemp. Antitax sentiment swelled as inflation relentlessly drove people into higher and higher tax-rate brackets without really having made them richer—the dreaded phenomenon known as "bracket creep." In some locales, inflation helped produce a real estate boom that brought large increases in real estate values and hence property taxes at a time when incomes were stagnating. The most dramatic manifestation of antitax sentiment came in the great California tax revolt of 1978, when voters handily approved Proposition 13, which capped the maximum rate of property taxation and prohibited the state and the local California governments from raising existing taxes or imposing new ones without a two-thirds majority vote in the affected jurisdiction. The cut in property taxes put additional money in people's pockets, but did so without altering the incentive to save and invest more, which was the most distinctive feature and the raison d' être of the new supply-side emphasis. Nevertheless, Kemp characterized the California initiative as sounding "a coast-to-coast appeal for a solution to oppressive tax rates," and his staff economist later wrote that Kemp-Roth "got a big boost" from the way that the debate over Prop 13 influenced the general political and economic climate.[33] A less noticed but equally significant straw in the wind was the passage in the fall of 1978 of a capital gains tax cut that effectively reduced the maximum tax rate on capital gains from roughly 49 to 28 percent. The capital gains cut was enacted by strong bipartisan majorities in both houses despite the opposition of the Carter administration, whose spokesmen reviled the proposal as the "Millionaire's Relief Act of 1978."[34]

Despite such favorable developments, at decade's end Kemp-Roth remained stuck in the legislative mill. Republicans had rallied to the cause but could not pass their program. On the several occasions when they managed to bring their handiwork to a vote, Kemp-Roth was defeated. But in another sense, Kemp and his allies had succeeded wildly in seizing control of the debate about the future shape of the economy and direction of policy. While Humphrey-Hawkins slipped quietly into the oblivion of studied inaction and outright evasion and while industrial policy remained the stuff of academic debate rather than the guiding principle of public policy, the Kemp-Roth tax cut proposal became an important vehicle for the fundamental reconsideration of the Keynesian demand-side analysis and prescription that had dominated national economic policy since the end of World War II. As the 1970s came to an end, the casting about for an alternative path to growth narrowed down to the promise of a supply-side revolution.

II. The Supply-Side Intellectual Revolution

The tax-cutting approach of Kemp-Roth gained influence in part because of the sustenance and support it derived from developments within the discipline of economics itself. The rise of a number of new theoretical insights emerging from the routine cut and thrust of intellectual life, together with the apparent inadequacy of existing theory to explain and deal with stagflation, resulted in a fierce challenge to the Keynesian analytical orthodoxy. Once this challenge had weakened the regnant demand-side paradigm, the way was open for the rise of a new, alternative school of supply-side economic analysis, of which Kemp-Roth quickly became the showcase policy embodiment.

The challenge to the Keynesian paradigm, which unfolded largely within the economics profession's mainstream channels of discussion, came in three distinct waves.[35] The first began with warnings in the late 1960s that the conventional wisdom regarding the mutual exclusivity of stagnation and inflation was simply wrong. The established view held that there existed a trade-off between unemployment and inflation—when the one decreased, the other rose. This relationship appeared to be forcefully demonstrated in the work of a New Zealand economist working at the London School of Economics, A. W. Phillips, who in the late 1950s observed that British statistics indicated that wages and unemployment had varied inversely over a long period. His quantification of this tendency became the well-known Phillips curve, and American scholars soon discerned a similar pattern in the U.S. data. From the Phillips curve, Keynesians drew the implicit lesson that they could use discretionary fiscal and monetary policy to fine-tune the economy along the curve and in that way achieve an acceptable level of unemployment at a moderate level of inflation.[36]

In his 1967 presidential address to the American Economic Association, Milton Friedman devastated the conceptual underpinnings of the Phillips curve and struck the single most telling intellectual blow against the reigning Keynesianism. James Tobin, a prominent Keynesian and the 1981 recipient of the Nobel Prize in economics, described the published version of Friedman's address as "very likely the most influential article ever published in an economics journal."[37] Friedman argued that there existed a "natural rate of unemployment," which is dictated by the particular structural and institutional characteristics of the economy, especially the labor market, at any given point in time; to lower unemployment below the natural rate by trading off a bit of inflation was in the long run impossible. Any such attempt would require increasing rates of inflation and would in the end result in the disastrous condition of stagflation (although Friedman did not use that term), with high inflation and high unemployment coexisting in calamitous tandem. "There is always a temporary trade-off between inflation and unemployment," Friedman concluded, "[but] there is no permanent trade-off."[38] The hope of paying for a decrease in unemployment below the economy's "natural" or structural level with only a modicum of inflation was illusory. In other words, Friedman was calling into question Keynesianism's most basic policy prescription, the stimulation of demand in order to reduce unemployment. If Friedman was right—and he was—the activist Keynesian paradigm and the U.S. economy were in for serious trouble (as the subsequent experience of the 1970s seemed to prove).

The second wave of the assault on Keynesianism came in the 1970s in the work of the Nobel Prize-winning economist Robert Lucas and his followers of the so-called rational expectations school. Although they elaborated their theories in dauntingly dense and complex formulations, Lucas and his adherents pointed to a deceptively simple conclusion: they argued that predictable government intervention was destined to be futile and ineffectual because economic actors would anticipate it. For example, if government historically responded to recession by boosting demand, firms caught in a downturn would expect the government to do so again and be tempted simply to raise prices in anticipation of government action rather than allowing them to fall or increasing their output. Policy could successfully change behavior only by surprising or fooling economic actors, and, of course, the unpredictableness of a self-conscious policy of surprise carried with it still other dangers of instability. Thus, government activism of any sort was suspect. Little wonder, then, that the president of the Federal Reserve Bank of Minneapolis, Mark H. Willes, wrote, "Until the early 1970s, the economists who opposed the Keynesians had to be content with pulling a few fish off of their opponents' hooks. But when what has become known as the theory of rational expectations began to be developed, these economists found that they could simply dynamite all the fish in the lake."[39] Willes's comment understated the significance of Friedman's demolition of the Phillips curve, but captured well the contemporary judgment regarding the radical implications of the rational expectations approach. In his presidential address to the American Economic Association in 1976, Franco Modigliani called the incorporation of the rational expectations hypothesis into Friedman's critique "the death blow to the already battered Keynesian position."[40]

A third and final, somewhat more oblique attack on Keynesian orthodoxy came in the field that soon came to be called the New Public Finance. Led by such luminaries as Harvard's Martin Feldstein, this movement argued that existing tax disincentives—the ways in which the tax system discouraged desirable economic behavior—were greater than Keynesians admitted, that they seriously distorted saving and investment decisions, and that the inflation of the 1970s was exacerbating those effects by pushing individual and corporate taxpayers into ever-higher brackets based on inflationary, nominal rather than real, gains. By 1980, the work of the New Public Finance school—Feldstein, his Harvard colleague Lawrence Summers, and Stanford's Michael Boskin—had, according to Paul Krugman, "convinced many economists that U.S. taxes were in fact a significant obstacle to investment."[41]

By the end of the 1970s, the combined weight of these professional challenges had left the Keynesian paradigm in tatters. "By about 1980, it was hard to find an American academic macroeconomist under the age of 40 who professed to be a Keynesian," lamented Alan Blinder, himself an economist of such inclination at Princeton University. That this "intellectual turnabout" had transpired "in less than a decade" was, in his eyes, "astonishing."[42] With less sadness, Robert Lucas wrote in 1981 that Keynesianism was "in deep trouble, the deepest kind of trouble in which an applied body of theory can find itself: It appears to be giving wrong answers to the most basic questions of macroeconomic policy."[43] Pragmatists and policymakers in the middle, who gave allegiance wholly to neither Keynes nor his academic detractors, found themselves adrift on the currents of academic debate and real-world ineffectiveness. As Paul Volcker explained to a journalist, "We're all Keynesians now—in terms of the way we look at things. National income statistics are a Keynesian view of the world, and the language of economists tends to be Keynesian. But if you mean by Keynesian that we've got to pump up the economy, that all these relationships are pretty clear and simple, that this gives us a tool for eternal prosperity if we do it right, that's all bullshit."[44]

The weakening of the Keynesian consensus in both macroeconomics (because of intellectual challenges) and policy (because of the practical failure to deal effectively with stagflation) opened the way for the emergence of a new, competing approach to economic problems that would subordinate the Keynesian emphasis on the management of demand to a renewed attention to the problems of supply. The resultant "supply-side economics" was a complex mixture of intellectual insights from within the economic mainstream—often rediscovered ideas from the pre-Keynesian past—and prescriptions from the more highly and overtly politicized worlds of public policy and advocacy journalism.

Whereas the attacks on the existing Keynesian consensus had taken place within the economics discipline's traditional channels of professionally scrutinized theoretical disputation—in refereed journals and the like—the framing of the supply-side alternative occurred more in the rough-and-tumble of policy debate and was, therefore, a more haphazard and inchoate process. As late as 1981, one supply-sider has noted, "there were no distinctive supply-side texts, no courses, no distinguished scholar, and no school of supply-side economists."[45] Nevertheless, the formulation of supply-side economics has not lacked for chroniclers, and the recollections of the participants enable us to chart the development of the doctrine with some precision and confidence.

Just what constituted the essence of the supply-side approach that took shape as the Keynesian approach went into decline has been a matter of dispute. The champions of the new school have complained bitterly about being misquoted and mischaracterized. Notwithstanding such controversy, the basic outlines of their position are clear. First, they emphasized that supply matters greatly, an economic truism that had, in fact, been lost sight of since the triumph of Keynes, in the aftermath of which the chief economic problem had seemed to be the maintenance of sufficiently high aggregate demand to keep pace with the economy's recurrent tendency toward over-production. Supply-siders shifted attention back to the problem of produc-tivity and how to raise it. Second, in achieving this rediscovery of the relative significance of supply, the supply-siders also necessarily shifted attention away from macroeconomics, with its concern for aggregate behavior, and back to the behavior of discrete economic actors—individuals and firms. Third, following the logic of their broad suppositions, the supply-siders believed that the way to achieve prosperity without inflation was to expand supply by increasing the incentives for individuals to work, save, and invest: the surest way to achieve such results was to cut taxes, especially the existing high marginal rates—those tax rates that applied to the last dollar of income and that therefore most discouraged extra effort and enterprise. Such a tax reduction, they claimed, would raise real output—not by increasing demand but by operating on the supply side of the economy. Full-bore supply-siders went so far as to assert that such tax cuts would be so powerful as to actually generate more revenue than would be lost by the cuts themselves.[46]

The theoretical base for these supply-side ideas derived partly from the classical economics of the nineteenth century and partly from more recent developments at the margin of economic discourse in the early 1970s. At one level, the intellectual founders of the supply-side movement considered that they had chiefly "discovered a lost continent of [pre-Keynesian] eco-nomics." The foundation of the supply-side approach derived from the insights of Adam Smith, Jean-Baptiste Say, and Alfred Marshall. The point of good economics and good government, Say had asserted early in the nine-teenth century, was to stimulate production, not consumption. Supply-siders asserted that the enduring wisdom of Say's insight had been obscured by the wrenching experience of the Great Depression and the subsequent sway enjoyed by Keynes's emphasis on the necessity of maintaining aggre-gate demand. The "new" supply-side economics, wrote insider Norman Ture, was "merely the application of price theory—widely and tastelessly labeled microeconomics—in analysis of problems concerning economic aggregates—widely and tastelessly labeled as macroeconomics. . . . Its new-ness is to be found only in its applications to the public economic policy issues of contemporary American society."[47] Supply-side theory, the econo-mist Arthur Laffer agreed, was "little more than a new label for standard neoclassical economics."[48]

Laffer, who taught at the University of Southern California and had worked at OMB in the Nixon years, and Robert Mundell of Columbia University provided what little updating accompanied the modern formulation of supply-side theory in the 1970s. Both were academic outsiders. After having made significant contributions in the field of international economics early in his career, Mundell served as an eccentric, long-haired economic guru to the Right, organizing conferences at his own Italian villa, increasingly removed from the professional mainstream even as his influence among policy entrepreneurs grew; Laffer remained similarly aloof from the conventional world of academe, but became widely known by virtue of authoring the central heuristic device of the supply-side crusade, the so-called Laffer curve, which illustrated the truism that tax rates set too high were as ineffective at raising revenue as tax rates set too low. Laffer was, Martin Anderson, President Ronald Reagan's chief domestic and economic policy adviser, subsequently wrote, "the first person who took the simple idea of supply-side tax effects that has been around since the dawn of economics and painted a picture of it." It was indicative of the professional remove of the supply-side theoreticians that insiders would subsequently celebrate the fact that Laffer first drew the curve that bore his name on a paper cocktail napkin during a legendary meeting with a White House staffer from the Ford administration at the Two Continents Restaurant across the street from the Treasury Department in Washington. The chief attraction of the Laffer curve was its suggestion that a reduction of tax rates could conceivably pay for itself by generating more revenue, a generally dubious proposition that would ultimately make the device as controversial and professionally suspect as it was politically seductive—no small feat for a truism.[49]

In the mid-1970s, Mundell and Laffer spread their ideas by means of an ongoing, informal supply-side economics seminar-*cum*-dinner that convened at Michael I, a Wall Street area restaurant within yards of the American Stock Exchange in Manhattan. The other participants in the Michael I discussions included Jude Wanniski, an editorialist for the *Wall Street Journal*, who would serve as the emergent movement's energetic and hyperbolic publicist, and Robert Bartley, that newspaper's editor in chief. These two powerful business journalists quickly made the *Journal*'s op-ed page into, as Bartley put it, "a daily bulletin board" for supply-side ideas. Wanniski helped spread the supply-side message to Irving Kristol, a founding father of the neo-conservative movement then starting to blossom; soon the readers of Kristol's increasingly influential journal of opinion, *The Public Interest*, were exposed to approving discussions of supply-side doctrine. Wanniski penned the burgeoning movement's most complete manifesto in 1978, a book that he, with characteristic zeal, entitled *The Way the World Works*. The basic economic prescription formulated at Michael I and subsequently publicized in these neo-conservative forums was tight money to curb inflation and supply-side (i.e., incentive-creating) tax cuts for economic growth.

Meanwhile, the same supply-side approach to fiscal policy emerged independently in a very practical way on Capitol Hill (as we have seen in our discussion of Kemp-Roth in the previous section), where the staff economists Paul Craig Roberts and Bruce R. Bartlett worked with Representative Jack Kemp (and, later, other Republicans) to develop the supply-side ideas that eventuated in Kemp-Roth. Kemp proved to be the linchpin that joined the several wings of the supply-side crusade together. In 1975, Bartley met Kemp in Washington and upon his return to New York, told his *Wall Street Journal* colleague Wanniski, "You'd better get by and meet this guy Kemp; he's quite a piece of horseflesh." Wanniski sought out the young congressman and in short order introduced him to Laffer and Kristol. By mid-1976, the *Wall Street Journal* had begun to champion Kemp as the chief political spokesman for the new intellectual movement. As Kemp emerged as America's first supply-side politician and the movement's political drum major, both the New York theoreticians and publicists and the Washington political economists rallied around him, thereby giving the appearance of unity to a movement that had in reality appeared in different guises and in different places virtually simultaneously.[50]

By April 1976, the new movement had cohered sufficiently to gain its own appellation. In a paper delivered to a meeting of economists, Herbert Stein sketched a taxonomy of economic orientations that included a group he identified as "supply-side fiscalists." Contrary to the myth that soon grew up among supply-siders, a myth nurtured by the tendency of some movement faithful to accentuate their challenge to establishment economics, Stein did not intend the label to be pejorative (although he would quickly become a spirited critic of supply-side doctrine). Audacious pamphleteer that he was, Wanniski seized upon the label but dropped the term "fiscalist" as too limiting. Supply-side economics now had a name.[51]

That the movement deserved to be singled out as a new, valid, or useful contribution to the centuries-old effort to understand and better order the economic affairs of humankind was challenged from the start. To some critics, the supply-side vision was simply a repackaging of common knowledge; to others, it was a pseudoscience whose relationship to "real" economics was similar to the relationship of astrology to astronomy. Herbert

Stein argued that the supply-side dogma was old hat, both theoretically and practically. That supply constituted an important element in economic analysis was, he wrote, something commonly known since the first parrot had gotten a Ph.D. in economics for learning to say "supply and demand." He considered the Laffer curve argument a "shoddy" echo of the argument mounted by business conservatives in the early postwar years that tax cuts could work miracles—increase production, cure inflation, prevent a recession, raise revenue, and perhaps cure the common cold. "They were Lafferites before there was a Laffer curve," he told an audience of professional economists, "and possibly before there was a Laffer." In the hands of such business leaders, Stein recalled archly, supply-side propositions had been little more than "a way of arguing that what is good for us is good for you."[52] Supply-siders were guilty of restating the obvious and then using the resulting dogma to cloak their class and personal interests. The noted Keynesian economist Paul Krugman dismissed the supply-side movement as a collection of "cranks" pushing a political agenda rather than an economic analysis, less a valid school of conservative economic thought than a "cult" or "sect."[53]

These criticisms contained an undeniable kernel of truth. The supply-siders themselves admitted rather proudly that they were "basically returning to pre-Keynesian understandings."[54] They agreed they were restating the obvious, but saw that as an honorable task made necessary by the decades of misunderstanding that followed the unfortunate triumph of Keynesian macroeconomics. It is also clear that the supply-side movement was driven as much by ideological preferences, political expediency, and unquenchable optimism as by intellectual curiosity, scientific method, or empirical proof. The supply-side publicist Irving Kristol has written revealingly that he "was not certain of . . . [the doctrine's] economic merits but quickly saw its political possibilities." He championed the movement because it promised an alternative to traditional Republican root-canal economics, which usually trapped conservatives into "explaining to the populace, parent-like, why the good things in life that they wanted were all too expensive." Supply-side economics, he wrote in the mid-1990s, "offered neoconservatism an economic approach that promised steady economic growth—a sine qua non for the survival of a modern democracy."[55] For Kristol, the political appeal of supply-side economics outweighed any uncertainty regarding its theoretical validity or programmatic merit.

If such criticisms hit the mark regarding the most moderate formulations of supply-side economics, they registered even more tellingly against

more extreme expressions of the doctrine. Having already given the movement its generic name, Herbert Stein in 1981 identified what he perceived as
egregiously unsupportable oversimplifications of the doctrine as "punk supply-sidism." He applied the label to brands of supply-side doctrine that he
considered "extreme to the point of being bizarre," versions that offered both
a "universal explanation" and a "universal solution" and that in the process
crowded out more responsible, if more complicated and difficult, diagnoses
and prescriptions.[56] Indeed, moderate supply-siders shared some of Stein's
concern for the patent exaggerations of their most zealous brethren.

Paul Craig Roberts subsequently blamed Laffer and Wanniski for exag-
gerating the implications of the Laffer curve in suggesting that the government could cut taxes without worrying at all about the deficit. They
"covered the supply-side movement with hyperbole," he complained, and in
the process shifted attention from the central issue of the incentive-creating
effects of tax reduction to the distracting side issue of whether tax cuts
would automatically and immediately pay for themselves. This diversion,
agreed the economist William Niskanen, who served in Reagan's CEA from
1981 to 1985, "unfortunately trivialized the substantive contribution of the
focus on the micro effects of fiscal policy."[57] Even regarding those micro
effects, the enthusiasm of Laffer and Wanniski could be disconcerting.
When asked whether the incentive effects of reductions in marginal tax
rates might not be necessarily slow to appear, Laffer answered, "How long
does it take you to reach over and pick up a fifty dollar bill in a crowd?"
"That's how quick it is," Wanniski agreed, "if the incentive is there, the production is there."[58]

However, to dismiss moderate supply-siders as religious cultists or to
focus on "punk supply-sidism" obscures the crucial fact that the supply-
siders were not wholly isolated in their essential analysis and policy recommendations. As the 1970s wound down, the U.S. economy was in free fall,
beset by a dramatic drop-off in the rate of productivity growth and a highly
unstable rate of inflation. The dominant postwar policy paradigm, Keynesianism, was in tatters, under assault for both its intellectual inadequacy and
its practical ineffectiveness. In this setting, the supply-siders' emphasis on
the microeconomic foundations of economic activity and their prescription
of tight monetary policy to combat inflation and incentive-directed tax cuts
to stimulate economic growth found more than a little resonance. Whereas
supply-siders themselves have exaggerated their isolation by romanticizing
their role as a tiny band of brothers struggling bravely against a wrong-
headed establishment, liberals have exaggerated that isolation out of sheer

disdain for the supply-side approach. In truth, by the end of the 1970s sup-, ply-side ideas had a significant place in serious discussions of the U.S. political economy.

The congressional Joint Economic Committee (JEC) gave supply-side thinking an increasingly receptive hearing. In July 1977, the JEC began a three-and-one-half-year Special Study on Economic Change (SSEC), which sought to illuminate the changed economic conditions that had resulted in stagflation in the same way that the congressional Temporary National Economic Committee had sought in the late 1930s to get at the reasons for the stubborn duration of the Great Depression. At the outset of the study, Congressman Richard Bolling, a Missouri Democrat and the vice chairman of the JEC, observed that "conventional wisdom and established economic tools" appeared unequal to the "challenge of making sound policies in the economic sphere" and instructed the Special Study on Economic Change staff to develop "new policies and modes of adjustment."

Although the SSEC staff purposely avoided choosing a guiding motif at the beginning of its work, by the time of its final report two central themes had emerged: the suddenness and magnitude of the changes that had transformed the U.S. economy in the 1970s, and the compelling need to reject any "deliberate policies of slow growth or no growth" in favor of a strong pro-growth program. Recognizing that "traditional" demand management policies had proven ineffective against the "two-headed monster of inflation and stagnation" and that "the policies which will best promote growth in the economy of the 1980s and 1990s may be quite different from those which worked in other decades," the SSEC identified a supply-side approach (without using that label, however) as a major alternative. As described by the SSEC, such an alternative approach attributed stagnation largely to "government-induced barriers to work and production caused by high marginal tax rates and costly government regulation" and inflation largely to "the excess demand caused by government spending or increases in the money supply." Indeed, the SSEC's own very mild and cautiously worded recommendations echoed just such an analysis in calling for cuts in federal spending, a reduction in the rate of growth of the money supply, increased efforts to remove "unwarranted growth barriers" (i.e., government regulation), and "more incentives to save, invest, conduct research, innovate, produce."[59]

The JEC chairman Lloyd Bentsen, who would later serve as Bill Clinton's first treasury secretary, became an increasingly outspoken champion of the supply-side approach. In his introduction to the JEC's 1979 yearly economic report, Bentsen wrote that whereas the chief preoccupation of post-war economists had for thirty years been how to ensure an adequate level of aggregate demand, the dramatic changes of the 1970s had finally begun "to force the attention of the country and its economic experts on the supply side of the economy." A year later, he proclaimed "the start of a new era of economic thinking." "For too long," he told the press, "we have focused on short-run policies to stimulate spending, or demand, while neglecting sup-ply—labor, savings, investment and production. Consequently, demand has been overstimulated and supply has been strangled." To correct the policy imbalance, the JEC in its 1980 annual report recommended "a comprehen-sive set of policies designed to enhance the productive side, the supply side of the economy."[60]

From the other side of the partisan divide (but still within the moderate mainstream of American politics), Arthur Burns, a close economic adviser to Eisenhower and Nixon and later chairman of the Federal Reserve, pro-vided early support for a supply-side analysis, although his strong sense of fiscal rectitude prevented him from backing the particularly dramatic tax cuts proposed in Kemp-Roth. While at the Fed, Burns asserted in 1975 that "the economic mind of America" needed to be "reopened." "We need," he said, "a renaissance of economic thinking in our country." The heart of any such reorientation, Burns subsequently made clear, would be a shift in the focus of policy from demand to output. Martin Anderson, who would sub-sequently emerge as a key White House adviser and contributing architect of the Reagan Revolution, recalled that Burns was "the first person to intro-duce me to the essence of supply-side economic policy" while both served in the Nixon administration.[61]

Although the community of academic economists accorded supply-side analysis a distinctly mixed reception, Harvard's Martin Feldstein made the National Bureau of Economic Research (NBER) an outpost of supply-side emphasis, if not doctrine, when he became the organization's president in the mid-1970s. Feldstein's own research was wide-ranging; when he won the American Economic Association's prestigious John Bates Clark medal in 1977, the citation lauded his contributions in thirteen different subject areas; but unifying most of his scholarship was a deep interest in the elasticity, or incentives, effects of government policies. And incentive effects lay at the heart of supply-side economics. When the NBER held a two-day confer-ence in January 1980 to review the postwar experience of the U.S. economy, Feldstein reported approvingly that "there are at present some signs of growing public and governmental interest in increasing the rate of capital formation." "The Keynesian fear of saving that has dominated thinking . . . for more than thirty years is finally giving way," he told his audience, "to a concern about the low rates of productivity increase and of investment. . . . If the public begins to see more clearly the links between current policies and future consequences, there will be less reason to fear the unexpected consequences of myopic decisions."[62]

Even the Carter administration paid obeisance to the supply-side ideas that were in the air, although it did so grudgingly, haltingly, and to no discernible end. Carter's dalliance with industrial policy showed a concern for productivity, innovation, and competitiveness that was shared more by supply-siders than by traditional Keynesians. Just before the president sacked him in 1979, Treasury Secretary Michael Blumenthal testified before the JEC that the consensus underlying postwar economic policy—"that the major . . . concern . . . should be to manage aggregate demand to smooth out swings in the business cycle and assure steady increases in income and employment"— had broken down. Productivity growth was down, government spending was up, and tax rates were so high as to "stultify innovation and risk taking." He concluded that policymakers needed "to reorient economic policy to concentrate more heavily on the supply side, to reduce rigidities and inefficiencies that create supply constraints throughout the economy."[63]

Thus, by 1980 supply-side economics was both less and more than met the eye. While the claims of its champions were overwrought, so too were the denunciations of its detractors. It remained more a policy vision than a scientific analysis, but it seemed to fill a real void that was theoretical as well as practical. Much of the supply-side approach was already familiar to economists, and the parts that seemed freshest were, in fact, the doctrine's most dubious aspects. Supply-side thinking remained outside the mainstream, but its policy particulars and its conceptual underpinnings enjoyed notable support.

In retrospect, the emergence of the supply-side doctrine was highly significant. First, it offered policymakers a fundamental change in perspective, a new way in which to envision the nation's economic problems and their solutions. Second, it enabled the Republican Party to rebound from the disaster of Watergate; in Jude Wanniske's joyous phrase, the GOP was "reborn as a party of economic growth." Daniel Patrick Moynihan, now a Democratic senator from New York, had just this development in mind when he observed uneasily in July 1980, "Of a sudden, the GOP has become a party of ideas."[64] Finally, it gave to conservatives a powerful rationale for the policy agenda that would help them win the White House and undertake yet another ideological crusade in conjunction with (and under the cover of) a drive for economic growth, a crusade that this time sought to undo the modern American welfare state that had been born of the New Deal and so greatly augmented by the growth liberals' crusade of the 1960s.

III. Antistatist Growthmanship

"The GOP is in the process of rediscovering growth," Jack Kemp crowed in 1979, "and with the discovery is coming a political success it will not soon forget." There was a "tidal wave" coming, he predicted, similar to that which had sweep FDR into the presidency in 1932.[65] At the time, Kemp hoped he would be the Republican to ride that wave into the White House, but that was not to be; instead, the Republican to benefit from the confluence of his party's rebirth and Jimmy Carter's political self-destruction was a former movie star and governor of the nation's largest state, Ronald Reagan.

Reagan proved to be one of the most deceptive of America's presidents. The fact that he also appeared to be the most obvious and transparent of politicians merely deepened the enigma. Few national leaders in U.S. history have been at once so limited and so gifted. Reagan, who turned seventy just a few weeks after his first presidential inauguration, struck the longtime Washington insider Clark Clifford as "an amiable dunce," and, in truth, he was strikingly ill-informed and unanalytical. Blessed with a memory that was near-photographic when it worked but notoriously spotty in its overall performance, he compiled a record of embarrassing gaffes that included a much-talked-about failure even to recognize his secretary of housing and urban development, Sam Pierce, whom he mistakenly addressed as "Mr. Mayor" while greeting a delegation of visiting mayors to the White House half a year into his first term. (That Pierce was the only African American in the cabinet magnified the significance of Reagan's faux pas in the minds of liberal critics.)

Over time, Reagan's ignorance and intellectual laziness became the stuff of legend among both insiders and observers. An economic adviser has recalled rather delicately that the Californian had "a low tolerance for analysis"; Richard Darman, a White House adviser who spent several hours each day with Reagan during his first term, noted that the president was hardworking when pressed—he had "a compulsive insistence upon completing whatever work was given to him"—and was blessed with "a natural analytic facility," but observed that Reagan's capacity for hard work and talent for analysis had, over time, atrophied "because his charm, good looks, and memory served to get him a long way without additional effort."[66] In a similar vein, well-informed journalistic observers have concluded that Reagan's "biggest problem was that he didn't know enough about public policy to participate fully in his presidency—and often didn't realize how much he didn't know" and that the Reagan presidency would have been far more successful "had Reagan not been so lazy."[67]

Notwithstanding such weaknesses, Reagan's opponents learned quickly enough the cost of underestimating his leadership gifts. Speaker of the House Thomas P. "Tip" O'Neill greeted the incoming president during the transition with the derisive comment "Welcome to the big leagues!" When, within months, Reagan managed to defeat the Democratic majority in the House on a number of crucial votes, a constituent at home asked O'Neill what was happening. "I'm getting the shit whaled out of me," he replied. Jim Wright, the Democratic House majority leader, expressed a similar shocked disbelief in a June 1981 diary entry: "Appalled by what seems to me a lack of depth, I stand in awe nevertheless of . . . [Reagan's] political skill. I am not sure that I have seen its equal."[68] The big leagues, indeed!

O'Neill, Wright, and others often learned the hard way that Reagan's intellectual weaknesses were counterbalanced by a number of leadership strengths. The most basic of these was what the conservative columnist George Will described as Reagan's "talent for happiness," an unshakable optimism as infectious as it was deeply grounded. A classic example was one of Reagan's favorite stories during his early days in the White House (until reporters began to make it the butt of their own gibes). There were, it went, two youngsters, one an incurable malcontent and the other an incorrigible optimist. The boys' parents decided to temper their sons' inclinations by means of very different Christmas gifts. Given a roomful of toys, the malcontent just cried in the corner, certain that all his wonderful presents would soon break on him. Meanwhile, his brother, given a pile of horse manure, dove in with great relish, exclaiming with a huge grin as he dug into the manure, "I just know there's a pony in here somewhere!"

Reagan projected his personal penchant for positive thinking onto the broader canvas of American life as well. The nation's problems, he told the onlookers at his inauguration in 1981, required "our best effort and our willingness to believe in ourselves and to believe in our capacity to perform great deeds, to believe . . . we can and will resolve the problems which now confront us." "And after all," he added, in what was the most telling line of his entire speech, "why shouldn't we believe that? We are Americans."[69] On this foundation of sunniness rested a personality seemingly so at ease with itself, so engaging and winning, that even confirmed political adversaries felt its warm influence.

Reagan also had an unusual ability to cobble together his few core beliefs and ideas into something grander—a vision, which was itself made all the more coherent and powerful by its simplicity. There might be much that Reagan did not know, but he knew well the few big things that he hoped to achieve as president. Isaiah Berlin has reminded us of the observation by the Greek poet Archilochus that "the fox knows many things, but the hedgehog knows one big thing."[70] Nothing so set Reagan apart from Jimmy Carter as that difference between the fox and the hedgehog. Carter knew an astounding array of facts about how government worked; Reagan knew what he wanted. In the 1980 election, and likely in the larger judgment of history as well, this particular hedgehog bested that particular fox. Moreover, Reagan managed not only to focus on those central goals but also to sustain that focus over time. As Edwin Meese III, a close adviser throughout Reagan's government career in both California and Washington, has written, "He kept his eye on the main objective at all times—astonishingly so, considering the number and complexity of the issues involved."[71]

Finally, Reagan had the ability to communicate his agenda clearly and compellingly, not simply through the smoothness of his speaking delivery or by means of his impressive physical presence, but most important through his uncanny ability to manipulate the symbols and imagery of presidential leadership. Behind what sometimes appeared to be a shallow fondness for the pomp of office lay the fact that Reagan, as White House communications aide David Gergin noted, "understood, better than anyone since de Gaulle, the dramatic and theatrical demands of national leadership."[72] The former actor and his aides made the previously innocuous "photo op" into a potent instrument of governance. Reagan's carefully scripted projections of presidential imagery came to be seen, one political analyst has written, "as synonymous with the act of governing itself, as distinct from merely being adjuncts or backdrop."[73]

In his run for the presidency, Reagan put his various strengths in the service of a handful of simply stated but impressively large goals. The big things Reagan hoped to achieve—what he conceived as his heroic missions—are best remembered as the three "r's." First, he sought to revitalize the U.S. economy by defeating stagflation and moving back to the fast growth track of the earlier postwar decades. "The Republican program for solving economic problems is based on growth and productivity," he pro-

claimed to a rapt audience in accepting the presidential nomination at the
GOP national convention in July 1980. Second, he was determined to
restore U.S. military strength and international prestige. "No American
should vote," he told the assembled Republicans, "until he or she has asked:
Is the United States stronger and more respected now than it was three and
a half years ago? Is the world a safer place in which to live?" Finally, Reagan
meant to reverse what he perceived as the nation's drift in the direction of a
European welfare state by halting the growth of the federal government.
"Our federal government is overgrown and overweight," he declared to the
convention. Once elected, the new president added famously in his inaugural address that government was not the solution to the nation's problems so much as it was their cause.[74] The tasks of revitalization, restoration,
and reversal remained the lodestars by which Reagan steered his presidency,
consistently, albeit with uneven success, through two terms.

The economic program Reagan adopted to help achieve these large
ends—the three "r's"—further demonstrated the incoming administration's ability to focus at the outset on a few essentials and to sustain that
focus over time. In August 1979, Martin Anderson, Reagan's chief domestic
policy adviser, drafted the Reagan for President Campaign's "Policy Memorandum No. 1," which sketched out the economic strategy the Californian
would take to the voters. "It is time the United States began moving forward again," Anderson told the candidate, "with new inventions, new products, greater productivity, more jobs, and a rapidly rising standard of living
that means more goods and services for all of us." To regain the economy's
former momentum, Anderson suggested across-the-board tax cuts of at
least three years' duration in conjunction with the indexation of federal
income tax brackets; reduction in the rate of increase in federal spending;
the balancing of the federal budget; vigorous deregulation; and a consistent
monetary policy to deal with inflation.

Despite George Bush's stinging criticism during the primary campaign
that, when combined with the massive military buildup Reagan promised,
such a program constituted "voodoo economics," Reagan stuck to the blueprint laid out in Policy Memorandum No. 1. With only minor adjustments
and some change in emphasis—a slight downplaying of the balanced budget
goal, attainment of which was pushed farther into the future, and an under-
scoring of the immediate need to fight inflation—that early strategy was the
program President Ronald Reagan presented to the American people in February 1981. As Anderson later wrote, "Again and again, in the campaign, during the transition, and all during his tenure as president . . . [Reagan] adjusted

his economic plan to accommodate changes in the economy and political opposition in the Congress, but he did not adjust the blueprint." Both its champions and its critics labeled the blueprint Reaganomics.[75]

The rationale behind Reaganomics was varied. Several members of Reagan's Council of Economic Advisers have noted that there was much more agreement on what the administration should do than on why it should do those things.[76] The president's commitment to the regimen of tax cuts and spending constraints, tight money, and deregulation reflected, in large part, his own emotional and experiential view of economics. He abhorred big government and had a primordial dislike of high taxes rooted in his own experiences in the film industry. During his peak earning years as an actor at Warner Brothers, Reagan found himself in the 94 percent marginal tax bracket: "The IRS took such a big chunk of my earnings," he remembered, "that after a while I began asking myself whether it was worth it to keep on taking work. Something was wrong with a system like that." Moreover, the problem was not simply the confiscatory level of taxation but also the ultimate economic impact of such disincentives to work: "If I decided to do one less picture," Reagan later wrote, "that meant other people at the studio in lower tax brackets wouldn't work as much either; the effect filtered down, and there were fewer total jobs available."

When the Californian left acting to become an increasingly visible spokesman for American conservatism in the early 1960s, he told his audiences that the progressive income tax had come "directly from Karl Marx who designed it as the prime essential of a socialist state."[77] Reagan's disdain for the progressive income tax, together with his alarm at the growth of the federal government, predisposed him to favor the supply-side approach championed by Jack Kemp and his politico-intellectual allies. The practical preferences were marrow-deep, the theoretical rationale skindeep, but both counted. Reagan's sunny nature reinforced his inclinations, pushing him farther toward a doctrine suffused with an optimism as boundless as his own. "Jack [Kemp] was basically pushing on an open door," recalled Ed Meese, because Ronald Reagan "was a supply-sider long before the term was invented." For Reagan, such ideas were less economic doctrine than simple "common sense."[78]

It nevertheless helped immensely that Reagan's version of common sense coincided with an economic dogma that legitimated and bolstered his predilections. Supply-side economics provided a coherent, if controversial, rationale for Reagan's policies and exercised a decisive influence on a number of his key advisers. Martin Anderson, the author of the "Reagan for

President Campaign's Policy Memorandum No. 1," was an early convert to the supply-side approach and in 1976, while reviewing grant applications for the Richardson Foundation, helped Jude Wanniski get the funding that allowed him to leave the *Wall Street Journal* in order to write his supply-side tract *The Way the World Works*. During the race to the presidency, Anderson took what he called "the simple idea that was supply-side economics" and helped make it into "an important part of President Reagan's economic program."[79]

Supply-side ideas also influenced Reagan's "economic professionals" on the Council of Economic Advisers. In announcing the administration's Program for Economic Recovery in February 1981, Murray Weidenbaum, the first of Reagan's several CEA chairmen, noted that "in contrast to the inflationary demand-led booms of the 1970s, the most significant growth of economic activity will occur in the supply side of the economy." When the CEA later set forth the philosophical and intellectual underpinnings of the administration's economic program in the 1982 *Economic Report*, it embraced a supply-side perspective. While never persuaded that tax cuts would so stimulate economic activity as to automatically and immediately make up for lost revenue—Stein's "punk supply-sidism"—Weidenbaum and his CEA colleagues subsequently recalled that they nevertheless "really believed in supply-side economics."[80]

Shaped by both personal experience and economic doctrine, Reaganomics also had a larger inspiration and rationale. The Reagan program was, at bottom, yet another expression of postwar growthmanship. William Brock, the Republican Party chairman, later recalled the "very clear sense that . . . the basic aim of the policy we were trying to implement was to restore growth." Reaganomics, Kemp observed, was "really the classical prescription for economic growth." Thus, it was no coincidence that Reagan entitled his major 1980 campaign speech on economic policy "A Strategy for Growth: The American Economy in the 1980s." In his first presidential address on the economy, he reminded his live national television audience, "Our aim is to increase our national wealth so all will have more, not just redistribute what we already have [*sic*] which is just a sharing of scarcity."[81]

In this way, the Gipper finally achieved unambiguously what Richard Nixon had earlier attempted with characteristic indirection—he stole the Democrats' most potent politico-economic appeal and placed it at the center of his conservative Republicanism. Running for reelection in 1984, Reagan joyfully offered voters a choice "between two different visions of the future, two fundamentally different ways of governing—their government of pessimism, fear, and limits, or ours of hope, confidence, and growth."[82] Moreover, like both Nixon and the growth liberals before him, Reagan harnessed growth to a larger ideological crusade. The growth liberals had used growth to underwrite a new level and style of governmental activism at home and abroad; Nixon had sought to use it to reestablish a republic of Whiggish virtue; Reagan now turned to growth to help him dismantle the modern welfare state.

The apparent brilliance of Reagan's approach and much of its consequent appeal to conservatives lay in the fact that the same mechanisms that would spur economic growth—tax cuts, spending controls, and deregulation—would also serve to restrain the growth of the federal government. Reagan's disdain for government was real and ran deep. In January 1982, he complained in his diary that "the press is trying to paint me as trying to undo the New Deal. I remind them I voted for FDR four times." As Reagan saw it, the charge was off the mark, if only by a little: "I'm trying to undo the Great Society. It was LBJ's war on poverty that led us to our present mess." Believing that the federal government would "grow forever unless you do something to starve it," Reagan perceived his growth program to be both good economics and good ideology. "By cutting taxes," he later wrote, "I wanted not only to stimulate the economy but to curb the growth of government and reduce its intrusion into the economic life of the country." As both candidate and president, Reagan gave top priority to an economic program designed to stimulate economic growth and to achieve these larger, heroic objectives as well. The relationship between the goals was reciprocal: the tax and spending cuts designed to generate growth would shrink government, and the shrinkage of government would in turn contribute to still more growth. Once again, economic growth became both vehicle and camouflage for a larger ideological agenda.[83]

IV. Deficits and the Defunding of the Welfare State

The administration took full advantage of Reagan's single-mindedness in pursuing its economic agenda. It also benefited mightily from the surge of public affection for the president generated by his brave and graceful performance after an assassination attempt only weeks into his first term in the spring of 1981. The combination of purposefulness and luck enabled the administration to implement large parts of its economic program with a speed that stunned its Democratic opponents. In August, Congress passed the Economic Recovery Tax Act of 1981 (ERTA), which phased in a 23 percent cumulative reduction in personal income tax rates over three years, lowered immediately the top marginal personal income tax rate from 70 to 50 percent, committed the federal government to begin indexing the personal income tax for inflation in 1985, and liberalized depreciation guidelines and increased the business investment tax credit. It was the largest tax cut in U.S. history, and it was permanent.[84]

Reagan achieved similar success on the monetary front, although there he necessarily acted mainly by indirection while the notionally independent Federal Reserve took the lead. Encouraged by Reagan's campaign commitment to fight inflation unmercifully, the Fed, which had already adopted a more strictly monetarist policy approach in October 1979, tightened monetary policy soon after the 1980 election and again in May 1981. Most important, when critics both inside and outside the administration clamored for relief from the economic pain caused by the Fed's attempt to wring inflation out of the economy once and for all, Reagan protected the central bank politically. The president was "steadfast in supporting the Fed's stance of monetary restraint," Reagan confidant Edwin Meese has written: "He never wavered. . . . I was frequently involved in meetings with Federal Reserve Board chairman Paul Volcker, and the message was always the same—the president backed the board's approach." "If not us, who?" Reagan would ask his associates regarding the war against inflation, "If not now, when?"[85]

To the extent that the battle against inflation was psychological, and it was partly so, Reagan's firmness in firing the 11,400 air traffic controllers who went out on strike over a pay dispute in August 1981 made an important symbolic contribution. As Volcker later recalled, "The significance was that someone finally took on an aggressive, well-organized union and said no." Equally important for the campaign against inflation, Reagan's strong action against the air traffic controllers dramatically established his determination and willingness to court short-term risks and to absorb short-term costs in the pursuit of larger goals or principles. The decision to fight the 1982 midterm elections under the slogan "Stay the Course" and the subsequent reappointment of Volcker to a new term as Fed chairman in 1983 drove home the anti-inflation message. Although the Fed's tight money campaign came at an exceedingly high price in both joblessness and lost production—the policy played a major role in bringing about the sharpest recession of the postwar era in 1981–82—the payoff was considerable: in 1982, the consumer price index increased only 3.8 percent, and it remained in that vicinity for the remainder of the decade. As the economist Michael Mussa has observed, "the demon of inflation . . . had finally been tamed."[86]

The administration also made some initial progress in the attempt to reduce the growth of federal spending and to further the efforts, already under way and often far advanced during the Carter years, to reduce the extent of federal regulation. Reagan's first budget proposal, presented in February 1981 for fiscal year 1982, called for spending cuts of slightly more than $45 billion; in the end, the legislative package passed in August was estimated to trim spending by $35 billion. The latter figure was sufficient to cause the Democratic chairman of the House Budget Committee to claim that the reduction in spending constituted "the most monumental and historic turnaround in fiscal policy that has ever occurred."[87] In its drive to deregulate the economy, the new administration immediately created a task force on regulatory reform under the leadership of Vice President George Bush, terminated the price controls on oil remaining from the 1970s, put a blanket hold on the imposition of new regulations, and filled important posts with champions of regulatory relief.[88]

However, the administration's substantial initial progress in all these areas was quickly overtaken and overshadowed by a budgetary crisis that developed even as the basic building blocks of Reaganomics were being put into place in the summer of 1981. Weeks before the president signed the Economic Recovery Tax Act of 1981 into law, OMB director David Stockman warned of a brewing fiscal disaster. From the outset Stockman, a former Michigan congressman, had been a driving force in the framing and implementation of Reaganomics. He possessed, his compatriot Martin Anderson has written, "the zeal of a newly born-again Christian, the body of a thirty-four-year-old, and the drive to work fourteen-hour days, including Saturdays and some Sundays." His personality wore better with some people than with others—Treasury Secretary Donald Regan thought him "arrogant and antidemocrat"—but his intellectual grasp of budgetary matters impressed both friend and foe and made him a powerful figure in White House circles and beyond. Nobody in the administration, perhaps the whole government, knew as much about the budget, and in early August 1981 Stockman told Reagan and his top aides, "The scent of victory is still in the air, but I'm not going to mince words. We're heading for a crash landing on the budget. We're facing potential deficit numbers so big that they could wreck the president's entire economic program."[89]

The problem that Stockman presented to the seemingly barely comprehending president and his aides was real, and it quickly got worse. The administration's predicament could be stated all too simply: Revenue growth lagged more than originally anticipated but spending continued to rise. The widening gap between intake and outgo threatened to eventuate in a round of the biggest deficits in peacetime U.S. history. The reasons for the fiscal debacle were somewhat more complicated than the distressingly simple arithmetic that underlay them. On the revenue side of the fiscal equation, several factors were at work. First, the administration won not simply the largest tax cut in the nation's history, but a tax cut far larger overall than even it had originally envisioned. Tax-cutting was obviously a political exercise—there were benefits to be gained and disadvantages to be avoided—and, once under way, the process touched off a congressional frenzy, a bidding war in which both political parties courted support by offering special tax relief for favored constituencies. Consequently, the Economic Recovery Tax Act of 1981 came to include not merely the massive reductions in the personal income tax a la Kemp-Roth but also a host of lesser "ornamental" tax breaks, income tax indexation (a big revenue loser when it corrected the individual income tax structure for inflation from 1985 onward), and large cuts in business, estate, and gift taxes.[90]

In addition, the administration had based its initial budget projection of a balanced budget by fiscal year 1984 on a very optimistic forecast, which came to be known as the "Rosy Scenario." As it turned out, economic growth—and hence revenue growth—was much slower than projected, in part because the much-heralded incentive effects of supply-side policies proved both less potent and less immediate in their impact than some had predicted, and in part because when the Fed constricted the money supply to battle inflation, it helped trigger a recession in 1981-82 that further weakened the flow of revenue. Ironically, even the Fed's success in bringing down inflation worked against the administration's hope for a balanced budget, since the slackening of inflation meant less bracket creep in the tax system and consequently less revenue, even before indexation took effect.[91]

Developments on the spending side of the ledger proved similarly disastrous to the administration's initial projections of a balanced budget by 1984. As revenues lagged, expenditures continued to grow. Here, too, the reasons were several. First, even the most dedicated budget slashers within the administration found that gutting the modern welfare state was easier said than done. Stockman was a true radical, an ideologue who wanted a revolutionary reduction in the size and scope of the federal government, what he later termed "a frontal assault on the American welfare state." But, as he himself admitted, his "blueprint for sweeping, wrenching change in national economic governance would have hurt millions of people in the short run." To his disappointment, Stockman discovered that although Reagan genuinely wanted to slow the growth of the federal apparatus, the president was temperamentally "too kind, gentle, and sentimental" for the kind of draconian expenditure reductions his budget director thought necessary to balance the budget and dismantle the existing welfare state. Liberals took a rather different view, complaining that Reagan's cuts in domestic spending signaled "the return of social Darwinism," this time presided over by a former movie actor playing "Herbert Hoover with a smile." The truth actually lay somewhere in between these contrasting assessments. Real spending for nondefense programs other than interest on the national debt did grow in the Reagan years, but at an average annual rate—less than 1 percent—far below that of previous postwar decades.[92]

Reagan was committed to slowing the growth of established federal programs, but he carefully avoided pledges to abolish outright any specific existing ones. Here, as elsewhere, he preferred the protective cover of his unique combination of rhetorical generalities about government being the problem, not the solution, and anecdotal specificity about Cadillac-driving welfare queens and feckless bureaucrats. Although he lacked his budget director's command of fiscal detail, he was savvy enough to recognize Stockman's call for "the ruthless dispensation of short-run pain in the name of long-run gain" as political dynamite. After all, Stockman had been appointed OMB director; Reagan had been elected president. He and his political advisers entertained hopes for a second term, and their aversion to bloated government, although genuine, was not so great as to incline them to political suicide attacks. When on one occasion Stockman did manage to engineer Reagan's acquiescence in a plan to cut Social Security benefits to early retirees (those who left the workforce at age 62 instead of 65), the resulting political firestorm persuaded the president and his advisers that Social Security was, in Niskanen's phrase, "a minefield for the administration." Consequently, the White House placed such middle-class entitlements as Social Security and Medicare off-limits to budget cutters, preferring to believe, erroneously, that large budget reductions could be made just by cutting out waste and fraud.[93]

Moreover, when the administration did move to trim discretionary spending, it encountered resistance from both within and without that in the long run often proved overpowering. When Stockman sought to trim what he called the "vast local transportation pork barrel"—federal funding for the local building and upkeep of streets, roads, and mass transit—he found himself in a losing battle with Transportation Secretary Drew Lewis, most of Congress, and a huge constituency of state and local officials, contractors, and unions. "In the end," the budget director ruefully recounted later, "the transportation sector of the pork barrel never even knew the Reagan Revolution had tilted at it." "It was a dramatic case of everything staying the same," he added, "but it would be only one of many."[94]

Finally, the administration compounded its budget-cutting woes by implementing a massively expensive military buildup even more energetically than the candidate had promised in the 1980 campaign. The additional impetus behind the buildup as it actually unfolded came in part from the determination to defeat the Soviet Union by outspending it. Lawrence J. Korb, an assistant secretary of defense in 1981–84, maintains that the buildup "was based not on military need but upon a strategy of bankrupting the Soviet Union." Nevertheless, Stockman was originally heartened by the appointment of Caspar W. Weinberger as secretary of defense. Weinberger's tightfistedness as Nixon's budget director and secretary of health, education, and welfare had earned him the nickname Cap the Knife, and Stockman hoped that Weinberger would be willing to trim some of the more exuberant plans for rearmament. Reagan's budget director supported the military buildup in the abstract but wanted some defense spending reductions because he thought the defense effort embodied some egregious waste, because he was increasingly desperate for spending cuts wherever they could be found, and because he hoped that cuts in defense spending would "provide political lubricant" for cuts elsewhere. In the event, however, Weinberger proved a fierce champion of the military machine; to Stockman's horror, Cap the Knife had become Cap the Shovel. So successfully did he fight off OMB oversight of the defense budget that William Niskanen of the CEA subsequently characterized the resulting administration defense budget as "little more than a stapled package of the budget requests from each service." The pace of military spending slowed in his second term, but overall Reagan presided over an unparalleled peacetime defense buildup that totaled nearly $2 trillion.[95]

In this fashion, a combination of ineluctable arithmetic and the vagaries of politics immersed the Reagan presidency in a tide of red ink. By the end of the administration's second year, the fiscal picture was, Stockman later admitted, "an utter, mind-numbing catastrophe." It worsened with time. The final Reagan record on deficits was unprecedentedly bad: all eight of the administration's budgets ran deficits, the smallest $127.9 billion (current dollars) in fiscal year 1982 and the largest $221.2 billion in fiscal year 1986; in fiscal year 1983 the deficit reached a peacetime record of 6.3 percent of GNP; and, overall, the national debt tripled on Reagan's watch, from $914 billion in fiscal year 1980 to $2.7 trillion in fiscal year 1989. James M. Poterba, an MIT economist, has estimated that one-third of the deficit growth under Reagan resulted from tax reduction, two-thirds from expenditure growth in the form chiefly of increased transfer payments to individuals, increased interest payments on federal borrowing, and increased defense spending.[96]

The reaction to this budgetary distress was a series of grudging tactical retreats that came to dominate federal budget policy for the remainder of the 1980s and beyond. For the most part, the impetus for these efforts to recapture a measure of fiscal probity came from fiscal moderates and old-style budget-balancers in Congress, abetted by those of Reagan's advisers, the budget wizards Stockman and his OMB deputy Richard Darman foremost among them, who too late recognized that their original economic design contained, in the so-called out years of their own projections, the seeds of fiscal havoc. Reagan himself was most often a passive spectator or, at best, a hesitant participant in the subsequent attempts at correction, while the unrepentant "punk supply-siders" among his advisers and elsewhere vigorously opposed them. The salvaging effort took the form chiefly of corrective tax increases (the Tax Equity and Fiscal Responsibility Act of 1982 [TEFRA], the 1983 Social Security Amendments, the Deficit Reduction Act of 1984 [DEFRA], and the Omnibus Budget Reconciliation Act of 1987 [OBRA]) and spending control measures (Gramm-Rudman-Hollings, passed in 1985, and Gramm-Rudman of 1987) that set precise deficit targets and specified the mechanisms to achieve them. In the end, these efforts, rather than eliminating the deficit as a problem, merely underscored the fact that record budget deficits and the tripled national debt had become the central economic and political realities of the Reagan era.

As a result of the unprecedented red ink, the decade from the mid-1980s through the mid-1990s may well be remembered as the era of the budget. Between 1982 and 1995, the federal government was forced twelve times technically to halt operations, however briefly, for lack of funds. Former presidents Gerald Ford and Jimmy Carter warned Reagan's Republican successor, George Bush, before his inauguration that the federal deficit had come to dominate decision making "in Congress, in the White House, throughout the Federal government." By the end of the 1980s, wrote the political scientists Joseph White and Aaron Wildavsky, the budget had become "to our era what civil rights, communism, the depression, industrialization, and slavery were at other times." Extravagant perhaps, but New

York's Democratic senator Daniel Patrick Moynihan agreed that the deficit had become "the first fact of national government."[97]

The overriding political consequence of this defining fact of governance was its shattering impact on the sort of federal activism strongly identified with Democratic liberalism. The Reagan administration's persistent efforts to dismantle social programs by restricting eligibility, slashing benefits, and privatizing activities met with only uneven success, but where direct assault failed, fiscal policy succeeded by indirection: Reagan's budget deficits effectively defunded the welfare state. The recurring deficits and growing national debt forced liberals to scurry to protect existing social programs from budget cuts and made it almost impossible for them to mount new efforts at the federal level. The fiscal crisis was "Reagan's revenge," complained the liberal historian Alan Brinkley, "a back door for doing what many on the right had been unable to achieve with their frontal assaults in the 1950s and 1960s." As Reagan White House aide Tom Griscom observed with palpable satisfaction, "You can no longer just say, 'Well, let's do this and not worry about either where the money is going to come from or whether we are going to have to take away from another program or shift priorities.'" Reduced support for existing programs and the forestalling of new ones further hurt liberalism by contributing to a general loss of faith by voters in the capacity of government to address national concerns. To the horror of liberals, Reagan's economic ineptitude seemed to weaken their programmatic potency and political appeal![98]

Daniel Patrick Moynihan believed this outcome deliberate. The senator from New York favored a supply-side tax cut of some sort in 1981 in order to improve incentives and boost investment, but he distrusted the promises of the enthusiastic supply-siders around Reagan, observing that they bore the same relationship to genuine conservatives that anarchists did to liberals. Moynihan realized almost immediately that the ERTA of 1981 was too large, and he predicted presciently that it would result in crushing deficits. Within weeks of the ERTA's passage, he asked a New York business audience, "Do we really want a decade in which the issue of public discourse, over and over and over, will be how big must the budget cuts be in order to prevent the deficit from being even bigger. Surely, larger, more noble purposes ought to engage us."[99]

By the end of 1983 the senator became convinced, partly on the basis of conversations with Stockman, who had been a Moynihan protégé (and that family's live-in babysitter) while studying at Harvard Divinity School, that "the early Reagan deficits had been deliberate, that there had been a hidden agenda." Writing in *The New Republic* in December, Moynihan argued that the deficits for the president's initial budgets were "purposeful," although he conceded that they "were expected to disappear" in later years.[100] When doubters scoffed at Moynihan's conspiracy theory, he repeated and clarified his charge in the Marnold Lecture at New York University in 1986:

To double the national debt in five years was a disaster. Who would deliberately bring about a disaster? Nonsense. Agreed. But that was not . . . [my] argument. The disaster was not deliberate: the deficits were. Which is to say that the deficits were meant to spur action, which however did not occur, thereby resulting in disaster. A nice distinction but not, I should have thought, impenetrably subtle.[101]

Over time, however, the crucial distinction between intentional initial deficits and the unintended ultimate outcome of an unbroken series of record deficits occasionally blurred in Moynihan's writing. By the mid-1990s, he wrote more generally of "the intentional nature of the Reagan deficits" and implied a larger conspiracy: "They created a crisis. . . . First, the tax cuts of 1981 followed by the severe recession of 1982. Next, the development within the incumbent [Reagan] administration of a grand strategy of using deficits to bring about a reduction in the size of government, followed by a disinclination to cut specific programs." Indeed, Moynihan argued that, even into the 1990s, "the deficit, with the accompanying debt service, was doing the job that had been expected from the tax cuts."[102]

Was Moynihan's charge accurate? Had there been a conspiracy purposely to generate huge deficits in order to bring the welfare state to its knees by "starving the beast"? Stockman denied the charge, asserting that both the administration's "rosy scenario" forecast and the Congressional Budget Office projections used by Congress in developing the ERTA of 1981 had predicted falling deficits under the administration's budget proposals; he also denied that anyone within the administration really believed they were creating huge deficits that could be used effectively to discipline congressional spending. In other words, the deficits were too much of a surprise to have been put to the conspiratorial uses suggested by Moynihan. Stockman's deputy at OMB, Richard Darman, called Moynihan's charge "way overdrawn," but granted that both Reagan and Stockman had believed that the threat or reality of reduced revenue could be used to rein in the spending habits of the profligate Congress.[103]

Moynihan was indeed onto something. Stockman's denial notwithstanding, it is clear that a number of conservatives thought that the way to arrest the growth of the welfare state was to cut off its revenue and let the threat of any subsequent deficits help move Congress to restrain expenditures. For too long, they believed, Republicans had attacked the burgeoning liberal state by trying to curb spending, an approach that left them at the disadvantage of opposing popular liberal "give-away" programs and then, when defeated, calling for tax increases to cover the excesses of Democratic big spenders. To the critics, that approach was tantamount to "root-canal economics" and had all the political appeal of a trip to the dentist. As was often the case, Milton Friedman was in the forefront of those calling for a change in strategy. As early as 1967, he wrote in his *Newsweek* column that "those of us who believe that government has reached a size at which it threatens to become our master rather than our servant" needed to oppose any tax increase and accept larger deficits as "the lesser of evils." The Chicago economist served on Reagan's pre-election Economic Policy Coordinating Committee and then on the president's Economic Policy Advisory Board, and weeks after Reagan's inauguration, he put an even finer point on the idea in another *Newsweek* column: "If the tax cut threatens bigger deficits, the political appeal of balancing the budget is harnessed to reducing government spending rather than to raising taxes. That . . . is the way that President Reagan proposes to follow."[104]

Reagan was not merely conversant with the idea that the size-of-government problem was best addressed from the tax, rather than the spending, side—while governor of California he had, in fact, pioneered that approach in an episode that has subsequently been largely forgotten. In late 1972, Reagan brought together a group of advisers at the Century Plaza Hotel in Los Angeles to discuss how to limit government growth. At his prompting, a small committee, directed by Lew Uhler of the governor's staff and including William Niskanen and Anthony Kennedy (later, members respectively of the CEA and the Supreme Court), drafted a tax control measure that would amend the state constitution to limit future taxes to a fixed percentage of total personal income (proceeding through stages to a final cap of 7 percent of total personal income) and require a two-thirds majority vote in both houses of the state legislature for future tax increases. When the state legislature refused to put the proposed amendment to a vote of the people, Reagan and his allies took their measure to the voters in the form of an initiative, Proposition 1.

The governor barnstormed the state with Milton Friedman to drum up support for what he described as "an idea whose time has come." "We must impose some reasonable fiscal restraints," Reagan told a receptive business audience as the battle over Prop 1 spilled over into 1973. "You can lecture your teenagers about spending too much until you are blue in the face, or you can accomplish the same goal by cutting their allowance. We think it is time to limit government's allowance—to put a limit on the amount of money they can take from the people in taxes. This is the only way we will ever bring government spending under control."[105]

The voters defeated Prop 1 in November 1973 by a margin of 54–46 percent, but the battle over Reagan's proposed amendment launched the modern tax limitation movement. Lew Uhler went on to help found the National Tax Limitation Committee, which he subsequently led in a struggle for a national balanced budget amendment that continued for over two decades; and by the end of the 1970s, tax limitation proposals won approval in California, Michigan, and Missouri. By 1981, the tax-limitation approach to curbing government spending was much in the air; Ronald Reagan had helped put it there.[106]

Thus, in the loose sense foreshadowed by the earlier Prop 1 experience, the Reagan administration was determined to use the specter of budget deficits to force Congress to control spending. Reagan himself continued to believe that cutting government's allowance would force more responsible spending behavior. Despite his occasional denial, Stockman obviously thought along precisely this line. As he recalled in his political memoir (published even before the Reagan red ink had dried), the OMB director realized as early as mid-February 1981 that a looming budget deficit "would become a powerful battering ram. It would force Congress to shrink the welfare state. It would give me an excuse to come back to them [for spending cuts] again and again."[107] As conspiracies go, however, this one was, for those willing to read between the lines of public pronouncements, a rather poorly kept secret. Repeating his familiar trope, Reagan himself told the National Association of Manufacturers in a March 1982 speech that "increasing taxes only encourages government to continue its irresponsible spending habits. We can lecture it about extravagance till we're blue in the face, or we can discipline it by cutting its allowance."[108] It was the threat of budget deficits that gave this disciplinary tactic its coercive power. On numerous occasions throughout 1981, Reagan publicly warned that "without [the spending cuts requested by the administration] . . . we will have . . . added red ink, an unbalanced budget, and more inflationary pressure in the next few years."[109]

But the budgetary politics of the 1980s were also more complicated than Moynihan's charge of conspiracy allowed. Attitudes were ambivalent and ambiguous, sometimes even schizophrenic. Those most responsible for the fiscal carnage of the 1980s certainly did not welcome the deficits when they first appeared. When the threat of red ink failed to elicit the spending cuts needed to balance the budget and the large deficits became reality, some of the key plotters in Moynihan's supposed conspiracy panicked. Stockman, who later joked that he was one-half supply-sider and the other half "recidivist Hooverite," quickly became a leading exponent of tax increases to staunch the fiscal hemorrhaging. This offended the more zealous supply-siders: Wanniski commented acidly, "Stockman was part of the small band of revolutionaries, and he went over"; Edwin Meese complained that the OMB director became "a tax-hike mole in a tax-cutting government."[110] Stockman, however, was not the only one spooked by the emergent deficit overhang.

Reagan, too, grew worried, as his diary entries over the course of 1982 indicate. In January, the president was resolute: "I told our guys I couldn't go for tax increases," he wrote. "If I have to be criticized, I'd rather be criticized for a deficit rather [sic] than for backing away from our economic program." But after a budget briefing on election day in November (an off-year contest that saw the Republicans lose twenty-five seats in the House), his tone was more distressed: "We really are in trouble. Our one time projections, pre-recession, are all out the window and we look at $200 billion deficits if we can't pull some miracles." In early January 1983, he shared his growing anguish with his Budget Review Board: "We can't live with outyear deficits. I don't care if we have to blow up the Capitol, we have to restore the economy."[111]

Expressing his concern several weeks later in his 1983 State of the Union address, the president himself broke with his hard-core supply-side supporters, calling the deficit problem "a clear and present danger to the basic health of our Republic" and proposing a standby tax "because we must ensure reduction and eventual elimination of deficits over the next several years." At the time of his 1984 reelection campaign, Reagan considered cutting the deficit and balancing the budget the chief domestic tasks for his second term.[112] Even Treasury Secretary Donald Regan, one of the administration's most dedicated supply-siders, came to believe that the projected $221 billion deficit for fiscal year 1986 meant the administration had "reached the danger point."[113]

Although Reagan had long recognized the political usefulness of the deficit threat, there is compelling reason, beyond the clear evidence of his growing concern already cited, to doubt that he purposely engineered the series of deficits that actually occurred. The administration wanted the intimidation of potential deficits, not the reality of actual ones. For one thing, the advisers closest to the president were convinced that the supply-side tax cut would so boost growth as to leave the federal government with more, not less, revenue after the tax cuts. As Stockman wrote derisively, "The whole California gang had taken . . . [the Laffer curve] literally (and primitively)." The revenue increase generated by the tax cut was called "reflow," a label that gave wishful thinking the aura of economic science.[114] Those who worried about the lost revenue were deemed not sufficiently appreciative of the "reflow" principle.[115] Throughout 1981, Reagan invoked the reflow concept, pointing reassuringly to historical precedent to prove his point. "There's still that belief on the part of many people," he observed sadly but wisely to reporters in February 1981, "that a cut in tax rates automatically means a cut in revenues. And if they'll only look at history, it doesn't. A cut in tax rates can very often be reflected in an increase in government revenues because of the broadening of the base of the economy."[116]

In Reagan's case, the stubborn belief in reflow was both an intellectual infatuation with punk supply-sidism and a particularly vivid example of the way that his unquenchable optimism significantly influenced public policy. It also captured just how quintessentially—and powerfully—economic growth continued to express both personal and national optimism at the beginning of the 1980s. In December 1981, the president complained to an interviewer about those "who kind of chickened a little" in the face of yawning deficit projections, whereas his "own feeling—you could call it optimism—is, we haven't even seen the [supply-side tax cut] program work yet." Martin Feldstein, chair of the CEA in 1982–84, has remarked that, despite the Council's increasingly grim deficit projections, Reagan "continued to hope that higher growth would come to his rescue."[117]

Moreover, in this case Reagan's optimism was determinative. It cannot be dismissed as the affectation of a figurehead leader, who specialized in presidential pomp and public relations while leaving the heavy lifting of policymaking to staffers. Rather, the president himself called the shots that determined the parameters of policy. For example, it was Reagan who decided in the summer of 1981 that the administration would not compromise with those congressional Democrats who insisted that the third year of the Reagan personal income tax cut be made contingent on further progress in reducing spending. "I can win this," he told Murray Weidenbaum, who served as the first chair of Reagan's CEA, and thus the die was cast. "I wonder," the economist later mused, "if we would have those remaining triple-digit budget deficits if he had compromised."[118]

Even as growth failed him and the unprecedented deficits began to pile up, Reagan's optimism held firm and he put the best face possible on developments. Weidenbaum observed the remarkable evolution of the president's thought: "In the beginning, he said that big deficits would not occur because dismal scientists were underestimating the strength of the American economy. When the deficits came about, his initial reaction was that they would shrink as the economy recovered. When they endured, he shifted to a third explanation. After all, deficits served a useful purpose: They keep the liberals from voting on big new spending programs."[119]

Of course, in the end, Reagan was correct: the unprecedented string of huge deficits did prove exceedingly friendly to his antistatist inclinations. Although Stockman would criticize the president for lacking the nerve to deliver a killing blow to the welfare apparatus and other conservatives would bemoan the resilience of federal spending programs and the political clout of their constituencies, the fact is that Reagan's deficit overhang severely limited the ability of liberals to expand existing programs or establish new ones. Although the administration's record of programmatic retrenchment was uneven, fiscal defunding succeeded. The introduction of costly, new social policy initiatives became virtually unthinkable. The welfare state was not dismantled, but it was put on hold, as much through inadvertence as by conspiratorial design.

V. The Several Ironies of Reaganomics

It is one of the great ironies of the 1980s that Reagan's stumbling success in his ideological endeavor to limit the perceived leftward drift of government came at the expense of his economic goal of accelerated long-term growth. The deficits that effectively prevented any substantive extension of the welfare state (beyond the inertial advance of middle-class entitlements) at the same time compromised the drive to make the economy more productive. The administration's record on growth was lackluster. It is a further irony that when the deficits generated by the administration's supply-side approach helped the economy recover from the 1981–82 recession, they succeeded because they boosted demand in the short run; the impact of the deficits on the supply side of the economy—investment and productivity—operated in the long run to undercut economic growth.

The economic impact of the large Reagan deficits was substantial, but just how substantial and to what degree harmful have proven to be controversial questions. It will not do to oversimplify a complex matter. Even among professional economists, there was much empirical and analytical uncertainty regarding the effect of the Reagan budget "disasters." William Niskanen, a veteran of Reagan's CEA, wrote in 1988 that although economists had been studying the economic effects of government borrowing for years, "the economics community has probably never been more confused about this issue." Another economist noted that the confusion was compounded by the fact that virtually everyone who approached the topic of Reagan's deficit spending had "some kind of ax to grind." Consequently, professional opinion ranged widely: some said large deficits mattered little, if at all; others saw in them the road to ruin.[120]

If the Reagan deficits were indeed harmful, the damage they did was not immediately obvious to the casual eye. In truth, Reagan's economic record was not nearly so catastrophic as liberal critics insisted. The administration's initial tax cuts helped fuel the recovery from the 1981-82 recession by substantially increasing consumer spending, and the economy subsequently enjoyed what was to become the longest peacetime expansion in U.S. history (to that point). Most important, the Reagan expansion was sustained alongside a significant decline in inflation. Even Charles L. Schultze, Carter's CEA chairman, admitted that "the reduction in inflation was worth the pain" of the 1981–82 recession.[121] The conventional wisdom that large deficits fueled inflation proved in this case to be wrong. A massive inflow of foreign capital appeared to mitigate the immediate impact of the deficits on investment in the United States. This was surely not the immediate meltdown some critics predicted.

Nevertheless, the massive deficits constituted a real problem in several regards. First, they required drastically increased interest payments, which themselves came to constitute a significant source of increased federal spending (no small irony!), further distending subsequent budgets in a compounding fashion. Second, as the Harvard economist Benjamin Friedman has written, "Deficits absorb saving. When more of what we save goes to finance the deficit, less is available for other activities that also depend on borrowed funds. . . . The more of our saving the deficit absorbs, the harder everyone else must compete for the rest and the higher interest rates go." Thus, the sustained large deficits kept real interest rates (that is, interest rates corrected for inflation) high even after the Federal Reserve eased monetary policy to deal with the 1981–82 recession, and those high real interest rates, both short-term and long-term, in turn caused both business and individual net investment (relative to income) to lag significantly in the Reagan years. The end result was, in Friedman's words, an "extraordinary shrinkage of America's capital formation in the 1980s."[122] Third, the string of deficits meant that government subsequently skimped on the sorts of long-term investment in infrastructure and human capital (education and training) required for future economic growth. Finally, the deficits left policymakers with little fiscal purchase for fine-tuning the economy for either growth or stability. Without very much discretionary fiscal income to manipulate through spending and taxing decisions, "all that is left is monetary policy," wrote the economic journalist Thomas Friedman, "[which] is like trying to play a piano with only the black keys."

Thus, in the name of growth, the Reagan administration ended up damping one of the chief postwar engines of growth. Paul Krugman of MIT concluded that, all told, the Reagan deficits constituted "a moderate drag on U.S. economic growth." The administration's policies were, he wrote, "if anything biased against long-term growth." Ironically, the administration's vaunted supply-side approach ended up working more to boost demand in the short run than to effect long-term growth by increasing investment and productivity on the supply side. If this was less than the calamity claimed by Democratic partisans, it was nevertheless a rather incongruous and disappointing outcome for an administration embarked on a supply-side growth crusade.[123]

Moreover, the stultifying impact of the Reagan deficits was broadly psychological as well as narrowly economic. If economic activity does indeed have a psychological component—as notions such as Keynes's "animal spirits," consumer confidence, and depression and boom mentalities all imply—then the symbolic impact of the budget woes of the 1980s must also be taken into account. The deficit overhang became a problem to the extent that it seemed to reflect on the order and legitimacy of the nation's political household. The deficits were threatening in part simply because the political system seemed unable to control them.[124] That failure placed a cloud of uncertainty over both the economic and political future. How could Americans be certain inflation was really dead, and could be kept that way, when the federal government could not keep its own financial house in order? In the face of such a failure of character and nerve, how could anyone be certain U.S. policymakers and politicians would ever be able to do the things that were necessary but also difficult and painful? And without some semblance of reassurance regarding inflation, how could long-term interest rates be brought down from their unusually high level? The failure to control the budget deficits of the 1980s inevitably left hanging the fundamental question of whether the government could be trusted to control itself. Without such confidence, vigorous and sustained economic growth would remain problematic.

In a moment of self-flagellation, Stockman summed up the budget policy of the 1980s as "$1.5 trillion worth of cumulative deficits, radical deterioration of our internal and external financial health, and a political system that became so impaired, damaged, fatigued, and bloodied by coping with it year after year that it now functions like the parliament of a banana republic."[125] In a curious way, Reagan's budget director managed to overstate his capacity for harm just as he had earlier exaggerated his capacity for good. Nevertheless, his evaluation suggests an equivocal outcome indeed for a president who had proclaimed famously in the 1984 election campaign that under his leadership it was morning again in America.

Slow Drilling in Hard Boards

In the 1990s, the pursuit of economic growth took yet
another twist. Having campaigned for election as a
self-proclaimed New Democrat who combined liberal
sensibilities with hard-headed real-
ism and fiscal practicality, President
Bill Clinton displayed a centrist,
highly expedient style of leadership
that generated both extraordinary controversy and considerable practical success. Self-consciously seeking to
"build a bridge to the 21st century big enough, wide
enough, and strong enough for all of us to walk across together," the
Arkansan tacked and trimmed his way toward the new
millennium with a show of political flexibility and prag-
matism of a sort not seen since the heyday of FDR.[1]
Clinton's opportunism sowed despair among his liberal
supporters and consternation among his political opponents. Nowhere was the style more clearly demonstrated than in the realm of political economy. The
result was an eclectic approach to growth that reflected less the preconceptions of an ideological program than the lessons, both positive and negative,
of a half century's experience with growth policy.

I. Strategies of Growth: Public Investment versus Deficit Reduction

The economy got Bill Clinton elected in 1992. The incumbent Republican
George Bush had wrapped himself in the mantle of his predecessor and,

promising to consolidate the Reagan Revolution, had during the 1988 campaign dramatically pledged, "Read my lips: No new taxes." But the federal deficits kept coming, and under the pressure of the Gramm-Rudman-Hollings deficit reduction legislation passed in the mid-1980s to deal with the skyrocketing Reagan deficits, Bush felt compelled to renege on his promise. Grudgingly, he worked with Democratic congressional leaders to pass a tax hike in 1990. Hard-core conservatives cried foul, and neither Bush's management of the spectacular coalition victory in the Gulf War, nor his subsequent admission in early 1992 that breaking his no-tax pledge had been a mistake, could assuage their anger. An economic downturn solidified the resentment of the GOP's right wing.

As the 1992 campaign unfolded, Clinton's advisers sensed that the Republican president was vulnerable on the issue of the domestic economy. In the Democratic campaign headquarters that insiders nicknamed the War Room, James Carville, one of Clinton's chief political strategists, posted the phrase "The economy, stupid" to ensure that everyone remembered to emphasize the Democrats' most compelling argument. In the event, the mild recession combined with lingering uneasiness about budget deficits, rising health care costs, and slipping international economic competitiveness to drive a crucial portion of the normal Republican presidential constituency into the arms of the Democratic challenger and the third-party spoiler Ross Perot. After his narrow electoral victory, Clinton observed, "The economy is why we started down this road . . . [and] the economy is why the American people gave me the chance . . . to turn this country around."[2]

The Clinton team put growth at the center of its economic thinking from the beginning. Publicized during the campaign under the title "Putting People First," Clinton's "national economic strategy" called for a program of massive public investment in human capital and physical infrastructure—the "most dramatic economic growth program since the Second World War."[3] Public investment of this supply-side sort (as opposed to public spending conceived of as a contribution to aggregate demand) had a pedigree that went back to the public power and rural electrification initiatives of the New Deal and the developmental program of public investment espoused by Alvin Hansen in his more optimistic phase during World War II, which liberals at the beginning of the 1990s were newly rediscovering.[4]

The most influential champion of public investment among Clinton's advisers was the diminutive Robert Reich, a Rhodes scholar contemporary of the president's. Armed with a law degree and a talent for persuasion but innocent of formal advanced training in the field of economics, Reich had emerged over the course of the 1980s as a key liberal policy entrepreneur in the area of the political economy. An outspoken advocate of industrial policy, he came to see public investment as a politically more attractive means to the same ends: "The only becoming-richer strategy," he wrote at the end of the Reagan Revolution, "is to invest in our future productivity."[5] And now, in the early 1990s, as Reich recounted in his engaging but self-serving memoir, Clinton had actually *used* my ideas."[6]

The public investment strategy had strong appeal. Six Nobel laureates in economics endorsed "Putting People First," and at the economic summit convened by the president-elect in Little Rock at the end of 1992, the Princeton economist Alan Blinder sounded the "very simple theme" that "inadequate investment in our people, in the quality of our workforce, has been a big part of the problem we've been hearing about, and that correcting that should be a big part of the solution." It was, Clinton responded, "sort of preaching to the choir when you make this argument to me."[7]

Not surprisingly, Clinton asked Reich to head his economic policy team during the transition and then named him secretary of labor in the new cabinet, while Blinder joined the Council of Economic Advisers, which in turn would be chaired by another champion of public investment, Laura d'Andrea Tyson. At the newly created National Economic Council (Clinton's effort to construct an agency that would coordinate economic policy for the global economy in the same way that the National Security Council had worked to coordinate security policy for the purposes of the Cold War), deputy director Gene Sperling represented a strong public investment point of view. Outside the formal governmental structure, Clinton's favored political consultants, James Carville and Paul Begala, plumped hard for greater public investment.

A competing view of national economic priorities exerted a powerful counterinfluence on the administration, however. It held that deficit reduction was the nation's top priority. During the struggle for the Democratic nomination in 1992, former Massachusetts senator Paul Tsongas hammered away with a single-minded intensity at the pressing need for deficit reduction.[8] The same message drove Ross Perot's third-party run at the presidency. "The debt," Perot told voters, "is like a crazy aunt we keep down in the basement. All the neighbors know she's there, but nobody wants to talk about her."[9] Largely because of the efforts of Tsongas and Perot, Americans confronted the extraordinary deficits hanging over the U.S. economy more directly than ever before. Political commentators seemed to agree that continuing large budget deficits had several consequences and that all of them were bad.

Large deficits limited long-term growth, because they inevitably carried with them the perceived threat of future inflation and so encouraged investors to insist on historically high, growth-restraining long-term interest rates as a hedge against inflation. Moreover, large deficits sucked up available funds that otherwise would go into private investment to contribute to the future standard of living. In a sense, they represented a form of inter-generational larceny: the present borrowed wildly in order to avoid reductions in its own public and private consumption (in the form of either spending cuts or tax increases) and then passed on the bill to the future—their children. Finally, large deficits required large interest payments, and these of necessity diverted spending from more pressing societal needs and made the institution of new government programs, including public investment of the sort advocated by Reich and his allies, exceedingly difficult.

The key struggle in Clinton's first term occurred in the realm of national economic policy, not in the areas of gay rights or health care reform that garnered more immediate public attention. The battle pitted the administration's advocates of public investment against its champions of deficit reduction.[10] The so-called deficit hawks inside the Clinton camp included Treasury Secretary Lloyd Bentsen, OMB Director Leon Panetta and Deputy Director Alice Rivlin, and National Economic Council Director Robert Rubin. They argued not that public investment was unwise—on that issue their opinions varied—but rather that deficit reduction deserved top priority. In the gritty effort to devise an overall economic policy, they consistently urged greater deficit reduction, even at the cost of forgoing some of Clinton's prized public investment projects.

The administration's deficit hawks enjoyed two strong sources of external support: one an individual, the head of the Federal Reserve, the other that amorphous institution known as the bond market. A month after the election, Federal Reserve chairman Alan Greenspan met privately with Clinton in Little Rock and told the incoming president that credible deficit reduction was the sure path to lower long-term interest rates, and that lower rates would in turn generate accelerated growth, more jobs, and a rising stock market. The mechanism that would translate assurances about deficit reduction into lower rates was the bond market. That seemingly mysterious and vaguely sinister force was essentially the loose, inchoate conglomeration of bankers, financiers, money managers, and investors who amassed and oversaw the more than $10 trillion in long-term debt that kept U.S. capitalism afloat in 1993.[11] It was a vague collectivity unified by function and self-interest: Its members represented massive accumulated wealth that was lent out for long periods, and they shared a strong desire to see that their loans were repaid without costly losses due to inflation. They were, historically, the sound money faction. When the so-called bond market spoke, it was incumbent on a president who claimed to be a "New Democrat"—both pro-growth and pro-business—to listen.

The dispute over whether to emphasize public investment or deficit reduction was extended and bitter. The issue was one of emphasis, but the stakes were high and the outcome promised to establish a fundamental aspect of the Clinton presidency. Clinton's populist political consultants were horrified at the prospect of a conservative turn. They believed that too much deficit reduction would sacrifice vigorous growth, which served especially society's less well-off, in order to minimize inflation as a favor to the well-to-do. Begala called Budget Director Panetta "the poster boy of economic constipation," and James Carville began addressing Rubin as "Nick," pretending to confuse him with George Bush's treasury secretary, Nicholas Brady. "I used to think if there was reincarnation," Carville complained to journalists, "I wanted to come back as the president or the pope or a .400 baseball hitter. But now I want to come back as the bond market. You can intimidate everybody."[12] As the administration leaned toward increased deficit reduction, Clinton bewailed a rightward drift that he himself was overseeing: "I hope you're all aware we're the Eisenhower Republicans here," he railed sarcastically to his advisers. "We stand for lower deficits and free trade and the bond market. Isn't that great?"[13] Yet he believed also that the nation had "lost control over our financial affairs" and that the deficit was "like a bone in our throat." In the end, Clinton decided to side with the deficit hawks. When Congress finally passed the administration's economic program in August 1993, Reich complained that his original public investment proposals had been reduced to "a tiny morsel."[14]

The administration won the battle for congressional approval of its economic program, but the advocates of public investment feared that their side had lost the larger war for the soul of the Clinton presidency. The administration was, Reich noted, now locked in a "conceptual prison." "In due time," he worried, "we will end up incarcerated in a 'balanced' budget. . . . [And] a balanced budget will require massive cuts in spending."[15] In actuality, the pressure to go beyond cutting the deficit to actually balancing the budget did intensify over the next several years. The Republicans used the issue in 1994 to help them gain control of Congress for the first time since the early Eisenhower years and they continued to press for reductions in the scale and scope of government spending; in 1997, the administration and its congressional opposition agreed to a long-term plan to reach a balanced budget by the year 2002. (Events moved even more quickly, however, and the federal government actually achieved a budget surplus in 1998.)

Reich was by this time long gone, however. He left the administration in 1996, still smarting from the outcome of the earlier, defining struggle. All too many of the labor secretary's paleoliberal fears had been realized; his Oxford chum's opportunism and fundamentally moderate instincts, not his vestigial idealism, were determinative. After the defeat of public investment as the top priority of the administration's economic program, Reich became increasingly alienated. Toward the end of his Washington stint, he later recalled, he felt "as though I'm on another planet, far out in the solar system, beyond Pluto, where it's very cold and dark and the air is very thin, where I'm weightless and alone, unable to make myself heard, barely able to see the tiny speck of light that I used to call the sun."[16] At his last official meeting with the president, he observed that Clinton was stating publicly that the major task of his second administration would be to balance the federal budget. "But the deficit is down to almost *nothing*," Reich exclaimed. "The whole goddamn budget is an *accounting* number. What about the *poor*? They're bearing the brunt of deficit reduction. And what about the *investments*? Four years ago you proposed an extra fifty billion dollars a year, and it's vanished."[17] But, as the secretary knew all too well, the battle had passed him by.

The policy package that emerged from the early struggle to establish economic priorities was an eclectic mix. Debt reduction, by means of tax increases and spending cuts, was clearly the centerpiece. Public investment in infrastructure and human resources was never entirely abandoned but remained subordinate; it continued to resurface in a variety of guises, many aimed at educational assistance. Congressional opposition and the recovery from the Bush recession rendered moot Clinton's campaign call for short-term, demand-side stimulus in the form of public works spending. Similarly, candidate Clinton's promise of a middle-class tax cut became a casualty of the effort at deficit reduction, but President Clinton's tactical dance of maneuver with the Republican opposition inevitably led to further skirmishes over who could best help their preferred constituencies by reducing taxes in some focused fashion while still appearing to be resolute deficit-cutters. The passage of the North American Free Trade Act anchored a vigorous push to expand U.S. trade abroad. To help those at the bottom of the economic ladder, who seemed to be falling ever farther behind as inequality continued to worsen, the administration fought successfully to expand the earned income credit and unemployment compensation and to increase the national minimum wage.

Two aspects of the Clinton agenda stood out and imposed an overall coherence on this somewhat confusing array of initiatives. First, it was clear that this Democratic administration was domesticating the supply-side approach of the Reagan revolution by bringing that approach into the policy mainstream, in much the same way that Republicans beginning with Eisenhower had gradually absorbed first the informal lessons and later the explicit techniques of the Keynesian revolution. Clinton's chief concern was how to increase the capacity of the economy to produce more. The advocates of public investment and the deficit hawks had in essence debated which should get top priority—making labor more productive through education and training workers or making capital more productive by shifting it from government to private hands; however, both approaches aimed at the supply side of the economic equation. "Our growth policies are supply side," said Joseph E. Stiglitz, the chairman of Clinton's CEA, in mid-1996. Paul David, an economist at Stanford University, noted that "both the Democrats and the Republicans are campaigning [in 1996] on the assumption that the problem of demand had been solved and full employment can be maintained."[18] Demand-side fiscal Keynesianism of the sort that had propelled the initial, liberal formulation of postwar growthmanship was hardly visible on the public policy horizon.

Second, it was equally clear that when the pace of economic activity required fine-tuning, it would be provided via the Federal Reserve. That made Alan Greenspan the single most visible and arguably most influential economic policymaker in the world. Reich called him, ruefully, "the most powerful man in America."[19] Named to the Fed chairmanship in 1987 by President Reagan and renominated by both Bush and Clinton, Greenspan had risen to prominence in a highly idiosyncratic fashion. Born and raised in New York City, he originally set out to become a musician, training for several years at the Juilliard School and touring briefly as a professional clarinetist with the Henry Jerome swing band. After a year on the road, however, he realized that he was destined to be an average musician, and so he turned to another keen interest: business finance.

Greenspan graduated with honors in economics from New York University and began graduate work, but interrupted his academic training to start a business consulting firm and become rich. (He finally received his Ph.D. from New York University in 1977.) Along the way, he fell into a close relationship with two important mentors: the economist and public servant

Arthur Burns and the charismatic Objectivist philosopher Ayn Rand. The two gave him an abiding regard for free market capitalism and an equally strong aversion to inflation. In the late 1960s, Greenspan joined the Nixon presidential campaign and remained an informal adviser to the administration; he succeeded Herbert Stein as chairman of the CEA in 1974; and after Nixon's resignation, he served President Gerald Ford in that capacity for the duration of his term.[20]

The Clinton administration alternately wooed, cajoled, and subtly threatened Greenspan and the Fed to keep short-term interest rates low to offset the contractionary impact of deficit reduction, while waiting for that same deficit reduction gradually to drive down long-term rates. Both the White House and the Fed chairman desired the maximum sustainable economic growth consistent with controlling inflation, and their convergence of interests was symbolically displayed by Greenspan's being seated next to Hillary Rodham Clinton in the House of Representatives gallery at the president's first State of the Union address, in February 1993. For the most part, Greenspan cooperated with administration policy. "We're trying to have a more restrictive fiscal policy and our hope is we'll have room for a more expansive monetary policy," he observed in May 1993.[21]

Although there were inevitable moments of tension, especially when the Fed raised the short-term rates in 1994 and 1995 to combat what it perceived as threatening signs of inflation, both the unelected central bank and the highly political Clinton administration were committed to growth with low inflation; both believed that deficit reduction and cautious monetary oversight constituted the best available path to that goal. Consequently, Clinton surprised no one when in 1996 he reappointed Greenspan to another four-year term; the president and the Federal Reserve chairman were, the chief executive later joked, "the odd couple."[22] In announcing his decision to retain Greenspan, Clinton observed that the administration had enjoyed "a respectful and productive relationship with the Federal Reserve" and that "together our efforts have helped to create a climate for sustained economic growth, the lowest combination of unemployment, inflation, and mortgage rates in 27 years."[23]

II. Disciplined Growth and the End of the Postwar Era

The Clinton administration's economic record was by many measures impressive, and the performance of the economy undergirded a national resurgence that seemed to make premature several decades of talk about an American climacteric. Instead, the mid-1990s witnessed a moment of American triumphalism, the likes of which had not been seen, one journalist observed, since the heady days of the Marshall Plan. "The U.S. economy," he reported, "has become the world's beau ideal—its champion of growth, fiscal responsibility and technical progress." The editors of the New Republic cooed that Clinton was "presiding over what will be seen in future decades as a golden age in American history." Pollsters at the University of Michigan's Survey Research Center found Americans more confident about the economy than at any time since 1952.[24] As the twentieth century approached its close, the United States stood as the world's only true superpower, with unmatched economic and military might, unrivaled influence as a political and economic model, and perhaps the most far-reaching global cultural hegemony in history.

In mid-1997, the New York Times published in its Sunday magazine a collection of essays by foreign writers entitled "How the World Sees Us" that captured the spirit of the moment. The collection served as a remarkable cultural window on the end of the postwar era, an arresting, matching-bookend complement to the famous 1952 Partisan Review symposium "Our Country and Our Culture" that had seemed to capture the cultural tenor of the postwar era's beginning. The arresting quality of both exercises, the one an embrace of American culture by its own intellectuals, the other an appreciation from afar by an international cadre, was their underlying tone of affirmation. While more than a few contributors took their opportunity to mock American foibles, the message of the New York Times essays was that the United States mattered. As Josef Joffe expressed it in the lead essay (entitled "America the Inescapable"), "Whichever heap you choose, America sits on top of it." "America has the world's most open culture," he continued, "and therefore the world is the most open to it. . . . That makes for a universalist culture with a universal appeal. . . . We live in an 'American age,' meaning that American values and arrangements are most closely in tune with the new Zeitgeist."[25] And no small part of America's appeal and impact as world model came from the performance of the U.S. economy.

The statistics of economic performance seemed to support Joffe's characterization of the United States as "No. 1 and soaring."[26] In mid-1997, when he wrote, the stock market stood at an all-time record high; unemployment at 4.8 percent, the lowest level since November 1973; and inflation at around 3 percent, its steady level the past four years. (Each of these numerical indicators of economic well-being would improve further in the next two years.) Meanwhile, serious observers suggested that the most commonly used measure of inflation, the government's consumer price index, over-stated reality and noted that the so-called core rate of inflation (omitting the volatile categories of food and energy costs) was at its lowest level in over three decades. Turning a significant fiscal corner, the Congressional Budget Office in early 1998 projected a budget surplus for fiscal year 1998, the first since 1969, and forecast growing surpluses over the next decade.[27]

Economic growth, as measured by yearly change in the real gross domestic product, registered 2.3 percent in 1993, 3.5 percent in 1994, 2.3 percent in 1995, 3.4 percent in 1996, and 3.9 percent in 1997—moderate growth by earlier postwar standards of performance but steady nonetheless (and perhaps more impressive if the government's deflators really did exaggerate the rate of inflation and consequently understate the economy's real rate of growth).[28] In June 1997, *Fortune* magazine declared that the U.S. economy was stronger than ever before in the nation's history.[29] Moreover, what was already the third-longest economic expansion in U.S. history seemed to many economists to be sparking an incipient global boom. "This is an important historical moment," said Jeffrey Sachs, an economist at Harvard; he predicted that, barring a major extraneous shock such as a large-scale war or environmental disaster, "economic growth will raise the living standards of more people in more parts of the world than at any prior time in history."[30]

Not surprisingly, the Clinton administration basked in the reflected light of the economic good news. Robert Rubin, who left the National Economic Council to become treasury secretary, stated in early 1997 that "the most likely scenario far and away is a continuation of solid growth and low inflation as far into the future as you feel comfortable in making this kind of judgement."[31] Shortly after his reelection, Clinton said, "If we can keep interest rates down with the deficit-reduction package and a balanced budget, keep investing in education and technology and keep expanding trade, I'm not sure we'll be as victimized by the business cycle as we have been in the past. We may be able to have much more stable and much longer-term growth than we ever had before." Fed chairman Greenspan told Congress in mid-1998 that the combination of strong growth, low unemployment, and low inflation was "as impressive [a performance] as any I have witnessed in my near half-century of daily observation of the American economy."[32]

Despite the good news on many fronts and by many measures, there remained strong pressure from a variety of sources for more vigorous growth. What the economist Paul Krugman called "the growth sect" found adherents all along the political spectrum in its mid-1990s incarnation.[33] On the right stood a large segment of American business. Both the Chamber of Commerce of the United States and the National Association of Manufacturers argued that policymakers at the White House and the Fed were giving too much weight to the struggle against inflation and consequently settling for too low a level of economic growth. In 1995 the NAM board of directors unanimously demanded a commitment to higher growth. The group resolved that "the common assumption that the economy cannot exceed annual growth rates of 2.5 percent without risking a resurgence of inflation does not reflect changed economic realities"; the NAM called a target range of 3.0 to 3.5 percent in GPD growth "realistic and appropriate."[34] *Business Week* advocated what it called "a strong pro-growth position," arguing that U.S. productivity was higher and inflation lower than government statistics indicated and that the global economy now served more effectively than before to constrain prices; in light of these new realities, it believed faster growth without renewed inflation to be both possible and desirable.[35]

For a season, the Republican Party appeared to identify with such concerns, partly out of rational conviction, partly because of the kind of ideological inertia running over from the 1980s, and partly, no doubt, because they could find little other purchase for an issue-oriented economic critique of a Democratic president whose slipperiness and resilience matched even that of his famously "Teflon-coated" predecessor, Ronald Reagan. The matter crystallized as a partisan issue during the 1996 presidential campaign. First, the publisher Malcolm S. "Steve" Forbes ran for the Republican nomination on an unabashedly 1980s-style tax-cutting, pro-growth platform. Forbes's combination of personal loopiness and supply-side zealotry was easy enough to mock—Herbert Stein commented sharply that America "could afford Ronald Reagan once . . . [but] we cannot afford him again"— but Forbes's ideas managed to outlive his candidacy.[36]

When former senator Bob Dole, long a champion of fiscal probity and deficit reduction and a leader of what some derided as the "political-economy-as-root-canal-surgery" faction within the Republican Party, won the nomination, he surprised nearly everyone by picking as his vice presidential running mate the hyperkinetic cheerleader of the Republican growth tribe, Jack Kemp. Dole had already declared that if elected, he would "liberate the great engine of free enterprise"; the addition of Kemp to the ticket and the decision to build the Republican campaign around the proposal of a massive 15 percent tax cut gave Dole's somewhat ambiguous earlier pro-growth declaration an unmistakable supply-side inflection.[37] Not even the defeat of the Dole-Kemp ticket at the polls could extinguish the call for faster growth.

For example, Forbes created an "issues advocacy" group, Americans for Hope, Growth and Opportunity, that operated its own Internet web page and toll-free telephone hotline in an effort to keep alive both his hyper-growth economic message and his future presidential aspirations.

Meanwhile, congressional Republicans used their control of the Joint Economic Committee to drive home the message that the Clinton administration was "robbing America of its full growth potential." Taxes were high and real median family incomes stagnant. "We can do better," the committee majority exhorted, borrowing a page from Democratic rhetoric of yore: "Only vigorous growth will produce hope, opportunity and higher living standards for everyone." The JEC's own prescription for faster growth called for reduced taxes, less government spending, less burdensome regulation, and more freedom for people to make their own decisions about saving and investing.[38]

Those on Clinton's left voiced an equally loud, if not quite so widespread, demand for more vigorous growth. A small group of Senate Democrats—Tom Harkin of Iowa, Paul Wellstone of Minnesota, Bryon Dorgan of North Dakota, and Harry Reid of Nevada—excoriated Fed chairman Greenspan in particular for stifling the U.S. economy in order to combat inflation. "We have had growth," admitted Harken. "It has been comparatively about a C average. If we are happy with a C average in America, fine. I am not." "What we have," Wellstone complained, "is a policy that works great for bondholders, great for Wall Street, but does not work well for families in our country." Behind the fiery rhetoric of the small band of prairie populists lay two decades of both stagnant middle- and working-class incomes and increasing income inequality. Wage stagnation and income inequality exacerbated each other, the stagnation making the inequality an ever more volatile source of resentment and concern.[39]

The Left's call for faster growth also reflected the influence of sophisticated arguments mounted by a minority of liberal economists advocating faster growth. Robert Eisner, a former president of the American Economic Association, aimed his fire directly at the Fed and only obliquely at "some political leaders" (a transparent nod at intellectual candor, while avoiding the specific public indictment of a sitting, nominally liberal, Democratic president for not fighting hard enough for progressive ideals) for their acquiescence in "the dismal argument that economic growth cannot be allowed to become too rapid." At the heart of that misguided argument, Eisner maintained, was the mistaken but "still-dominant dogma" of the NAIRU—the non-accelerating inflation rate of unemployment, also known as the natural rate of unemployment.[40]

The idea that there was a natural rate of unemployment, dictated by a host of historically determined and time-specific economic factors, was framed most famously by Milton Friedman in his 1967 presidential address to the American Economic Association, and the concept was fleshed out and accepted by many economists in the following two decades. As a consequence, mainstream economists and policymakers believed that any attempt to expand the economy that drove unemployment down below the NAIRU level—calculated to be in the neighborhood of 5.5 to 6.5 percent in the early 1990s—would ineluctably, and ultimately, disastrously, raise inflation. Eisner called NAIRU "one of the more bizarre and costly turns in the development of economic science," and believed it to be a misconception rooted in bad theory and unsubstantiated by the historical record.[41] Eisner's indictment of the pessimism underlying the NAIRU concept was complemented by his own unusually strong optimism, which prompted him to remark at Clinton's preinaugural Little Rock economic summit that unemployment during the Vietnam War had been as low as 3 percent and "there's no reason we have to have a war to have unemployment that low."[42]

Lester Thurow of the Massachusetts Institute of Technology took a similar pro-growth message to a larger popular audience. Possessing a style that relied more on compelling analogies and arresting metaphors than on the arcane, increasingly mathematical hypotheses of academic economics, Thurow commanded $30,000 a speech and wrote sweeping analyses of the global economy that often became best-sellers. The *Economist* placed him in the company of John Kenneth Galbraith as "the most widely read establishment economist of the left in America." In a 1996 work entitled, with characteristic bravura, *The Future of Capitalism*, he labeled inflation "an extinct volcano" and asserted that "important structural changes" in the global economy now made its reignition "impossible."[43] The demise of inflation opened up the possibility that expansionary federal policy could itself rachet up productivity and so achieve faster growth. Keynesian measures, either increased federal spending or lower interest rates, could stimulate the economy in ways that would, in turn, excite advances in productivity. Increased demand would, in this way, be translated into increased supply. "Productivity," Thurow maintained, "comes out of an economy that is pushed. It is the result of what people do in response to the opportunities that growth makes possible, not the cause of growth."[44] In short, the government needed to step on the gas in the traditional Keynesian fashion.

Sometimes the pressure for faster growth came from the White House itself. As the 1996 presidential election loomed, Clinton became exasperated at the Fed's seemingly single-minded pursuit of price stability, which had resulted in seven credit-tightening rate hikes over the course of 1994-95. In February 1996, he nominated the New York investment banker Felix Rohatyn to the post of Fed vice chairman, in part to make the case for faster growth within the central bank. When Senate Republicans forced Rohatyn to withdraw in the face of strong opposition, Clinton publicly called for a national debate "about whether there is a maximum growth rate we can have over any period of years without inflation." The conventional wisdom, the president noted, placed that rate at about 2.5 percent. But, he declared, "there are a lot of people, including . . . Republican executives in the manufacturing sector[,] . . . who believe that global competition will keep down inflation, and that higher productivity, driven by technology and Americans working more effectively, will permit higher growth rates in the next 10 years than in the past 25."[45] Treasury Under Secretary Lawrence Summers subsequently added that the administration "cannot and will not accept any 'speed limit' on American economic growth. It is the task of the economic policy to grow the economy as rapidly, sustainably and inclusively as possible."[46]

A majority of American economists, however, questioned whether much faster growth without inflation was possible. Official statistics showed productivity growth in the business sector at 1.5 percent in 1996, with no gain the previous year (1995) and only small gains in 1994 (0.4 percent) and 1993 (0.2 percent).[47] As Paul Krugman of MIT noted, even if productivity growth were outpacing the official statistics designed to track it, as Clinton seemed to imply, that would hardly justify efforts to speed up growth, because estimates of growth and productivity were based on the same data and underestimating productivity would necessarily mean that growth was *already* faster than previously believed. Moreover, Krugman spoke for the skeptics in doubting that the official statistics were in fact missing a productivity revolution. The promised payoff of a "silicon revolution" appeared to lie at some point in the future; perhaps it was in the nature of such technological revolutions that their full impact lagged behind expectations and predictions, or perhaps the positive contribution of these technologies had been offset by other diseconomies accompanying their adoption. Nor was there persuasive evidence that global competition prevented inflation in the 70 percent of the U.S. economy that did not compete in world markets. "In short," Krugman concluded, "there is no good reason to believe that the speed limit on the economy had been raised."[48] Writing in the *New Republic*, Matthew Miller put an even finer point on the argument by pointing out that growth potential "is a function of two things: the growth of the labor force [slightly over 1 percent per year] and the growth in productivity [also slightly over 1 percent]. Arguments about growth have to work through one or both of these factors to be credible. . . . Together, these rates produce today's 'gloomy' view of potential growth of 2.2 to 2.5 percent. It's not rocket science or conspiracy. It's math."[49]

If the math regarding growth was inexorable—and those who believed that the global economy was now governed by a "new paradigm" believed otherwise—the desire for faster growth was nevertheless understandable. After all, the rate of growth from the Civil War to 1973 had averaged 3.4 percent a year, but since 1973 only 2.3 percent. The accumulated loss of this one-third decline in growth in the two decades after 1973—the difference between what the historical rate of growth would have yielded and the actual performance of the economy—has been estimated by Jeffrey Madrick at $12 trillion.[50] A loss of wealth that large was stunning enough; when viewed against the demands that were sure to be made on Americans and their economy in the foreseeable future, it became truly alarming.

Life in twenty-first-century America promised challenges aplenty for citizens and policymakers alike, as needs pressed ever more tightly against resources, and many of the most vexed and vexing issues would be those for which faster growth offered considerable relief. Of the ominous problems confronting Americans in the foreseeable future, none would be more threatening than the growing gap between rich and poor. For three decades, the well-off and well-educated in the United States had steadily pulled away from the poor and unskilled. There were many reasons for the development. Kevin Phillips, a longtime Republican strategist, created a stir in 1990 by blaming the rising inequality on the class warfare policies of Ronald Reagan; but as inequality actually accelerated in the early years of the Clinton presidency, it became clear that although government policies might exacerbate the trend on the margins through sins of both commission and omission, the main causes of the widening gap between rich and poor lay in technological change and global competition.[51]

Although faster growth alone could not reverse the trend, the advocates of faster growth believed that their policies could at least cushion the blow by reducing unemployment, creating a tighter labor market wherein workers had more bargaining power and generating the resources needed to support more generous social welfare and long-term public investment programs. Without such indirect relief or a more direct attack, increasing inequality threatened to deny America's claim to be the world's first middle-class society. Without "a huge program of re-educating and retraining . . .

investments in research and high-tech infrastructure and a willingness to run the economy with tight labor markets so that labor shortages push wages upward," wrote Lester Thurow, the United States would revert to a Spencerian survival-of-the-fittest capitalism and spiral slowly downward into a social order resembling nothing so much as the darker portions of the Middle Ages. "If we lose our middle class and become a two-tiered society," Robert Reich warned, "we not only risk the nation's future prosperity but also its social coherence and stability."[52]

The siren song of faster growth held out the promise of relief from a myriad of other problems as well. The demographic demands of the immediate future greatly strengthened the allure of growth. The future financial strain of supporting the nation's middle-class welfare state entitlements, in particular social security and Medicare, with ever fewer workers and ever more beneficiaries was as predictable as it was inescapable. In 1967, Paul Samuelson had written that "the beauty about social insurance is that it is actuarially unsound," relying as it did on population increase and economic growth to pay for benefits that outran contributions. "A growing nation," he commented archly, "is the greatest Ponzi game ever contrived."[53] The temptation to use faster growth to keep the game going was considerable. Faster growth also would help ease the economic and social integration of the continuing flood of immigrants to the United States; help propel the United States into the warm, sunlit uplands of the global economy foreseen by optimistic free traders; help protect the American competitive position that so concerned pessimistic economic nationalists; and help mitigate what some critics insisted was a "broad degradation of standards . . . all around us."[54]

The allure of such possibilities made it all the more difficult for liberals to reconfigure their doctrine to alter their long-standing reliance on growth. Admitting that liberals stood "largely discredited in the public mind," Jacob Weisberg recommended that they rehabilitate their creed by relearning the habits of restraint that guided their Progressive forebears. Among other things, that meant that liberals had to "forswear spending beyond our means, period." New initiatives would be allowable only if existing programs were cut back or new efficiencies found, or if made possible by the additional resources generated by growth: "Government must increase the size of the pie if it wants to do more," Weisberg wrote.[55] But this represented a reversion to liberalism's old escape clause rather than a step toward redefinition. In another meditation on the role of the state in the quest for a better society at the end of the twentieth century, Derek Bok, the former president of Harvard University, counted growth among the handful of basic societal goals that government needed to continue to advance. The payoff from growth continued to excite the liberal imagination: "A 1 percent addition to our growth rate over [two decades]," Bok wrote, "could wipe out the budget deficit, restore the viability of our Social Security program, increase the incomes of all families, and still leave enough money in additional tax revenues to extend health insurance to every American and fully pay for a host of other social programs that are now only partially funded or about to be cut back."[56]

One of the most striking aspects of the Clinton administration was its resistance, however wavering and ambivalent, to the blandishments of faster growth. Clinton continued to believe that some further acceleration of growth was possible, because "the globalization of our economy, the impact of technologies, improved management, increased productivity, and a greater sophistication among working people about the relationship between their incomes and the growth of their companies—all are giving us greater capacity for growth. A lot is coming through productivity, and a greater sophistication among working people about the relationship between their incomes and the growth of their companies—all are giving us greater capacity for growth. A lot is coming through productivity that so far we haven't been able to easily measure."[57]

Clinton undoubtedly welcomed faster growth, for all the reasons his critics on the right and left clamored for it. What made Clinton's new liberalism genuinely different from its postwar ideological ancestors, and from the leadership of his immediate Republican presidential predecessors, was the determination to keep the pursuit of growth within the bounds dictated by the bitter experience of several decades of disastrous inflation and debilitating fiscal irresponsibility. The approach seemed to work economically and politically, although it did not shield the administration from pressure by those who wanted to pick up the economic pace (nor, entirely, from the ravages of personal scandal, although the administration's economic success surely helped protect Clinton from those who brought his impeachment and sought to remove him from office for his actions in the Monica Lewinsky affair). The insistence that growth be disciplined and sustainable left economic policy more a tricky technical matter than the vehicle for liberal and conservative crusades it had been throughout the postwar era.

It remained possible that the Clinton administration would yield to the pressure for faster growth or that the Federal Reserve would come to share Clinton's hopeful belief that changed economic circumstances now allowed a faster sustainable rate of growth consistent with low inflation than had been true in the recent past. Testifying on the state of the economy before a House subcommittee in mid-July 1997, Greenspan left open the possibility that the economy might have moved into a new era that would allow a higher level of noninflationary growth. "From the Federal Reserve's point of view," he declared, "the faster the better."[58] Nevertheless, the resolution of the new-era/faster-growth issue promised to rest more on a technical assessment than on grand ideological visions, and for the foreseeable future policymakers will seek to ensure that their growth targets meet the primary economic criterion of sustainability and the political criterion of the appearance of discipline.

Clinton's disciplined brand of post-ideological growthmanship was still worthy of the name, but his attenuation of that old creed represented a difference sufficiently great as to be a change in kind rather than merely of degree. While Nixon and Carter, each in his own way, sought to lead the United States into what they perceived as a new era of limits, Clinton, without fanfare, had actually taken the nation there. After the long, heroic phase of the American presidency that coincided with the crises of the Great Depression, World War II, and the Cold War, Clinton managed—partly by the accident of personal scandal and partly by design—to downsize the presidency, inadvertently diminishing its dignity and self-consciously scaling down both its role and the expectations surrounding it. "F.D.R.'s mission," he told his chief speech writer in 1998, "was to save capitalism from its own excesses. Our mission has been to save government from its own excesses so it can again be a progressive force."[59]

The administration's economic program, social welfare policy, and posture in world affairs all bespoke the change. It was confirmed, in a backhanded way, by Clinton's insistence, particularly noticeable after the 1994 Republican electoral takeover of Congress, on using the bully pulpit of the presidency to establish himself as, depending on one's own political lights, the nation's moral leader or national nanny. In either case, this preachy posture was largely explained by the old chestnut "talk is cheap," a fact that Clinton hoped to turn to his advantage in a time of downsized vision and capacity.

The shift from the previous regimes of hyperactive growthmanship to the new, chastened variety helped mark the end of an era. The postwar epoch was defined by four great national projects: first, the Cold War; second, the struggle at home for full citizenship for African Americans, women, and a host of other minority groups; third, in the sociocultural realm, the cultivation of a set of values perhaps best described as "expressive individualism"; and, fourth, the pursuit—initially successful, later not—of exuberant economic growth.

All four projects have, at about the same time, effectively come to an end or been significantly recast. The collapse of the Soviet empire and the victory of the West in the Cold War constituted perhaps the most spectacular outcomes. No less significant has been the transmogrification, evident in the mid-1990s, of the pursuit of equality, expressive individualism, and growth. The struggle for equality has shifted from grand, idealistic campaigns for inclusion on a number of racial, gender, and other fronts to a congeries of smaller-bore struggles to hammer out, in virtually every aspect of American life, workable arrangements for a centrifugally diverse, multicultural society. Race relations have come to be seen less as a problem that good intentions and heroic action could speedily resolve than as a vexed and vexing reality to be wrestled with by all for the foreseeable future. The debate over affirmative action in the mid-1990s, for example, appears to be as much a traditional struggle for group advantage as it is a crusade driven by clear-cut moral imperatives. On the cultural front, the values of expressive individualism are increasingly counterbalanced by calls for greater community and more responsibility, a trend likely to accelerate as senescent baby boomers contemplate the implications of expressive individualism for a society with a rapidly growing elderly population. A value system that flourished on the disco floor seems somehow less well suited to life in a nursing home.

Meanwhile, the pursuit of growth has evolved into an essentially technocratic endeavor, still central but now more circumscribed than before. Growth remains an important societal goal, but is, for the historical moment, conceived of in a longer time frame (therefore the emphasis on sustainability), evaluated according to lower expectations, and harnessed more closely than before to the need for price stability and a measure of fiscal probity. Henceforth, the pursuit of growth promises to be less the stuff of grand crusades by Left and Right and more (to borrow a phrase Max Weber used long ago to describe politics in general) the slow drilling of hard boards.[60] The twenty-first century might well be no better—indeed, it could easily be worse—than that half century after World War II we label the postwar era. But it will be different. Postwar America is over.

8

Conclusion

Discussing the demise of historical epochs is risky business. History is littered with the premature reports of one thing or another's extinction: John Maynard Keynes wrote an influential essay entitled "The End of Laissez-Faire" in 1926; two years later, Herbert Hoover declared that the United States was about to extinguish poverty; in the 1980s, Ronald Reagan announced the passing of the mixed economy; and in the 1990s, Bill Clinton announced the end of both the era of big government and "welfare as we know it." Obviously, it pays to be cautious and specific in writing such obituaries. The postwar period is over, but the political economy of growth will continue to play out and will undoubtedly evolve in the future in ways that will surprise us. The pursuit of growth has changed, but it has hardly been ended. History seldom admits of final punctuation in such matters.

It therefore behooves us to keep the past in mind even as we move ahead. Mark Twain once wrote that history does not repeat itself, but it rhymes. One good reason for studying the past is to make ourselves more sensitive to these rhyming patterns. Attention to the historical record sharpens our perceptual acuity: it extends the range of our hearing and enhances our ability to discern not only the rhythms of the past but also the rustlings in our own day. To have the proverbial "sense of history" is to have an acquaintance with how things happened yesterday and, thus, an informed "feel" for how they might happen today and tomorrow.

With Twain's observation in mind, it is useful to consider four fundamental conclusions that emerge from the present study: first, that the pursuit of exuberant economic growth was *central* to the history of the
postwar period; second, that growthmanship was *protean*, serving not simply as an end in itself but also to advance a strikingly variable array of other
purposes; third, that the process of policymaking for growth was *complex* in
ways that defy some of the conventional wisdom about the workings of
political economy; and fourth, that, as a historical phenomenon, the pursuit
of growth proved to be much more *tricky and dangerous* in its execution and
consequences than policymakers anticipated.

Regarding centrality, the history of postwar America can be viewed,
profitably if not exclusively, in terms of a succession of growth regimes,
running from the initial formulation of growthmanship in the 1940s
through the ascendancy of a full-blown growth liberalism in the 1960s,
Richard Nixon's embrace of growth for the purposes of national rejuvenation in the aftermath of the 1960s, the retreat from growth under both economic and cultural pressures in the 1970s, the reassertion and partisan
domestication of growth by Ronald Reagan and the Republicans in the
1980s, and the emergence of a diluted but still influential technocratic brand
of growthmanship in the 1990s. Looking at the recent past in this way, we
learn important particulars from all of these individual episodes—the shift
from scarcity to abundance as the United States emerged from the Great
Depression and World War II, the aspirations and problems of liberals who
sought to redefine their creed to take advantage of the new economic environment, the complex nature of both Richard Nixon and his presidency, the
causes and symptoms of the national malaise of the 1970s, and so on—but
we also find among these episodes skeins and connections that serve to tell
a larger story about how the struggle to achieve greater growth and the failure to do so influenced both the political economy and the larger contours
of postwar American history. An examination of the political economy of
1968 illustrates how intertwined economic affairs were with the other significant domestic and international currents of the day. Neither such particular episodes nor the bigger story they tell stand as the whole of postwar
American history, but they do, arguably, lie near the center of that history.
We ignore them at our peril.

The centrality of growthmanship in all its various manifestations also
raises the issue of historical dynamics. What drove American political history in the postwar era? Many commentators argue that the postwar political culture has been shaped most profoundly by cultural and social issues. In

1970, Ben Wattenberg and Richard Scammon published *The Real Majority*, in which they advanced not only a seminal interpretation of voting behavior in the 1960s but a general theory of the elections as well. They argued that politics was driven increasingly by what they labeled "the social issue," matters of cultural values and social behavior that had become coequal with economic concerns in determining the shape of the American political landscape. Their argument was powerful and their insight has since exerted an important influence on how Americans think about their political system and how politicians seek election and behave in office. Michael Barone recently reiterated the point, writing that "in the United States politics more often divides Americans along cultural than along economic lines."[1]

Surely Wattenberg, Scammon, and Barone are right in contending that cultural politics matter. One wonders, however, whether their insight has not been embraced too fervently, leaving us with a one-dimensional way of thinking about public affairs that now overemphasizes the cultural determinants of political life and loses sight of the enduring, albeit never exclusive, significance of such "traditional" concerns as political economy. If much political behavior, especially electoral behavior, is determined by cultural issues—and who, in the heyday of identity politics, can doubt that?—public policy, a slightly but significantly different aspect of civic culture, continues to be dictated directly and influenced indirectly by the substance of political economy. The overlap among economics, politics, and policy has indeed mattered, not just in the 1992 election ("The economy, stupid") but throughout the postwar period.

The present study's second overarching conclusion is that the growth-manship we have traced was strikingly protean. Growth was pursued as a goal in its own right in a variety of theoretical and practical ways. Some sought to achieve it via policies directed at the demand side; others relied on supply-side initiatives. These approaches differed in both their conceptual underpinnings and their practical implications. Most significant, leaders and policymakers pursued growth as a means of achieving a striking variety of other ends. Postwar liberals saw growth as the vehicle for transformative social change; Richard Nixon viewed growth as a way to overcome the ravages of liberal decay. Jimmy Carter looked upon balanced growth as a way to accommodate a new era of limits; Ronald Reagan considered unbounded growth a way to transcend limits and at the same time arrest the drift toward a European-style social democracy. Throughout, growth politics took a variety of forms for a variety of purposes: domestic liberal reform, conservative restoration, world leadership and international influence, global economic preeminence, national moral rehabilitation, and simple political success and electoral victory.

Growth promised a way to solve old problems and to advance new ideological agendas. It offered both a way to achieve these ends and a way to legitimate them. The historian Ellis Hawley, in his classic study of the political economy of the New Deal, noted that one key to effective cartelization in the 1930s was the ability of those who sought government sanction for their self-interested restrictionist arrangements to wrap their cause in a politically attractive symbol or value.[2] Farmers sought to increase their group market power in the name of soil conservation; union workers did the same in the name of social justice; independent retailers sought protection from price-cutting chains in the name of defending small-town America's way of life; the giant oil companies that set production quotas claimed to be conserving a vital natural resource.

During the New Deal years, concepts such as conservation, competition, social justice, and something as amorphous as "the American way of life" often served to advance, and sometimes to disguise, other purposes, which themselves varied greatly in their political, economic, and moral content. In the postwar period, growth was added to the list, as both liberals and conservatives sought to transform the political culture and used the cause of economic growth to both further and legitimate their efforts. The striking characteristic of all such symbols, economic growth included, was their plasticity, the fact that they could be reshaped, molded, and used for a variety of vastly different ideological purposes. A lesson suggested by Hawley's work and reinforced by the present study is that any claim based on, or justified by, such symbols deserves careful scrutiny by citizen and scholar alike.

In this and other ways, the pursuit of growth in the postwar has also been more complex than some formulas for making sense of the modern political economy have allowed. In the oft-quoted concluding lines of *The General Theory*, John Maynard Keynes wrote that "the ideas of economists and political philosophers, both when they are right and when they are wrong, are more powerful than is commonly understood. Indeed, the world is ruled by little else. Practical men, who believe themselves to be quite exempt from any intellectual influences, are usually the slaves of some defunct economist. Madmen in authority, who hear voices in the air, are distilling their frenzy from some academic scribbler of a few years back. . . . Sooner or later, it is ideas, not vested interests, which are dangerous for good or evil."[3] We have seen proof throughout our story that ideas do have consequences—but not in the inexorable, rather simple fashion implied by Keynes.

Several qualifications and modifications to Keynes's dictum are in order. The study of postwar growthmanship makes it clear that the ideas that mattered first and arguably mattered most did not emerge from the store of theoretical knowledge we generally identify as the scientific substance of economics. Rather, at important points, economic science counted for less than what Joseph Schumpeter called "Vision." Schumpeter defined Vision as "a preanalytic cognitive act that supplies the raw material" for economic analyzing and theorizing. Vision, he wrote, "teaches us to *see* things in a light of which the source is not to be found in the facts, methods, and results of the pre-existing state of science." Vision is not rigorously scientific but rather "ideological almost by definition."[4] It was precisely this sort of insight, rather than the dictates of existing economic science, that led Leon Keyserling to renounce scarcity economics and reorient public policy toward growth after World War II; that led Richard Nixon to attempt to mobilize the nation to prevail in the then-emergent global economic order; and that caused a cadre of supply-siders to challenge the prevailing but compromised political-economic orthodoxy of the late 1970s.

Furthermore, Keynes's "academic scribblers" were overshadowed at critical points in the postwar pursuit of growth by those who might more accurately be called "policy entrepreneurs"—individuals such as Leon Keyserling, Walter Heller, and Jack Kemp and the supply-side publicists—who influenced developments not by virtue of their generation of new economic knowledge or the direct exercise of public authority but through their ability to inject into the public policy dialogue their particular Schumpeterian Vision. Their effectiveness rested not simply on the quality and timeliness of their ideas but also on their ability to shepherd those ideas through the public policy process. They were, in the sense of yet another Schumpeterian concept, public policy "entrepreneurs," who through their mastery of bureaucratic maneuver and presentation brought innovation to the public sector in a fashion similar to that of private-sector entrepreneurs whose innovations propelled capitalism forward in Schumpeter's famous "gales of creative destruction."[5]

Finally, Keynes erred in omitting the role of experiential learning from his schema. In pursuing economic growth, policymakers adjusted their techniques and even their goals to take into account new knowledge, changed circumstances, and, most especially, their own and others' practical experience. For example, Keyserling's embrace of growth owed more to the practical reality of postwar prosperity than it did to economic theory. Nixon based his decision to pump up the economy in order to help ensure his reelection in 1972 in part on what he held to be the lesson of the impact of rising unemployment on his previous run for the presidency in 1960. The development of supply-side economics was an attempt to come to grips with the observed theoretical and practical inadequacies of Keynesianism. By century's end, the accretion of scientific knowledge and policy experience had bred a new eclectic mix that seemed to make up in effectiveness what it lacked in purity and elegance. "In 1994 one might say," Herbert Stein wrote, "'We are all Keynesian-monetarist-supply-side-traditionalists now, and no one any longer knows what that means.'" Experience taught, he noted, that "deficits and surpluses, tax rates and subsidy programs, and the money supply all matter." The catch was that "we don't know, within considerable limits, how much they matter."[6]

Clinton's disciplined growthmanship offers a final example of such learning. Dick Morris, at one time a close political adviser, reported that the Arkansan was "haunted" from the outset by the memory of Jimmy Carter's failed presidency.[7] Indeed, Clinton's identity as a New Democrat has been, in the area of political economy, forged as much by the avoidance of past sins as by the pursuit of a positive vision of the future. Overall, Clinton pursued an economic strategy that attempted to avoid the mistakes of his predecessors. Thus, he struggled to find some middle path between Carter's overtly fatalistic acceptance of limits and Reagan's stubbornly optimistic denial of them: "We simply cannot go gently into a good night of limited economic expectations, slow growth, no growth in living standards, and a lesser future for our children. It is not the American way," Clinton declared in 1993.[8] But his own emphasis on "sustainability" did, in fact, recognize limits and draw back from the growth crusades of the past. In announcing the 1997 bipartisan balanced budget and tax-cut agreement, Clinton stressed that he was "determined never again to repeat the mistakes of the past, when we mortgaged our economy to reckless policies."[9] Of course, experience was never a perfect guide; throughout the postwar era, the nature of problems seldom remained static, and the tendency to overcorrect for past mistakes of omission and commission made learning always a perilous process.

Because the matter of growth was at once elemental, complex, and variable, policymaking for growth yielded decidedly mixed and surprisingly far-reaching results. The record of U.S. economic growth in the postwar period is hardly unimpressive, but it is unclear how much credit goes to the policymakers, how much to the innate strength of the world's largest capitalist economy, how much to dumb luck and inertia. No scholarly discipline possesses the analytical tools to settle the issue. History can, however, instruct us concerning the broader consequences of growthmanship, which in practice proved both tricky and dangerous.

The results of the various efforts to push the pace of economic growth were on several occasions nothing short of pernicious. Growth liberalism helped engineer the longest economic expansion to that point and underwrote one of the most fruitful episodes of social reform in American history, but it also encouraged an overreach that contributed significantly to the American debacle in Vietnam, that excited expectations of reform at home that any administration would have been hard-pressed to fulfill, and that planted the seeds of an inflation that would plague the U.S. economy for a generation. Richard Nixon's Whig growthmanship, which he hoped would lead the nation into a new post–Cold War era while undoing the spiritual damage of the 1960s, instead exacerbated the inflationary legacy he had inherited and contributed to the onset of a ruinous stagflation that weakened national institutions in ways that would reverberate to the end of the century. Nixon's failure ushered in a painful period of drift and uncertainty that in turn prepared the way for the risorgimento growthmanship of Ronald Reagan.

The so-called Reagan Revolution finally squeezed most of the inflationary energy out of the economy, at the cost of the most serious recession of the postwar years, and encouraged the beginning of a long-term restructuring of the economy that would later yield substantial efficiencies. In addition, the expansiveness of Reaganomics encouraged a national security posture that arguably contributed to the Western victory in the Cold War.[10] Once again, however, the costs of these gains were considerable: at the very least, a failure to arrest the dramatic surge in inequality resulting from technological change and global economic competition, together with the generation of gigantic budget deficits, the overhang from which effectively ruled out any new governmental efforts to address pressing national needs—this more a defect in liberal than conservative eyes—and which in themselves came ultimately to dampen growth and constitute an acute problem for subsequent policymakers. To be sure, postwar economic growth enriched the lives of Americans in ways so fundamental and pervasive that they are easy to overlook. But the unintended costs of the crusades for exuberant growth that we have examined were manifestly real and considerable as well.

There is reason to believe that policymakers have at last recognized, at least for a season, that such crusades bring with them danger as well as promise. The emphasis on the sustainability of growth at century's end reflects this hard-won knowledge. Under Clinton, the pursuit of growth has approached the sort of practical problem-solving-by-deft-technique that Keynes had in mind when, in a fit of unusual but admirable professional humility, he declared that economists ought to be like dentists.[11] The history of growthmanship in the postwar era confirms the great theoretician's point.

Yet it remains true that the acceptance of limits in the pursuit of growth brings its own painful consequences. Growth has often been America's "out"—the way, many believed, that the nation could somehow square the circle and reconcile its love of liberty with its egalitarian pretensions. Without the promise of particularly rapid growth to resolve this tension at the core of the American enterprise, we are at century's end left with a task fully challenging enough to test, and perhaps again to tap, whatever reserves of national genius and greatness we carry with us into the new millennium.

N⊙tes

Preface

1. Maurice Stans to Paul McCracken, 7 December 1970, WHCF:SMOF: McCracken: Box 28, Nixon President Materials, National Archives, Washington, D.C. (hereafter, NPM).
2. *New York Times*, 16 December 1970.
3. U.S. Presidents, *Public Papers of the Presidents*, Richard Nixon, 1970, 1134–36. Galbraith's comments on the cult of production are found in *The Affluent Society* (Boston, 1958), esp. ch. 9.
4. Alan Wolfe, *America's Impasse: The Rise and Fall of the Politics of Growth* (New York, 1981), 10.
5. Adam Smith, *An Inquiry Into the Nature and Causes of the Wealth of Nations* (New York, 1937), 69.
6. David M. Wrobel, *The End of American Exceptionalism: Frontier Anxiety from the Old West to the New Deal* (Lawrence, Kans., 1993).

Prologue

1. Twelve Southerners, *I'll Take My Stand: The South and the Agrarian Tradition*, introd. by Louis D. Rubin Jr. (Baton Rouge, La., 1977). See also Paul Conkin, *The Southern Agrarians* (Knoxville, Tenn., 1988).
2. Lyle Lanier, "Discussion: The Agrarian-Industrial Metaphor," in *A Band of Prophets: The Vanderbilt Agrarians After Fifty Years*, ed. William C. Havard and Walter Sullivan (Baton Rouge, La., 1982), 167; John Crowe Ransom, "Reconstructed But Unregenerate," in *I'll Take My Stand*, 8, 12.
3. James C. Cobb, *The Selling of the South: The Southern Crusade for Industrial Development, 1936–1980* (Baton Rouge, La., 1982), 5–63; idem, *Industrialization and Southern Society, 1877–1984* (Lexington, Ky., 1984), 27–50.
4. Quoted in Howard P. Segal, *Technological Utopianism in American Culture* (Chicago, 1985), 122; "Toward a New System," *The Nation*, 7 September 1932, 205; and William E. Akin, *Technocracy and the American Dream: The Technocrat Movement, 1900–1941* (Berkeley, Calif., 1977), 150.

5. Quoted in Segal, *Technological Utopianism*, 122.

6. Alan Brinkley, *Voices of Protest: Huey Long, Father Coughlin, and the Great Depression* (New York, 1982), 157–58.

7. U.S. Presidents, *Public Papers of the Presidents of the United States*, Herbert Hoover, 1929 (Washington, 1974), 11 (hereafter *Public Papers*); Franklin D. Roosevelt, *The Public Papers and Addresses of Franklin D. Roosevelt*, comp. Samuel Rosenman, 13 vols. (New York, 1938–50), 1:645.

8. Roosevelt, *Public Papers and Addresses*, 1:743, 750–52.

9. Hoover's speech of 31 October 1932 from Aaron Singer, ed., *Campaign Speeches of American Presidential Candidates, 1928–1972* (New York, 1976), 103–21; Hoover, *The Challenge to Liberty* (New York, 1934); Alfred M. Landon, *America at the Crossroads* (New York, 1936), 13–15; Theodore Rosenof, *Dogma, Depression, and the New Deal* (Port Washington, N.Y., 1975), 113.

10. Harry Hopkins, "The Future of Relief," *New Republic*, 10 February 1937, 8.

11. Corrington Gill, *Wasted Manpower: The Challenge of Unemployment* (New York, 1939), 277, 274, 255.

12. Alvin Hansen, "Economic Progress and Declining Population Growth," *American Economic Review* 29 (March 1939): 4. See also Robert M. Collins, *The Business Response to Keynes, 1929–1964* (New York, 1981), passim. The most sophisticated treatment of Hansen's thought is Theodore Rosenof, *Economics in the Long Run: New Deal Theorists and Their Legacies, 1933–1993* (Chapel Hill, N.C., 1997).

13. Richard Gilbert et al., *An Economic Program for American Democracy* (New York, 1938); Elliott Roosevelt, ed., *F.D.R.: His Personal Letters*, 4 vols. (New York, 1947–50), 4:857–58.

14. Quoted in Arthur M. Schlesinger Jr., *The Age of Roosevelt: The Coming of the New Deal* (Boston, 1958), 64; Mordecai Ezekiel, *$2500 a Year: From Scarcity to Abundance* (New York, 1936), viii-ix. See also Schlesinger, *The Age of Roosevelt: The Politics of Upheaval, 1935–36* (Boston, 1960), 215–18; and Ezekiel, *Jobs for All Through Industrial Expansion* (New York, 1939).

15. Quoted in Schlesinger, *Coming of the New Deal*, 62–63; Henry A. Wallace, *New Frontiers* (New York, 1934), 28–29, 34, 47.

16. Alan Brinkley, *The End of Reform: New Deal Liberalism in Recession and War* (New York, 1995), 86.

17. Jordan A. Schwarz, *The New Dealers: Power Politics in the Age of Roosevelt* (New York, 1993), xi-xvii.

18. Ibid., 83; Bruce J. Schulman, *From Cotton Belt to Sunbelt: Federal Policy, Economic Development, and the Transformation of the South* (New York, 1991), 91–94. See also Alan Brinkley, "Liberals and Public Investment: Recovering a Lost Legacy," *The American Prospect* (Spring 1993): 81–86.

19. Richard Lowitt, *The New Deal and the West* (Bloomington, Ind., 1984), 225–27; Gerald D. Nash, *The American West Transformed: The Impact of the Second World War* (Bloomington, Ind., 1985), chs. 1–2; idem, *World War II and the West: Reshaping the Economy* (Lincoln, Nebr., 1990); Mark S. Foster, "Giant of the West: Henry J. Kaiser and Regional Industrialization, 1930–1950," *Business History Review* 59 (Spring 1985): 1–23.

20. Quoted in Patrick J. Maney, *"Young Bob" La Follette: A Biography of Robert M. La Follette, Jr., 1895–1953* (Columbia, Mo., 1978), 206. See also John E. Miller, *Governor Philip F. La Follette, The Wisconsin Progressives, and the New Deal* (Columbia, Mo., 1982), ch. 7.

21. Quoted in Rosenof, *Dogma, Depression, and the New Deal*, 92.

22. Roosevelt, *Public Papers and Addresses*, 6:5.

23. John Morton Blum, *From the Morgenthau Diaries: Years of Urgency, 1938–1941* (Boston, 1964), 41; Herbert Stein, *The Fiscal Revolution in America* (Chicago, 1969), 120–23; James Patterson, *Congressional Conservatism and the New Deal* (Lexington, Ky., 1967), 288–324.

24. Brinkley, *End of Reform*, 86–91; Ellis Hawley, *The New Deal and the Problem of Monopoly: A Study in Economic Ambivalence* (Princeton, 1966), 187–269.

25. Jeffrey L. Meikle, *Twentieth Century Limited: Industrial Design in America, 1925–1939* (Philadelphia, 1979), 189–90. See also Helen A. Harrison et al., *Dawn of a New Day: The New York World's Fair, 1939/40* (New York, 1980).

26. Keynes to J. M. Clark, 26 July 1941; and Walter Salant to Joseph Dorfman, 8 June 1971, both in Box 1, Walter Salant MSS, Harry S. Truman Presidential Library (hereafter HSTL).

27. See Bryd L. Jones, "The Role of Keynesians in Wartime Policy and Postwar Planning, 1940–1946," *American Economic Review* 62 (May 1972):125–33; John Kenneth Galbraith, "The National Accounts: Arrival and Impact," in U.S. Bureau of the Census, *Reflections of America: Commemoration of the Statistical Abstract Centennial* (Washington, 1980), 75–80; and John Brigante, *The Feasibility Dispute: Determination of War Production Objectives for 1942 and 1943* (Washington, D. C., 1950).

28. Quoted in Richard A. Lauderbaugh, *American Steel Makers and the Coming of the Second World War* (Ann Arbor, Mich., 1976), 78.

29. John Kenneth Galbraith, "The National Accounts," 77.

30. I. F. Stone, *Business As Usual* (New York, 1941), 122.

31. Quoted in Lauderbaugh, *American Steel Makers*, 82.

32. Bruce Catton, *The War Lords of Washington* (New York, 1948), 46.

33. John Kenneth Galbraith, *A Life in Our Times: Memoirs* (Boston, 1981), 149.

34. The best account is Lauderbaugh, *American Steel Makers*, 87–107. See also Gerald T. White, *Billions for Defense: Government Financing of the Defense Plant Corporation During World War II* (University, Ala., 1980).

35. U.S. Bureau of the Budget, *The United States at War: Development and Administration of the War Program by the Federal Government* (Washington, D. C., 1946), 339–53; and Walter Wilcox, *The Farmer in the Second World War* (Ames, Iowa, 1947), 45.

36. Russell Weigley, *The American Way of War* (New York, 1973), 146.

37. Ronald Schaffer, *Wings of Judgment: American Bombing in World War II* (New York, 1985), 166; Winston S. Churchill, *The Hinge of Fate* (Boston, 1950), 346. See also Kent Roberts Greenfield, *American Strategy in World War II: A Reconsideration* (Baltimore, 1963), 74.

38. Richard M. Leighton, "The American Arsenal Policy in World War II: A Retrospective View," in *Some Pathways in Twentieth-Century History*, ed. Daniel R. Beaver (Detroit, 1969), 221–22.

39. Ibid., 225, 251; John Craf, *A Survey of the American Economy, 1940–1946* (New York, 1947), 178.

40. R. Elberton Smith, *The Army and Economic Mobilization* (Washington, D. C., 1959), 9–11; Robert H. Connery, *The Navy and Industrial Mobilization in World War II* (Princeton, N.J., 1951), 3; Frederic C. Lane, *Ships for Victory: A History of Shipbuilding Under the U.S. Maritime Commission in World War II* (Baltimore, 1951), 4. The statistic for cargo vessels and tankers is for the period 1939–45.

41. Donald M. Nelson, *Arsenal of Democracy: The Story of American War Production* (New York, 1946), 259.

42. "National Industrial Conference Board Round-table, May 26, 1943," Box 18, Transcripts, Records of the National Industrial Conference Board, Hagley Library, Wilmington, Delaware.

43. U.S. National Resources Planning Board, *Security, Work, and Relief Policies* (Washington, D. C., 1942), 545.

44. U.S. National Resources Planning Board, *National Resources Development: Report for 1943. Part I. Post-War Plan and Program* (Washington, D. C., 1943), 4.

45. Frederic A. Delano et al. to FDR, 24 August 1943, OF 1092, Franklin D. Roosevelt Presidential Library, Hyde Park, New York.

46. Hansen to Gerhard Colm, 11 July 1944, Box 1, Gerhard Colm MSS, HSTL.

47. Hansen to David McCord Wright, 30 July 1945, HUG (FP)-3.50, Box 2, Alvin Hansen MSS, Harvard University.

48. Roosevelt, *Public Papers and Addresses of Franklin D. Roosevelt*, 12:574–75; 13:369–78.

49. Theodore Rosenof, "The Economic Ideas of Henry A. Wallace, 1933–1948," *Agricultural History* 41 (April 1967): 143–53; John Morton Blum, "Portrait of the Diarist," in Blum, ed., *The Price of Vision: The Diary of Henry A. Wallace, 1942–1946* (Boston, 1973), 3–49; Henry A. Wallace, *Sixty Million Jobs* (New York, 1945); and Norman D. Markowitz, *The Rise and Fall of the People's Century: Henry A. Wallace and American Liberalism, 1941–1943* (New York, 1973).

50. Walter P. Reuther, "Reuther Challenges `Our Fear of Abundance,'" *New York Times Magazine*, 16 September 1945, 8.

51. Paul Hoffman, speech to the National Association of Manufacturers, 6 December 1944, Box 2, Edwin Nourse MSS, HSTL.

52. Quoted in Herman E. Krooss, *Executive Opinion* (Garden City, N.Y., 1970), 306–7.

53. Richard S. Tedlow, *New and Improved: The Story of Mass Marketing in America* (New York, 1990), 328–35.

54. U.S. Presidents, *Public Papers*, Harry S. Truman, 1946, 125.

Chapter 1

1. Memo, "Postwar Employment," 9 October 1944, Box 1, Colm MSS, HSTL.

2. Committee for Economic Development, *Taxes and the Budget: Program for Prosperity in a Free Economy* (New York, 1947), 10.

3. Chester Bowles, *Promises to Keep: My Years in Public Life, 1941–1969* (New York, 1971), 161–62.

4. Chester Bowles, *Tomorrow Without Fear* (New York, 1946), 44.

5. CEA to Truman, 13 December 1946, Box 1, John D. Clark MSS, HSTL.

6. Craufurd D. Goodwin, "Attitudes toward Industry in the Truman Administration: The Macro Origins of Micro-Economic Policy," paper presented at the Truman

Centennial Symposium, Woodrow Wilson Center, September 1984. See also Edwin
Nourse, "The Professional Background of the First Chairman of the Council of
Economic Advisers," August 1963, Box 1, Nourse MSS, HSTL.

7. Erwin C. Hargrove and Samuel A. Morley, eds., *The President and the Council of Economic Advisers: Interviews with CEA Chairman* (Boulder, Colo., 1984), 79.

8. U.S. Council of Economic Advisers, *First Annual Report to the President* (Washington, D. C., 1946), 9, 12.

9. U.S. Council of Economic Advisers, *Second Annual Report to the President* (Washington, D. C., 1947), 7.

10. Ibid.

11. Ibid., 27.

12. Ibid., 10, 19.

13. U.S. Council of Economic Advisers, *Business and Government: Fourth Annual Report to the President* (Washington, D. C., 1949), 3, 5, 6, 7.

14. Leon Keyserling to John D. Clark, 26 November 1956, in Box 5, Keyserling Papers, HSTL; and Keyserling Oral History Memoir, HSTL. See also Keyserling, "New Economics for New Problems," 4 December 1951, OF 396, Box 1076, HSTL.

15. Leon Keyserling, "Economic Outlook for Sales Management," May 1949, General File/Keyserling, President's Secretary's File, HSTL.

16. Gerhard Colm, Memo, 4 May 1950, OF 396, Box 1076, HSTL.

17. Charles S. Maier, "The Politics of Productivity: Foundations of American International Economic Policy After World War II," *International Organization* 31 (Autumn 1977): 629.

18. Michael J. Hogan, *The Marshall Plan: America, Britain, and the Reconstruction of Western Europe, 1947–1952* (New York, 1987), 23.

19. Quoted in David W. Ellwood, *Rebuilding Europe: Western Europe, America, and Postwar Reconstruction* (London, 1992), 229.

20. U.S. Presidents, *Public Papers*, Harry S. Truman, 1949, 3. Compare, for example, the State of the Union Address and the Special Message to Congress on the President's Economic Report in January with July's Report to the American People on the State of the National Economy, ibid., 1–7, 13–26, 369–74.

21. Ibid., 494. On Keyserling's overall influence, see Lester H. Brune, "Guns and Butter: The Pre-Korean War Dispute Over Budget Allocations," *American Journal of Economics and Sociology* 48 (July 1989): 357–71; Alonzo L. Hamby, "The Vital Center, the Fair Deal, and the Quest for a Liberal Political Economy," *American Historical Review* 77 (June 1972): 653–78; Donald K. Pickens, "Truman's Council of Economic Advisers and the Legacy of New Deal Liberalism," in Harry S. Truman, *The Man from Independence*, ed. William F. Levantrosser (New York, 1986), 245–63.

22. Edwin G. Nourse, *Economics in the Public Service: Administrative Aspects of the Employment Act* (New York, 1953), 243–46; CEA to Truman, 14 January 1949, and "Draft of Interagency Working Group: A Bill," 15 January 1949, both in OF 396, Box 1076, HSTL.

23. Nourse, *Economics in the Public Service*, 246–48; and the diary entries for 18 June and 6 July 1949, Box 6, Nourse MSS, HSTL.

24. Steve Fraser, "The `Labor Question,'" in *The Rise and Fall of the New Deal Order, 1930–1980*, ed. Steve Fraser and Gary Gerstle (Princeton, N.J., 1989), 57; and Nelson

Lichtenstein, "From Corporatism to Collective Bargaining: Organized Labor and the Eclipse of Social Democracy in the Postwar Era," ibid., 122–52.

25. Nelson Lichtenstein, *The Most Dangerous Man in Detroit: Walter Reuther and the Fate of American Labor* (New York, 1995), 271–90.

26. U.S. Presidents, *Public Papers*, Harry S. Truman, 1950, 462.

27. U.S. Presidents, *The Economic Report of the President, 1950* (Washington, D. C., 1950), 2.

28. John Lewis Gaddis, *Strategies of Containment: A Critical Appraisal of Postwar American National Security Policy* (New York, 1982). On Keyserling's role, see Fred M. Kaplan, "Our Cold-War Policy, Circa '50," *New York Times Magazine*, 18 May 1980, 34 ff. The text of NSC-68, with helpful commentary, is in Ernest R. May, ed., *American Cold War Strategy: Interpreting NSC 68* (Boston, 1993), 23–82 (quotation from 46).

29. Leon Keyserling Oral History Memoir, HSTL.

30. See Edward S. Flash Jr., *Economic Advice and Presidential Leadership: The Council of Economic Advisers* (New York, 1965), 39–61; Keyserling, "Production: America's Great Non-Secret Weapon," 23 October 1950; and CEA to Truman, 12 September 1950 and 19 October 1950, all in OF 985, Box 1564, HSTL.

31. Quoted in Flash, *Economic Advice*, 45.

32. Nourse to Truman, 29 July 1946, quoted in Nourse, *Economics in the Public Service*, 106–7; Nourse "Economics in the Public Service," 23 January 1947, OF 985, Box 1564, HSTL.

33. Nourse, "Economics in the Public Service," 23 January 1947, OF 985, Box 1564, HSTL.

34. Nourse to Donald Wallace, 3 May 1948, Box 5, Nourse MSS, HSTL.

35. John D. Clark, "The President's Economic Council," unpublished manuscript [1948], chapter 7: 44–45, 53, in Box 2, Clark MSS, HSTL.

36. Keyserling to Nourse, 14 August 1948, Box 5, Nourse MSS, HSTL.

37. Roy Blough to William Frank, 23 September 1950, Box 9, Roy Blough MSS, HSTL.

38. Leon Keyserling Oral History Memoir, HSTL.

39. Paul Samuelson, "Economic Growth," in Robert C. Merton, ed., *The Collected Scientific Papers of Paul Samuelson*, 3 vols. (Cambridge, Mass, 1972), 3:704.

40. R. F. Harrod, "Scope and Method of Economics," *Economic Journal* 48 (September 1938): 405; idem, "An Essay in Dynamic Theory," *Economic Journal* 49 (March 1939): 14–33; idem, *Towards a Dynamic Economics* (London, 1948); Evsey D. Domar, "Capital Expansion, Rate of Growth, and Employment," *Econometrica* 14 (April 1946): 137–47; idem, "Expansion and Employment," *American Economic Review* 37 (March 1947): 34–55; and idem, "The Problem of Capital Accumulation," *American Economic Review* 38 (December 1948):777–94.

41. Moses Abramovitz, "Economics of Growth," 133, 153; Harold F. Williams, "Comment," 182; and Simon Kuznets, "Comment," 180, all in Bernard F. Haley, ed., *A Survey of Contemporary Economics, Volume II* (Homewood, Ill., 1952). On Samuelson's text, see the comments of Robert J. Gordon in *The American Economy in Transition*, ed. Martin Feldstein (Chicago, 1980), 159.

42. Nourse, Daily Diary, 2 September 1949, Box 6, Nourse MSS, HSTL.

43. Nourse to Bertram Gross, 24 February 1953, Box 1, Nourse MSS, HSTL.

44. Keyserling, "Congressional Testimony of March 12, 1952," OF 985, Box 1564, HSTL. See also Keyserling to J. M. Clark, 1 April 1950, Box 5, Keyserling MSS, HSTL.

45. Keyserling, "New Economics for New Problems," 4 December 1951, OF 396, Box 1076, HSTL.

46. Nourse, Daily Diary, 26 November 1946, Box 3, Nourse MSS, HSTL.

47. Hargrove and Morley, eds., *Interviews with CEA Chairmen*, 58.

48. Joseph Feeny to Truman, 26 January 1950; and Truman to Secretary of the Treasury, 31 January 1950, both in OF 396, HSTL.

49. Donald Wallace to Nourse, July, 1947, Box 1, Nourse MSS, HSTL. See also Nourse to Wallace, 3 May 1948, Box 5, Nourse MSS, HSTL.

50. Nourse to Paul Douglas, 2 August 1949, in Daily Diary 1949, Box 6, Nourse MSS, HSTL.

51. Roy Blough to William Hewett, 1 November 1950; and Blough to Paul Parker, 26 December 1950, both in Box 9, Blough MSS, HSTL.

52. Nourse, *Economics in the Public Service*, 210.

53. Pickens, "Truman's Council of Economic Advisers," 250–51; Nourse quoted in Michael J. Hogan, *A Cross of Iron: Harry S. Truman and the Origins of the National Security State, 1945–1954* (New York, 1998), 279.

54. Hogan, *Cross of Iron*, 279–84.

55. Leon Keyserling Oral History Memoir, HSTL.

56. J. L. Fisher to Keyserling, 14 February 1952, in Box 11, Blough MSS, HSTL.

57. W. W. Rostow, *The Process of Economic Growth*, 2nd ed. (New York, 1962), v; Simon Kuznets, "Comment," 180.

58. Stuart Rice to Henry A. Wallace, 22 December 1944, Box 32, Stuart Rice MSS, HSTL.

59. The discussion of national income accounting that follows is based on Paul Studenski, *The Income of Nations. Part I, History* (New York, 1961); Edgar Z. Palmer, *The Meaning and Measurement of the National Income and of Other Social Accounting Aggregates* (Lincoln, Nebr., 1966); John W. Kendrick, "The Historical Development of National-Income Accounts," *History of Political Economy* 2 (Fall 1970): 284–315; and Carol S. Carson, "The History of the United States National Income and Product Accounts: The Development of an Analytical Tool," *The Review of Income and Wealth* 21 (June 1975): 153–81.

60. CEA to Truman, 4 April 1947, Box 1, Clark MSS, HSTL.

61. John D. Clark, "The President's Economic Council," unpublished manuscript [1948], chapter 4, 23, in Box 3, Clark MSS, HSTL.

62. Walter Salant to Staff, 16 April 1947, Box 2, Walter Salant MSS, HSTL.

63. On the history of federal statistical programs, see Bureau of the Budget, Office of Statistical Standards, "Functions and Operations," November 1952, Box 12, Rice MSS, HSTL.

64. On the wartime use of statistics, see the correspondence in Box 32, Rice MSS, HSTL.

65. Bureau of the Budget, Division of Statistical Standards, "Statistical Requirements in the Readjustment Period: Detailed Plans for a Government-wide Program," 1 November 1944, Box 13, Rice MSS, HSTL.

66. Rice to Assistant Director, Bureau of the Budget, 25 November 1944, Box 7; Harold D. Smith to Truman, 25 April 1945, Box 8, both in Rice MSS, HSTL.

67. See, for example, the memo "Integrity of Government Statistics: 1946 Controversy," Box 114, Rice MSS, HSTL.

68. Rice to Frederick J. Lawton, 2 February 1949, Box 8, Rice MSS, HSTL.
69. This trichotomy is borrowed from Milton Moss, "Changing Boundaries of Federal Statistics," March 1969, Box 164, Rice MSS, HSTL.
70. Nourse, *Economics in the Public Service*, 166–67.
71. Gerhard Colm, "The Nation's Economic Budget: A Tool of Full Employment Policy," in National Bureau of Economic Research, *Studies in Income and Wealth*, vol. 10 (New York, 1947), 89.
72. George Soule, *New York Times Book Review*, 1 February 1948, 29.
73. Gerhard Colm to Staff, 14 October 1947, Box 4, Nourse MSS, HSTL.
74. Nourse, *Economics in the Public Service*, 233.
75. "The Operations of the Council of Economic Advisers," 15 May 1950, Box 11, Blough MSS, HSTL; National Bureau of Economic Research, *Long-Range Economic Projection* (Princeton, N.J., 1954).
76. Hargrove and Morley, eds., *Interviews with CEA Chairmen*, 73.
77. Keyserling to Committee of Experts on the New England Economy, 15 May 1950, OF 396, Box 1076, HSTL.
78. Flash, *Economic Advice*, 62–99; Leon Keyserling Oral History Memoir, HSTL; and Hargrove and Morley, eds., *Interviews with CEA Chairmen*, 52–54, 77–84.
79. Walter Heller, *New Dimensions of Political Economy* (Cambridge, Mass., 1966), 29.
80. Truman to Keyserling, 15 January 1953 and 19 September 1963, both in Box 1, Keyserling MSS, HSTL; Alonzo Hamby, *Man of the People: A Life of Harry S. Truman* (New York, 1995), 500–501.
81. The Wardman Park group is discussed in Cabell Phillips, *The Truman Presidency* (Baltimore, 1966), 162–65; and the Leon Keyserling and C. Gerard Davidson Oral History Memoirs, HSTL.
82. Jonathan Hughes, *The Vital Few: The Entrepreneur and American Economic Progress*, expanded ed. (New York, 1986), ix.
83. W. Robert Brazelton and Willadee Wehmeyer, "Leon H. Keyserling and Mary Dublin Keyserling, Growth and Equity: Over Fifty Years of Economic Policy and Analysis, From Roosevelt and Truman to Bush," unpublished manuscript (1989), 16–17, Keyserling MSS, HSTL.
84. The best treatment of postwar optimism and the consumer culture, indeed the best synthetic guide to early postwar history, is James T. Patterson, *Grand Expectations: The United States, 1945–1974* (New York, 1996).

Chapter 2

1. Alvin H. Hansen, *The Postwar American Economy: Performance and Problems* (New York, 1964), 5.
2. Andrew Hacker, ed., *U/S: A Statistical Portrait of the American People* (New York, 1983), 13–14.
3. *The Statistical History of the United States from Colonial Times to the Present* (Stamford, Conn., 1965), 462.
4. Quoted in William Leuchtenburg, *A Troubled Feast: American Society Since 1945*, rev. ed. (Boston, 1979), 55.

5. John Updike, *Verse* (Greenwich, Conn., 1965), 55.

6. Norman Mailer, "Superman Comes to the Supermart," *Esquire*, November 1960, 119–27.

7. *Statistical History*, 143, 158.

8. Ibid., 409, 422.

9. Ibid., 143, 158.

10. Peter John de la Fosse Wiles, *Distribution of Income: East and West* (Amsterdam, 1974), xiv, 48.

11. Paul Samuelson, *Economics*, 8th ed. (New York, 1970), 110.

12. *Statistical History*, 166.

13. Ibid., 168.

14. Quoted in Stephen E. Ambrose, *Eisenhower: The President* (New York, 1984), 249.

15. Calculated from statistics in Herbert Stein, *Presidential Economics: The Making of Economic Policy from Roosevelt to Reagan and Beyond* (New York, 1984), 381.

16. On the debate regarding the CEA's future, see Raymond J. Saulnier, *Constructive Years: The U.S. Economy Under Eisenhower* (Lanham, Md., 1991), 26–30.

17. For a succinct summary, see Erwin C. Hargrove and Samuel A. Morley, eds., *The President and the Council of Economic Advisers: Interviews with CEA Chairmen* (Boulder, Colo., 1984), 89–94, 123–26.

18. Arthur F. Burns, "Progress Toward Economic Stability," *American Economic Review* 50 (March 1960): 1.

19. Keyserling manuscript, "Stabilizing Prosperity: Our Foremost Test," with cover letter to Edwin Nourse and John Clark, 17 May 1948, Box 5, Keyserling MSS, HSTL; Raymond J. Saulnier, *The Strategy of Economic Policy* (New York, 1963), 21. The views of Eisenhower's economic advisers are cogently discussed in Iwan W. Morgan, *Eisenhower Versus 'The Spenders': The Eisenhower Administration, the Democrats and the Budget, 1953–60* (New York, 1990), ch. 1.

20. Dwight D. Eisenhower, *The White House Years: Waging Peace, 1956–1961* (Garden City, N.Y., 1965), 462.

21. U.S. Presidents, *Public Papers*, Dwight D. Eisenhower, 1959 (Washington, D.C., 1960), 125.

22. U.S. Presidents, *Economic Report of the President, 1962* (Washington, D.C., 1962), 113.

23. Harold G. Vatter, *The U.S. Economy in the 1950s: An Economic History* (New York, 1963), 8.

24. U.S. Presidents, *Economic Report of the President, January 1961* (Washington, 1961), 44. See also Raymond J. Saulnier, "Anti-Inflation Policies in President Eisenhower's Second Term," paper delivered before the American Historical Association, 30 December 1973, in White House Central Files:Staff Member and Office Files:Herbert Stein, Box 25, NPM.

25. Leon H. Keyserling, "Full Employment," in *Guide to Politics, 1954*, ed. Quincy Howe and Arthur M. Schlesinger Jr. (New York, 1954), 9, 10, 13.

26. Steven M. Gillon, *Politics and Vision: The ADA and American Liberalism, 1947–1985* (New York, 1987), 113.

27. Keyserling to John Clark, 22 December 1959, Box 5, Keyserling MSS, HSTL; Sidney Hyman, "Can a Democrat Win in '60?" *The Reporter*, 5 March 1959, 14. Keyserling's DAC experience is discussed in Morgan, *Eisenhower Versus "The Spenders,"* 32–33, 42–48.

28. Eisenhower, *Waging Peace*, 377; Nixon quoted in Stephen Ambrose, *Nixon: The Education of a Politician, 1913–1962* (New York, 1987), 487; Stans quoted in "Russian v. U.S. Growth," *Time*, 14 December 1959, 90; Henry Hazlitt, "Rates of Growth," *Newsweek*, 25 August 1958, 73; Hazlitt, "Wrong Aims and Means," *Newsweek*, 9 March 1959, 100; Hazlitt, "The 'Growth' Game," *Newsweek*, 2 March 1959; 73.

29. Quoted in U.S. Congress, Joint Economic Committee, *Comparisons of the United States and Soviet Economies, Papers Submitted by Panelists Appearing Before the Subcommittee on Economic Statistics, Pts. 1–3* (Washington, D.C., 1959), 549.

30. Walter Lippmann, "America Must Grow," *Saturday Evening Post*, 5 November 1960, 92.

31. Quoted in U.S. Congress, Joint Economic Committee, *Comparisons of the United States and Soviet Economies, Papers*, 549; U.S. Congress, Joint Economic Committee, *Comparisons of the United States and Soviet Economies, Hearings* before the Joint Economic Committee, 86th Cong., 1st sess., 1959.

32. Legislative Reference Service, *Soviet Economic Growth: A Comparison with the United States*, A Study Prepared for the Subcommittee on Foreign Economic Policy of the Joint Economic Committee (Washington, D.C., 1957), 24.

33. Ibid., 24, 136.

34. U.S. Congress, Joint Economic Committee, *Comparisons of the United States and Soviet Economies, Hearings*, 6.

35. Ibid., 11.

36. "Russian v. U.S. Growth," *Time*, 14 December 1959, 90.

37. Domar quotation from U.S. Congress, Joint Economic Committee, *Comparisons of the United States and Soviet Economies, Hearings*, 247; Lovestone and Peterson quotations from U.S. Congress, Joint Economic Committee, *Comparisons of the United States and Soviet Economies, Papers*, 567, 525.

38. *Prospect for America: The Rockefeller Panel Reports* (Garden City, N.Y., 1961), xv, 251, 251–333 passim.

39. *The National Purpose* (New York, 1960), v, 120, 38, 133.

40. *Goals for Americans: The Report of the President's Commission on National Goals* (New York, 1960), 10–11.

41. Paul H. Douglas and Howard Shuman, "Growth Without Inflation," *New Republic*, 26 September 1960, 22.

42. William R. Allen, "Thoughts on Economic Growth: The Full and Efficient Use of Resources," *New Republic*, 6 June 1960, 13, 16.

43. James Tobin, "Growth Through Taxation," *New Republic*, 25 July 1960, 15, 18.

44. Leon H. Keyserling, "Investment and Consumption," *New Republic*, 10 October 1960, 17–19.

45. Quoted in Arthur M. Schlesinger Jr., *A Thousand Days: John F. Kennedy in the White House* (Boston, 1965), 625.

46. Quoted in Richard Goodwin, *Remembering America: A Voice from the Sixties* (Boston, 1988), 99.

47. The Democratic platform is reprinted in Arthur M. Schlesinger Jr., ed., *History of American Presidential Elections, 1789–1968* (New York, 1971), 4:3482.

48. Quoted in Ambrose, *Education of a Politician*, 486.
49. Richard M. Nixon, *Six Crises* (Garden City, N.Y., 1962), 310.
50. *New York Times*, 27 September 1960.
51. The so-called Compact of Fifth Avenue is reprinted in Theodore White, *The Making of the President, 1960* (New York, 1961), 434–36.
52. "Statements of the Candidates on Growth," *New Republic*, 10 October 1960, 16.
53. Goodwin, *Remembering America*, 132.
54. Walter Heller, ed., *Perspectives on Economic Growth* (New York, 1968), ix.
55. *New York Times*, 24 December 1960.
56. Council of Economic Advisers Oral History Memoir, 34, 49. John F. Kennedy Presidential Library, Boston, Massachusetts (hereafter JFKL).
57. James Tobin, "Economic Growth as an Objective of Government Policy," *American Economic Review* 54 (1964): 1.
58. U.S. Presidents, *Public Papers*, John F. Kennedy, 1961, 20.
59. W. W. Rostow, *The Diffusion of Power: An Essay in Recent History* (New York, 1972), 123.
60. Hargrove and Morley, eds., *Interviews with CEA Chairmen*, 196.
61. James Tobin, *The New Economics One Decade Older* (Princeton, N.J., 1974), 3, 13.
62. Walter Heller, *New Dimensions of Political Economy* (Cambridge, Mass., 1966), 11; Heller, ed., *Perspectives on Economic Growth*, 3; Heller to JFK, 28 March 1962, Box 5 and JFK to Secretary of the Treasury et al., 21 August 1962, Box 17, Walter Heller MSS, JFKL.
63. U.S. Presidents, *Public Papers*, John F. Kennedy, 1961, 41.
64. Heller, *New Dimensions of Political Economy*, vii-viii.
65. The phrase is from Heller, *New Dimensions of Political Economy*, 70.
66. James Tobin, "The Political Economy of the 1960s," in *Toward New Human Rights: The Social Policies of the Kennedy and Johnson Administrations*, ed. David C. Warner (Austin, Tex., 1977), 35.
67. Theodore H. White, *In Search of History* (New York, 1978), 492–93. See also Michael Barone, *Our Country: The Shaping of America from Roosevelt to Reagan* (New York, 1990), 388.
68. Rostow, *Diffusion of Power*, 112.
69. Tobin, "Political Economy of the 1960s," 33; Johnson quoted in Goodwin, *Remembering America*, 258.
70. Walter Heller speech, Madison, Wisconsin, 13 November 1961, Box 17, Heller MSS, JFKL; Heller, *New Dimensions*, 11.
71. U.S. Presidents, *Public Papers*, John F. Kennedy, 1961, 404.
72. Walter A. McDougall, *The Heavens and the Earth: A Political History of the Space Age* (New York, 1985), 225.
73. Quoted in John M. Logsdon, *The Decision to Go to the Moon: Project Apollo and the National Interest* (Cambridge, Mass., 1970), 36.
74. McDougall, *The Heavens and the Earth*, 308, 362.
75. John Lewis Gaddis, *Strategies of Containment: A Critical Appraisal of Postwar American National Security Policy* (New York, 1982), 134, 147. See also Richard A. Melanson, "The Foundations of Eisenhower's Foreign Policy: Continuity, Community, and Consensus," in *Revolutionary Eisenhower: American Foreign Policy in the 1950s* (Urbana, Ill., 1987), 31–64.

76. U.S. Department of State, *Foreign Relations of the United States, 1952–1954*, Diplomatic Papers, vol. 2, pt. 1, National Security Affairs (Washington, D.C., 1984), 236.

77. On the "New Look" policy, see Russell F. Weigley, *The American Way of War: A History of United States Military Strategy and Policy* (New York, 1973), ch. 17; Glenon H. Snyder, "The 'New Look' of 1953," in Warner R. Schilling et al., *Strategy, Politics, and Defense Budgets* (New York, 1962); and Stephen E. Ambrose with Richard H. Immerman, *Ike's Spies: Eisenhower and the Espionage Establishment* (New York, 1981).

78. Dulles quoted in Saki Dockrill, *Eisenhower's New-Look National Security Policy, 1953–61* (London, 1996), 217; NSC-162/2 quoted in Michael J. Hogan, *A Cross of Iron: Harry S. Truman and the Origins of the National Security State, 1945–1954* (New York, 1998), 407; James Tobin, "Defense, Dollars, and Doctrines," *The Yale Review* 47 (March 1958): 324–25. It should be noted, however, that Hogan sees more continuity than change between the Truman and Eisenhower national security policies.

79. Henry A. Kissinger, "Strategy and Organization," *Foreign Affairs*, April 1957, 379–94.

80. Ambrose, *Education of a Politician*, 551; Weigley, *American Way of War*, 428–29.

81. Maxwell D. Taylor, *The Uncertain Trumpet* (New York, 1960), 6.

82. U.S. Presidents, *Public Papers*, Lyndon B. Johnson, 1963–64, 1:494.

83. Schlesinger Jr., ed., *History of Presidential Elections*, 4:3471; John F. Kennedy, *A Compendium of Speeches, Statements, and Remarks Delivered During His Service in the Congress of the United States*, Senate Document 79, 88th Cong., 2d sess. (Washington, D.C., 1964), 929.

84. Theodore Sorensen, *Kennedy* (New York, 1965), 608.

85. Weigley, *American Way of War*, 448.

86. Gaddis, *Strategies of Containment*, ch. 7; Townsend Hoopes, *The Limits of Intervention: An Inside Account of How the Johnson Policy of Escalation in Vietnam Was Reversed* (New York, 1973), 17–18; Sorensen, *Kennedy*, 632–33.

87. U.S. Department of Defense, *Annual Report for Fiscal Year 1962* (Washington, D.C., 1963), 3; Gaddis, *Strategies of Containment*, 226.

88. Gaddis, *Strategies of Containment*, 261.

89. James Gavin, *War and Peace in the Space Age* (London, 1959), 128; Taylor, *Uncertain Trumpet*, 24.

90. Schlesinger Jr., *A Thousand Days*, 315–16.

91. Memorandum, Rostow to Kennedy, 29 March 1961, quoted in George McT. Kahin, *Intervention: How America Became Involved in Vietnam* (New York, 1986), 131.

92. U.S. Presidents, *Public Papers*, Lyndon B. Johnson, 1963–64, 2:953.

93. Ibid., 1:114, 822.

94. Robert H. Haveman, ed., *A Decade of Federal Antipoverty Programs: Achievements, Failures, and Lessons* (New York, 1977), 11.

95. Tobin, "Political Economy of the 1960s," 33; Okun is quoted in Hargrove and Morley, eds., *Interviews with CEA Chairmen*, 275.

96. Goodwin, *Remembering America*, 270.

97. Doris Kearns, *Lyndon Johnson and the American Dream* (New York, 1976), 222.

98. Tobin, "Political Economy of the 1960s," 35.

99. Sar A. Levitan and Robert Taggart, *The Promise of Greatness* (Cambridge, Mass., 1976), 29.

100. Walter Lippmann, column, *Washington Post*, 19 March 1964, sec. A.

101. U.S. Council of Economic Advisers, *Economic Report of the President, 1964* (Washington, D.C., 1964), 77.

102. Carl M. Brauer, "Kennedy, Johnson, and the War on Poverty," *Journal of American History* 69 (June 1982): 108.

103. Lester C. Thurow, "Discussion," in *Decade of Federal Antipoverty Programs*, ed. Haveman, 118.

104. Joseph A. Kershaw, "The Attack on Poverty," in *Poverty in America*, ed. Margaret S. Gordon (San Francisco, 1965), 56.

105. Ibid., 57.

106. James Tobin, *National Economic Policy: Essays* (New Haven, Conn., 1966), vii.

107. See, for example, David E. Shi, *The Simple Life: Plain Living and High Thinking in American Culture* (New York, 1985).

108. Burns quoted in Walter P. Reuther, "Goals for America," in *National Priorities: Military, Economic, and Social* (Washington, D.C., 1969), 66.

109. Arthur M. Schlesinger Jr., "Where Does the Liberal Go from Here?" *New York Times Magazine*, 4 August 1957, 7, 38.

110. Arthur M. Schlesinger Jr., "The Shape of National Politics to Come," in Box 22, Leon Keyserling MSS, HSTL.

111. John Kenneth Galbraith, *A Life in Our Times: Memoirs* (Boston, 1981), 325; idem, *The Affluent Society* (New York, 1958), 152–53.

112. Leon Keyserling, "Eggheads and Politics," *New Republic*, 27 October 1958, 13–17 (quoted material appears on p. 16). See also "Galbraith and Schlesinger Reply to Leon Keyserling," ibid., 10 November 1958, 14–15; Keyserling, "Leon Keyserling on Economic Expansion: A Communication," ibid., 17 November 1958, 16–17; and correspondence among the principals in Box 38, John Kenneth Galbraith Papers, JFKL, and Box 22, Keyserling MSS, HSTL.

113. Schlesinger Jr., *A Thousand Days*, 657.

114. Quoted in Raymond A. Bauer, ed., *Social Indicators* (Cambridge, Mass., 1966), xii.

115. U.S. Presidents, *Public Papers*, Lyndon B. Johnson, 1963–64, 1:704.

116. U.S. Presidents, *Public Papers*, Lyndon B. Johnson, 1966, 1:246–47. See also Bertram M. Gross, "Preface: A Historical Note on Social Indicators," in *Social Indicators*, ed. Raymond A. Baver, ix-xviii; and Otis Graham Jr., *Toward a Planned Society: From Roosevelt to Nixon* (New York, 1976), ch. 4.

117. U.S. Department of Health, Education, and Welfare, *Toward A Social Report* (Ann Arbor, Mich., 1970).

118. Samuel P. Hays, *Beauty, Health, and Permanence: Environmental Politics in the United States, 1955–1985* (New York, 1987), 54–55.

119. Martin V. Melosi, "Lyndon Johnson and Environmental Policy," in *The Johnson Years: Volume Two*, ed. Robert A. Divine (Lawrence, Kans., 1987), 121.

120. John F. Kennedy, "Preface," in Stewart Udall, *The Quiet Crisis* (New York, 1963), xiii; Schlesinger Jr., *A Thousand Days*, 659.

121. U.S. Presidents, *Public Papers*, Lyndon B. Johnson, 1965, 2:1101.

122. Quoted in Melosi, "Johnson and Environmental Policy," 117. On Lady Bird Johnson's role, see Lewis L. Gould, *Lady Bird Johnson and the Environment* (Lawrence, Kans., 1988).

123. Lyndon Baines Johnson, *The Vantage Point: Perspectives of the Presidency, 1963–1969* (New York, 1971), 324.
124. U.S. Presidents, *Public Papers*, Lyndon B. Johnson, 1965, 1:199–201.
125. Levitan and Taggart, *Promise of Greatness*, 21.
126. Johnson quoted in Jack Valenti, *A Very Human President* (New York, 1975), 345. On the crucial July 1965 troop commitment, see Larry Berman, *Planning a Tragedy: The Americanization of the War in Vietnam* (New York, 1982); and Kahin, *Intervention*, 347–401.

Chapter 3

1. *Time*, 22 March 1968, 24.
2. Fred Smith to Fowler, 16 March 1968, Henry Fowler Papers, Box 82, Lyndon B. Johnson Presidential Library, Austin, Texas (hereafter LBJL); *Time*, 22 March 1968, 24; Edward Fried Oral History Memoir (hereafter OHM), p. 19, LBJL.
3. *Time*, 22 March 1968, 24; March 29, 1968, 81.
4. Joseph W. Barr OHM, Tape 2, p. 8, LBJL; Fried OHM, p. 19, LBJL; Walt Rostow to LBJ, memo, 15 March 1968, Memos to the President, National Security File, Box 31, LBJL.
5. Introductions to the Bretton Woods regime include Alfred E. Eckes Jr., *A Search for Solvency: Bretton Woods and the International Monetary System, 1941–1971* (Austin, Tex., 1975), ch. 6; John S. Odell, *U.S. International Monetary Policy: Markets, Power, and Ideas as Sources of Change* (Princeton, 1982), 80–88; Robert Solomon, *The International Monetary System, 1945–1981*, updated ed. (New York, 1982), ch. 2; and Michael D. Bordo, "The Bretton Woods International Monetary System: A Historical Overview," in *A Retrospective on the Bretton Woods System: Lessons for International Monetary Reform*, ed. Michael D. Bordo and Barry Eichengreen (Chicago, 1993), 3–85.
6. Alvin H. Hansen, *The Postwar American Economy: Performance and Problems* (New York, 1964), 74–75.
7. U.S. Presidents, *Public Papers*, John F. Kennedy, 1961, 58.
8. Dwight D. Eisenhower, *The White House Years: Waging Peace, 1956–1961* (Garden City, N.Y., 1965), 603–7, quotation from 606.
9. Arthur M. Schlesinger Jr., *A Thousand Days: John F. Kennedy in the White House* (Boston, 1965), 654; Theodore C. Sorensen, *Kennedy* (New York, 1965), 407–10; George Ball OHM, Interview 2, pp. 28–30, LBJL; *Public Papers*, John F. Kennedy, 1961, 57–66.
10. On the Kennedy program, see Hansen, *Postwar American Economy*, 76–77; Amy Elisabeth Davis, "Politics of Prosperity: The Kennedy Presidency and Economic Policy" (Ph.D. diss., Columbia University, 1988), 186–210, 384–428; and Robert V. Roosa, *The Dollar and World Liquidity* (New York, 1967), 3–39.
11. Gardner Ackley OHM, Tape 2, p. 47, LBJL.
12. Frederick Deming OHM, Tape 2, p.7, LBJL.
13. U. S. Department of the Treasury, *Maintaining the Strength of the U.S. Dollar in a Strong Free World Economy* (Washington, D.C., 1968), 9, 47.
14. Arthur Okun OHM, Tape 2, p. 4, LBJL.

15. The statistics are from Arthur Okun, Cabinet Meeting Minutes, May 29, 1968, Cabinet Papers, Box 13, LBJL.

16. Gardner Ackley to Johnson, memo, 27 December 1965, WHCF, CF, FI 4, LBJL.

17. U.S. Presidents, *Public Papers*, Lyndon B. Johnson, 1966, 1:48.

18. U.S. Presidents, *Public Papers*, Lyndon B. Johnson, 1967, 2:733. For a good discussion of LBJ's efforts in 1966 to control inflation without a tax hike, see Joseph A. Califano Jr., *The Triumph and Tragedy of Lyndon Johnson: The White House Years* (New York, 1991), 137–48. Regarding the struggle to develop a tax program, see Harvey C. Mansfield Sr., *Illustrations of Presidential Management: Johnson's Cost Reduction and Tax Increase Campaigns* (Austin, Texas, 1988); Henry Fowler OHM, Tape 3, p. 9, LBJL; and "Chronology of President Johnson's Tax Proposals, 1965–66," Aides Files, Califano, Box 54, LBJL.

19. Gardner Ackley OHM, Tape 1, p.34, and Tape 2, p. 17, LBJL. The quotation is from the latter.

20. Arthur Okun OHM, Tape 2, p. 13, LBJL.

21. Gardner Ackley OHM, Tape 2, p. 42, LBJL. In March 1966 McNamara strongly opposed Treasury Secretary Fowler's suggestion of a public review of the need for a tax increase, fearing that such would incite Congress to cut Great Society programs. See Joe Califano to LBJ, 22 March 1966, Confidential File, FG 795, Box 41, LBJL.

22. Lyndon Baines Johnson, *The Vantage Point: Perspectives of the Presidency, 1963–1969* (New York, 1971), chap. 19 passim; Arthur M. Okun, *The Political Economy of Prosperity* (Washington, D.C., 1970), 71. On the important role played by the chief economic editorialists of the *New York Times* and *Washington Post*, see Walter Heller OHM, Tape 2, pp. 47–48, LBJL. The Gallup poll is in *New York Times*, 24 January 1968.

23. Gardner Ackley OHM, Tape 1, p. 32, LBJL.

24. See, for example, "Our Congressmen—Who Is Best? Who Is Worst?" *Pageant Magazine*, November, 1964, 6–14; and Julius Duscha, "The Most Important Man on Capitol Hill Today," *New York Times Magazine*, 25 February 1968, 30ff.

25. Wilbur Cohen OHM, Tape 2, p. 6, LBJL.

26. Quoted from Sorensen, *Kennedy*, 426.

27. Wilbur Mills OHM, Tape 1, p. 37, LBJL.

28. Ibid., Tape 1, p. 38. See also p. 21 for similar sentiments.

29. Wilbur Mills, speech, "Expenditures and Taxes in the Context of Today's Problems," 20 November 1967, Cabinet Papers, Box 11, LBJL.

30. Duscha, "Most Important Man on Capitol Hill," 72.

31. Wilbur Mills, speech, "Some International and Domestic Aspects of Tax and Expenditure Policy," 3 December 1968, Box 420, Wilbur Mills Papers, Hendrix College, Conway, Arkansas.

32. Wilbur Mills, speech at Hazen, Arkansas, 15 March 1968, Box 420, Mills Papers.

33. Wilbur Mills to B. Freeland, 19 October 1967, Box 509, Mills Papers.

34. Wilbur Mills, "Statement . . . on the Necessity for Establishing Controls over the Future Course of Federal Spending," 6 October 1967, Box 425, Mills Papers; and Wilbur Mills to H. Hodge, 25 June 1968, Box 509, ibid.

35. Charles L. Schultze to Johnson, memo, 16 September 1967, Aides Files, Califano, Box 54, LBJL.

36. The discussion that follows draws heavily on "The Gold Crisis, Nov. 1967–March 1968," undated manuscript, and "Gold Crisis—1967: Chronology and Annotated Index of Documents," undated manuscript, both in National Security File, National Security Council History, Box 53, LBJL.

37. Frederick Deming OHM, Tape 2, p. 18, LBJL. A high-level British perspective on the 1967 sterling devaluation episode is found in Harold Wilson, *A Personal Record: The Labour Government, 1964–1970* (Boston, 1981), ch. 23.

38. The Group of Ten was created in 1961 to enlarge the lending resources of the IMF. Its members—the United States, Britain, Germany, France, Italy, the Netherlands, Belgium, Sweden, Canada, and Japan—agreed to provide additional money to the IMF and to communicate together regarding developments in the international monetary system.

39. Henry Fowler to Johnson, memo, 12 November 1967, National Security File, National Security Council History, Box 53, LBJL.

40. Henry Fowler to Johnson, memo, 13 November 1967, ibid.

41. Gardner Ackley to Johnson, memo, 27 November 1967, ibid. The gold pool has been described by one of the policymakers who helped create it as "a little bit like a cartel, but in the interests of the world monetary system." See Robert Roosa, OHM, Tape 1, pp. 23–26, LBJL.

42. "Memorandum of Conversation: Highlights of Meeting of Deming Group with Secretary Fowler on Gold Policy," 24 November 1967, National Security File, National Security Council History, Box 53, LBJL. Deming, however, flew to Frankfurt and on 26 November negotiated a renewed agreement among the seven remaining members of the gold pool (Belgium, Germany, Italy, the Netherlands, Switzerland, Britain, and the United States—France, an original member, had dropped out earlier in 1967) to maintain a firm line on the gold price in London. See Gardner Ackley to Johnson, memo, 27 November 1967, ibid.

43. Cabinet Meeting Minutes, 20 November 1967, Cabinet Papers, Box 11, LBJL. For similar sentiments, see E. Ernest Goldstein OHM, Tape 3, p. 2, LBJL.

44. Press release, "Statement by the President," 18 November 1967, National Security File, National Security Council History, Box 53, LBJL. The overall strategy and Fowler's quoted remarks are from "Notes on the President's Meeting with Bipartisan Leadership," 20 November 1967, Meeting Notes File, Box 2, LBJL. See also "Notes on the President's Meeting with the Leadership," 19 November 1967, ibid.

45. "Gold Pool Activity," attachment I to "The Gold Crisis, Nov. 1967–March 1968," manuscript, n.d., National Security File, National Security Council History, Box 53, LBJL.

46. "Gold Pool Activity"; and Walt Rostow to Johnson, memo, 12 December 1967, both ibid.

47. Summary of telephone call, Hubert Ansiaux to William McChesney Martin, Friday, 15 December 1967; and Walt Rostow to Johnson, 15 December 1967, both ibid.

48. U.S. Presidents, *Public Papers*, Lyndon B. Johnson, 1968–69, 1:8–13; "The Balance of Payments Program of New Year's Day, 1968," manuscript, n.d., and "The President's Balance of Payments Message of January 1, 1968: Chronology and Annotated Documents," both in National Security File, National Security Council History, Box 54, LBJL; and Frederick Deming OHM, Tape 2, pp. 8–16.

49. Gardner Ackley to Johnson, memo, 6 January 1968, National Security File, National Security Council History, Box 54, LBJL.

50. Gardner Ackley to Johnson, memo, 21 December 1967. See also "Minutes of the Cabinet Committee on Balance of Payments," 21 December 1967, both ibid.

51. *New York Times*, 1 March 1968.

52. Walt Rostow to Johnson, 14 March 1968, National Security File, National Security Council History, Box 53, LBJL.

53. Walt Rostow to Johnson, 23 January 1968, ibid.

54. Ernest Goldstein to Johnson, memo, 24 January 1968, National Security File, National Security Council History, Box 54, LBJL; and Walt Rostow to Johnson, memo, 14 February 1968, Box 53, ibid.

55. "The Gold Crisis," National Security File, National Security Council History, Box 53, LBJL; Joseph Barr OHM, Tape 2, pp. 9–10, LBJL; and Frederick Deming OHM, Tape 2, pp. 30–34, LBJL.

56. "Gold Pool Activity," National Security File, National Security Council History, Box 53, LBJL.

57. The pressures building early in 1968 are well treated in "The Gold Crisis," National Security File, National Security Council History, Box 53, LBJL. On the continued weakness of sterling, see Barbara Ward Jackson, memo, 23 January 1968; Gardner Ackley to Johnson, memo, 24 January 1968; and Walt Rostow to Johnson, memo, 23 January 1968, all ibid.

58. Henry Fowler to Johnson, memo, 4 March 1968; and Walt Rostow to Johnson, memo, 8 March 1968, both ibid.

59. Bundy quoted from "The Dollar Is Not as Bad as Gold," *Time*, 12 January 1968, 16.

60. Walt Rostow to Johnson, memo, 12 March 1968, Diary Backup, Box 92, LBJL.

61. The discussion that follows relies heavily on "The Gold Crisis," National Security File, National Security Council History, Box 53, LBJL.

62. Henry Fowler OHM, p. 33, LBJL.

63. Rusk to Amconsul Frankfurt and others, telegram, 15 March 1968, National Security File, National Security Council History, Box 53, LBJL.

64. Johnson to Kiesinger, telegram, 15 March 1968, National Security File, National Security Council History, Box 53, LBJL. The administration's rationale for opposing any increase in the official price of gold is found in T. Page Nelson to Hunt, 16 February 1968, Fowler Papers, Box 83, LBJL.

65. "Communiqué," 17 March 1968, National Security File, National Security Council History, Box 53, LBJL. See also the discussion in Solomon, *The International Monetary System*, 119–24. Solomon was a participant at the Washington meeting and helped draft its final communiqué.

66. *Time*, 29 March 1968, 80.

67. Arthur Okun OHM, p. 23, LBJL. On Carli's role, see Frederick Deming OHM, Tape 2, p. 29, LBJL.

68. "Communiqué," 17 March 1968, National Security File, National Security Council History, Box 53, LBJL.

69. Sorensen, *Kennedy*, 407.

70. Ibid.; Odell, *U.S. International Monetary Policy*, 129; T. P. Nelson to Fowler, 3 July 1967, Fowler Papers, Box 84, LBJL. Martin's remark is from *Congressional Record—Senate*, 26 June 1967, S 8875.

71. U.S. Presidents, *Public Papers*, Johnson, 1968–69, 1:33; Joseph Barr OHM, Tape 2, p. 10, LBJL.

72. "Communiqué," 17 March 1968, National Security File, National Security Council History, Box 53, LBJL.

73. Odell, *U.S. International Monetary Policy*, 129; Solomon, *The International Monetary System*, 128–50; and Frederick Deming OHM, Tape 2, pp. 34–45, LBJL.

74. "The Dollar Is Not as Bad as Gold," *Time*, 12 January 1968, 17; "Gold Fever Rises to Record Heat," *Business Week*, 16 March 1968, 31.

75. Henry Fowler OHM, Tape 3, p. 31, LBJL.

76. Arthur Okun to Johnson, memo, 23 March 1967, National Security File, National Security Council History, Box 53, LBJL. On the outcome of the tax struggle, see Kettl, "Economic Education of Lyndon Johnson," 70–71; and Charles Zwick OHM, Tape 2, pp. 5–9, LBJL.

77. Wilbur Mills OHM, p. 35, LBJL.

78. Johnson, *The Vantage Point*, 451; Wilbur Mills, speech at England, Arkansas, 27 August 1968, Box 420, Mills Papers; Frederick Deming OHM, Tape 1, p. 34, LBJL.

79. U.S. Presidents, *Public Papers*, Johnson, 1968–69, 1:545–46.

80. Arthur Okun to Johnson, memo, 29 July 1968, WHCF, EX FI9, Box 53, LBJL; Okun, Notes for Cabinet Meeting, 5 September 1968, Cabinet Papers, Box 14, LBJL.

81. Joseph Barr OHM, Tape 1, p. 28, LBJL.

82. Gordon, *Economic Instability and Growth*, 179–85.

83. Robert Eisner, "Fiscal and Monetary Policy Reconsidered," *American Economic Review* 59 (December 1969): 897–905; and Eisner, "What Went Wrong?" *Journal of Political Economy* 79 (May-June 1971): 629–41.

84. Wilbur Mills OHM, p. 12, LBJL.

85. Solomon, *The International Monetary System*, 176 ff.

86. See Thomas L. Friedman, "A Nixon Legacy Devalued By a Cold War Standard," *New York Times*, 1 May 1994.

87. "Notes of the President's Foreign Affairs Luncheon," 30 January 1968, Tom Johnson's Notes of Meetings, Box 2, LBJL.

88. Clark Clifford OHM, Tape 4, p. 33, LBJL.

89. William Westmoreland, cable MAC 01049, 22 January 1968, National Security File, Memos to the President (Rostow), Box 27, LBJL.

90. William Westmoreland, cable MAC 0161, 4 February 1968, ibid., Box 28.

91. Peter Braestrup, *Big Story: How the American Press and Television Reported and Interpreted the Crisis of Tet 1969 in Vietnam and Washington*, 2 vols. (Boulder, Colo., 1977).

92. George Christian OHM, p. 9, LBJL.

93. Earle Wheeler to Johnson, memo, 27 February 1969, Tom Johnson's Notes of Meetings, Box 2, LBJL. The origins of the February 1968 troop request have been the stuff of controversy. See "The Origins of the Post-Tet 1968 Plans for Additional American Forces in RVN." 9 November 1970, DSDUF File, Box 3, LBJL; William C. Westmore-

land, *A Soldier Reports* (New York, 1976), 350–59; Mark Perry, *Four Stars* (Boston, 1989), 173–89; and Clark Clifford, *Counsel to the President: A Memoir* (New York, 1991), 472–83.

94. "Notes of the President's Meeting with Senior Foreign Policy Advisers," 4 March 1968, Tom Johnson's Notes of Meetings, Box 2, LBJL.

95. Charles Zwick to Johnson, 2 March 1968, Clifford Papers, Box 1, LBJL.

96. Clark Clifford OHM, Tape 3, p. 15, LBJL.

97. "Notes of the President's Meeting with Senior Foreign Policy Advisers," 9 February 1968, Tom Johnson's Notes of Meetings, Box 2, LBJL.

98. "Notes of the President's Meeting with Senior Foreign Policy Advisers," 4 March 1968, ibid.

99. Henry Fowler to Johnson, memo, 1 March 1968, National Security Council History, Box 53, LBJL; "Difficulties and Negative Factors in the Course of Action," n.d., Tab. G, Box 1, Clifford Papers, LBJL. See also Henry Fowler, "Economic and Financial Problems and Measures," memo, 3 March 1968, ibid.

100. Walt Rostow to Johnson, 11 March 1968, National Security File, Memos to the President (Rostow), Box 30, LBJL.

101. Hobart Rowen, "Gold, Dollar Threats Affecting War Policy," *Washington Post*, 24 March 1968; Edwin L. Dale Jr., "The Gold Rush," *New Republic*, 23 March 1968.

102. Clifford, *Counsel to the President*, 498.

103. "Notes of the President's Meeting with His Foreign Advisers at The Tuesday Luncheon," 19 March 1968, Tom Johnson's Notes of Meetings, Box 2, LBJL.

104. Mike Mansfield, "Reports of Requests for an Additional 200,000 Men in Vietnam," memo, 13 March 1968, National Security File, Meeting Notes File, Box 2, LBJL.

105. Quoted from Larry Berman, *Lyndon Johnson's War: The Road to Stalemate in Vietnam* (New York, 1989), 193.

106. Dean Acheson, "Confidential Memorandum: DA's Views Regarding Vietnam as of March 26, 1968 (As expressed at the State Department and White House on March 26, 1968)," Series IV, Box 67, Dean Acheson Papers, Yale University Library, New Haven, Connecticut.

107. Dean Acheson to John Cowles, 14 March 1968, Box 88, ibid.

108. Clifford, *Counsel to the President*, 518.

109. Johnson, *Vantage Point*, 406.

110. A first-rate scholarly account of the Tet decisions is David M. Barrett, *Uncertain Warriors: Lyndon Johnson and His Vietnam Advisers* (Lawrence, Kans., 1993), ch. 4. Detailed, firsthand accounts include Johnson, *Vantage Point*, ch. 17; and Clifford, *Counsel to the President*, chs. 27–28.

111. "Notes of the President's Meeting with General Earle Wheeler, JCS, and General Creighton Abrams," 26 March 1968, Tom Johnson's Notes of Meetings, Box 2, LBJL.

112. Ibid.

113. Ibid.

114. A limited reserve call-up of twenty thousand men took place shortly thereafter, in May 1968. Stanley Resor OHM, p. 19, LBJL. Resor was secretary of the army from 1968 to 1971.

115. This interpretation appears fleetingly in David Halberstam, *The Best and the Brightest* (New York, 1971), 604, but scholars have since pursued at least four other emphases

in explaining the March 1968 decision to deescalate. Don Oberdorfer, *Tet* (Garden City, N.Y., 1971), views the policy shift as the inevitable, or at least predictable, result of the shock generated by the Tet Offensive. Several studies emphasize the palace revolt of a handful of administration doves led by Clark Clifford. See Townsend Hoopes, *The Limits of Intervention* (New York, 1969), and Herbert Y. Schandler, *The Unmaking of a President: Lyndon Johnson and Vietnam* (Princeton, 1977). The significance of the defection of the so-called Establishment is stressed in Walter Isaacson and Evan Thomas, *The Wise Men: Six Friends and the World They Made* (New York, 1986). The impact of the antiwar movement has been emphasized in Melvin Small, *Johnson, Nixon, and the Doves* (New Brunswick, N.J., 1988), 129–32; Tom Wells, *The War Within: America's Battle Over Vietnam*, 4, 261; and Tom Hayden, *Reunion: A Memoir*, 501. There are elements of truth in all of these competing interpretations, but to the extent that they neglect the dimension of political economy presently under discussion, their explanatory power falls short. The most complete and compelling account to date is Lloyd Gardner, "Lyndon Johnson and Vietnam: The Final Months," in *The Johnson Years, Volume Three: LBJ at Home and Abroad*, ed. Robert A. Divine (Lawrence, Kans., 1994), 198–238. Halberstam notes correctly that the war never cost more than 3.5 percent of GNP, and concludes that it was not the war but rather "the essentially dishonest way in which it was handled" that "destroyed the economy" (610). The present chapter seeks to establish what other influences and problems, in addition to duplicity, were at work in the political economy of the war.

116. U.S. Presidents, *Public Papers*, Lyndon B. Johnson, 1968–69, 1:404.

117. Daniel Patrick Moynihan, *Maximum Feasible Misunderstanding* (New York, 1969); Wilbur Cohen OHM, Tape 3, p. 10 end Tape 4, pp. 5, 9.

118. See, for example, "Notes on Meeting of the President with Senator Robert Kennedy, April 3, 1968," and "Memorandum of Conversation: The President, Senator Robert F. Kennedy, Theodore Sorensen, Charles Murphy, and W. W. Rostow, 10:00 a.m., April 3, 1968," both in Diary Backup, Box 94, LBJL.

119. "Notes of the President's Meeting with Lyle Denniston, Bob Walters, and Jack Horner of the Washington Evening Star," 15 November 1967, Tom Johnson's Notes of Meetings, Box 1, LBJL.

120. Califano, *Triumph and Tragedy of Lyndon Johnson*, 258; U.S. Presidents, *Public Papers*, Lyndon B. Johnson, 1968–69, 1:46–53, 248–63, 509–10.

121. U.S. Presidents, *Public Papers*, Lyndon B. Johnson, 1967, 2:733–40; Cabinet Meeting Minutes, 20 November 1967, Cabinet Papers, Box 11, LBJL.

122. Joe Califano to Johnson, 20 November 1967, Cabinet Papers, Box 11, LBJL.

123. Cabinet Meeting Minutes, 6 December 1967, Cabinet Papers, Box 12, LBJL. See also Sargent Shriver to Johnson, 22 December 1967, Aides Files, Califano, Box 8, LBJL. On Johnson's backing and filling at this point, see also Califano, *Triumph and Tragedy of Lyndon Johnson*, 255–56.

124. Quoted from "The Monetary System Buys Some More Time," *Business Week*, 23 March 1968, 30.

125. Cabinet Meeting Minutes, 1 May 1968, Cabinet Papers, Box 13, LBJL.

126. *Report of the National Advisory Commission on Civil Disorders* (New York, 1968), passim; *New York Times*, 2 March 1968, 15; Cabinet Meeting Minutes, 13 March 1968, Cabinet Papers, Box 13, LBJL.
127. Califano, *Triumph and Tragedy of Lyndon Johnson*, 261.
128. "Notes on Meeting with Negro Editors and Publishers," 15 March 1968, Diary Backup, Box 93, LBJL; Johnson, *Vantage Point*, 173.
129. George Meany to Johnson, 29 December 1967, Aides Files, Califano, Box 8, LBJL; Joe Califano to Johnson, 28 March 1968, Box 16, ibid. See also Victor Riesel, "Inside Labor: Inside the White House: Labor Chiefs Warn LBJ: Budget Slash Plays Into Hands of Kennedy and McCarthy," syndicated column dated 16 May 1968, in Box 17, ibid.
130. Joe Califano to Johnson, 29 May 1968, Aides Files, Califano, Box 17, LBJL.
131. Joe Califano to Johnson, 3 April 1968, ibid.
132. Barefoot Sanders to Johnson, 5 April 1968, Diary Backup, Box 95, LBJL.
133. Joe Califano to Johnson, 10 April 1968, Aides Files, Califano, Box 16, LBJL.
134. Califano, *Triumph and Tragedy of Lyndon Johnson*, 282–83.
135. Johnson, *Vantage Point*, 451.
136. Arthur Okun to Johnson, 27 April 1968, Diary Backup, Box 97, LBJL.
137. Joe Califano to Johnson, 20 May 1968, Aides Files, Califano, Box 54, LBJL.
138. Johnson, *Vantage Point*, 453.
139. Minutes of Special Cabinet Meeting, 14 May 1968, Cabinet Papers, Box 13, LBJL.
140. Wilbur Mills, Remarks to Little Rock Rotary Club, 29 August 1968, Box 420, Mills Papers.
141. Califano, *Triumph and Tragedy of Lyndon Johnson*, 288.
142. Sar A. Levitan and Robert Taggart, *The Promise of Greatness* (Cambridge, Mass., 1976), 21.
143. Irwin Unger and Debi Unger, *America in the 1960s* (St. James, N.Y., 1993), 45.

Chapter 4
1. Seymour Martin Lipset and William Schneider, *The Confidence Gap: Business, Labor, and Government in the Public Mind* (New York, 1983).
2. U.S. Presidents, *Public Papers*, Richard Nixon, 1970, 8–16.
3. *Earth Day—The Beginning: A Guide for Survival Compiled and Edited by the National Staff of Environmental Action* (New York, 1970), unnumbered page.
4. Garrett DeBell, ed., *The Environmental Handbook: Prepared for the First National Environmental Teach-In* (New York, 1970), 328, 318.
5. *Earth Day—The Beginning*, 91.
6. William Nordhaus and James Tobin, "Is Growth Obsolete," in National Bureau of Economic Research, *Economic Growth: Fiftieth Anniversary Colloquim V* (New York, 1972), 1.
7. U.S. Presidents, *Public Papers*, Jimmy Carter, 1979, 2:1238.
8. *Washington Post*, 25 March 1973; Stephen Ambrose, *Nixon: Ruin and Recovery, 1973–1990* (New York, 1991), 94.

9. Henry Kissinger, *White House Years* (Boston, 1979), 55–56.

10. Quoted in Kenneth W. Thompson, ed., *Portraits of American Presidents*, vol. 6, *The Nixon Presidency: Twenty-two Intimate Perspectives of Richard M. Nixon* (Lanham, Md., 1987), 139.

11. Arthur M. Schlesinger Jr., *Kennedy or Nixon: Does It Make Any Difference?* (New York, 1960), 3; Rusher quoted in Thompson, ed., *The Nixon Presidency*, 192. In a similar vein, Allen J. Matusow finds political calculation, albeit of a sometimes sophisticated nature, the unifying theme of Nixon's leadership. See his excellent study of economic policy in Matusow, *Nixon's Economy: Booms, Busts, Dollars, and Votes* (Lawrence, Kans., 1998), 1–6, 180–81.

12. Lippmann in *Washington Post*, 25 March 1973; Ehrlichman quoted in Tom Wicker, *One of Us: Richard Nixon and the American Dream* (New York, 1991), 410.

13. This point is central to Tom Wicker's interpretation in *One of Us*, 410–11. A good introduction to the Whig ideology is Daniel Walker Howe, *The Political Culture of the American Whigs* (Chicago, 1979).

14. Thomas Brown, *Politics and Statesmanship: Essays on the American Whig Party* (New York, 1985), 217.

15. Regarding the American System, see Clement Eaton, *Henry Clay and the Art of American Politics* (Boston, 1957), 46; on Clay's invention of the phrase "self-made man," see John G. Cawelti, *Apostles of the Self-Made Man: Changing Concepts of Success in America* (Chicago, 1965), 43–46.

16. Garry Wills, *Nixon Agonistes: The Crisis of the Self-Made Man* (Boston 1970), 175.

17. Richard Nixon, *In the Arena: A Memoir of Victory, Defeat, and Renewal* (New York, 1990), 107.

18. For an incisive treatment of Nixon's 1968 acceptance speech, see Wills, *Nixon Agonistes*, ch. 9.

19. Herbert Stein, *Presidential Economics: The Making of Economic Policy from Roosevelt to Reagan and Beyond* (New York, 1984), 135.

20. William Safire, *After the Fall: An Inside View of the Pre-Watergate White House* (Garden City, N.Y., 1975), 135.

21. Richard Nixon, *RN: The Memoirs of Richard Nixon* (New York, 1978), 414; William E. Leuchtenburg, *In the Shadow of FDR: From Harry Truman to Bill Clinton*, 2nd ed., rev. and updated (Ithaca, N.Y., 1993), 169.

22. Quoted in Erwin C. Hargrove and Samuel A. Morley, eds., *The President and the Council of Economic Advisers: Interviews with CEA Chairman* (Boulder, Colo., 1984), 367.

23. Quoted in Richard P. Nathan, *The Plot that Failed: Nixon and the Administrative Presidency* (New York, 1975), 160–61.

24. Quoted in A. James Reichley, *Conservatives in an Age of Change: The Nixon and Ford Administrations* (Washington, D.C., 1981), 72.

25. Elliot L. Richardson, "Capacity for Greatness," in *Richard M. Nixon: Politician, President, Administrator*, ed. Leon Friedman and William F. Levantrosser (New York, 1991), 4.

26. Nixon, *RN*, 562.

27. Kissinger, *White House Years*, 951.

28. Quoted in James Reston, *The Lone Star: The Life of John Connally* (New York, 1989), 394.

29. John Connally, *In History's Shadow: An American Odyssey* (New York, 1993), 233. On Connally's governorship, see ibid., 217–33 and Reston, *Lone Star*, 291.

30. H. R. Haldeman, *The Haldeman Diaries: Inside the Nixon White House* (New York, 1994), 444.

31. Ibid., 397, 444, 546–47; Nixon, *RN*, 769; Reston, *Lone Star*, 459; and Herbert Parmet, *Richard Nixon and His America* (Boston, 1990), 616–17.

32. Kissinger, *White House Years*, 57.

33. Quoted in ibid., 952.

34. U.S. Presidents, *Public Papers*, Richard Nixon, 1969, 19. See Laurence W. Martin, "Military Issues: Strategic Parity and Its Implications," in Robert E. Osgood et al., *Retreat from Empire: The First Nixon Administration* (Baltimore, 1973), 137–71.

35. Statistics in Reichley, *Conservatives in an Age of Change*, 347. See also Lawrence J. Korb, *The Fall and Rise of the Pentagon: American Defense Policies in the 1970s* (Westport, Conn., 1979); and John M. Collins, *American and Soviet Military Trends: Since the Cuban Missile Crisis* (Washington, D.C., 1978).

36. U.S. Presidents, *Public Papers*, Richard Nixon, 1970, 9.

37. Robert E. Osgood, "Introduction: The Nixon Doctrine and Strategy," in Osgood et al., *Retreat from Empire*, 3.

38. Kissinger, *White House Years*, 136, 130.

39. John Lewis Gaddis, *Strategies of Containment: A Critical Appraisal of Postwar American National Security Policy* (New York, 1982), 292–97.

40. Quoted in Henry Brandon, *The Retreat of American Power* (Garden City, N.Y., 1973), 82.

41. Henry Kissinger, "Central Issues in American Foreign Policy," in *Agenda for the Nation*, ed. Kermit Gordon (Washington 1968), 74.

42. Walter Russell Mead, *Mortal Splendor: The American Empire in Transition* (Boston, 1987), 53. For concurring views from Britain, see Stephen Barber, *America in Retreat* (New York, 1971), and Brandon, *Retreat of American Power*.

43. Nixon, *RN*, 353, 352.

44. Theodore White, *The Making of the President, 1972* (New York, 1973), 358.

45. Quoted in "Nixon Goal: A Leaner but Stronger Government," *National Journal*, 16 December 1972, 1911.

46. U.S. Presidents, *Public Papers*, Richard Nixon, 1969, 644.

47. Timothy Conlan, *New Federalism: Intergovernmental Reform from Nixon to Reagan* (Washington, D.C., 1988), 81–83.

48. See, for example, Wicker, *One of Us*; and Joan Hoff, *Nixon Reconsidered* (New York, 1994).

49. Conlan, *New Federalism*, 20, 19.

50. Nixon's handwritten notes for the 6 July 1971 briefing are in President's Personal Files, Box 67, NPM. Quotes are from U.S. Presidents, *Public Papers*, Richard Nixon, 1971, 802–13. The briefing is discussed in Hoff, *Nixon Reconsidered*, 158–59, 164–65; and

John B. Judis, *Grand Illusion: Critics and Champions of the American Century* (New York, 1992), 210–13.

51. U.S. Presidents, *Public Papers*, Richard Nixon, 1971, 802–13.

52. Ibid., 890.

53. U.S. Presidents, *Public Papers*, Richard Nixon, 1969, 1; Paul McCracken to Nixon, 17 November 1969, WHCF:SMOF:McCracken:Box 91, NPM.

54. CEA to Cabinet Committee on Economic Policy, 8 November 1969, WHCF:SMOF: McCracken:Box 2, NPM.

55. U.S. Presidents, *The Economic Report of the President, February, 1970*, ch. 3, "Uses of the National Output."

56. William Safire to Nixon, 19 June 1969, White House Special Files:Central Files:BE Business/Economics, Box 2, NPM.

57. Quoted in Stephen Ambrose, *Nixon: The Triumph of a Politician, 1962–1972* (New York, 1989), 297.

58. Murray Weidenbaum to Donald Webster, 26 June 1969, WHCF:SMOF: McCracken: Box 91, NPM.

59. Herbert Stein to McCracken, WHCF:SMOF:Stein:Box 1, NPM.

60. Stein [as acting CEA Chair] to Nixon, 1 July 1969, WHCF:SMOF:McCracken:Box 91, NPM.

61. McCracken, "Notes: Remarks at Cabinet Meeting, March 20, 1969," handwritten, WHCF:SMOF:McCracken:Box 1, NPM.

62. U.S. Congress, Joint Economic Committee, *The 1969 Economic Report of the President, Hearings*, before the Joint Economic Committee, 91st Cong., 1st sess., pt. 2, 284–304.

63. Statistics in Wyatt C. Wells, *Economist in an Uncertain World: Arthur F. Burns and the Federal Reserve, 1970–78* (New York, 1994), 35. On gradualism, see F. Gerard Adams, "The Economic Road from Johnson to Nixon," *Wheaton Quarterly* (Summer 1969): 19–24; Arthur Okun, "Political Economy: Some Lessons of Recent Experience," *Journal of Money, Credit, and Banking* 4 (February 1972): 23–39; Stein, *Presidential Economics*, ch. 5; Reichley, *Conservatives in an Age of Change*, 205–17; and Neil De Marchi, "The First Nixon Administration: Prelude to Controls," in *Exhortation and Controls: The Search for a Wage-Price Policy, 1945–1971* (Washington, D.C., 1975), 295–352.

64. Herbert Stein, *On the Other Hand . . . : Essays on Economics, Economists, and Politics* (Washington, D.C., 1995), 65.

65. Richard Nixon, *Six Crises* (Garden City, N.Y., 1962), 309–11.

66. Nixon quoted in Joanne S. Gowa, *Closing the Gold Window: Domestic Politics and the End of Bretton Woods* (Ithaca, N.Y., 1983), 166; and in John Ehrlichman, *Witness to Power: The Nixon Years* (New York, 1982), 254.

67. Moynihan quoted in Thompson, ed., *The Nixon Presidency*, 52.

68. McCracken, "Notes for Quadriad Meeting, 15 December 1969," WHCF:SMOF: McCracken: Box 2, NPM.

69. McCracken to Nixon, 17 February 1970, and McCracken, "Cabinet Meeting, 18 May 1970" [handwritten notes], both WHCF:SMOF:McCracken:Box 1, NPM; "[Handwritten] Notes of Meeting with the President, 2 July 1970 (San Clemente)" WHCF:SMOF:Ehrlichman:Box 4, NPM.

70. McCracken to Nixon, 23 August 1970, WHCF:SMOF:McCracken:Box 2, NPM.

71. Stein to Kennedy, McCracken, and Shultz, 21 December 1970, WHCF:SMOF: Stein:Box 1, NPM.

72. U.S. Presidents, *Public Papers*, Richard Nixon, 1970, 1090.

73. Kissinger, *White House Years*, 951.

74. Quoted in Safire, *Before the Fall*, 504.

75. Kissinger, *White House Years*, 951.

76. Quoted in Wells, *Economist in an Uncertain World*, 61, and Ehrlichman, *Witness to Power*, 254.

77. Robert Aaron Gordon, *Economic Instability and Growth: The American Record* (New York, 1974), 174–75.

78. U.S. Presidents, *Public Papers*, Richard Nixon, 1971, 52.

79. Ibid., 80.

80. Quoted in Stein, *Presidential Economics*, 173.

81. Stein to Kennedy, McCracken, and Shultz, 25 January 1971, WHCF:SMOF:Stein:Box 1, NPM; McCracken to Nixon, 27 January 1971, WHCF:SMOF:McCracken:Box 42, NMP.

82. Samuelson quoted in Wells, *Economist in an Uncertain World*, 64; Arthur Okun, "Political Economy: Some Lessons of Recent Experience," 30.

83. Stein to McCracken, 8 February 1971, WHCF:SMOF:Stein:Box 1, NPM.

84. Nixon, *RN*, 517.

85. McCracken to Nixon, 5 March 1971, WHCF:SMOF:McCracken:Box 2, NPM. See also Murray Weidenbaum to Troika, 22 February 1971; and Stein and Art Laffer to Troika, 19 February 1971, both in WHCF:SMOF:McCracken:Box 3, NPM.

86. McCracken to Nixon, 17 June 1971, WHCF:SMOF:McCracken:Box 3, NPM.

87. Quoted in Sherman J. Maisel, *Managing the Dollar* (New York, 1973), 287.

88. Stein, "Memo for the President's Files re Quadriad Meeting of 21 May 1971 [document dated 5 June 1971]," WHCF:SMOF:Stein:Box 1, NPM.

89. Gowa, *Closing the Gold Window*, 147–49.

90. Burns quoted in Ehrlichman, *Witness to Power*, 253–54; McCracken to Nixon, 27 January 1971, WHCF:SMOF:McCracken:Box 42, NPM.

91. Gowa, *Closing the Gold Window*, 147–49; Robert Solomon, *The International Monetary System, 1945–1981*, updated ed. (New York, 1982), 176–85; John S. Odell, *U.S. International Monetary Policy: Markets, Power, and Ideas as Sources of Change* (Princeton, 1982), 202.

92. Odell, *U.S. International Monetary Policy*, 252; Gowa, *Closing the Gold Window*, 148.

93. Gowa, *Closing the Gold Window*, 26.

94. U.S. Presidents, *Economic Report of the President, 1972* (Washington, D.C., 1972), 22.

95. Nixon quoted in Haldeman, *Diaries*, 341. Except where noted, the following treatment of the Camp David meeting is based on the firsthand accounts in ibid., 340–46; Connally, *In History's Shadow*, 237–41; Safire, *Before the Fall*, 509–28; and on the scholarly reconstructions in Alfred E. Eckes Jr., *A Search for Solvency: Bretton Woods and the International Monetary System* (Austin, 1975); Odell, *U.S. International Monetary Policy*; Solomon, *International Monetary System*; and Gowa, *Closing the Gold Window*.

96. Safire, *Before the Fall*, 510.

97. Nixon, *RN*, 518.
98. Haldeman, *Diaries*, 335–36; Nixon, *RN*, 518.
99. Haldeman, *Diaries*, 340. Regarding the scale and nature of the British request, see Solomon, *International Monetary System*, 185; and Matusow, *Nixon's Economy*, 148.
100. Burns quoted in Safire, *Before the Fall*, 513; Shultz to Nixon, 18 May 1971 (emphasis in the original), WHSF:CF:BE 5:Box 2, NPM.
101. Stein [as acting CEA chairman] to Nixon, 20 August 1971, WHCF:SMOF: McCracken:Box 42, NPM.
102. McCracken to Nixon, 8 September 1971, WHCF:SMOF:McCracken:Box 43, NPM.
103. U.S. Presidents, *Public Papers*, Richard Nixon, 1971, 886–90.
104. "Memorandum to Safire from the President," 14 August 1971, President's Personal Files, Box 68, NPM.
105. U.S. Presidents, *Public Papers*, Richard Nixon, 1971, 898, 900, 905, 911, 925, 936, 944.
106. Nixon, *RN*, 522.
107. Nixon, *Six Crises*, 310–11.
108. Nixon quoted in Donald F. Kettl, *Leadership at the Fed* (New Haven, Conn., 1986), 125 (emphasis in the original); Patrick J. Buchanan, *Conservative Votes, Liberal Victories* (New York, 1975), 119–20.
109. Peter G. Peterson, *The United States in the Changing World Economy*, 2 vols. (Washington, D.C., 1971), I:cover letter, I:7, II-1.
110. U.S. Presidents, *Public Papers*, Richard Nixon, 1971, 942–43.
111. U.S. Presidents, *Public Papers*, Richard Nixon, 1969, 2.
112. Nixon, *RN*, 762–63.
113. Haldeman, *Diaries*, 338.
114. Nixon quoted in Parmet, *Nixon and His America*, 614. Driving dream references are found in U.S. Presidents, *Public Papers*, Richard Nixon, 1970, 15; and *Public Papers*, Richard Nixon, 1971, 21, 51.
115. Nixon's handwritten notes for 6 July 1971 Kansas City briefing in President's Personal Files, Box 67, NPM.
116. Haldeman, *Diaries*, 346.
117. "Memorandum to Safire from the President," 14 August 1971, President's Personal Files, Box 68, NPM.
118. McCracken to Nixon, 19 October 1971, WHCF:SMOF:McCracken:Box 43, NPM; Stein quoted in Wells, *Economist in an Uncertain World*, 84; Stein, *On the Other Hand*, 67.
119. Stein to Nixon, 28 February 1972, WHCF:SMOF:Stein:Box 45, NPM.
120. Kettl, *Leadership at the Fed*, 127–31; Wells, *Economist in an Uncertain World*, 84–85, 89–90, 98–101.
121. Reichley, *Conservatives in an Age of Change*, 226.
122. Stein quoted in *President and the Council of Economic Advisers*, ed. Hargrove and Morley, 395; Reichley, *Conservatives in an Age of Change*, 226; Alan Blinder, *Economic Policy and the Great Stagflation* (New York, 1979), 142, 181.
123. The interpretation of fiscal and monetary policy in 1972 as essentially political— committed to "buying the election"— is found in Sanford Rose, "The Agony of the

Federal Reserve," *Fortune*, July 1974, 90ff.; and Edward R. Tufte, *Political Control of the Economy* (Princeton, N.J., 1978). Kettl, *Leadership at the Fed*, ch. 5, and Wells, *Economists in an Uncertain World*, ch. 5, defend monetary policy in 1972 from the charge. Stein defends fiscal policy in *Presidential Economics*, 183–85. Samuelson is quoted in Lester A. Sobel, ed., *Inflation and the Nixon Administration, Volume 2, 1972–74* (New York, 1975), 45.

124. Stein to Nixon, 28 February 1972, WHCF:SMOF:Stein:Box 45, NPM; Friedman to Stein, 16 March 1972, WHCF:SMOF:Stein:Box 20, NPM; Shultz to Nixon, 18 April 1972, President's Personal Files, Box 15, NPM; Stein to Nixon, 3 April 1972, WHCF:SMOF:Stein:Box 45, NPM; Stein, *Presidential Economics*, 185.

125. Robert J. Gordon, "Postwar Macroeconomics: The Evolution of Events and Ideas," in *The American Economy in Transition*, ed. Martin Feldstein (Chicago, 1980), 151.

126. Stein to Nixon, 5 December 1973, WHCF:SMOF:Stein:Box 46, NPM; Stein, "The Economy in the State of the Union Message," n.d., WHCF:SMOF:Stein:Box 2, NPM.

127. U.S. Presidents, *Public Papers*, Richard Nixon, 1974, 455, 608.

128. U.S. Presidents, *Public Papers*, Richard Nixon, 1973, 697; Ambrose, *Nixon: Ruin and Recovery*, 154; Henry Kissinger, *Years of Upheaval* (Boston, 1982), 105.

129. Ambrose, *Nixon: Ruin and Recovery*, 755, 279, 289.

130. Kissinger, *Years of Upheaval*, 1195–96.

131. Raymond Price, *With Nixon* (New York, 1977), 369.

132. Otto Eckstein, *The Great Recession: With a Postscript on Stagflation* (Amsterdam, 1978), 109. On the harmful effects of the NEP's controls, see Blinder, *Great Stagflation*, ch. 6.

133. Angus Maddison, *The World Economy in the 20th Century* (Paris, 1989), 65. The discussion that follows is based on Maddison and W. W. Rostow, *The Barbaric Counter-Revolution: Cause and Cure* (Austin, Tex., 1983), passim.

134. John E. Schwarz, *America's Hidden Success: A Reassessment of Public Policy from Kennedy to Reagan*, rev. ed. (New York, 1988), 116–32.

135. Edwin Mansfield, "Technology and Productivity in the United States," in *American Economy in Transition*, ed. Feldstein, 564–68.

136. On imports, see Bennett Harrison and Barry Bluestone, *The Great U-Turn: Corporate Restructuring and the Polarizing of America* (New York, 1988), 8–9. On exports, see William H. Branson, "Trends in United States International Trade and Investment since World War II," in *American Economy in Transition*, ed. Feldstein, 195–203.

Chapter 5

1. John Kenneth Galbraith, *The Affluent Society* (New York, 1958), 156.

2. Martin J. Wiener, *English Culture and the Decline of the Industrial Spirit, 1850–1980* (New York, 1981).

3. Ezra J. Mishan, *The Costs of Economic Growth* (New York, 1967), xii, 171.

4. Ibid., 161, 166; Peter Laslett, *The World We Have Lost: England Before the Industrial Age* (New York, 1965), 22; E. F. Schumacher, *Small Is Beautiful: Economics as if People Mattered* (New York, 1973), 21, 57, 8.

5. Theodore Roszak, *The Making of a Counter Culture: Reflections on the Technocratic Society and Its Youthful Opposition* (Garden City, N.Y., 1969).

6. Guy Strait, "What Is a Hippie?" in *"Takin' It to the Streets": A Sixties Reader*, ed. Alexander Bloom and Wini Breines (New York, 1995), 312.
7. Schumacher, *Small Is Beautiful*, 297.
8. David Shi, *The Simple Life: Plain Living and High Thinking in American Culture* (New York, 1985), 269–70.
9. Ronald Inglehart, *The Silent Revolution: Changing Values and Political Styles Among Western Publics* (Princeton, N.J., 1977), 3; David Riesman et al., *The Lonely Crowd: A Study of the Changing American Character*, abridged ed. with a 1969 preface (New Haven, Conn., 1989), xvi; Daniel Bell, *The Cultural Contradictions of Capitalism* (New York, 1976), 7, 37.
10. Riesman, *Lonely Crowd*, 250, 304.
11. Robert N. Bellah et al., *Habits of the Heart: Individualism and Commitment in American Life* (Berkeley, 1985), 49.
12. Charles A. Reich, *The Greening of America* (New York, 1970); Peter Clecak, *America's Quest for the Ideal Self: Dissent and Fulfillment in the 60s and 70s* (New York, 1983), 7; Tom Wolfe, "The `Me' Decade and the Third Great Awakening," *New York*, 23 August 1976, 26–40; Peter Marin, "The New Narcissism," *Harper's*, October 1975, 45–56; Christopher Lasch, *The Culture of Narcissism: American Life in an Age of Diminishing Expectations* (New York, 1978); Daniel Yankelovich, *New Rules: Searching for Self-Fulfillment in a World Turned Upside Down* (New York, 1981).
13. A superior overview of the shift from conservation to environmentalism is Samuel P. Hays, "Three Decades of Environmental Politics: The Historical Context," in *Government and Environmental Politics: Essays on Historical Developments Since World War Two*, ed. Michael Lacey (Baltimore, 1989), 19–79. Hays argues that, contrary to the popular stereotype, the emergent environmental movement was favorably disposed toward modern science and technology. That may (or may not) be true, but the attitude of environmentalists toward economic growth per se was consistently negative.
14. Rachel Carson, *Silent Spring* (Boston, 1962); John C. Whitaker, *Striking a Balance: Environment and Natural Resources Policy in the Nixon-Ford Years* (Washington, D.C., 1976), 264.
15. Hazel Erskine, "The Polls: Pollution and Its Costs," *Public Opinion Quarterly* (Spring 1970): 120–21.
16. *New York Times*, 16 January 1972.
17. Robert Cameron Mitchell, "From Conservation to Environmental Movement: The Development of the Modern Environmental Lobbies," in *Government and Environmental Politics*, ed. Lacey, 96.
18. U.S. Presidents, *Public Papers*, Richard Nixon, 1970, 12.
19. John Maddox, *The Doomsday Syndrome* (New York, 1973), 10. See also William Tucker, *Progress and Privilege: America in the Age of Environmentalism* (New York, 1982); and Mary Douglas and Aaron Wildavsky, *Risk and Culture: An Essay on the Selection of Technical and Environmental Dangers* (Berkeley, Calif., 1982).
20. Todd R. LaPorte and Daniel Metlay, "Technology Observed: Attitudes of a Wary Public," *Science*, 11 April 1975, 121–27.
21. Barry Commoner, *Closing the Circle: Nature, Man, and Technology* (New York, 1971), 141, 265, 268, 270.

22. Kenneth E. Boulding, "The Economics of the Coming Spaceship Earth," in *Environmental Quality in a Growing Economy*, ed. Henry Jarrett (Baltimore, 1966); Linda Hanley, "Ain't No Time to Wonder Why . . . Whoopie! We're All Gonna Die," in *Student Voices/One*, ed. Christopher R. Reaske and Robert F. Wilson Jr. (New York, 1971), 83.

23. "A Blueprint for Survival," *The Ecologist*, January 1972, 1.

24. *Time*, 24 January 1972, 32.

25. Bowen Northrup, "Club of Rome—75 Powerful Men Who Want to Save the World," *Science Digest*, April 1973, 22–26; and John McCormick, *Reclaiming Paradise: The Global Environmental Movement* (Bloomington, Ind., 1989), ch. 4.

26. Donella Meadows et al., *The Limits to Growth: A Report for the Club of Rome's Project on the Predicament of Mankind* (New York, 1972), 142, 145.

27. Ibid., 168–69.

28. Ibid., 29.

29. On the mass-marketing of *Limits*, see Robert Gillette, "The Limits to Growth: Hard Sell for a Computer View of Doomsday," *Science*, 10 March 1972, 1088–92. The publication statistic is from McCormick, *Reclaiming Paradise*, 82. Peccei is quoted in Willem L. Oltmans, ed., *On Growth* (New York, 1974), 472.

30. Paul Verghese, "Develop—But Don't Grow!" *Christian Century*, 6 June 1973, 653; George J. Church, "Can the World Survive Economic Growth?" *Time*, 14 August 1972, 56–57; Boulding quoted in Mancur Olson, "Introduction," *Daedalus* (Fall 1973): 3. The *Daedalus* issue is devoted to discussion of the limits to growth issue and is a good source of commentary.

31. The critical literature on the debate surrounding *The Limits to Growth* is vast. A representative sample includes McCormick, *Reclaiming Paradise*, ch. 4; Francis Sandbach, "The Rise and Fall of the Limits to Growth Debate," *Social Studies of Science* (1978): 495–520; H.S.D. Cole et al., eds., *Thinking About the Future: A Critique of "The Limits to Growth"* (London, 1973); *Business Week*, 11 March 1972, 97–98; Kenneth E. Boulding, "Yes, the Wolf Is Real," *New Republic*, 29 April 1974, 27–28; Stuart Chase, "The Club of Rome and Its Computer," *Bulletin of the Atomic Scientists*, March 1973, 36–39.

32. Carl Kaysen, "The Computer That Printed Out W*O*L*F*," *Foreign Affairs*, July 1972, 665.

33. Christopher Freeman, "Malthus with a Computer," in *Thinking About the Future*, ed. Cole et al., 8.

34. Henry C. Wallich, "More on Growth," *Newsweek*, 13 March 1972, 86.

35. Henry Simmons, "Systems Dynamics and Technocracy," in *Thinking About the Future*, ed. Cole et al., 192–208. The quoted material is from 207.

36. Quoted in Maurice Goldsmith, "Meadows Unlimited or Caveat Computer," *Bulletin of the Atomic Scientists*, May 1973, 18.

37. Quoted in Oltmans, ed., *On Growth*, 472; *Business Week*, 11 March 1972, 98.

38. Leonard Silk, "On the Imminence of Disaster," *New York Times*, 14 March 1972.

39. Quoted in Oltmans, ed., *On Growth*, 48.

40. Walt W. Rostow, "Economic Growth: Past and Future," in *Growth in America*, ed. Chester Cooper (Westport, Conn., 1976), 50.

41. U.S. Presidents, *Public Papers*, Richard Nixon, 1973, 93, 102.

42. Ibid., 583.

43. Mihajlo Mesarovic and Eduard Pestel, *Mankind at the Turning Point: The Second Report of the Club of Rome* (New York, 1974).

44. Edison Electrical Institute, "We Stand at a Decisive Moment in America's Growth," in Records of the White House Conference on Balanced National Growth and Economic Development, Record Group 220 (hereafter White House Conference), Box 21, Jimmy Carter Presidential Library, Atlanta, Georgia (hereafter JCPL).

45. Quoted in Otis Graham, *Toward a Planned Society: From Roosevelt to Nixon* (New York, 1976), 200.

46. U.S. National Goals Research Staff, *Toward Balanced Growth: Quantity with Quality* (Washington, D.C., 1970), passim.

47. Daniel P. Moynihan, "The Third Generation and the Third Century: Choices Concerning the Quality of American Life," in Commission on Critical Choices for Americans, *Qualities of Life: Critical Choices for Americans, Volume VII* (Lexington, Mass., 1976), 405; Moynihan to Ehrlichman and Haldeman, 24 July 1970, WHSF:SMOF:Ehrlichman:Box 21, NPM; Stein to Moynihan, 29 May 1970, WHCF:SMOF:Stein:Box 24, NPM.

48. Nelson A. Rockefeller, "Overview: Critical Choices and Emergent Opportunities," in Commission on Critical Choices for Americans, *Vital Resources: Critical Choices for Americans, Volume I* (Lexington, Mass., 1977), xxx, xxxii.

49. Commission on Critical Choices for Americans, *Values of Growth: Critical Choices for Americans, Volume VI* (Lexington, Mass., 1976), xxi-xxii, xiii.

50. Ibid., xiii.

51. Neal R. Peirce, "A Town Meeting on Jobs and Growth," *Washington Post*, 30 January 1978.

52. "White House Conference on Balanced National Growth and Economic Development: Working Document," revised as of 13 October 1977, White House Conference, Box 6, JCPL.

53. "White House Conference . . . : Introduction [for Advisory Committee]," 3 January 1978, White House Conference, Box 1, JCPL.

54. Kreps speech to White House Governors' Conference, 9 January 1978, White House Conference, Box 19, JCPL.

55. Thomas Oliphant, "Economic Balance: A Clash Over Definition," *Boston Globe*, 31 January 1978.

56. Quoted in Neal R. Peirce, "A `Hell of an Experiment' in Resolving Economic Growth Dilemmas," *National Journal*, 21 January 1978, 103.

57. Carmen Delgado Votaw to Michael Koleda, 29 December 1977, White House Conference, Box 5, JCPL.

58. See, for example, Thomas Oliphant, "Sunbelt vs. the Frostbelt," *Boston Globe*, 25 September 1977.

59. *New York Times*, 3 February 1978.

60. Kreps speech to White House Conference, 29 January 1978, White House Conference, Box 2, JCPL.

61. Mike McManus column in *Newsday*, quoted in Michael S. Koleda speech, San Francisco, 10 April 1978, White House Conference, Box 19, JCPL.

62. Quoted in *The Chronicle for Higher Education*, 13 February 1978.
63. The administration's objectives for the conference are discussed at length and Watson quoted in Peirce, "A 'Hell of an Experiment,'" 103–5.
64. See, for example, the coverage in the *New York Times* and *Wall Street Journal*, 3 February 1978.
65. U.S. Presidents, *Public Papers*, Jimmy Carter, 1978, 1:268–69.
66. Rockefeller to Kreps, 29 May 1978, White House Conference, Box 1, JCPL.
67. Koleda speech, San Francisco, 10 April 1978, White House Conference, Box 19, JCPL.
68. White House Conference on Balanced National Growth and Economic Development, Final Report, July 1978, appendix, Volume 1, 210.
69. The OECD and IMF reports and the Gallup poll are discussed in Lester A. Sobel, ed., *Inflation and the Nixon Administration, Volume 2, 1972–74* (New York, 1975), 280; the domestic inflation statistics are from John Robert Greene, *The Presidency of Gerald R. Ford* (Lawrence, Kans., 1995), 67; Ford's speech in U.S. Presidents, *Public Papers*, Gerald R. Ford, 1974, 9.
70. Office of the White House Press Secretary, Transcript, White House Conference on Inflation, 5 September 1974, 36 (transcript copy in Research Library, Federal Reserve Bank of Boston).
71. Ibid., 37, 107, 109.
72. U.S. Presidents, *The Conference on Inflation, September 27–28, 1974* (Washington, D.C., 1974), 255, 259, 261.
73. Quoted in A. James Reichley, *Conservatives in an Age of Change: The Nixon and Ford Administrations* (Washington, D.C., 1981), 335, 383–84.
74. U.S. Presidents, *Public Papers*, Gerald R. Ford, 1974, 733.
75. Quoted in Hobart Rowen, *Self-Inflicted Wounds: From LBJ's Guns and Butter to Reagan's Voodoo Economics* (New York, 1994), 110.
76. Burns quoted in ibid., 118; Greenspan quoted in Erwin C. Hargrove and Samuel A. Morley, eds., *The President and the Council of Economics Advisers: Interviews with CEA Chairmen* (Boulder, Colo., 1984), 443; Ford quoted in Alan Blinder, *Hard Heads, Soft Hearts: Tough Minded Economics for a Just Society* (Reading, Mass., 1987), 51.
77. Quoted in Reichley, *Conservatives in an Age of Change*, 400–401. Burns's role is discussed in Wyatt C. Wells, *Economist in an Uncertain World: Arthur F. Burns and the Federal Reserve, 1970–78* (New York, 1994), 200–203.
78. Text of presidential debate in Sidney Kraus, *The Great Debates: Carter vs. Ford, 1976* (Bloomington, Ind., 1979), 458, 457.
79. W. Carl Biven, "Economic Advice in the Carter Administration," in *The Presidency and Domestic Policies of Jimmy Carter*, ed. Herbert D. Rosenbaum and Alexej Ugrinsky (Westport, Conn., 1994), 616.
80. U.S. Presidents, *Public Papers*, Jimmy Carter, 1977, 1:47–55, quote from 1:71.
81. Robert Kuttner, *The Life of the Party: Democratic Prospects in 1988 and Beyond* (New York, 1987), 154; the unnamed Washington insider is quoted in Elizabeth Drew, *American Journal: The Events of 1976* (New York, 1977), 41; Stuart E. Eizenstat, "President Carter, the Democratic Party, and the Making of Domestic Policy," in *Presidency and Domestic Policies of Jimmy Carter*, ed. Rosenbaum and Ugrinsky, 6. The best discus-

sion of Carter's relationship to American liberalism is William E. Leuchtenburg, *In the Shadow of FDR: From Harry Truman to Bill Clinton*, 2nd ed., rev. and updated (Ithaca, N.Y., 1993).

82. Leo Ribuffo, "Jimmy Carter and the Selling of the President, 1976–1980," in *Presidency and Domestic Policies of Jimmy Carter*, ed. Rosenbaum and Ugrinsky, 158; Jimmy Carter, *Keeping Faith: Memoirs of a President* (New York, 1982), 21; U.S. Presidents, *Public Papers*, Jimmy Carter, 1977, 1:2; U.S. Presidents, *Public Papers*, Jimmy Carter, 1979, 2:1981.

83. Quoted in Erwin C. Hargrove, *Jimmy Carter as President: Leadership and the Politics of the Public Good* (Baton Rouge, La., 1988), 91.

84. Hargrove and Morley, eds., *President and the Council of Economic Advisers*, 463.

85. Carter, *Keeping Faith*, 77–78; Carter quoted in Joseph A. Califano Jr., *Governing America: An Insider's Report from the White House and the Cabinet* (New York, 1981), 124.

86. William Greider, *Secrets of the Temple: How the Federal Reserve Runs the Country* (New York, 1987), Part I; Carter, *Keeping Faith*, 527–28.

87. Statistics for 1980 from Burton I. Kaufman, *The Presidency of James Earl Carter, Jr.* (Lawrence, Kans., 1993), 168, 178; Michael Mussa, "U.S. Monetary Policy in the 1980s," in *American Economic Policy in the 1980s*, ed. Martin Feldstein (Chicago, 1994), 97.

88. Republican nomination acceptance speech in Ronald Reagan, *A Time for Choosing: The Speeches of Ronald Reagan, 1961–1982* (Chicago, 1983), 233.

89. Carter, *Keeping Faith*, 541.

90. Quoted in Steven M. Gillon, *The Democrats' Dilemma: Walter F. Mondale and the Liberal Legacy* (New York, 1992), 287.

91. The discussion of Carter's economic policy is based on Anthony S. Campagna, *Economic Policy in the Carter Administration* (Westport, Conn., 1995); Hargrove, *Jimmy Carter as President*, ch. 4; and Kaufman, *Presidency of James Earl Carter, Jr.*, passim.

92. Taylor Dark, "Organized Labor and the Carter Administration: The Origins of Conflict," in *Presidency and Domestic Policies of Jimmy Carter*, ed. Rosenbaum and Urgrinsky, 765.

93. Kaufman, *Presidency of James Earl Carter, Jr.*, 110–11.

94. Quoted in Hargrove, *Jimmy Carter as President*, 93.

95. Carter, *Keeping the Faith*, 102.

96. Quoted in Gillon, *Democrats Dilemma*, 205.

97. Califano, *Governing America*, 358–63; Kaufman, *Presidency of James Earl Carter, Jr.*, 52–55.

98. Kaufman, *Presidency of James Earl Carter, Jr.*, 102–5, 133–35; U.S. Presidents, *Public Papers*, Jimmy Carter, 1978, 2:1841.

99. Kaufman, *Presidency of James Earl Carter, Jr.*, 140, 181–95; Stuart E. Eizenstat, "President Carter, the Democratic Party, and the Making of Domestic Policy," in *Presidency and Domestic Policies of Jimmy Carter*, ed. Rosenbaum and Ugrinsky, 14.

100. Gillon, *Democrats' Dilemma*, 200; Mondale quoted ibid., 298.

101. Daniel Yankelovich and Bernard Lefkowitz, "The Public Debate on Growth: Preparing for Resolution," 18 May 1979, 1, in Records of the President's Commission for a National Agenda for the Eighties, Record Group 220 (hereafter Commission for a National Agenda), Box 13, JCPL; George Katona and Burkhard Strumpel, "A New Economic Era," *Public Opinion*, March-April 1978, 9.

102. The Harris Survey, 23 May 1977, White House Conference, Box 19, JCPL.

103. Yankelovich and Lefkowitz, "Public Debate on Growth," 29, Commission for a National Agenda, Box 13, JCPL.

104. White House Conference transcript, 30 January 1978, 48, White House Conference, Box 22, JCPL.

105. Hedley Donovan, *Roosevelt to Reagan: A Reporter's Encounters with Nine Presidents* (New York, 1985), 201–2.

106. See the superb account in Edward D. Berkowitz, "Jimmy Carter and the Sunbelt Report: Seeking a National Agenda," in *Presidency and Domestic Policies of Jimmy Carter*, ed. Rosenbaum and Ugrinsky, 33–44.

107. U.S. President's Commission for a National Agenda for the Eighties, *A National Agenda for the Eighties*, reprint (Englewood Cliffs, N.J., 1980), 1, 127–28.

108. "Executive Summary, Panel 2, The American Economy," ibid., 146–47.

109. "Executive Summary, Panel 8, The Quality of American Life," ibid., 189, 191.

110. Ibid., 22.

111. Amitai Etzioni, "America's Project," n.d. [1979], Box 7, Commission for a National Agenda, Box 7, JCPL.

Chapter 6

1. Hawkins quoted in Harvey L. Schantz and Richard H. Schmidt, "Politics and Policy: The Humphrey-Hawkins Story," in *Employment and Labor-Relations Policy*, ed. Charles Bulmer and John L. Carmichael Jr. (Lexington, Mass., 1980), 27; Wyatt C. Wells, *Economist in an Uncertain World: Arthur F. Burns and the Federal Reserve, 1970–78* (New York, 1994), 244.

2. "A Job for Everyone," *New Republic*, 27 March 1976, 4; Keyserling letter to the editor, *New Republic*, 1 May 1976; and Keyserling, "Memorandum In Re: Status of Humphrey-Hawkins Bill," 29 January 1976, Box 34, Keyserling MSS, HSTL. Regarding Keyserling's vigorous behind-the-scenes lobbying on behalf of Humphrey-Hawkins, see his correspondence with Walter Heller, Paul Samuelson, and George Schultze in Box 33, ibid.

3. Schantz and Schmidt, "Politics and Policy: The Humphrey-Hawkins Story," 25–39; Gary Mucciaroni, *The Political Failure of Employment Policy, 1945–1982* (Pittsburgh, Pa., 1990), 93–102; American Enterprise Institute, *Reducing Unemployment: The Humphrey-Hawkins and Kemp-McClure Bills* (Washington, D.C., 1976), 1–20.

4. Keyserling quoted in American Enterprise Institute, *Reducing Unemployment*, 15.

5. Keyserling, "Irresponsible Economics Under President Nixon and Areas of Democratic Responsibility: Presentation to H.R. Democratic Steering and Policy Committee," 18 June 1974, Box 32, Keyserling MSS, HSTL.

6. Ibid.

7. Milton Friedman, "Humphrey-Hawkins," *Newsweek*, 2 August 1976, 55.

8. Schultze quoted in Mucciaroni, *Political Failure of Employment Policy*, 97.

9. Quoted in A. James Reichley, *Conservatives in an Age of Change: The Nixon and Ford Administrations* (Washington, D.C., 1981), 398.

10. Quoted in American Enterprise Institute, *Reducing Unemployment*, 15–16.

11. "Economics and Morality: An Interview with Leon H. Keyserling," *Skeptic: The Forum for Contemporary History*, special issue number 6, 1975, 49.

12. Quoted in American Enterprise Institute, *Reducing Unemployment*, 16.

13. Quoted in Schantz and Schmidt, "Politics and Policy: The Humphrey-Hawkins Story," 36.

14. Keyserling, "What's Wrong with American Economics?" lecture, 9 October 1986, Box 39, Keyserling MSS, HSTL.

15. The best account of the American flirtation with industrial policy is Otis L. Graham Jr., *Losing Time: The Industrial Policy Debate* (Cambridge, Mass., 1992).

16. *Forging America's Future: Strategies for National Growth and Development, Report of the Advisory Committee on National Growth Policy Processes to the National Commission on Supplies and Shortages* (Washington, 1976), passim.

17. Richard H. K. Vietor, *Contrived Competition: Regulation and Deregulation in America* (Cambridge, Mass., 1994), 14–15.

18. Graham, *Losing Time*, 38–45. Eizenstat is quoted on 43.

19. Ibid., 44, 53.

20. "The Reindustrialization of America," *Business Week*, 30 June 1980, 86, 88.

21. Quoted in David E. Rosenbaum, "A Passion for Ideas," *New York Times*, 11 August 1996, 13.

22. Jack Kemp, *An American Renaissance: A Strategy for the 1980s* (New York, 1979), 49, 185.

23. Ibid., 49.

24. American Enterprise Institute, *Reducing Unemployment*, 21–23, 25–26.

25. Keyserling, "Comments on H.R. 13399 Kemp-McClure Bill ("Jobs Creation Act"), 14 September 1976, Box 34, Keyserling MSS, HSTL.

26. Paul Craig Roberts, *The Supply-Side Revolution: An Insider's Account of Policymaking in Washington* (Cambridge, Mass., 1984), 30–31; Kemp, *American Renaissance*, 37–39.

27. Kemp's speech to the 1976 Republican Convention is reprinted in Bruce R. Bartlett, *Reaganomics: Supply Side Economics in Action* (Westport, Conn., 1981), 219.

28. Ibid., 130.

29. Heller quoted in Robert L. Bartley, *The Seven Fat Years and How to Do It Again* (New York, 1992), 74; other quotations from Congress of the United States, Committee on the Budget, House of Representatives and Senate Budget Committee, United States Senate, *Leading Economists' Views of Kemp-Roth*, Joint Committee Print, 95th Cong., 2nd sess. (Washington, D.C., 1978), 13, 11, 123, 49, 45.

30. Congress of the United States, Committee on Ways and Means, U.S. House of Representatives, *Tax Reductions: Economists' Comments on H.R. 8333 and S. 1860, Bills to Provide for Permanent Tax Rate Reductions for Individuals and Businesses*, Committee Print, 95th Cong., 2nd sess. (Washington, D.C., 1978), 28, 59.

31. Ibid., 44, 86, 68.

32. Committee on the Budget, *Leading Economists' Views of Kemp-Roth*, 91.

33. Kemp, *American Renaissance*, 10; Bartlett, *Reaganomics*, 132, 144–45.

34. Bartlett, *Reaganomics*, 150–58. Quoted material from 153. Regarding the considerable political muscle put into the struggle to cut the capital gains tax, see Godfrey Hodgson, *The World Turned Right Side Up: A History of the Conservative Ascendancy in America* (Boston, 1996), 206–9.

35. The discussion that follows relies heavily on Paul Krugman's brilliant analysis in *Peddling Prosperity: Economic Sense and Nonsense in the Age of Diminished Expectations* (New York, 1994), 23–81. Different slants on the same phenomenon are found in James W. Dean, "The Dissolution of the Keynesian Consensus," in *The Crisis in Economic Theory*, ed. Daniel Bell and Irving Kristol (New York, 1981), 19–34; Robert Heilbroner and William Milberg, *The Crisis of Vision in Modern Economic Thought* (New York, 1995), 25–67; and Gregory Mankiw, "A Quick Refresher Course in Macroeconomics," *Journal of Economic Literature* 28 (December 1990): 1645–60.

36. A. W. Phillips, "The Relation Between Unemployment and the Rate of Change of Money Wage Rates in the United Kingdom, 1861–1957," *Economica* 25 (November 1958): 283–99; Paul Samuelson and Robert Solow, "Analytical Aspects of Anti-Inflation Policy," *American Economic Review* 50 (May 1960): 177–94.

37. Milton Friedman, "The Role of Monetary Policy," *American Economic Review* 58 (March 1968): 1–17. James Tobin, "The Natural Rate as New Classical Macroeconomics," in *The Natural Rate of Unemployment: Reflections on 25 Years of the Hypothesis*, ed. Rod Cross (New York, 1995), 40.

38. Friedman, "Role of Monetary Policy," 11.

39. Mark H. Willis, "'Rational Expectations' as a Counterrevolution," in *Crisis in Economic Theory*, ed. Bell and Kristol, 81. Seminal expressions of the rational expectations approach are John F. Muth, "Rational Expectations and the Theory of Price Movements," *Econometrica* 29 (July 1961): 315–35; Robert E. Lucas Jr., "Expectations and the Neutrality of Money," *Journal of Economic Theory* 4 (April 1972): 102–24; and Thomas J. Sargent, "Rational Expectations, the Real Rate of Interest and the Natural Rate of Unemployment," *Brookings Papers on Economic Activity* 2 (1973): 429–72.

40. Franco Modigliani, "The Monetarist Controversy, or Should We Forsake Stabilization Policies?" *American Economic Review* 67 (March 1977): 5.

41. Krugman, *Peddling Prosperity*, 72. See, for example, the essays by Feldstein, Summers, and Boskin in Martin S. Feldstein, ed., *Taxes and Capital Formation* (Chicago, 1987).

42. Alan S. Blinder, "The Rise and Fall of Keynesian Economics," *The Economic Record* (December 1988): 278.

43. Robert Lucas, "Tobin and Monetarism: A Review Article," *Journal of Economic Literature* 19 (June 1981): 559.

44. Quoted in William R. Neikirk, *Volcker: Portrait of the Money Man* (New York, 1987), 78.

45. William A. Niskanen, *Reaganomics: An Insider's Account of the Policies and the People* (New York, 1988), 19.

46. This distillation of supply-side doctrine is based on Roberts, *Supply-Side Revolution*; Bartley, *Seven Fat Years*; Michael K. Evans, *The Truth About Supply-Side Economics* (New York, 1983); and Herbert Stein, "Some 'Supply-Side' Propositions," *Wall Street Journal*, 19 March 1980.

47. Jude Wanniski, *The Way the World Works*, 3rd ed. (Morristown, N.J., 1989), 345; regarding Say's ideas, see Thomas Sowell, *Say's Law: An Historical Analysis* (Princeton, N.J., 1972); Ture quoted in Bartley, *Seven Fat Years*, 56–57.

48. Victor A. Canto, Douglas H. Joines, and Arthur B. Laffer, *Foundations of Supply-Side Economics: Theory and Evidence* (New York, 1983), xv.

49. Martin Anderson, *Revolution* (New York, 1988), 147. On the creation of the Laffer curve, see Bartley, *Seven Fat Years*, 57–58. The role of Laffer and Mundell is sketched acerbicly but compellingly in Krugman, *Peddling Prosperity*, ch. 3. See also Jude Wanneski, "The Mundell-Laffer Hypothesis—A New View of the World Economy," *The Public Interest* 39 (Spring 1975): 31–52.

50. Robert Bartley, "Jack Kemp's Intellectual Blitz," *Wall Street Journal*, 29 November 1979; Roberts, *Supply-Side Revolution*, 7–33.

51. Herbert Stein, *Presidential Economics: The Making of Economic Policy from Roosevelt to Reagan and Beyond* (New York, 1984), 241. Robert Bartley, "Introduction to the Third Edition," in Wanniski, *Way the World Works*, xii.

52. Herbert Stein, "Some 'Supply-Side' Propositions," *Wall Street Journal*, 19 March 1980; Stein, "My Life as a Dee-cline," in *On the Other Hand: Essays on Economics, Economists, and Politics* (Washington, D.C., 1995), 18; Stein, "Changes in Macroeconomic Conditions," in *The American Economy in Transition*, ed. Martin Feldstein (Chicago, 1980), 172–73.

53. Krugman, *Peddling Prosperity*, 89–92.

54. Robert Bartley, "Introduction to the Third Edition," in Wanniski, *Way the World Works*, xii.

55. Irving Kristol, *Neoconservatism: The Autobiography of an Idea* (New York, 1995), 36–37.

56. Herbert Stein, "Professor Knight's Law of Talk," *Wall Street Journal*, 14 October 1981.

57. Roberts, *Supply-Side Revolution*, 28; Niskanen, *Reaganomics*, 19.

58. Quoted in Haynes Johnson, *Sleepwalking Through History: America in the Reagan Years*, updated ed. (New York, 1992), 107.

59. "Remarks by Chairman Richard Bolling, SSEC Directors Meeting," 23 March 1978; Memo, "Special Study on Economic Change," 1 March 1979; Robert Ash Wallace to Bolling, 25 January 1979; Joint Economic Committee, "Special Study on Economic Change: Committee Report," n.d., typescript, all in Box 2, Robert Ash Wallace Papers, JCPL.

60. Congress of the United States, Joint Economic Committee, *Joint Economic Committee Report, 1979*, Senate Report No. 96–44, 96th Cong., 1st sess. (Washington, D.C., 1979), 3; Bentsen press release, quoted in Bartley, *Seven Fat Years*, 87; and Congress of the United States, Joint Economic Committee, *Joint Economic Committee Report, 1980*, Senate Report No. 96–618, 96th Cong., 2nd sess. (Washington, D.C., 1980), 1.

61. Burns quoted in Wells, *Economist in an Uncertain World*, 163; Anderson, *Revolution*, 143.

62. Feldstein, "Introduction," in Feldstein, ed., *American Economy in Transition*, 6. See also A. F. Ehrbar, "Martin Feldstein's Electric-Blue Economic Prescriptions," *Fortune*, 27 February 1978, 54–58; and Soma Golden, "Superstar of the New Economists," *New York Times Magazine*, 23 March 1980, 30 ff.

63. Quoted in Bartlett, *Reaganomics*, 8–9.

64. Wanniski, "Introduction to the Revised and Updated Edition," in *Way the World Works*, 345; Daniel Patrick Moynihan, *Miles to Go: A Personal History of Social Policy* (Cambridge, Mass., 1996), 10.

65. Kemp, *American Renaissance*, 10, 13.

66. William Niskanen in Kenneth W. Thompson, ed., *Reagan and the Economy: Nine Intimate Perspectives* (Lanham, Md., 1994), 30; Richard Darman, *Who's in Control? Polar Politics and the Sensible Center* (New York, 1996), 40.

67. Lou Cannon, *President Reagan: The Role of a Lifetime* (New York, 1991), 130; Fred Barnes, "Nap Master Ronnie," *New Republic*, 9 January 1989, 17.

68. O'Neill quoted in Laurence I. Barrett, *Gambling with History: Reagan in the White House*, updated ed. (New York, 1984), 82; and Cannon, *President Reagan*, 116. Wright quoted in Barrett, *Gambling with History*, 15.

69. George Will, "How Reagan Changed America," *Newsweek*, 9 January 1989; regarding the famous pony story, see Barrett, *Gambling with History*, 174; U.S. Presidents, *Public Papers*, Ronald Reagan, 1981, 4.

70. Isaiah Berlin, *The Hedgehog and the Fox: An Essay on Tolstoy's View of History*, rev. ed. (Chicago, 1993), 3.

71. Edwin Meese III, *With Reagan: The Inside Story* (Washington, D.C., 1992), 20. On Reagan's criteria for selection to the administration team, see 63.

72. Quoted in Dinesh D'Souza, *Ronald Reagan: How an Ordinary Man Became an Extraordinary Leader* (New York, 1997), 45.

73. Meg Greenfield, "Leadership by Presentation," *Newsweek*, 9 March 1998, 68. See also Michael K. Deaver with Mickey Herskowitz, *Behind the Scenes* (New York, 1988).

74. Reagan speech to the Republican National Convention, 17 July 1980, in *A Time for Choosing: The Speeches of Ronald Reagan, 1961–1982* (Chicago, 1983), 223, 231, 225; U.S. Presidents, *Public Papers*, Ronald Reagan, 1981, 1.

75. Anderson, *Revolution*, 114–21, 126; "White House Report on the Program for Economic Recovery, February 18, 1981," in U.S. Presidents, *Public Papers*, Ronald Reagan, 1981, 116–32.

76. William Niskanen, William Poole, and Murray Weidenbaum, "Introduction," in *Two Revolutions in Economic Policy: The First Economic Reports of Presidents Kennedy and Reagan*, ed. James Tobin and Murray Weidenbaum (Cambridge, Mass., 1988), 279.

77. Ronald Reagan, *An American Life* (New York, 1990), 231; Reagan speech to the Phoenix, Arizona, Chamber of Commerce, 30 March 1961, in *A Time for Choosing*.

78. Meese, *With Reagan*, 123, 121; Reagan, *An American Life*, 232.

79. Anderson, *Revolution*, 140–63 (quote from 163).

80. Niskanen, Poole, and Weidenbaum, "Introduction," 287. On the rejection of "the simple-minded supply-side approach," see Weidenbaum's comments in Thompson, ed., *Reagan and the Economy*, 13.

81. Brock quoted in Kenneth W. Thompson, ed., *The Reagan Presidency: Ten Intimate Perspectives of Ronald Reagan* (Lanham, Md., 1997), 114; Kemp quoted in *Recollections of Reagan: A Portrait of Ronald Reagan*, ed. Peter Hannaford (New York, 1997), 74; the Chicago speech is discussed in Anderson, *Revolution*, 122–139; U.S. Presidents, *Public Papers*, Ronald Reagan, 1981, 83.

82. U.S. Presidents, *Public Papers*, Ronald Reagan, 1984, 2:1174.

83. Reagan, *An American Life*, 316, 232.

84. Niskanen, *Reaganomics*, 73–76; Don Fullerton, "Inputs to Tax Policy-Making: The Supply-Side, the Deficit, and the Level Playing Field," in *American Economic Policy in the 1980s*, ed. Feldstein, 165–85.

85. Meese, *With Reagan*, 156; Reagan quoted in Daniel Yergin and Joseph Stanislaw, *The Commanding Heights: The Battle Between Government and the Marketplace That Is Remaking the Modern World* (New York, 1998), 334.

86. Volcker quoted in Neikirk, *Volcker: Portrait of the Money Man*, 110; Michael Mussa, "U.S. Monetary Policy in the 1980s," in *American Economic Policy in the 1980s*, ed. Feldstein, 111.

87. Quoted in James M. Poterba, "Federal Budget Policy in the 1980s" in *American Economic Policy in the 1980s*, ed. Feldstein, 246.

88. Vietor, *Contrived Competition*, 15–16.

89. Anderson, *Revolution*, 245; Donald T. Regan, *For the Record: From Wall Street to Washington* (San Diego, 1988), 156; David A. Stockman, *The Triumph of Politics: Why the Reagan Revolution Failed* (New York, 1986), 271.

90. Joseph White and Aaron Wildavsky, *The Deficit and the Public Interest: The Search for Responsible Budgeting in the 1980s* (Berkeley, Calif., 1989), ch. 8.

91. Regarding the Rosy Scenario, the fundamental underpinnings of the revenue hemorrhage, and the problem of income tax indexation, see Murray L. Weidenbaum, *Confessions of a One-Armed Economist* (St. Louis, 1983), 9–11, 14–18.

92. Stockman, *Triumph of Politics*, 8, 11; liberal complaints are quoted in D'Souza, *Ronald Reagan*, 102; Benjamin Friedman, *Day of Reckoning: The Consequences of American Economic Policy Under Reagan and After* (New York, 1988), 272–73.

93. Stockman, *Triumph of Politics*, 11; Niskanen, *Reaganomics*, 39.

94. Stockman, *Triumph of Politics*, 136–38.

95. Korb quoted in Daniel Patrick Moynihan, *Miles to Go*, 113; Stockman, *Triumph of Politics*, 106, 278, 297; Niskanen, *Reaganomics*, 33.

96. Stockman, *Triumph of Politics*, 356; Iwan W. Morgan, *Deficit Government: Taxing and Spending in Modern America* (Chicago, 1995), 148–49; Poterba, "Federal Budget Policy in the 1980s," 238–39. Experts continue to disagree how much responsibility the Reagan tax cuts bear for the subsequent deficits of the 1980s. Lawrence Lindsay, *The Growth Experiment: How the New Tax Policy is Transforming the U.S. Economy* (New York, 1990), 98, argues that tax reductions account for only a quarter of the rise in the deficits of the 1980s; Paul Krugman, *Peddling Prosperity*, 154, estimates that over 70 percent of the increase in the deficit results from tax changes.

97. Carter and Ford joint statement in *American Agenda: Report to the Forty-First President of the United States* (n.p., n.d.), 8; White and Wildavsky, *The Deficit and the Public Interest*, xv; Moynihan, *Miles to Go*, 95 (quote), 11, 126.

98. Alan Brinkley, "Reagan's Revenge," *New York Times Magazine*, 19 June 1994, 37; Griscom quote from *The Reagan Presidency: Ten Intimate Perspectives*, ed. Kenneth W. Thompson, 43. See also Charles L. Schultze, "Paying the Bills," in *Setting Domestic Priorities: What Can Government Do?*, ed. Henry J. Aaron and Charles L. Schultze (Washington, D.C., 1992), 295; Theda Skocpol, *Boomerang: Clinton's Health Security Effort and the Turn Against Government in U.S. Politics* (New York, 1996); and Paul Pierson, *Dismantling the Welfare State? Reagan, Thatcher, and the Politics of Retrenchment* (New York, 1994), 149–55, 162–64.

99. Daniel Patrick Moynihan, *Came the Revolution: Argument in the Reagan Era* (San Diego, 1988), 21, 31, 34 (quote).

100. Ibid., 151, 153.

101. Ibid., 279.

102. Daniel Patrick Moynihan, *Miles to Go*, 111, 113, 11. Sidney Blumenthal has since extended the reach of the conspiracy by analyzing the appearance of the same "insolvency mechanism" of tax-cutting in the 1996 presidential campaign. See his "Seeking Insolvency: The Strange Career of Supply-Side Economics," *World Policy Journal* 14 (Summer 1997): 19–29.

103. Stockman's comments are in "Summary of Discussion," *American Economic Policy in the 1980s*, ed. Feldstein, 287; Darman, *Who's in Control?*, 80.

104. *Newsweek*, 7 August 1967, 68; 23 February 1981, 70. See also Friedman, "The Kemp-Roth Free Lunch," *Newsweek*, 7 August 1978, 59; Elton Rayack, *Not So Free to Choose: The Political Economy of Milton Friedman and Ronald Reagan* (New York, 1987), 188–89; Milton and Rose D. Friedman, *Two Lucky People: Memoirs* (Chicago, 1998), 388–92; Jude Wanniski, "The Two Santa Claus Theory," *The National Observer*, 6 March 1976; George Will, "Reining In the Federal Spending Urge," *Washington Post*, 27 July 1978.

105. Quotes from Reagan speech to the American Textile Manufacturers Institute, 29 March 1973, in *A Time for Choosing*, 116, 118.

106. On the Prop 1 struggle and tax limitation movement, see Niskanen, *Reaganomics*, viii-ix; William Niskanen, "Organizing the Government for Policy-Making," in *Reagan and the Economy*, ed. Thompson, 28; Friedman and Friedman, *Two Lucky People*, 352–56, 389; Edmund G. Brown and Bill Brown, *Reagan: The Political Chameleon* (New York, 1976), 61–67; Alvin Rabushka and Pauline Ryan, *The Tax Revolt* (Stanford, Calif., 1982), 18; Clarence Y. H. Lo, *Small Property Versus Big Government: Social Origins of the Property Tax Revolt* (Berkeley, Calif., 1990), 1–2, 23.

107. Stockman, *Triumph of Politics*, 133.

108. U.S. Presidents, *Public Papers*, Ronald Reagan, 1982, 1:328.

109. U.S. Presidents, *Public Papers*, Ronald Reagan, 1981, 556–57. (See also 545, 546, 563, 571.)

110. Stockman's self-characterization is in Stockman, "Budget Policy," in *American Economic Policy in the 1980s*, ed. Feldstein, 275; Wanniski, "Introduction to the Second Edition," in *Way the World Works*, 360; Meese, *With Reagan*, 138.

111. Reagan quoted in Darman, *Who's in Control?*, 118.

112. U.S. Presidents, *Public Papers*, Ronald Reagan, 1983, 1:105; Reagan, *An American Life*, 325.

113. Reagan, *For the Record*, 327.

114. Stockman, *Triumph of Politics*, 272.

115. William Greider, *The Education of David Stockman and Other Americans* (New York, 1982), 100–101.

116. U.S. Presidents, *Public Papers*, Ronald Reagan, 1981, 139. For other examples, see ibid., 178, 200, 468, 510, 557–58, 567; and U.S. Presidents, *Public Papers*, Ronald Reagan, 1982, 1:182. Martin Anderson has argued that no one in the administration actually said that massive tax reductions would yield increased revenues, merely that the loss would be offset to a substantial degree by increased growth. On this count, he is quite simply wrong, as the above citations indicate. See Anderson, *Revolution*, 152–57.

117. Reagan quoted in Barrett, *Gambling With History*, 341; Martin Feldstein, "American Economic Policy in the 1980s: A Personal View," in *American Economic Policy in the 1980s*, ed. Feldstein, 59.

118. Weidenbaum in *Reagan and the Economy*, ed. Thompson, 7.

119. Ibid., 9.

120. Niskanen, *Reaganomics*, 112; Paul Krugman, *The Age of Diminished Expectations: U.S. Economic Policy in the 1990s*, rev. and updated ed. (Cambridge, Mass., 1994), 87. Examples of the argument (from the left and right, respectively) that deficits matter little are Robert Eisner, *The Misunderstood Economy: What Counts and How to Count It* (Boston, 1994), and Robert J. Barro, *Macroeconomics*, 2nd ed. (New York, 1987). David P. Calleo provides a "road to ruin" perspective in *The Bankrupting of America: How the Federal Budget Is Impoverishing the Nation* (New York, 1992).

121. Schultze quoted in Herbert D. Rosenbaum and Alexej Ugrinsky, eds., *The Presidency and Domestic Policies of Jimmy Carter* (Westport, Conn., 1994), 671.

122. Friedman, *Day of Reckoning*, 164, 171–75, 185.

123. Thomas Friedman, "It's a Mad, Mad, Mad, Mad World Money Market," *New York Times*, 8 May 1994; and Krugman, *Peddling Prosperity*, 167, 128. See also Krugman, *Age of Diminished Expectations*, 85–99; White and Wildavsky, *The Deficit and the Public Interest*, 331–54; and Herbert Stein, "The Fiscal Revolution in America, Part II: 1964–1994," in *Funding the Modern American State, 1941–1995: The Rise and Fall of the Era of Easy Finance*, ed. W. Elliott Brownlee (New York, 1996), 278–86.

124. White and Wildavsky, *The Deficit and the Public Interest*, 428.

125. Stockman, "Budget Policy," in *American Economic Policy in the 1980s*, ed. Feldstein, 270.

Chapter 7

1. U.S. Presidents, *Public Papers*, William J. Clinton, 1996, 2:2021.

2. William C. Berman, *America's Right Turn: From Nixon to Clinton*, 2nd ed. (Baltimore, 1998), 145–63; Herbert Parmet, *George Bush: The Life of a Lone Star Yankee* (New York, 1998), 429–36, 500–507; Bob Woodward, *The Agenda: Inside the Clinton White House* (New York, 1995), 47–48; Arthur H. Miller, "Economic, Character, and Social Issues in the 1992 Campaign," *American Behavioral Scientist* 37 (November-December 1993): 315–28; Seymour Martin Lipset, "The Significance of the 1992 Election," *PS: Political Science and Politics* (March 1993): 7–16. Clinton quoted in *President Clinton's New Beginning: The Complete Text . . . of the Historic Clinton-Gore Economic Conference, Little Rock, Arkansas, December 14–15, 1992* (New York, 1992), 3.

3. Bill Clinton and Al Gore, *Putting People First: How We Can All Change America* (New York, 1992), 7.

4. Jordan Schwarz, *The New Dealers: Power Politics in the Age of Roosevelt* (New York, 1993); Alan Brinkley, "Liberals and Public Investment: Recovering a Lost Legacy," *The American Prospect* (Spring 1993): 81–86; Theodore Rosenof, *Economics in the Long Run: New Deal Theorists and Their Legacies, 1933–1993* (Chapel Hill, N.C., 1997), 60–65, 167–70.

5. Robert B. Reich, *The Resurgent Liberal (and Other Unfashionable Prophecies)* (New York, 1989), 57. On Reich's conversion to public investment, see Conrad P. Waligorski, *Liberal Economics and Democracy: Keynes, Galbraith, Thurow, and Reich* (Lawrence, Kans., 1997), 144–45; and Louis Uchitelle, "An Old Liberal, a New Sermon," *New York Times*, 12 April 1990.

6. Robert B. Reich, *Locked in the Cabinet* (New York, 1997), 9. On the role of Reich's ideas in the Clinton campaign, see the account by Clinton's pollster in Stanley B. Greenberg, *Middle Class Dreams: The Politics and Power of the New American Majority*, rev. and updated ed. (New Haven, Conn., 1996), 225–28.

7. *President Clinton's New Beginning*, 8, 22, 25.

8. Paul E. Tsongas, *Journey of Purpose: Reflections on the Presidency, Multiculturalism, and Third Parties* (New Haven, Conn., 1995).

9. Ross Perot, *United We Stand: How We Can Take Back Our Country* (New York, 1992), 8.

10. The following is based largely on Woodward, *The Agenda*. According to presidential adviser George Stephanopoulos, Woodward had unusual access to the Clinton White House in the preparation of his study. Woodward personally interviewed many of the principals of his study, including Hillary Rodham Clinton and, secretly, the president himself. The book displeased the White House, but Stephanopoulos later characterized it as "a comprehensive and basically accurate account." George Stephanopoulos, *All Too Human: A Political Education* (Boston, 1999), 280–84 (quote from 284).

11. On the bond market, see Louis Uchitelle, "Why America Won't Boom," *New York Times*, June 12, 1994; and Amy Waldman, "Of Inhuman Bondage: The Bond Market Has Policymakers in Its Grip," *Washington Monthly* (January-February 1997): 17–21.

12. Woodward, *The Agenda*, 136, 275, 160.

13. Ibid., 185.

14. U.S. Presidents, *Public Papers*, William J. Clinton, 1993, 1:1192; Reich, *Locked in the Cabinet*, 119.

15. Reich, *Locked in the Cabinet*, 119.

16. Ibid., 200.

17. Ibid., 337.

18. Quotes from Louis Uchitelle, "How Both Sides Joined the Supply Side," *New York Times*, 25 August 1996.

19. Reich, *Locked in the Cabinet*, 333.

20. Steven K. Beckner, *Back from the Brink: The Greenspan Years* (New York, 1996), ch. 1.

21. Quoted in Beckner, *Back from the Brink*, 307.

22. Quoted in "Clinton and Greenspan: The Odd Couple," *Business Week*, 14 July 1997, 48.

23. U.S. Presidents, *Public Papers*, William J. Clinton, 1996, 1:315.

24. Michael Hirsh, "It's Rubin, Stupid," *Newsweek*, 30 June 1997, 36; "Shut Up and Smile," *New Republic*, 3 November 1998, 9; Louis Uchitelle, "The Dark Side of Optimism," *New York Times*, 8 March 1998.

25. Josef Joffe, "America the Inescapable," *New York Times Magazine*, 8 June 1997, 41, 43.

26. Ibid., 41.

27. Louis Uchitelle, "Just a Little Inflation, and Everybody's Happy," *New York Times*, 8 September 1996; Abby Joseph Cohen, "It Was a Very Good Year," *Washington Post*, 29 December 1996; "U.S. Jobless Rate Declines to 4.8%, Lowest Since 1973," *New York Times*, 7 June 1997; Richard W. Stevenson, "It's the Economy, Congress," *New York Times*, 13 July 1997; "Budget Surplus Nears, And Plans for It Appear," *New York Times*, 4 March 1998.

28. Growth figures from U.S. Presidents, *Economic Report of the President, 1998*, Table B-4, updated using figures from U.S. Department of Commerce, Bureau of Economic Analysis, available from http://www.bea.doc.gov/bea/dn/niptbl_d.htm#whereto (August 1998).

29. Kim Clark, "These Are the Good Old Days," *Fortune*, 9 June 1997, 74. The characterization is repeated on the magazine's cover.

30. Quoted in G. Pascal Zachary, "Global Growth Attains a New, Higher Level That Could Be Lasting," *Wall Street Journal*, 13 March 1997.

31. Quoted in John B. Judis, "The Second Rubin Administration," *New Republic*, 10 February 1997, 26.

32. Rubin and Clinton quoted in Richard W. Stevenson, "An Economy of Happily Ever After?" *New York Times*, 24 November 1996; Greenspan's testimony before the Committee on Banking, Housing, and Urban Affairs, U.S. Senate, 21 July 1998, at http://wwwbog.frb.us/boarddocs/hh/ (last updated 22 July 1998).

33. Paul Krugman, "Stable Prices and Fast Growth: Just Say No," *The Economist*, 31 August 1996, 19.

34. Louis Uchitelle, "U.S. Industry Group Assails Fiscal Policy," *New York Times*, 24 September 1995; and Uchitelle, "Just a Little Inflation, and Everybody's Happy," *New York Times*, 8 September 1996.

35. Quoted in Krugman, "Stable Prices and Fast Growth," 19.

36. Quoted in David Rosenbaum, "It's Reaganomics, Alive and Irresistible," *New York Times*, 11 February 1996.

37. Dole quoted in Louis Uchitelle, "It's a Slow-Growth Economy, Stupid," *New York Times*, 17 March 1996. On the Dole-Kemp ticket, see Richard W. Stevenson, "Kemp's Ideas Move to Core of Party," *New York Times*, 11 August 1996; Michael Wines, "A True Believer Who Won the Day," *New York Times*, 25 August 1996; and Elizabeth Kolbert, "Dole in Taking Kemp, Buried Bitter Past Rooted in Doctrine," *New York Times*, 29 September 1996.

38. U.S. Congress, Joint Economic Committee, "The Growth Debate: How Fast Can We Grow?" Joint Economic Committee web page (prepared August 1996), available from http://www.senate.gov/~jec/grwthdeb.html.

39. Harken quoted in "How Healthy Is This Economy? Why Not Ask the Democrats?" ibid.; Wellstone quoted in Beckner, *Back from the Brink*, 417; Frank Levy, *The New Dollars and Dreams: American Incomes and Economic Change* (New York, 1998).

40. Robert Eisner, "Who's Afraid of Jobs and Growth?" *New York Times*, 31 March 1996.

41. Robert Eisner, *The Misunderstood Economy: What Counts and How to Count It* (Boston, 1994), ch. 8. Quotation from 182.

42. *President Clinton's New Beginning*, 284.

43. Lester C. Thurow, *The Future of Capitalism: How Today's Economic Forces Shape Tomorrow's World* (New York, 1996), 185, 189.

44. Quoted in Louis Uchitelle, "Like Oil and Water: A Tale of Two Economists," *New York Times*, 16 February 1997.

45. *New York Times*, 17 February 1996.

46. Quoted in Beckner, *Back from the Brink*, 417.

47. U.S. Presidents, *Economic Report of the President, 1998*, Table B-50.

48. Quotation from Paul Krugman, "Stay on Their Backs," *New York Times Magazine*, 4 February 1996, 37. See also Krugman, "Stable Prices and Fast Growth," 19–22; Uchitelle, "It's a Slow Growth Economy"; and Stephen V. Oliver and William L Wachser, "Is a Productivity Revolution Under Way in the United States?" *Challenge: The Magazine of Economic Affairs* (November–December 1995): 18–30.

49. Matthew Miller, "Grow Up," *New Republic*, 13 May 1996, 22.

50. Jeffrey Madrick, *The End of Affluence: The Causes and Consequences of America's Economic Dilemma* (New York, 1995), 5.

51. Kevin Phillips, *The Politics of Rich and Poor: Wealth and the American Electorate in the Reagan Aftermath* (New York, 1990); "Income Desparity Between Poorest and Richest Rises," *New York Times*, 20 June 1996; Matthew Miller, "Wage War," *New Republic*, 30 September 1996, 16–20. For evidence that the trend toward greater inequality was manifested elsewhere as well, see Frederick R. Strobel, "Britain Goes Down the Path of Income Inequality," *Challenge: The Magazine of Economic Affairs* (November–December 1995): 35–39.

52. Lester Thurow, "Why Their World Might Crumble: How Much Inequality Can a Democracy Take?" *New York Times Magazine*, 19 November 1995, 78–79; Reich quoted in Keith Bradsher, "Productivity Is All but It Doesn't Pay Well," *New York Times*, 25 June 1995.

53. Quoted in Matthew Miller, "Uh-Oh: The Social Security Mess—and How to Fix It," *New Republic*, 15 April 1996.

54. Edward N. Luttwak, *The Endangered American Dream: How to Stop the United States from Becoming a Third World Country and How to Win the Geo-Economic Struggle for Industrial Supremacy* (New York, 1993), 18.

55. Jacob Weisberg, "Leaner, Cleaner Liberals," *New Republic*, 1 April 1996, 17, 25.

56. Derek Bok, *The State of the Nation: Government and the Quest for a Better Society* (Cambridge, Mass., 1996), 33.

57. Quoted in Dean Foust, "Alan Greenspan's Brave New World," *Business Week*, 14 July 1997, 49.

58. "Fed Chief's Remarks Spur Surge in Bonds" and "Greenspan Upbeat, but Cautious," *New York Times*, 23 July 1997.

59. Quoted in Jacob Weisberg, "The Governor-President," *New York Times Magazine*, 17 January 1999, 33.

60. The line is translated as "politics is a strong and slow boring of hard boards" in Max Weber, *Politics as a Vocation*, trans. H. H. Gerth and C. Wright Mills (Philadelphia, 1965), 55.

Chapter 8

1. Richard M. Scammon and Ben J. Wattenberg, *The Real Majority* (New York, 1972); Michael Barone, *One Country: The Shaping of America from Roosevelt to Reagan* (New York, 1990). See also Ben J. Wattenberg, *Values Matter Most: How Republicans or Democrats or a Third Party Can Win and Renew the American Way of Life* (New York, 1995).

2. Ellis Hawley, *The New Deal and the Problem of Monopoly: A Study in Economic Ambivalence* (Princeton, N.J., 1966), 272.

3. *The Collected Writings of John Maynard Keynes*, vol. 7, *The General Theory of Employment Interest and Money* (London, 1973), 383–84.

4. Joseph A. Schumpeter, *History of Economic Analysis* (New York, 1954), 41, 42.

5. Joseph A. Schumpeter, *Capitalism, Socialism and Democracy*, 3rd ed. (New York, 1950), ch. 7.

6. Herbert Stein, "The Fiscal Revolution in America, Part II," in *Funding the Modern American State, 1941–1995: The Rise and Fall of the Era of Easy Finance*, ed. W. Elliot Brownlee (New York, 1996), 285.

7. Dick Morris, *Behind the Oval Office: Winning the Presidency in the Nineties* (New York, 1997), 29.

8. U.S. Presidents, *Public Papers*, William J. Clinton, 1993, 1:1180.

9. "Excerpts From Remarks on Budget Deal," *New York Times*, 30 July 1997.

10. John Lewis Gaddis, "Hanging Tough Paid Off," *Bulletin of the Atomic Scientists* 45 (January–February 1989): 11–14.

11. See Stein, *On the Other Hand: Essays on Economics, Economists, and Politics* (Washington, D.C., 1995), 214; and Daniel Bell and Irving Kristol, eds., *The Crisis in Economic Theory* (New York, 1981), xiii.

Index

on Nixonomics, 126; on social
security, 229; on stagflation, 154
Sanders, Barefoot, 95
Santa Barbara oil spill, 137
Saulnier, Raymond J., 37, 43
Say, Jean-Baptiste, 183
Scammon, Richard, 235
Schlesinger, Arthur M., Jr., 58, 65,
102; and qualitative liberalism,
62–64
Schultze, Charles, 76, 158, 169, 211
Schumacher, E. F., 133–34
Schumpeter, Joseph, 237
Schwarz, Jordan, 8
Science Policy Research Unit
(University of Sussex), 142
Scott, Howard, 3
Scott, Peter, 139
Sears, Roebuck, 15–16
Security, Work, and Relief Policies
(NRPB), 14
"Shape of National Politics to
Come, The" (Schlesinger),
62–63
Shultz, George, 122, 127, 153, 154;
and NEP, 118–21
Sierra Club, 137
Silent Spring (Carson), 65, 136–37
Silk, Leonard, 143
Six Companies consortium, 8
Small Is Beautiful (Schumacher),
133–34
Smith, Adam, xi, 27, 183
Smith, "Cotton" Ed, 38
Social Security Amendments of
1983, 203
Social statistics, 64

Solomon, Anthony M., 78, 172
Solomon, Robert, 78
Solomon plan (for steel industry,
1977), 172
Sorensen, Theodore, 56
South: attitudes toward growth,
2–3; development of, 8
Special Drawing Rights, 83
Special Studies Project (Rocke-
feller Brothers Fund), 47
Special Study on Economic
Change (Joint Economic Com-
mittee), 188
Spence Economic Stability Bill of
1949, 23, 25
Sperling, Gene, 216
Stagflation, 159; defined, 113; in
1970s, 152–60
Stagnationist economics, 6, 20,
40–41
Stans, Maurice, 45, 54
Steel industry: controversy over
expansion of, 11–12
Stein, Herbert, 111, 113, 115, 224; on
economics in the 1990s, 238; on
Humphrey-Hawkins, 170; on
Kemp-Roth, 178; names supply-side economics, 185–86;
and NEP, 118–21; on Nixon, 103,
112; on punk supply-sidism,
187; on quality v. quantity, 147;
and Whig growthmanship,
125–28
Stiglitz, Joseph E., 220
Stockman, David: and Reagan
economic policy, 199–213 passim